Twin Star Exorcists

ONMYOJI

Twin Star Exorcists

ONMYOJI

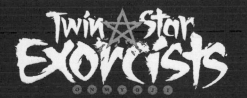

Twin★Star Exorcists

O N M Y O J I

10

STORY & ART
YOSHIAKI SUKENO

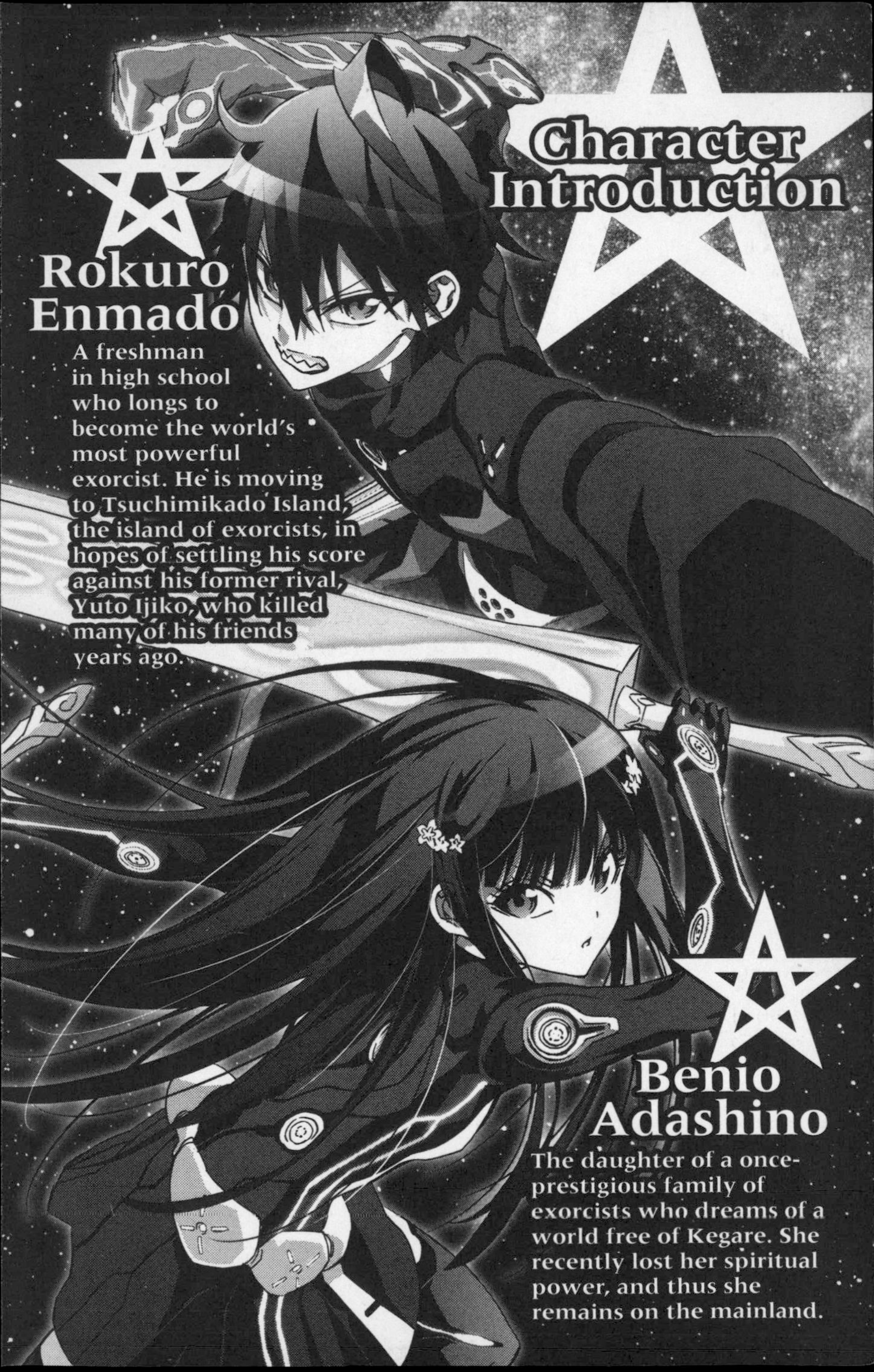
Character Introduction
Rokuro Enmado
A freshman in high school who longs to become the world's most powerful exorcist. He is moving to Tsuchimikado Island, the island of exorcists, in hopes of settling his score against his former rival, Yuto Ijiko, who killed many of his friends years ago.
Benio Adashino
The daughter of a once-prestigious family of exorcists who dreams of a world free of Kegare. She recently lost her spiritual power, and thus she remains on the mainland.

Shimon Ikaruga

One of the Twelve Guardians, he has the title of Suzaku. He deeply respects his mentor, Seigen.

Mayura Otomi

Rokuro's childhood friend. During a fierce battle in Magano, her commitment to protecting others earned her the spiritual protector White Tiger.

Sayo Ikaruga

The daughter of the prestigious Ikaruga Family of Tsuchimikado Island. She grew up with Shimon like real siblings. She has a big crush on Rokuro.

Yuto Ijika

Benio's twin brother. He was the mastermind behind the Hinatsuki Tragedy and has learned to use the Kegare curse for his own sinister purposes.

Arima Tsuchimikado

The Chief Exorcist of the Association of Unified Exorcists, an organization that presides over all exorcists. He received the Twin Star prophecy, which led him to play matchmaker with Rokuro and Benio.

The Mysterious Girl

The mysterious girl Rokuro saw in his subconscious, who referred to Rokuro as "My child..."

Story Thus Far...

Kegare are creatures from Magano, the underworld, and it is the duty of an exorcist to hunt, exorcise and purify them. Rokuro and Benio are the Twin Star Exorcists, fated to bear the Prophesied Child who will defeat the Kegare. They are attacked by Yuto, the perpetrator of the Hinatsuki Tragedy in which many young exorcists died. After a fierce battle, they manage to drive away—but not defeat—Yuto.

For two years, the unlikely pair live and train together in preparation for going to Tsuchimikado Island, the front line of the battle against the Kegare, to finish Yuto off. Sayo, the proctor of the Ascertainment Ritual to determine whether they are ready to go, comes to the mainland and is kidnapped by a Basara. With the help of Mayura, the Twin Stars manage to rescue her, but during the fierce battle, Benio mysteriously loses all her spiritual power.

Now Rokuro is heading for the island without his fellow Twin Star but accompanied by Mayura...

Twin Star Exorcists

ONMYOJI

EXORCISMS

10

ONMYOJI have worked for the Imperial Court since the Heian era. In addition to exorcising evil spirits, as civil servants they performed a variety of roles, including advising nobles by foretelling the future, creating the calendar, observing the movements of the stars, measuring time...

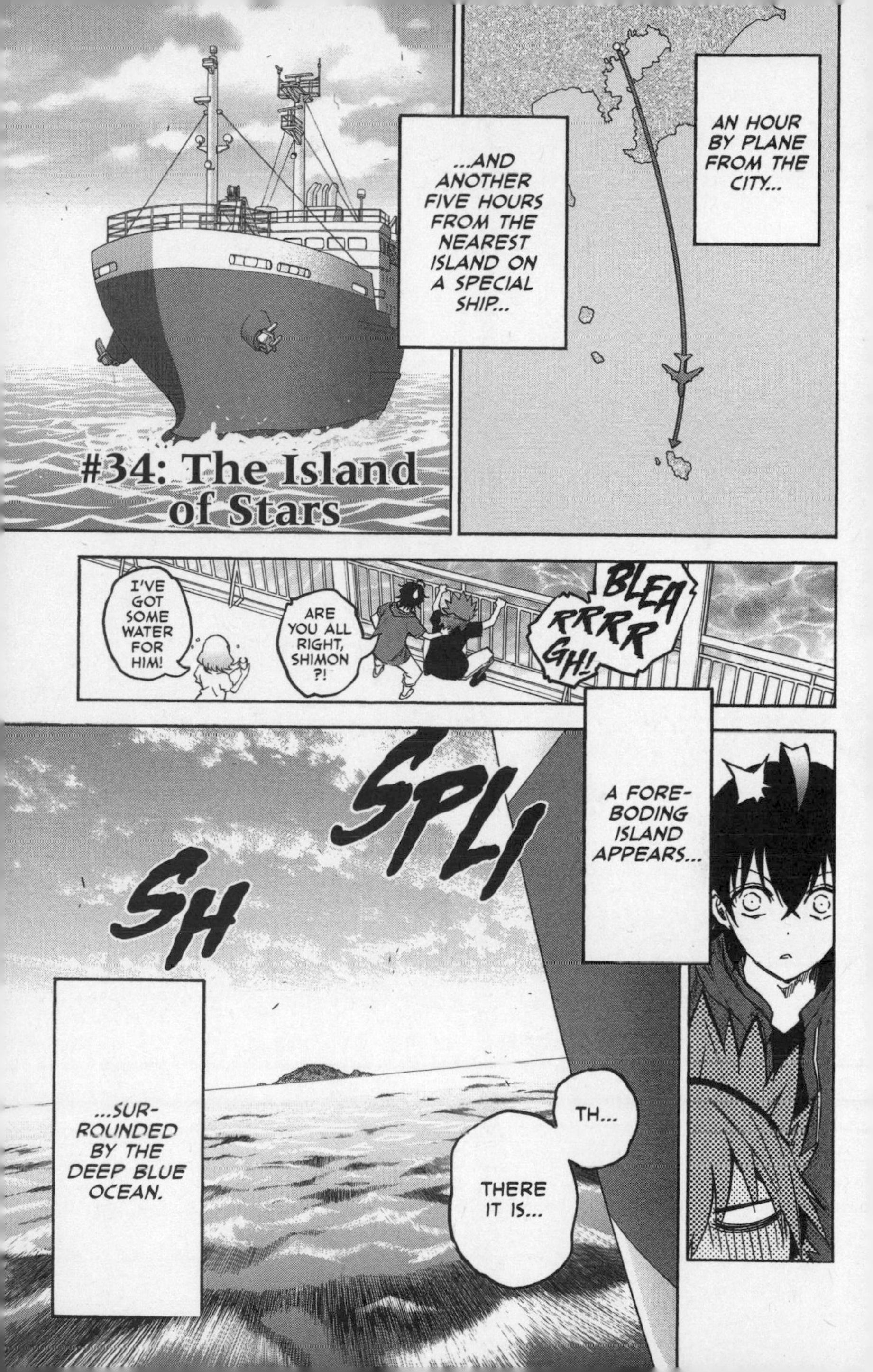
AN HOUR BY PLANE FROM THE CITY...
...AND ANOTHER FIVE HOURS FROM THE NEAREST ISLAND ON A SPECIAL SHIP...
#34: The Island of Stars
BLEARRRRGH!
ARE YOU ALL RIGHT, SHIMON?!
I'VE GOT SOME WATER FOR HIM!
A FORE-BODING ISLAND APPEARS...
SPLISH
TH...
THERE IT IS...
...SUR-ROUNDED BY THE DEEP BLUE OCEAN.

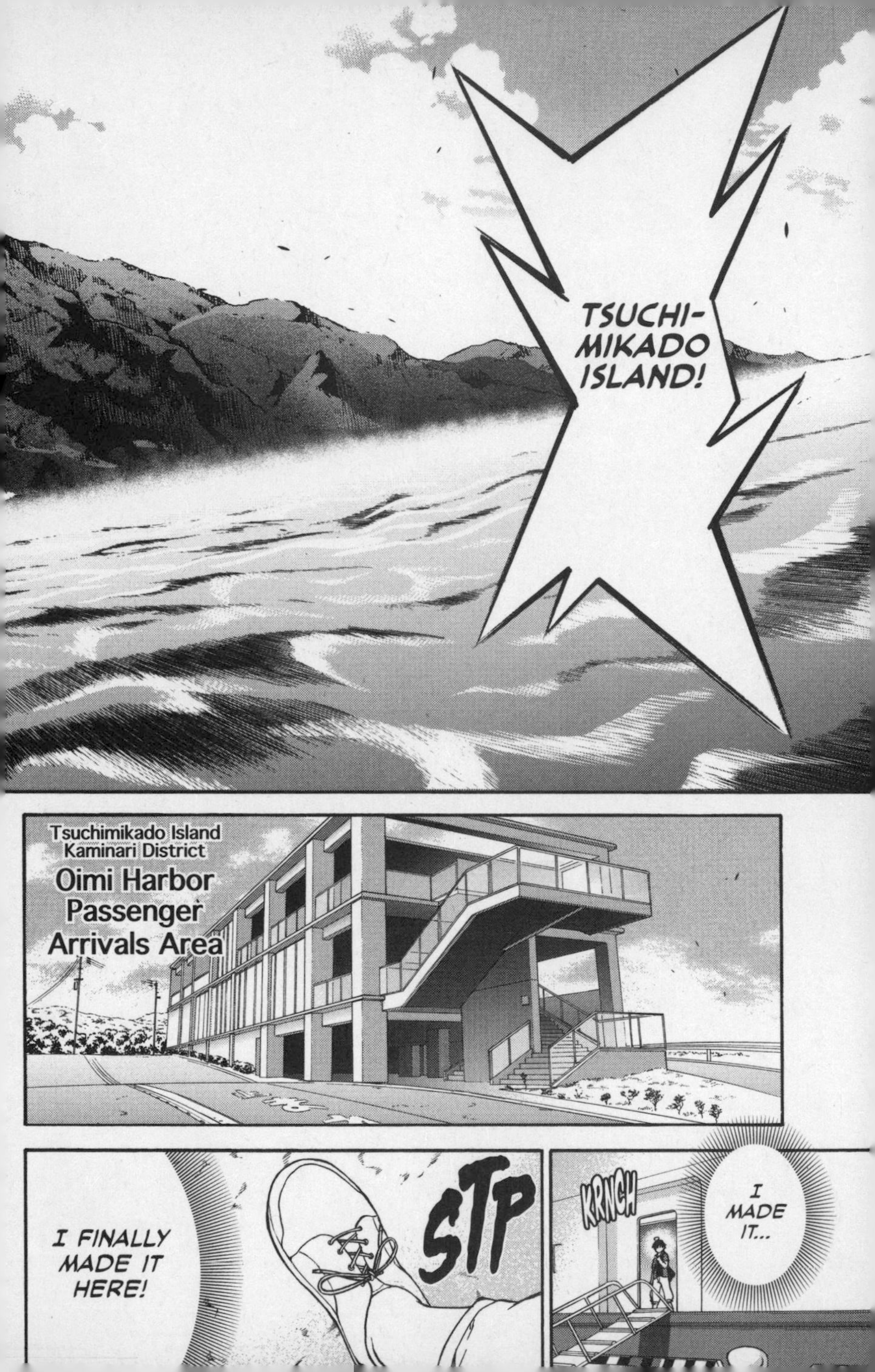
TSUCHI-MIKADO ISLAND!
Tsuchimikado Island Kaminari District
Oimi Harbor Passenger Arrivals Area
KRNCH
I MADE IT...
STP
I FINALLY MADE IT HERE!

#34: The Island of Stars

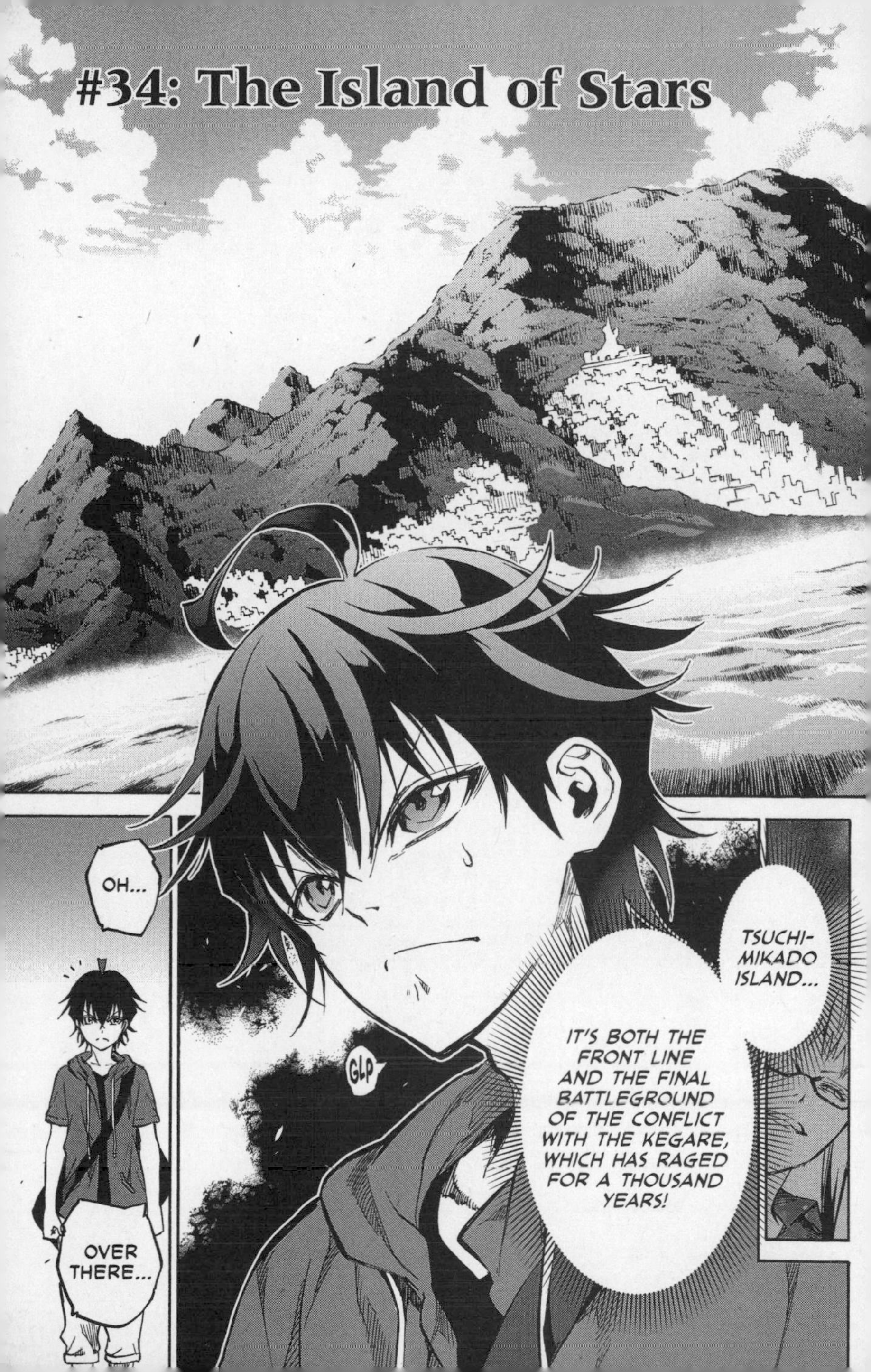
TSUCHI-MIKADO ISLAND...
IT'S BOTH THE FRONT LINE AND THE FINAL BATTLEGROUND OF THE CONFLICT WITH THE KEGARE, WHICH HAS RAGED FOR A THOUSAND YEARS!
GLP
OH...
OVER THERE...

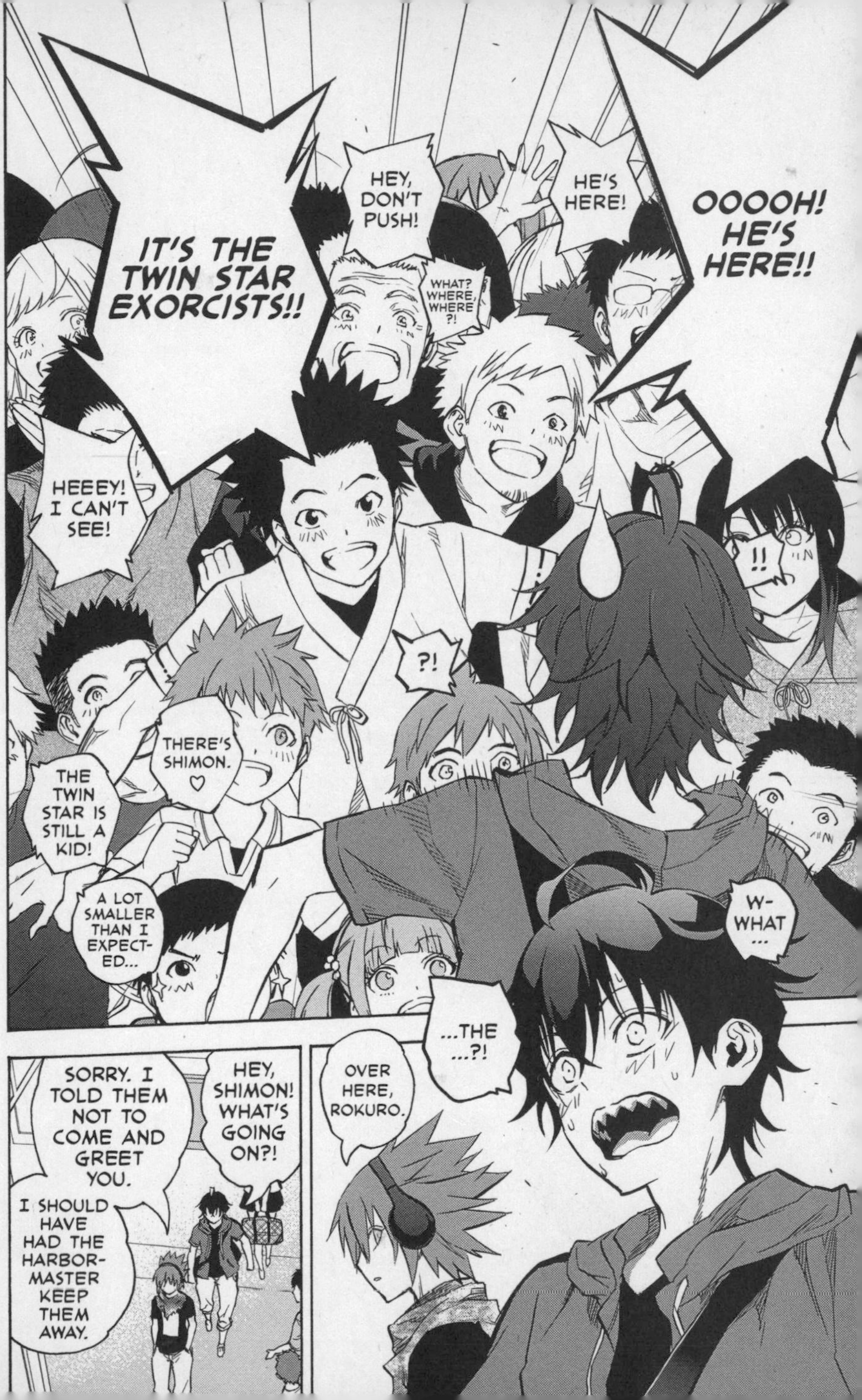
OOOOH! HE'S HERE!!
HE'S HERE!
HEY, DON'T PUSH!
IT'S THE TWIN STAR EXORCISTS!!
WHAT? WHERE, WHERE?!
HEEEY! I CAN'T SEE!
!!
?!
THERE'S SHIMON. ♡
THE TWIN STAR IS STILL A KID!
W-WHAT...
A LOT SMALLER THAN I EXPECTED...
...THE...?!
OVER HERE, ROKURO.
HEY, SHIMON! WHAT'S GOING ON?!
SORRY. I TOLD THEM NOT TO COME AND GREET YOU.
I SHOULD HAVE HAD THE HARBOR-MASTER KEEP THEM AWAY.

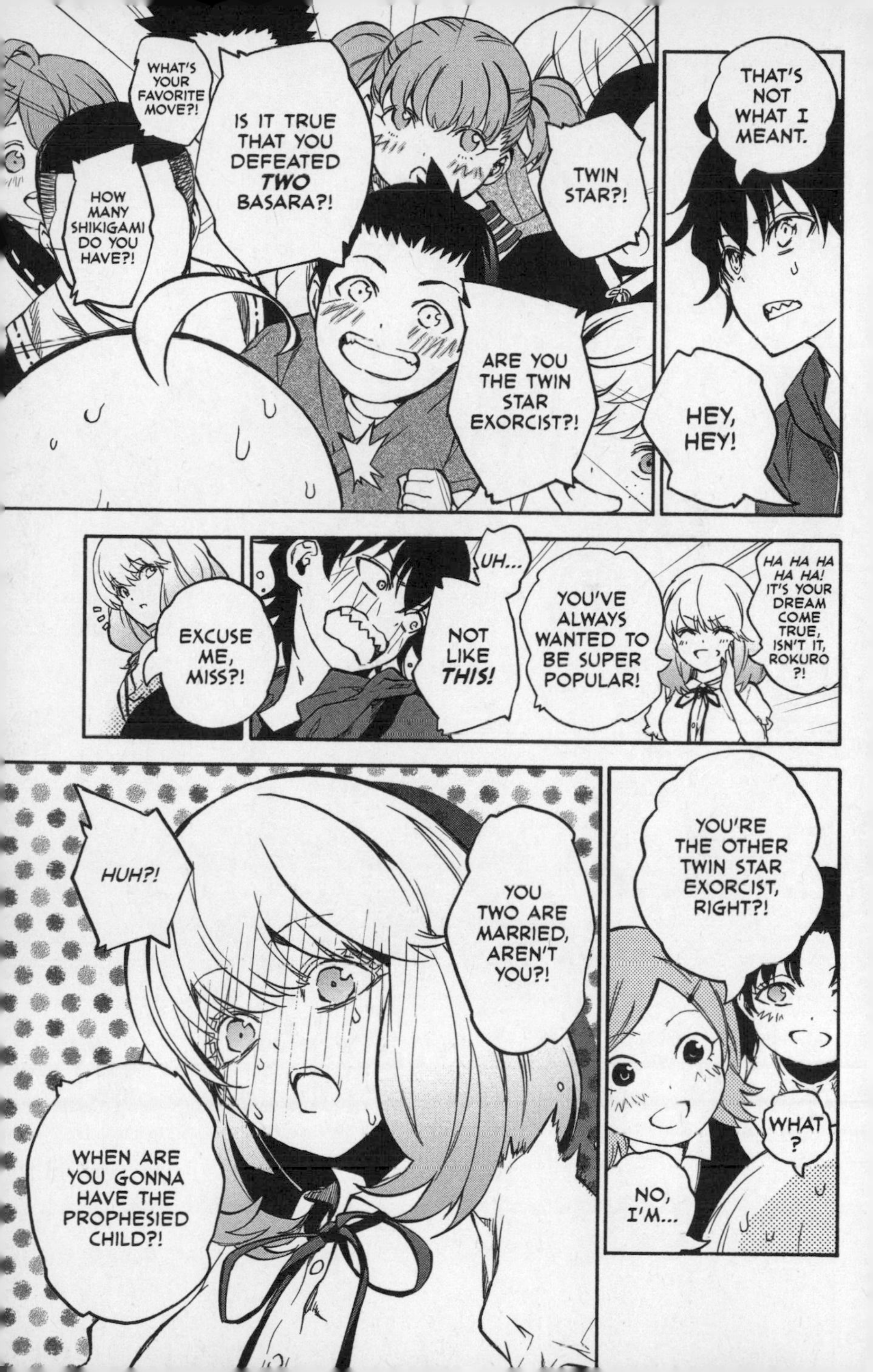
THAT'S NOT WHAT I MEANT.
HEY, HEY!
TWIN STAR?!
IS IT TRUE THAT YOU DEFEATED *TWO* BASARA?!
WHAT'S YOUR FAVORITE MOVE?!
HOW MANY SHIKIGAMI DO YOU HAVE?!
ARE YOU THE TWIN STAR EXORCIST?!
HA HA HA HA HA! IT'S YOUR DREAM COME TRUE, ISN'T IT, ROKURO?!
YOU'VE ALWAYS WANTED TO BE SUPER POPULAR!
UH...
NOT LIKE *THIS!*
EXCUSE ME, MISS?!
YOU'RE THE OTHER TWIN STAR EXORCIST, RIGHT?!
WHAT?
NO, I'M...
YOU TWO ARE MARRIED, AREN'T YOU?!
HUH?!
WHEN ARE YOU GONNA HAVE THE PROPHESIED CHILD?!

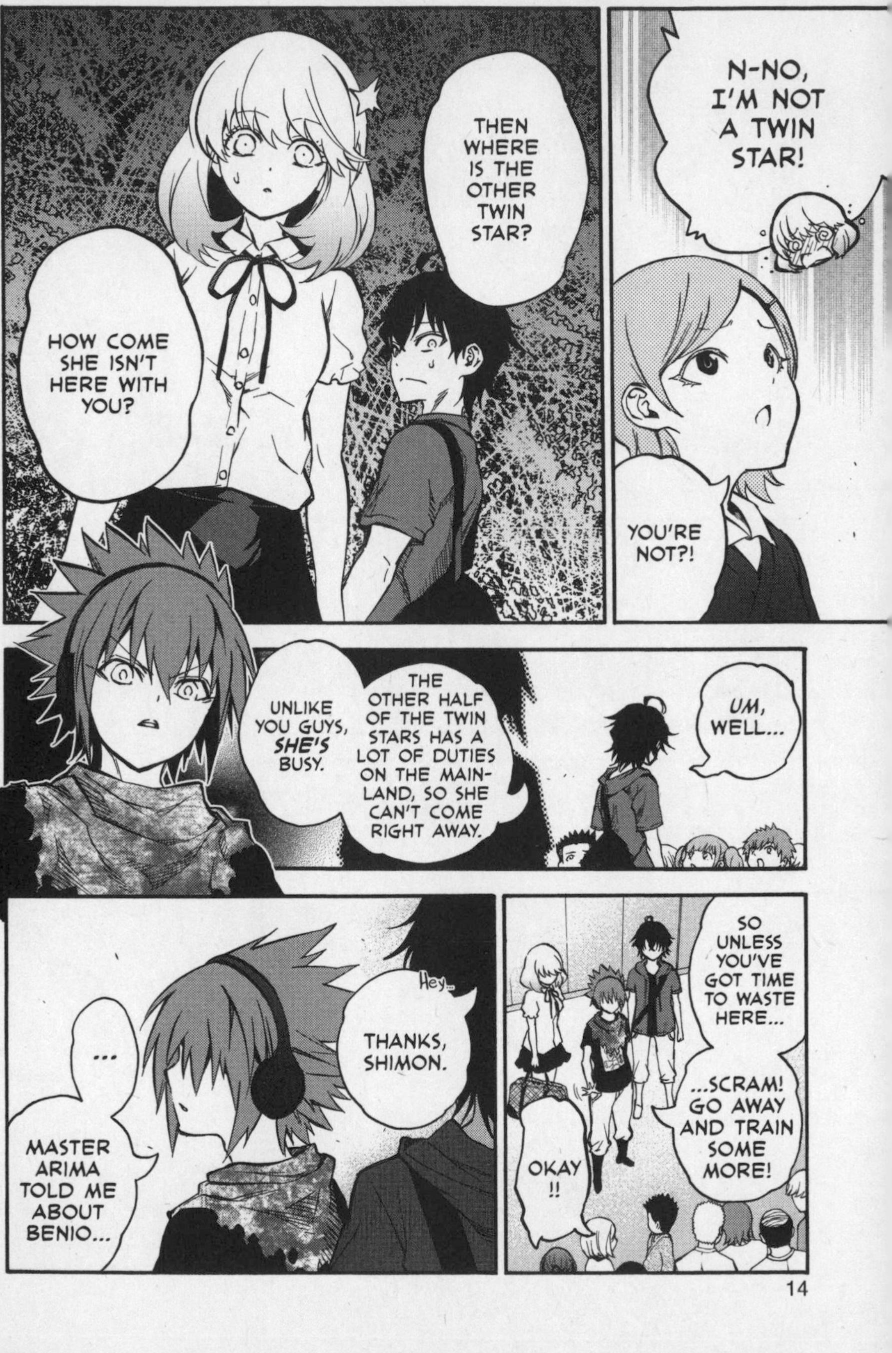
N-NO, I'M NOT A TWIN STAR!
YOU'RE NOT?!
THEN WHERE IS THE OTHER TWIN STAR?
HOW COME SHE ISN'T HERE WITH YOU?
UM, WELL...
THE OTHER HALF OF THE TWIN STARS HAS A LOT OF DUTIES ON THE MAIN-LAND, SO SHE CAN'T COME RIGHT AWAY.
UNLIKE YOU GUYS, SHE'S BUSY.
SO UNLESS YOU'VE GOT TIME TO WASTE HERE...
...SCRAM! GO AWAY AND TRAIN SOME MORE!
OKAY !!
Hey...
THANKS, SHIMON.
...
MASTER ARIMA TOLD ME ABOUT BENIO...

...

YOU DON'T NEED TO TELL THEM THE TRUTH.

NOT YET, ANYWAY...

?

Rokuro!

WHAT ARE YOU DOING? COME ON!

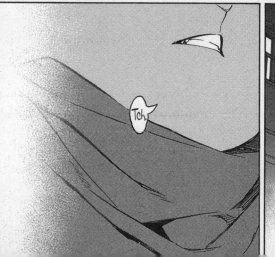

Tch.

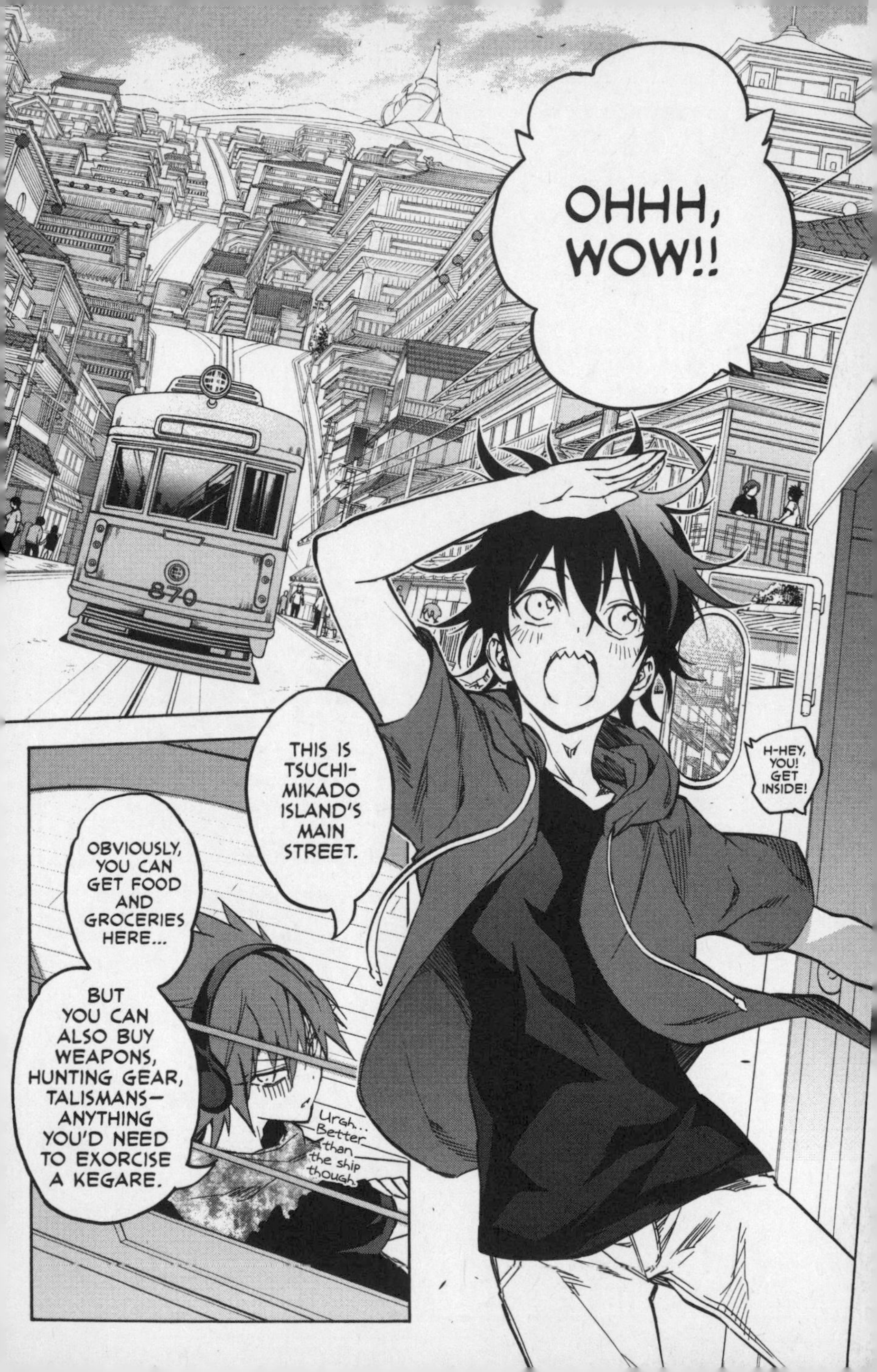
OHHH, WOW!!
H-HEY, YOU! GET INSIDE!
THIS IS TSUCHI-MIKADO ISLAND'S MAIN STREET.
OBVIOUSLY, YOU CAN GET FOOD AND GROCERIES HERE...
BUT YOU CAN ALSO BUY WEAPONS, HUNTING GEAR, TALISMANS—ANYTHING YOU'D NEED TO EXORCISE A KEGARE.
Urgh... Better than the ship though.

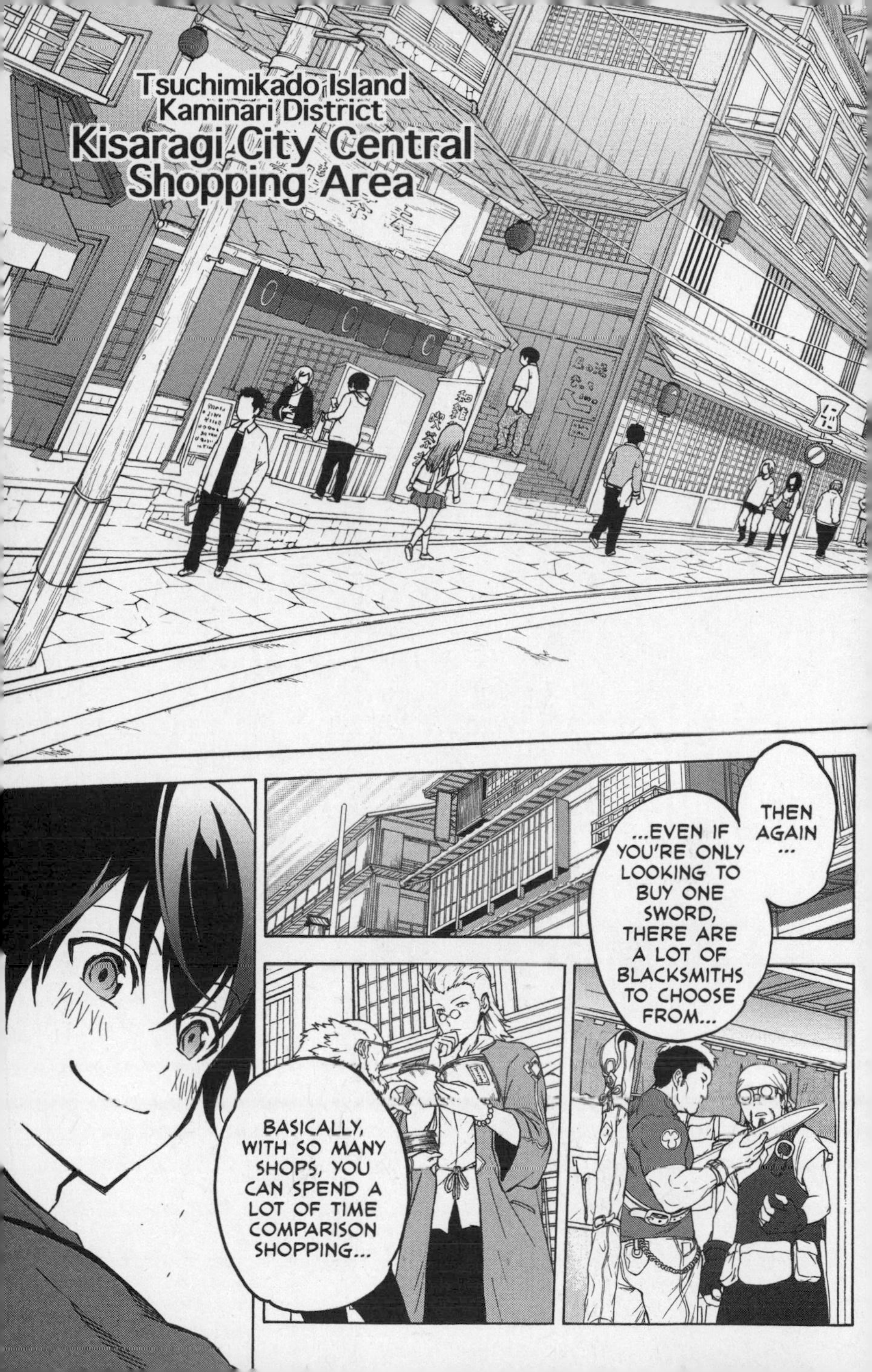
Tsuchimikado Island
Kaminari District
Kisaragi City Central Shopping Area
THEN AGAIN...
...EVEN IF YOU'RE ONLY LOOKING TO BUY ONE SWORD, THERE ARE A LOT OF BLACKSMITHS TO CHOOSE FROM...
BASICALLY, WITH SO MANY SHOPS, YOU CAN SPEND A LOT OF TIME COMPARISON SHOPPING...

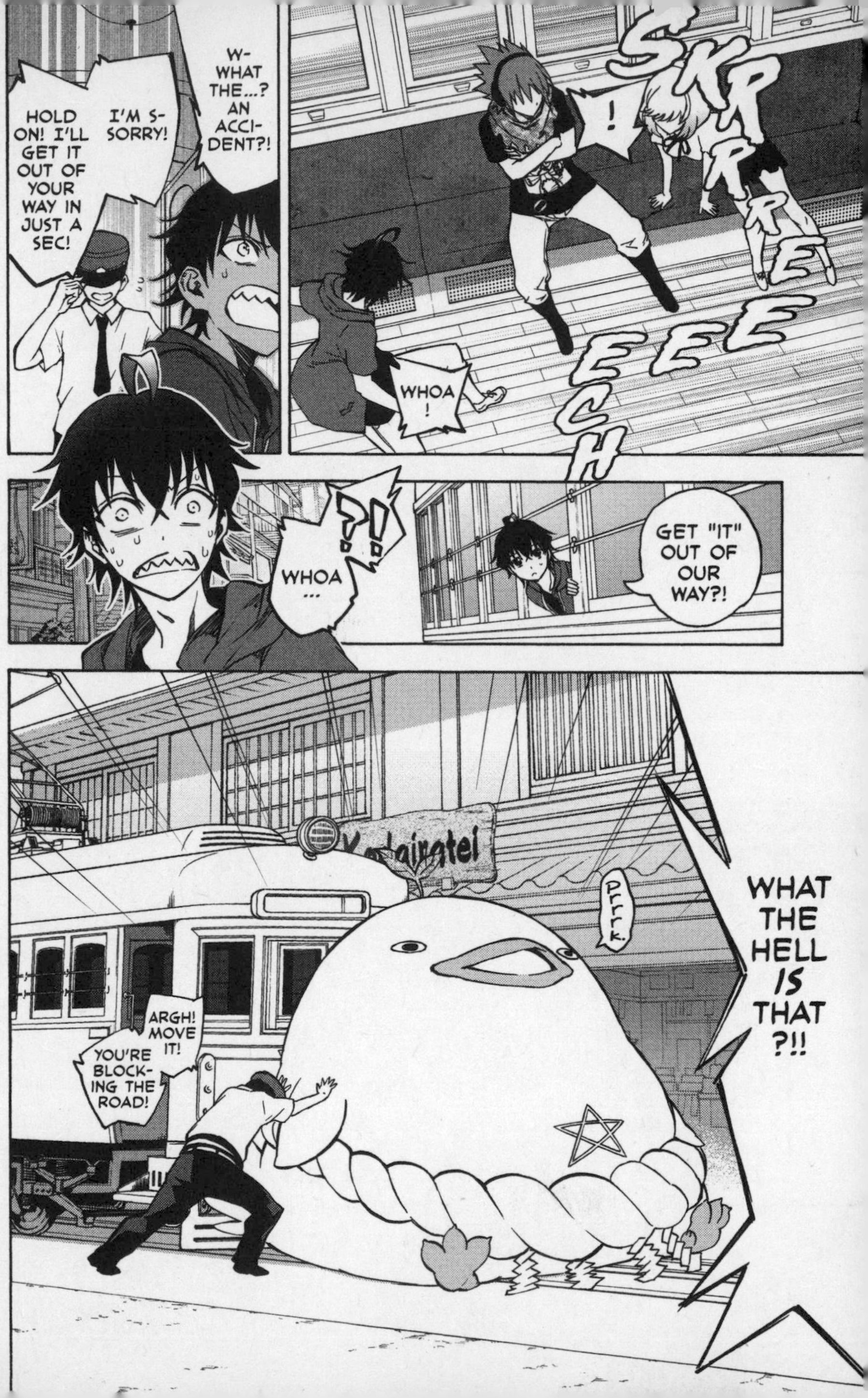
SKRREEEECH
!
WHOA!
W-WHAT THE...? AN ACCIDENT?!
I'M S-SORRY!
HOLD ON! I'LL GET IT OUT OF YOUR WAY IN JUST A SEC!
GET "IT" OUT OF OUR WAY?!
?!
WHOA...
Prrrk.
WHAT THE HELL IS THAT?!!
ARGH! MOVE IT!
YOU'RE BLOCKING THE ROAD!

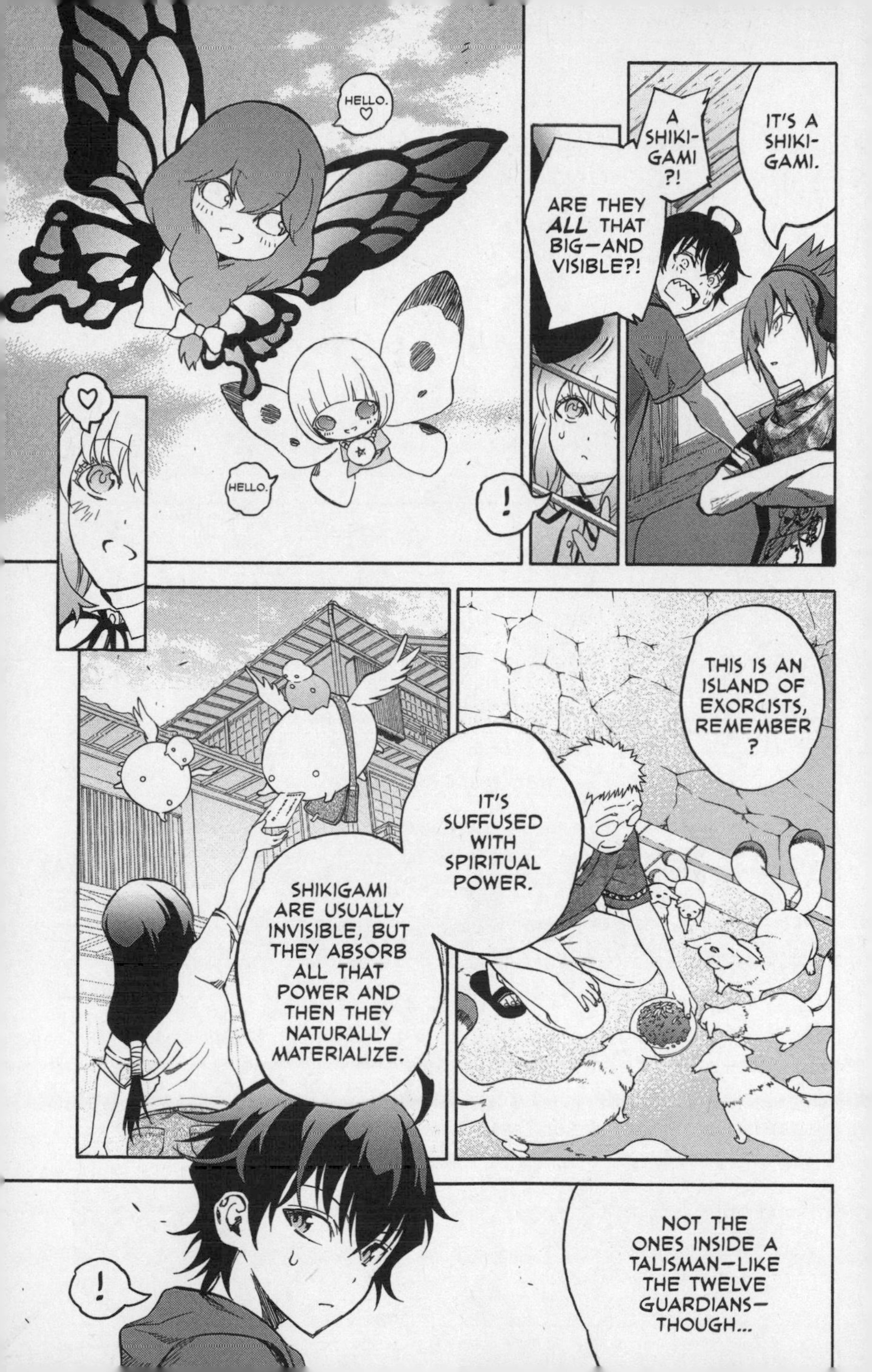
IT'S A SHIKIGAMI.
A SHIKIGAMI?!
ARE THEY ALL THAT BIG—AND VISIBLE?!
!
HELLO. ♡
HELLO.
♡
THIS IS AN ISLAND OF EXORCISTS, REMEMBER?
IT'S SUFFUSED WITH SPIRITUAL POWER.
SHIKIGAMI ARE USUALLY INVISIBLE, BUT THEY ABSORB ALL THAT POWER AND THEN THEY NATURALLY MATERIALIZE.
NOT THE ONES INSIDE A TALISMAN—LIKE THE TWELVE GUARDIANS—THOUGH...
!

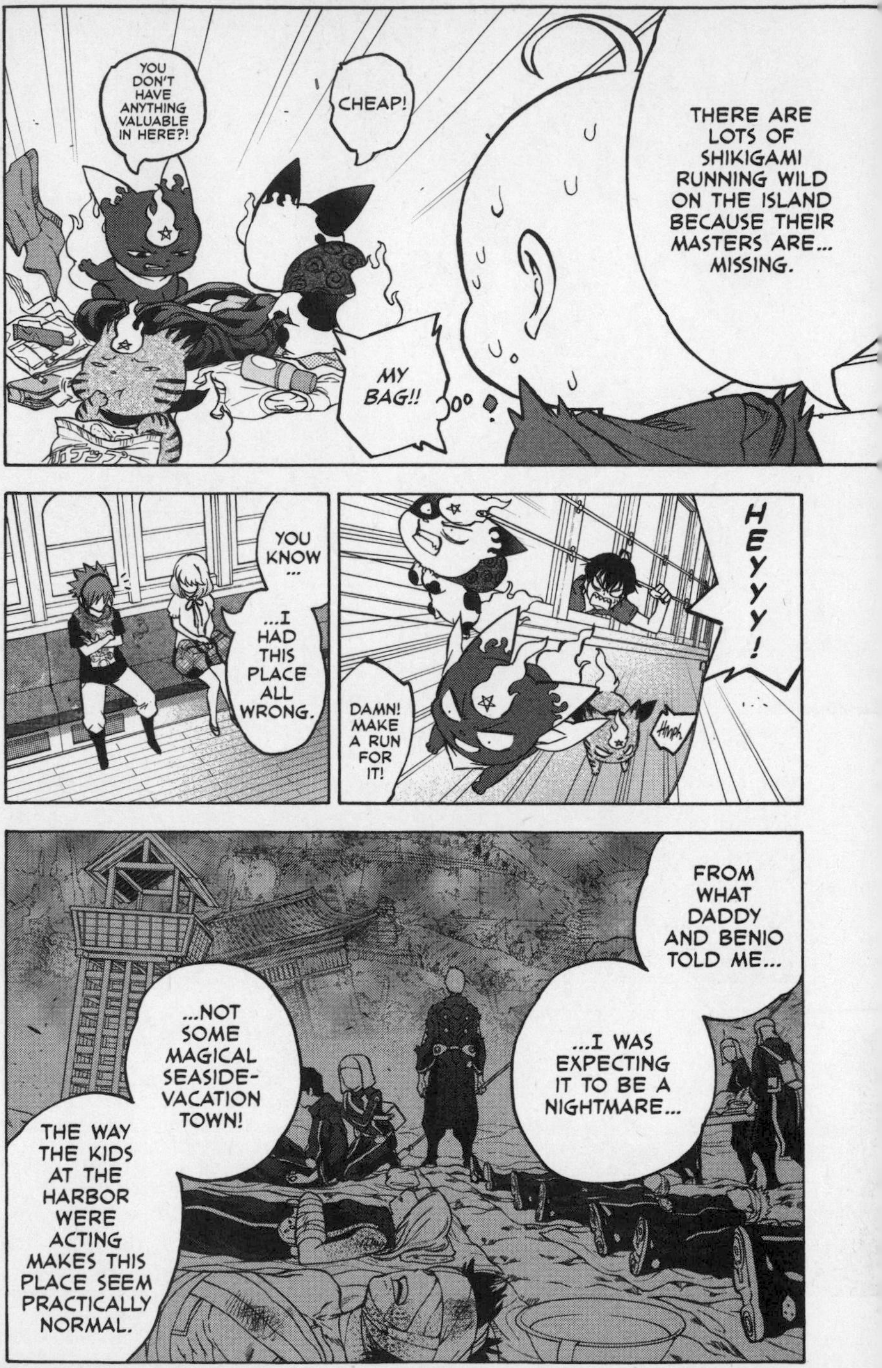
THERE ARE LOTS OF SHIKIGAMI RUNNING WILD ON THE ISLAND BECAUSE THEIR MASTERS ARE... MISSING.
MY BAG!!
CHEAP!
YOU DON'T HAVE ANYTHING VALUABLE IN HERE?!
HEYYY!
Hmph
DAMN! MAKE A RUN FOR IT!
YOU KNOW...
...I HAD THIS PLACE ALL WRONG.
FROM WHAT DADDY AND BENIO TOLD ME...
...I WAS EXPECTING IT TO BE A NIGHTMARE...
...NOT SOME MAGICAL SEASIDE-VACATION TOWN!
THE WAY THE KIDS AT THE HARBOR WERE ACTING MAKES THIS PLACE SEEM PRACTICALLY NORMAL.

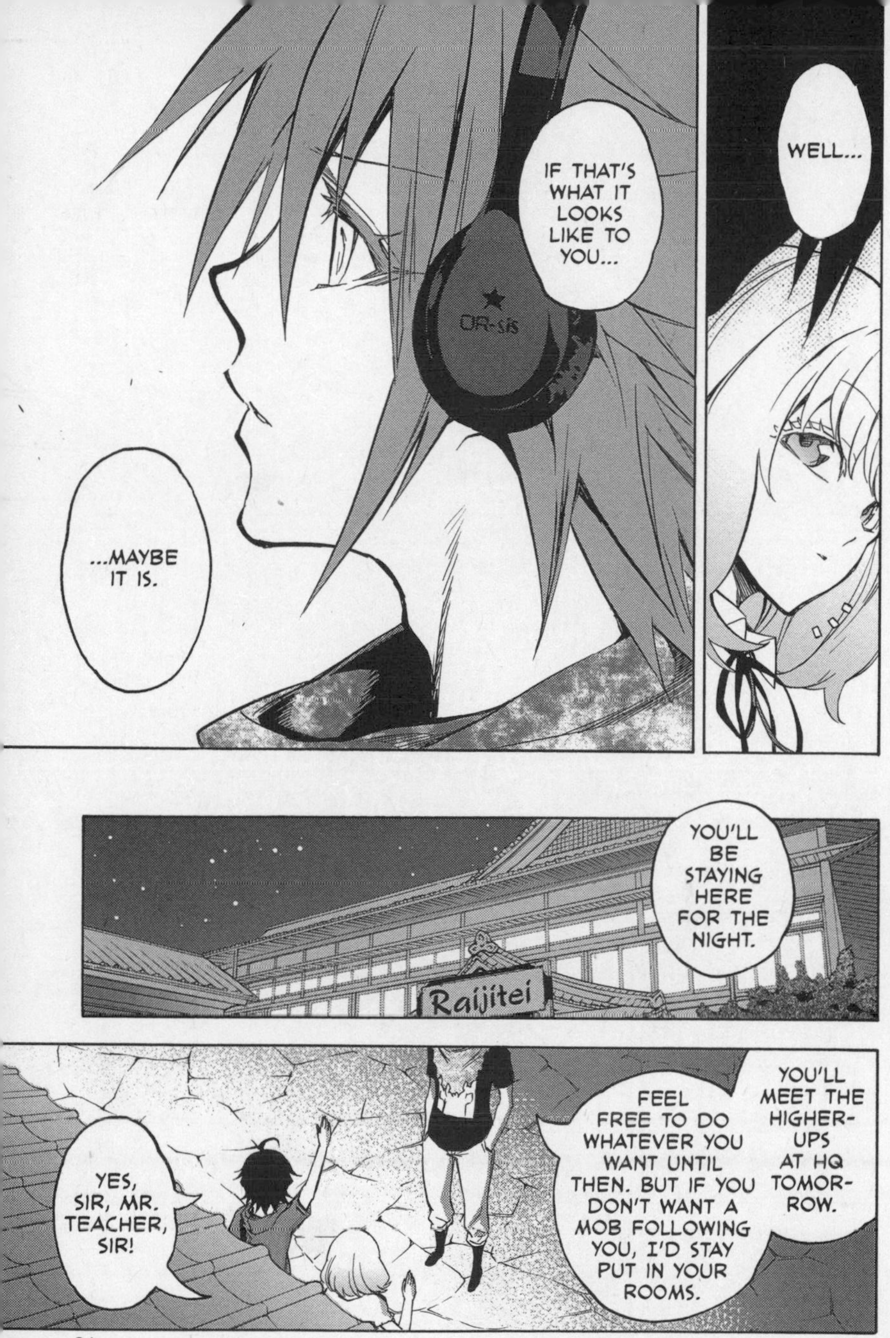
WELL...
IF THAT'S WHAT IT LOOKS LIKE TO YOU...
OR-sis
...MAYBE IT IS.
YOU'LL BE STAYING HERE FOR THE NIGHT.
Raijitei
YOU'LL MEET THE HIGHER-UPS AT HQ TOMORROW.
FEEL FREE TO DO WHATEVER YOU WANT UNTIL THEN. BUT IF YOU DON'T WANT A MOB FOLLOWING YOU, I'D STAY PUT IN YOUR ROOMS.
YES, SIR, MR. TEACHER, SIR!

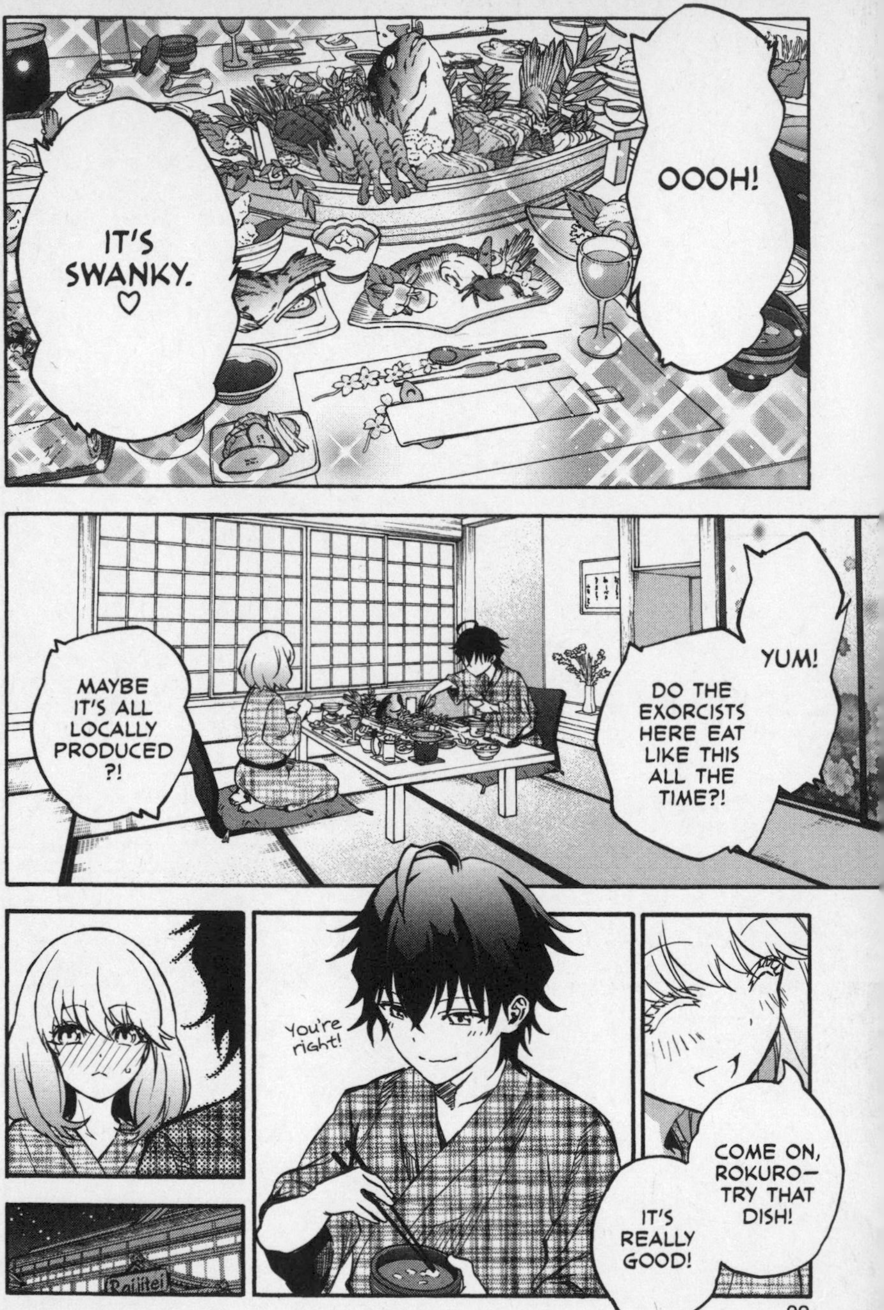
OOOH!
IT'S SWANKY. ♡
YUM!
DO THE EXORCISTS HERE EAT LIKE THIS ALL THE TIME?!
MAYBE IT'S ALL LOCALLY PRODUCED?!
COME ON, ROKURO— TRY THAT DISH!
IT'S REALLY GOOD!
You're right!

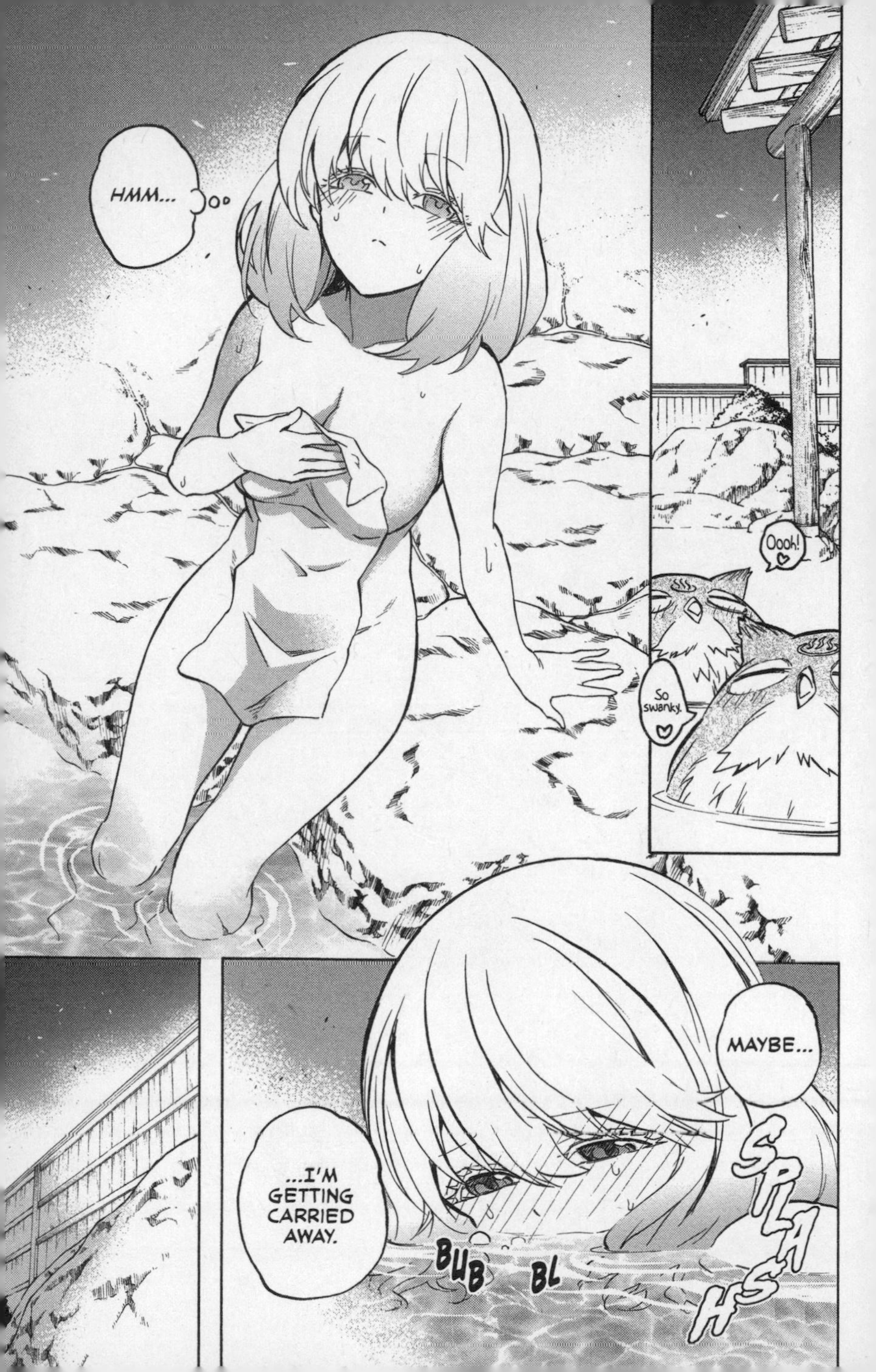
Oooh!
So swanky.
HMM...
MAYBE...
SPLASH
...I'M GETTING CARRIED AWAY.
BUB
BL

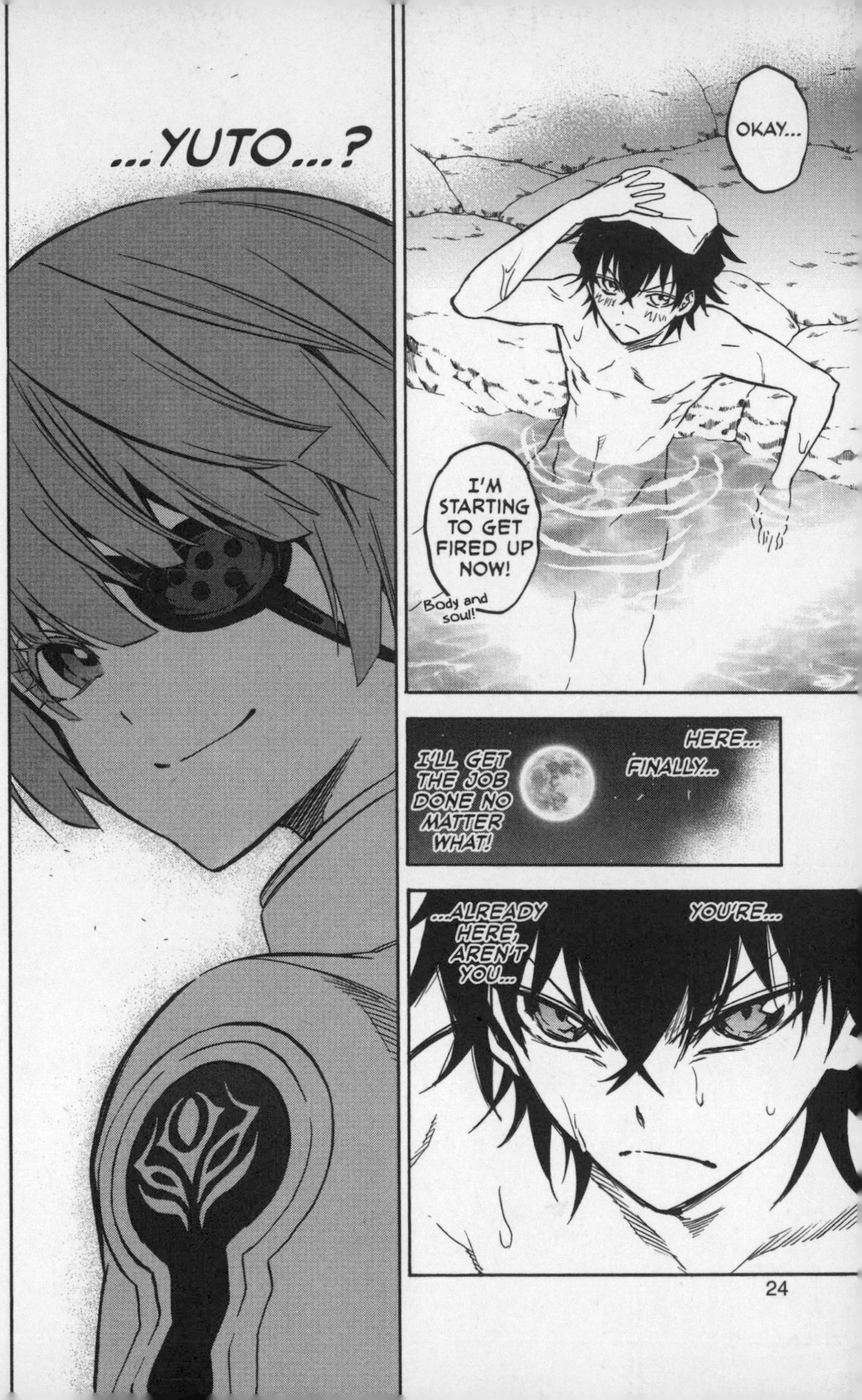
OKAY...
I'M STARTING TO GET FIRED UP NOW!
Body and soul!
HERE... FINALLY...
I'LL GET THE JOB DONE NO MATTER WHAT!
YOU'RE...
...ALREADY HERE, AREN'T YOU...
...YUTO...?

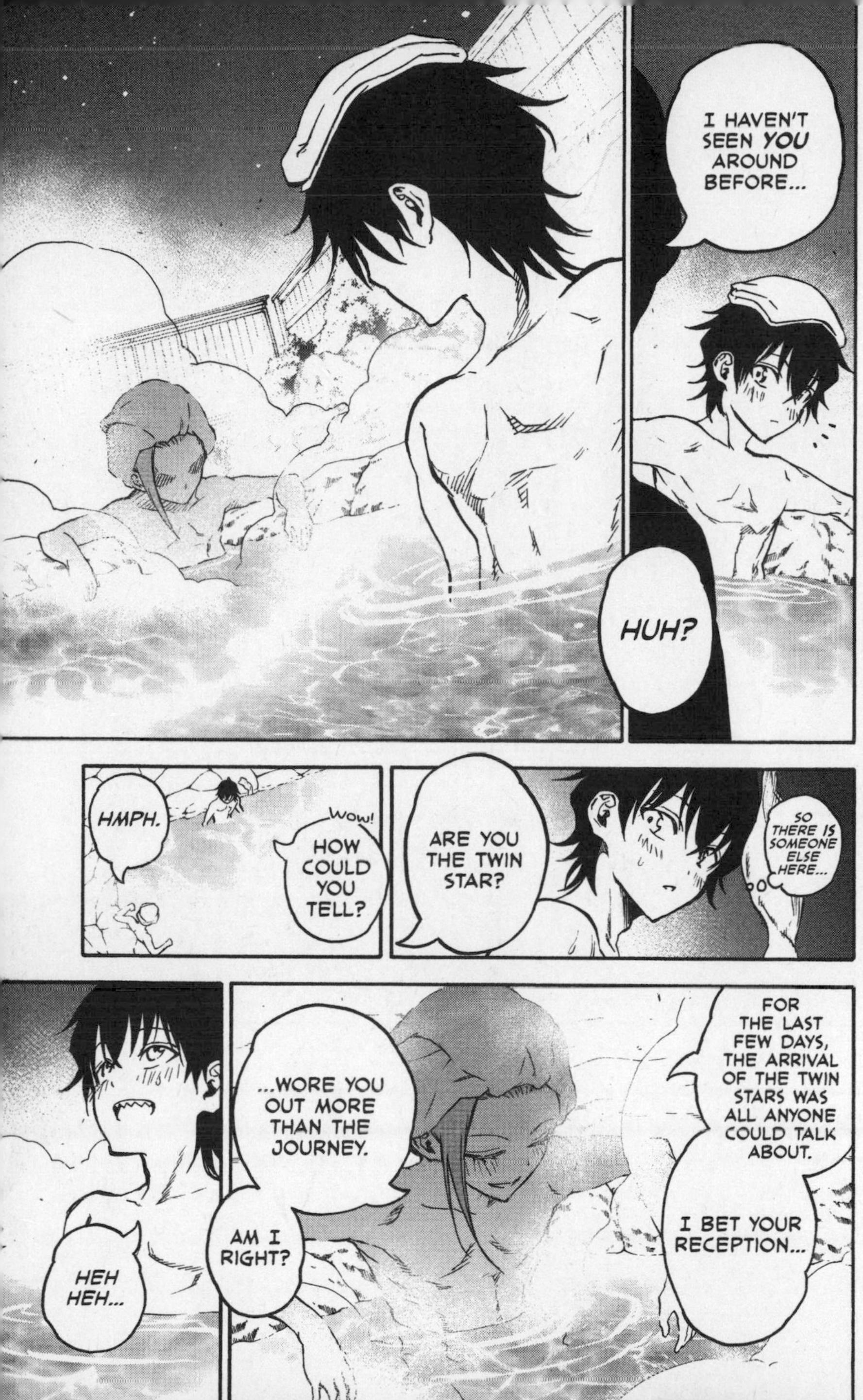
I HAVEN'T SEEN *YOU* AROUND BEFORE...
HUH?
SO THERE *IS* SOMEONE ELSE HERE...
ARE YOU THE TWIN STAR?
WOW!
HOW COULD YOU TELL?
HMPH.
FOR THE LAST FEW DAYS, THE ARRIVAL OF THE TWIN STARS WAS ALL ANYONE COULD TALK ABOUT.
I BET YOUR RECEPTION...
...WORE YOU OUT MORE THAN THE JOURNEY.
AM I RIGHT?
HEH HEH...

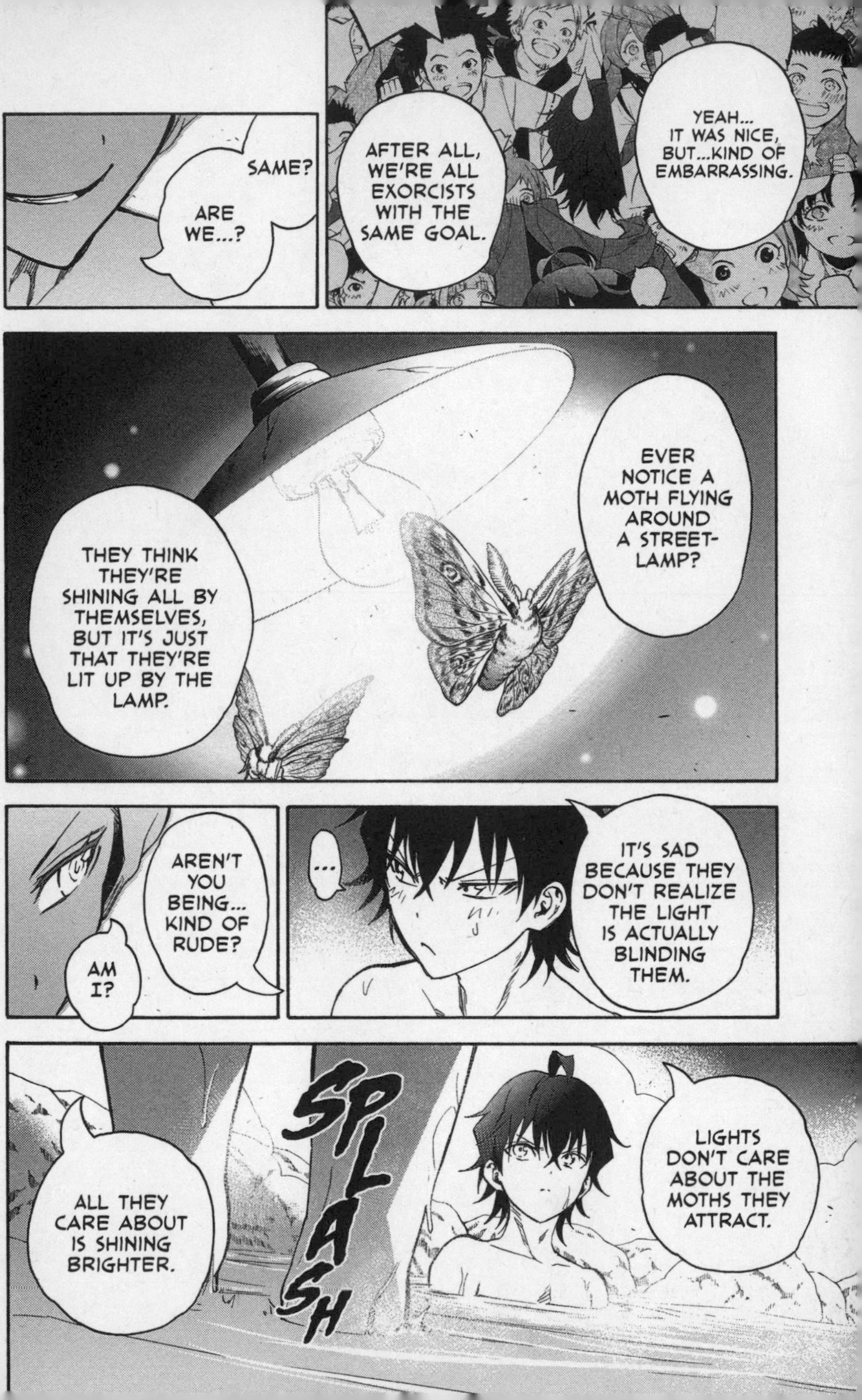
YEAH... IT WAS NICE, BUT...KIND OF EMBARRASSING.
AFTER ALL, WE'RE ALL EXORCISTS WITH THE SAME GOAL.
SAME?
ARE WE...?
EVER NOTICE A MOTH FLYING AROUND A STREET-LAMP?
THEY THINK THEY'RE SHINING ALL BY THEMSELVES, BUT IT'S JUST THAT THEY'RE LIT UP BY THE LAMP.
IT'S SAD BECAUSE THEY DON'T REALIZE THE LIGHT IS ACTUALLY BLINDING THEM.
...
AREN'T YOU BEING... KIND OF RUDE?
AM I?
LIGHTS DON'T CARE ABOUT THE MOTHS THEY ATTRACT.
SPLASH
ALL THEY CARE ABOUT IS SHINING BRIGHTER.

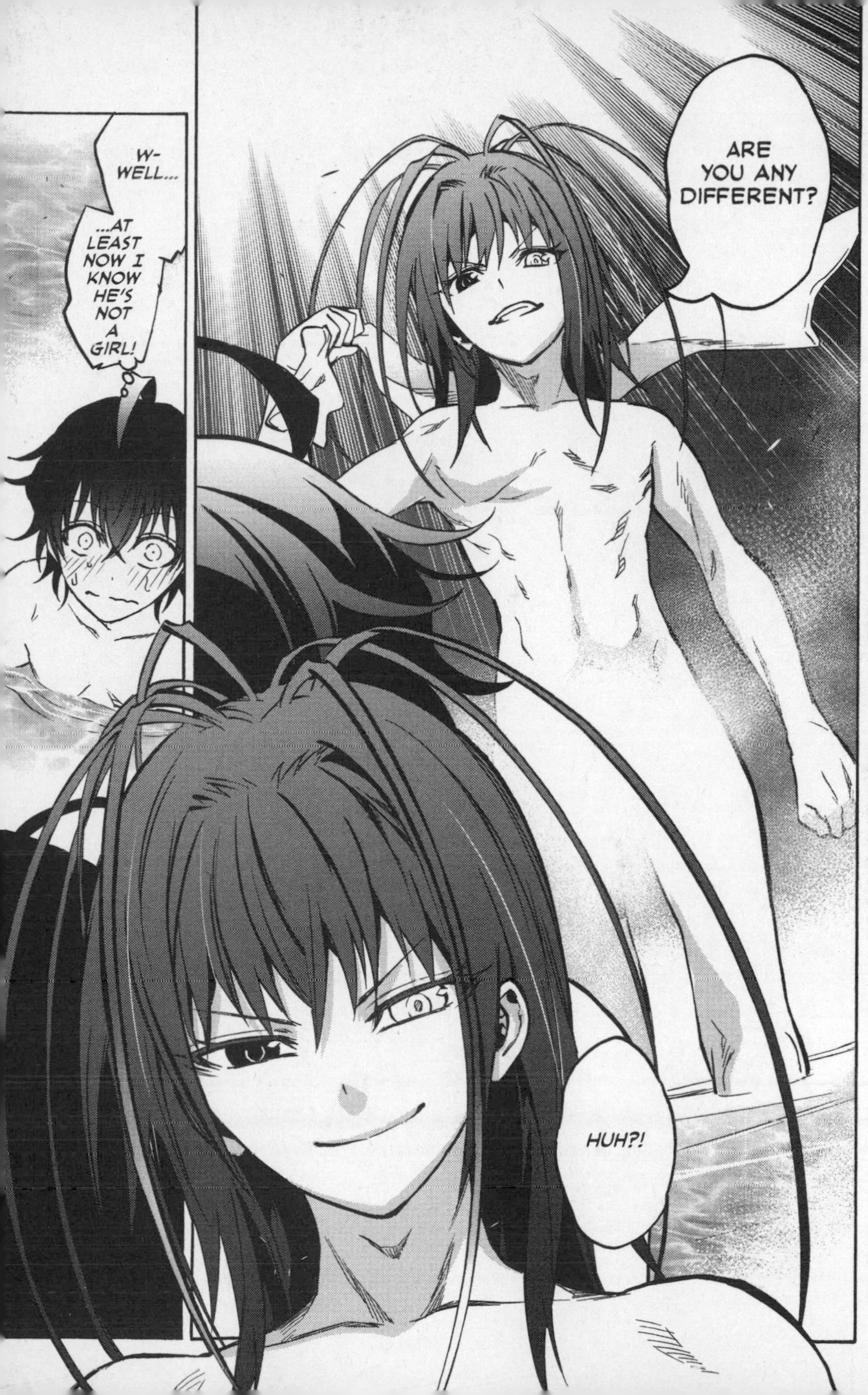
ARE YOU ANY DIFFERENT?
HUH?!
W-WELL...
...AT LEAST NOW I KNOW HE'S NOT A GIRL!

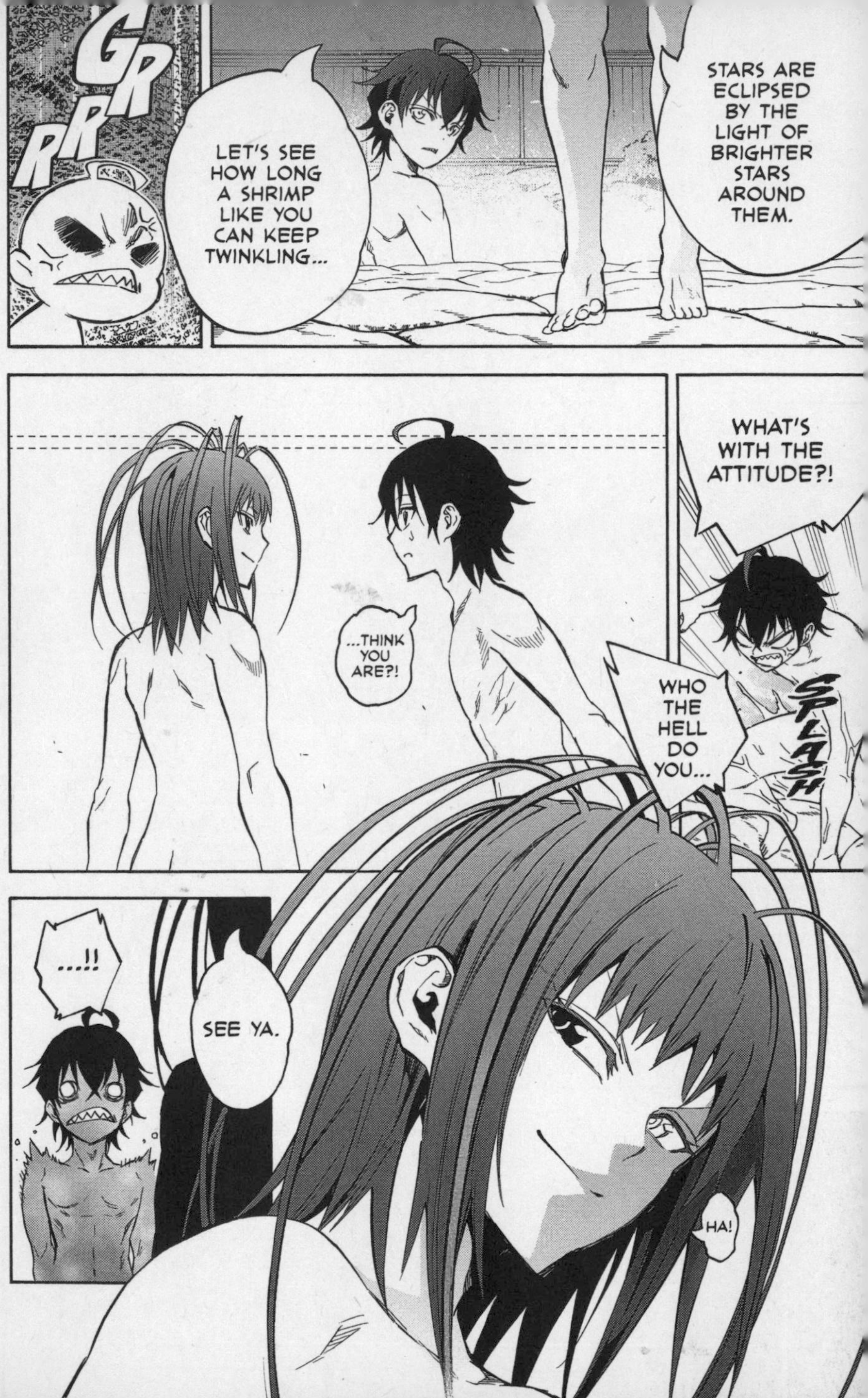
STARS ARE ECLIPSED BY THE LIGHT OF BRIGHTER STARS AROUND THEM.
LET'S SEE HOW LONG A SHRIMP LIKE YOU CAN KEEP TWINKLING...
GRRR
WHAT'S WITH THE ATTITUDE?!
SPLASH
WHO THE HELL DO YOU...
...THINK YOU ARE?!
HA!
SEE YA.
...!!

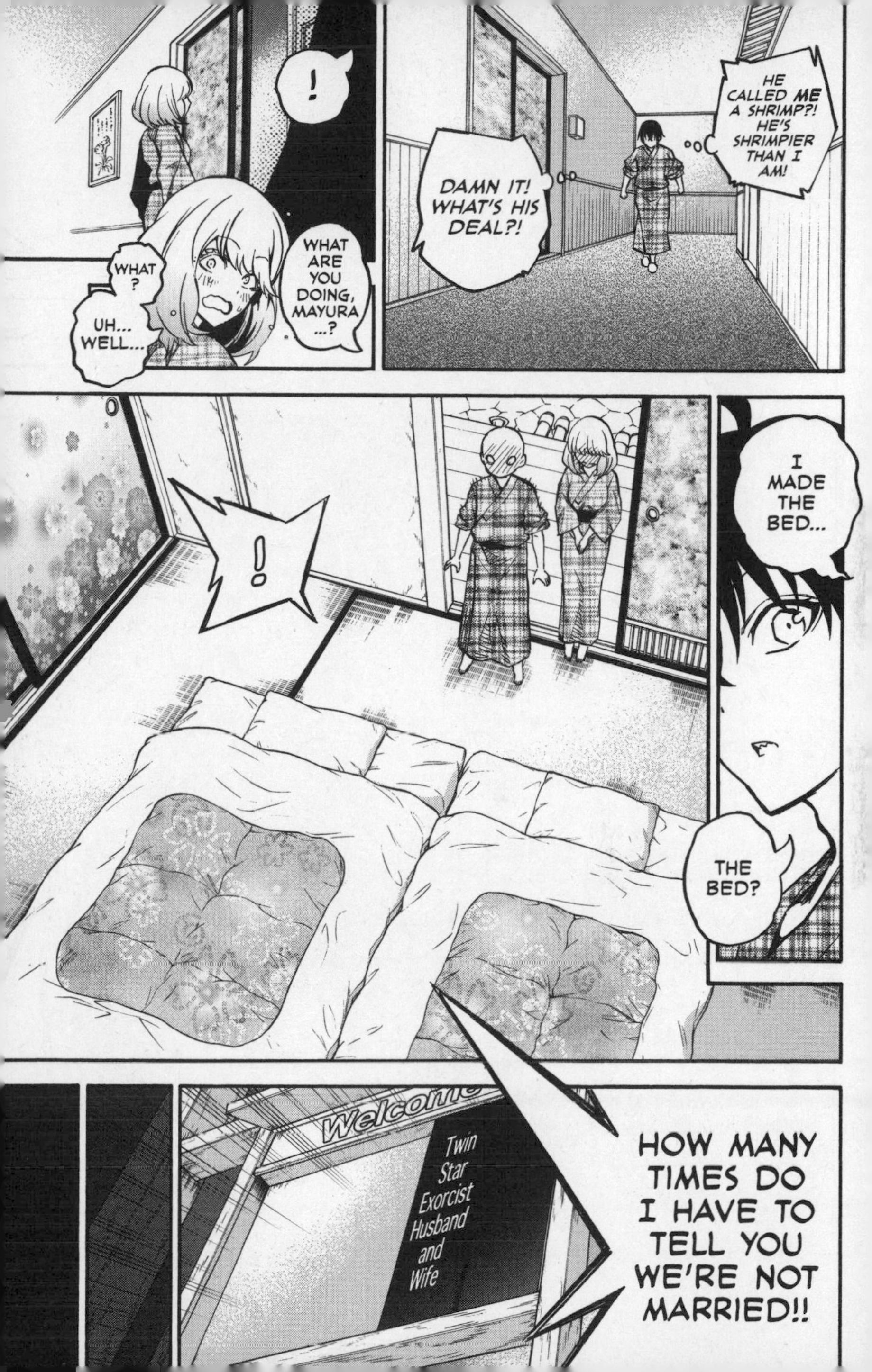
HE CALLED ME A SHRIMP?! HE'S SHRIMPIER THAN I AM!
DAMN IT! WHAT'S HIS DEAL?!
!
WHAT ARE YOU DOING, MAYURA...?
WHAT?
UH... WELL...
I MADE THE BED...
THE BED?
!
HOW MANY TIMES DO I HAVE TO TELL YOU WE'RE NOT MARRIED!!
Welcome
Twin Star Exorcist Husband and Wife

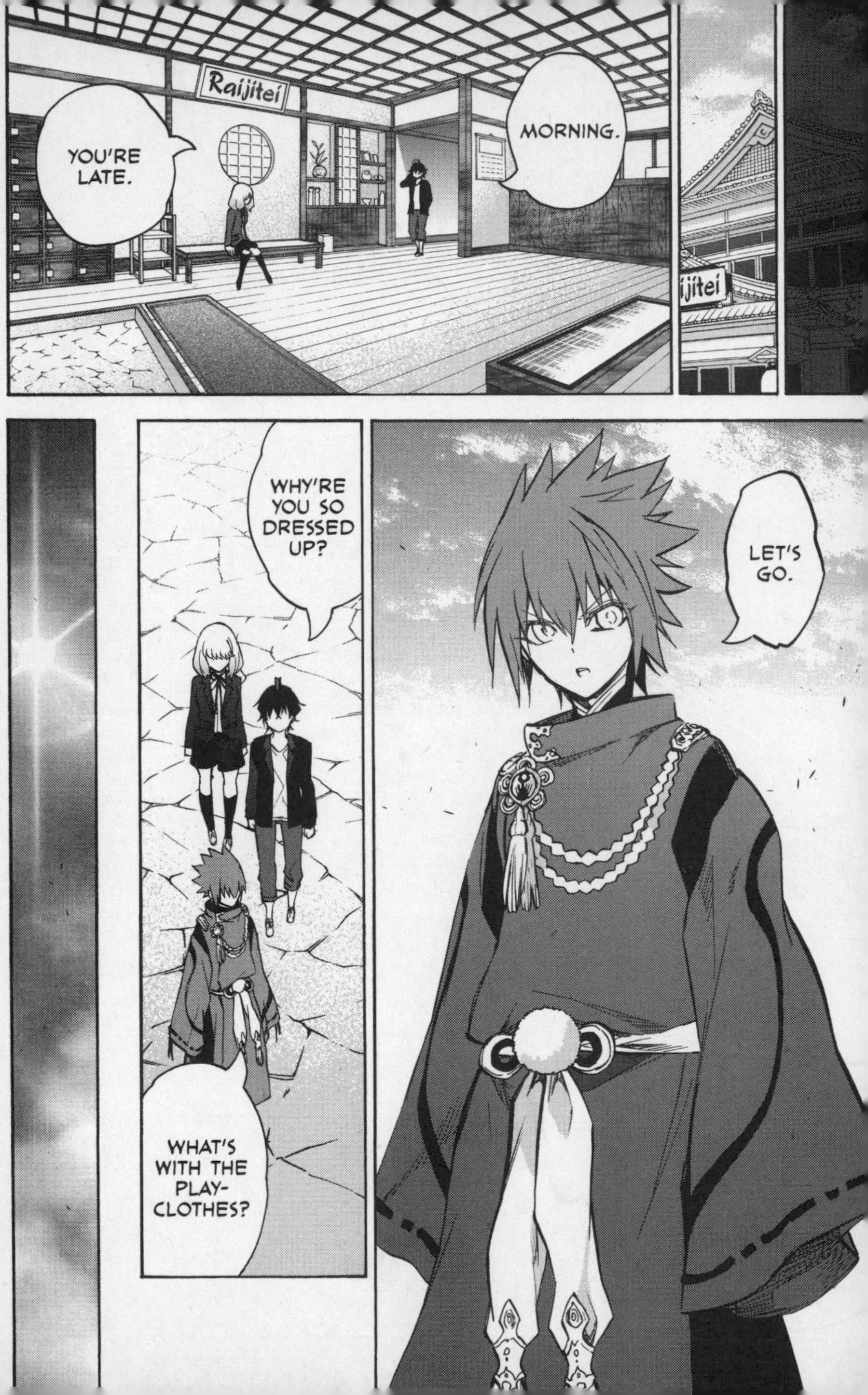
Raijitei
MORNING.
YOU'RE LATE.
LET'S GO.
WHY'RE YOU SO DRESSED UP?
WHAT'S WITH THE PLAY-CLOTHES?

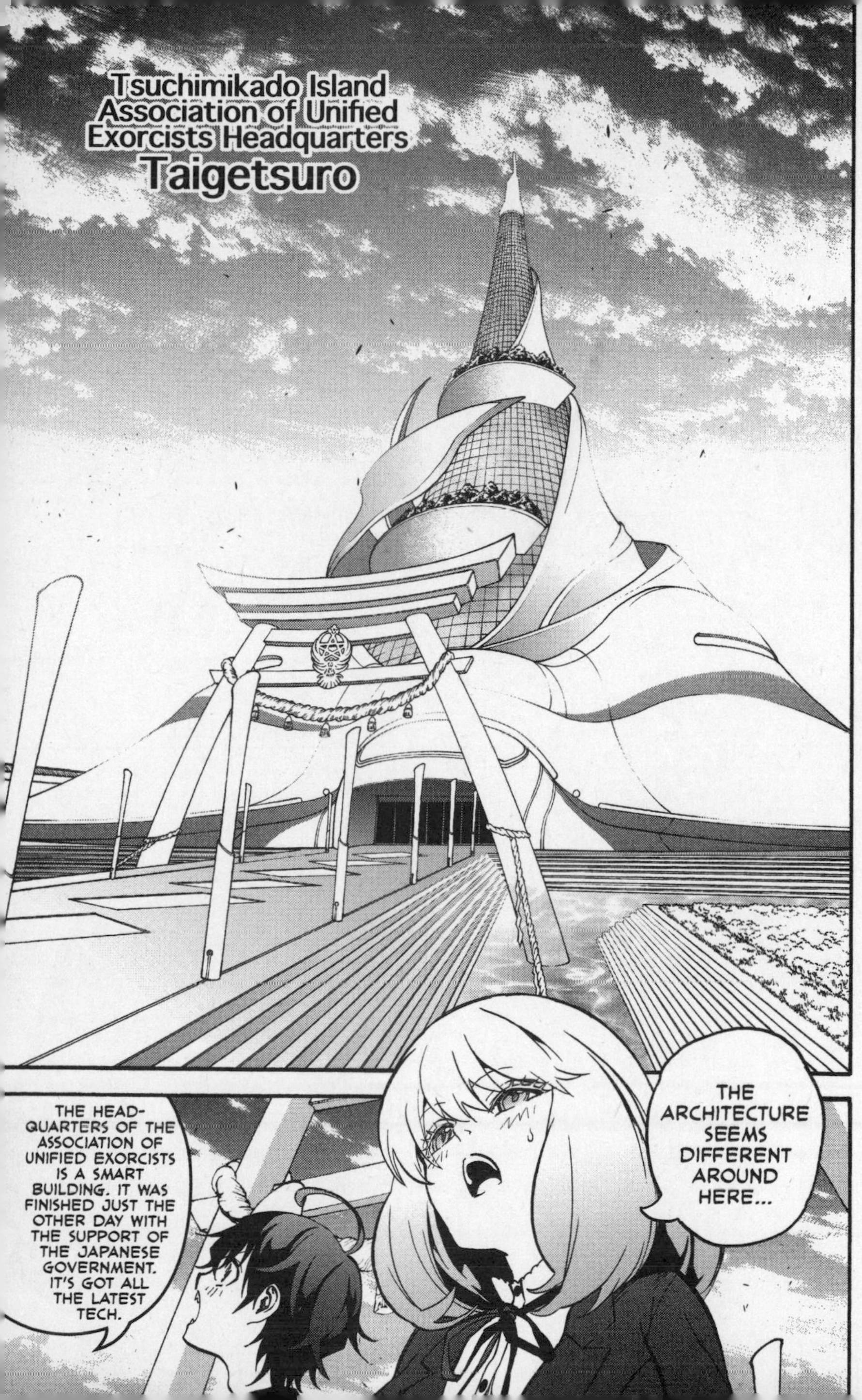
Tsuchimikado Island Association of Unified Exorcists Headquarters
Taigetsuro
THE ARCHITECTURE SEEMS DIFFERENT AROUND HERE...
THE HEAD-QUARTERS OF THE ASSOCIATION OF UNIFIED EXORCISTS IS A SMART BUILDING. IT WAS FINISHED JUST THE OTHER DAY WITH THE SUPPORT OF THE JAPANESE GOVERNMENT. IT'S GOT ALL THE LATEST TECH.

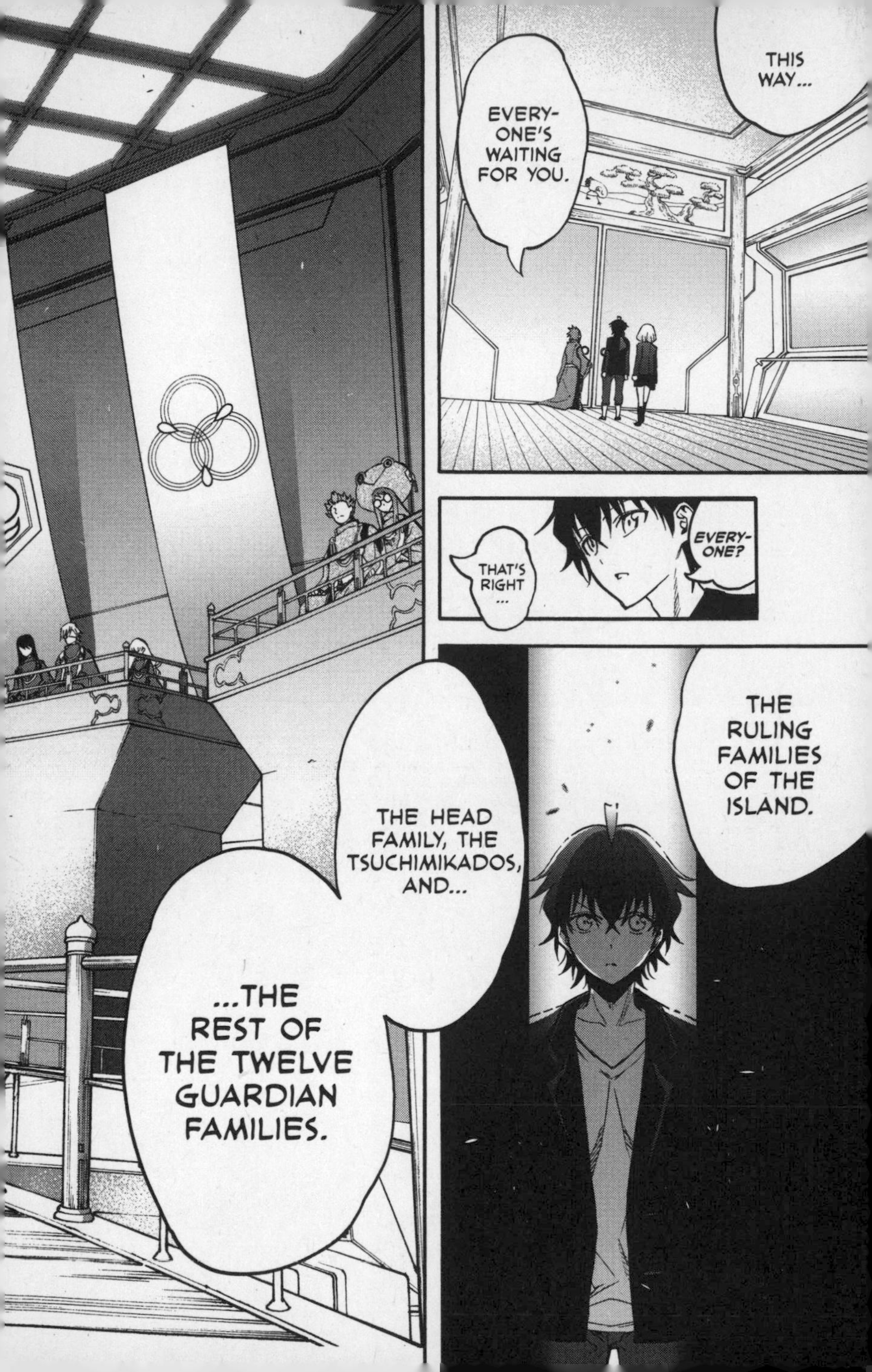
THIS WAY...
EVERY-ONE'S WAITING FOR YOU.
EVERY-ONE?
THAT'S RIGHT...
THE RULING FAMILIES OF THE ISLAND.
THE HEAD FAMILY, THE TSUCHIMIKADOS, AND...
...THE REST OF THE TWELVE GUARDIAN FAMILIES.

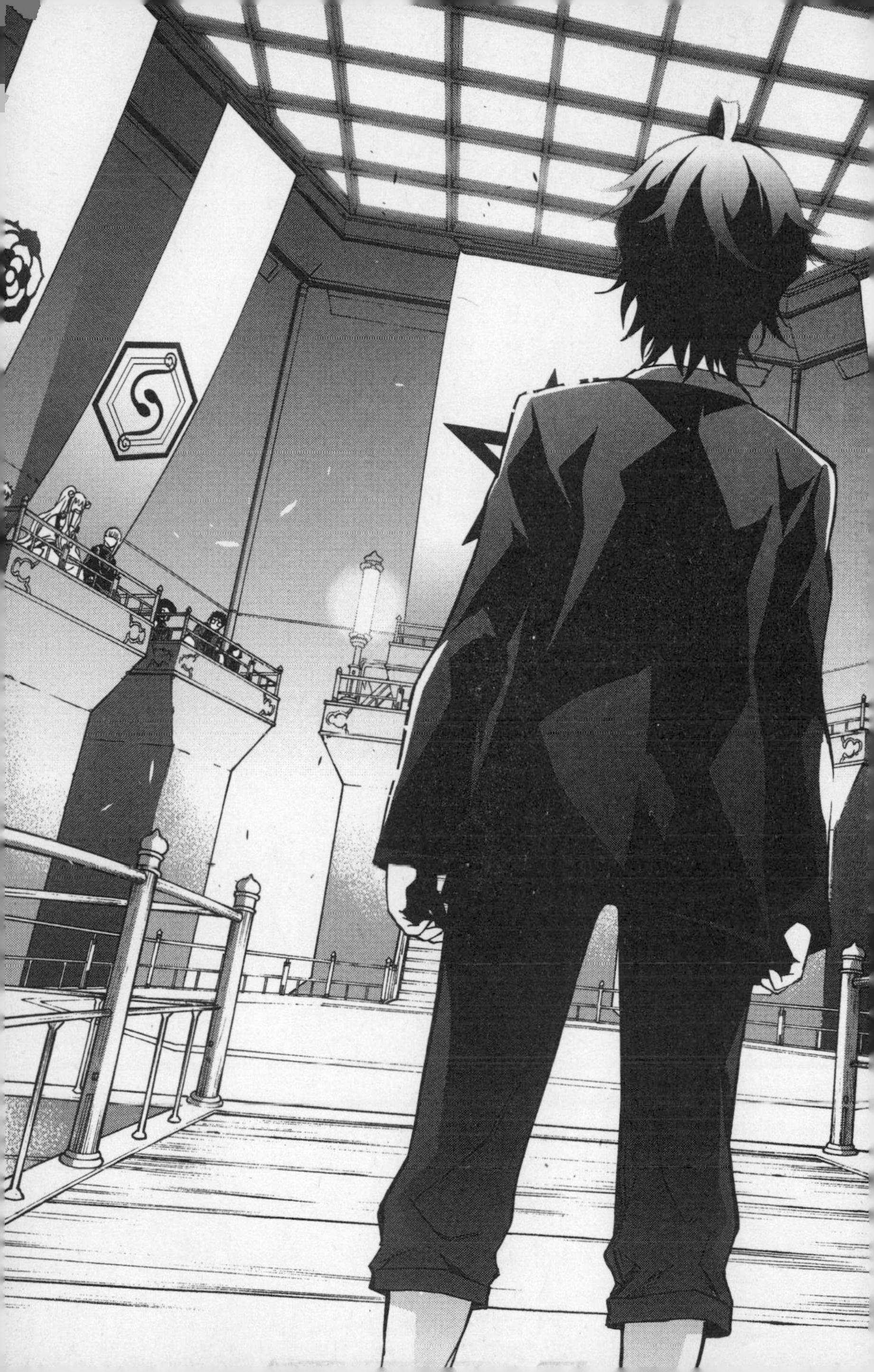

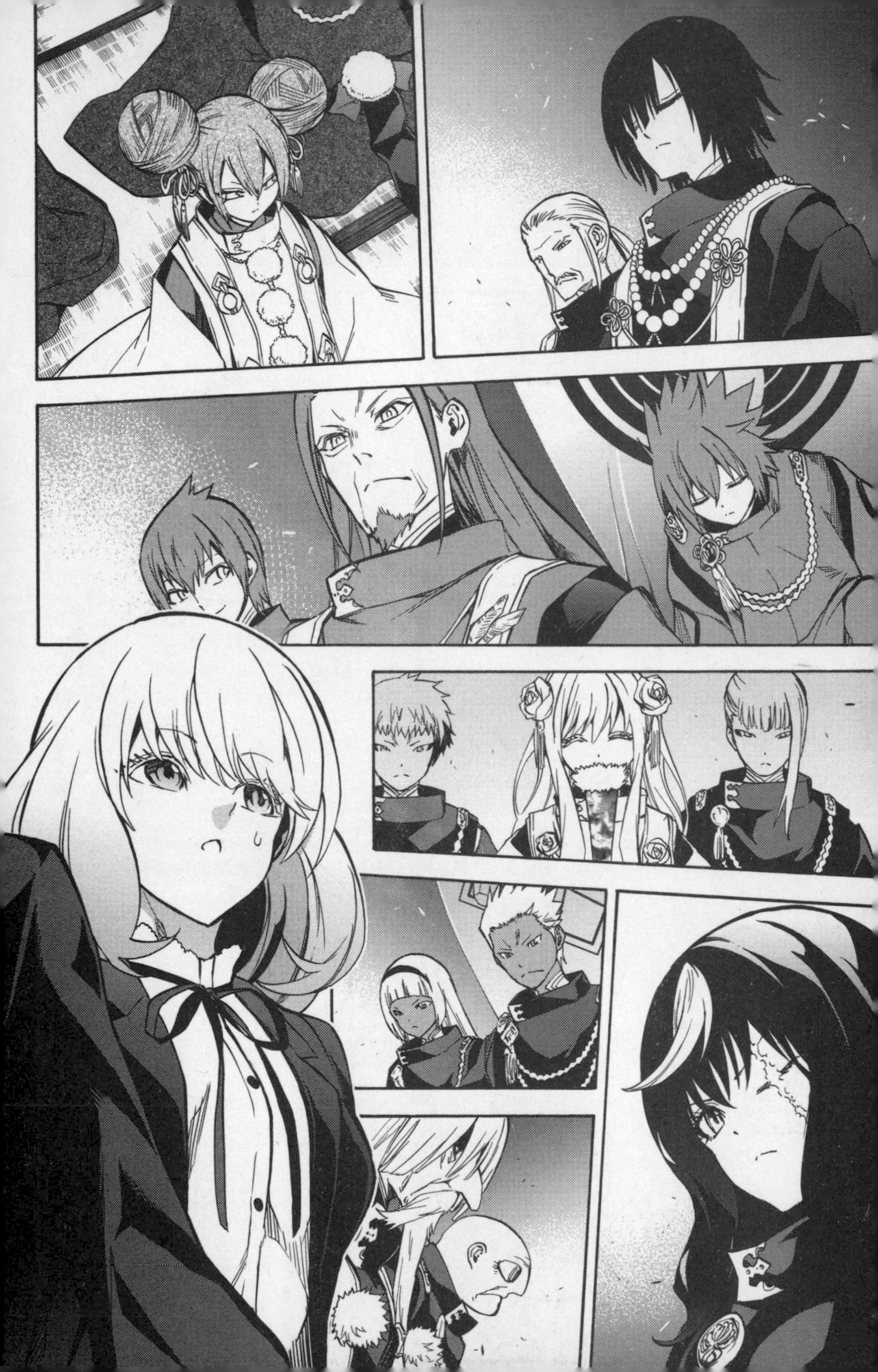

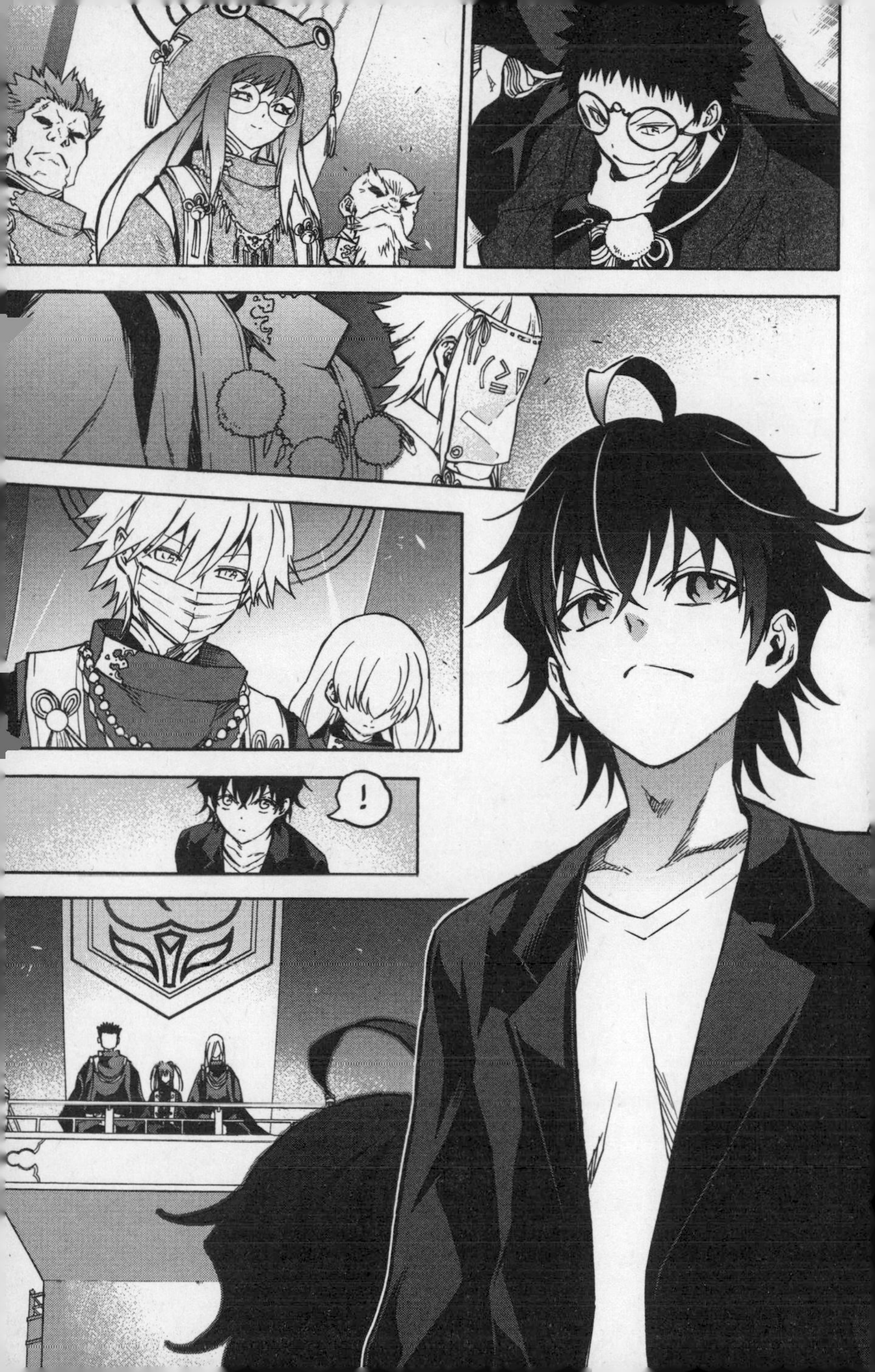
!

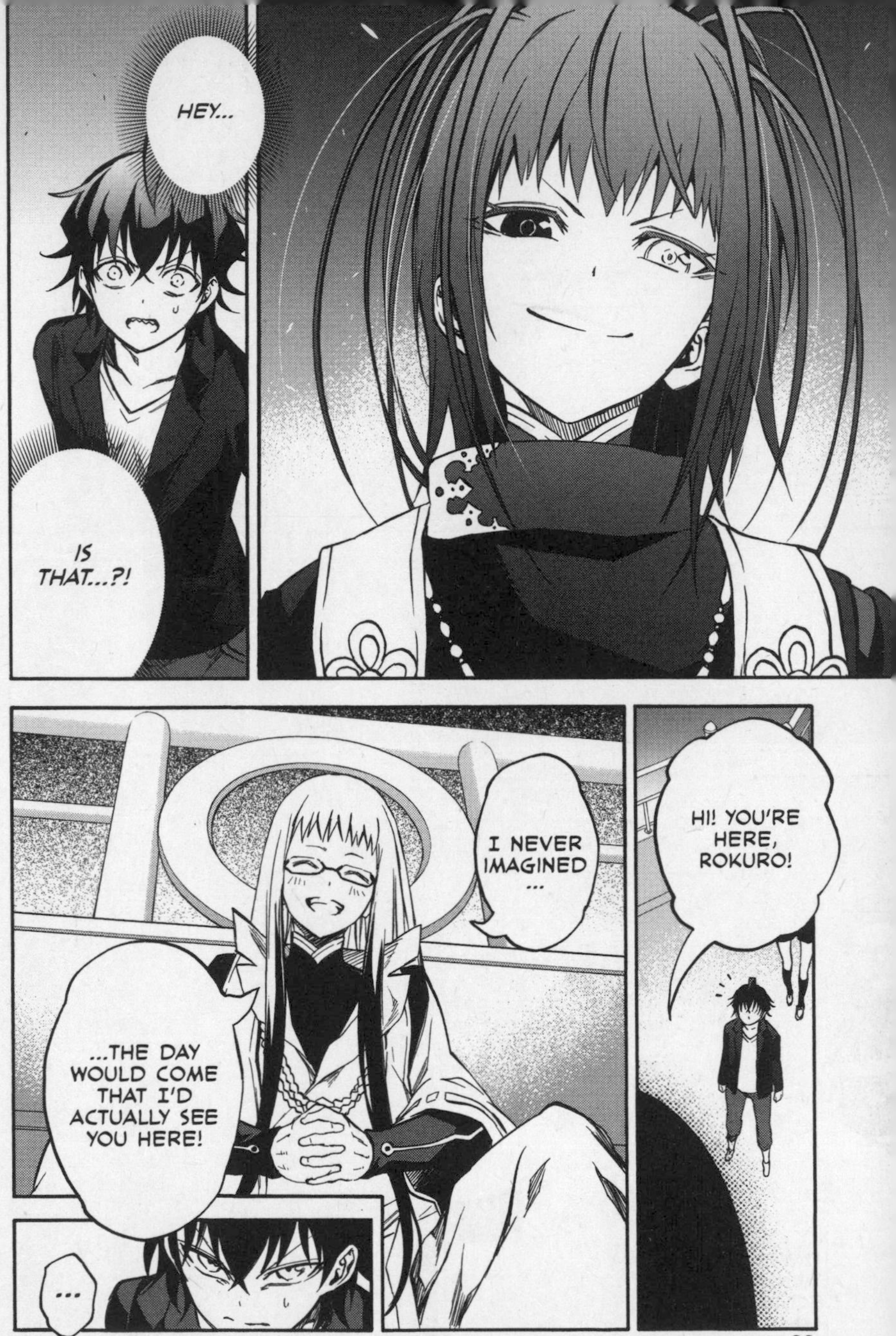
HEY...
IS THAT...?!
HI! YOU'RE HERE, ROKURO!
I NEVER IMAGINED ...
...THE DAY WOULD COME THAT I'D ACTUALLY SEE YOU HERE!
...

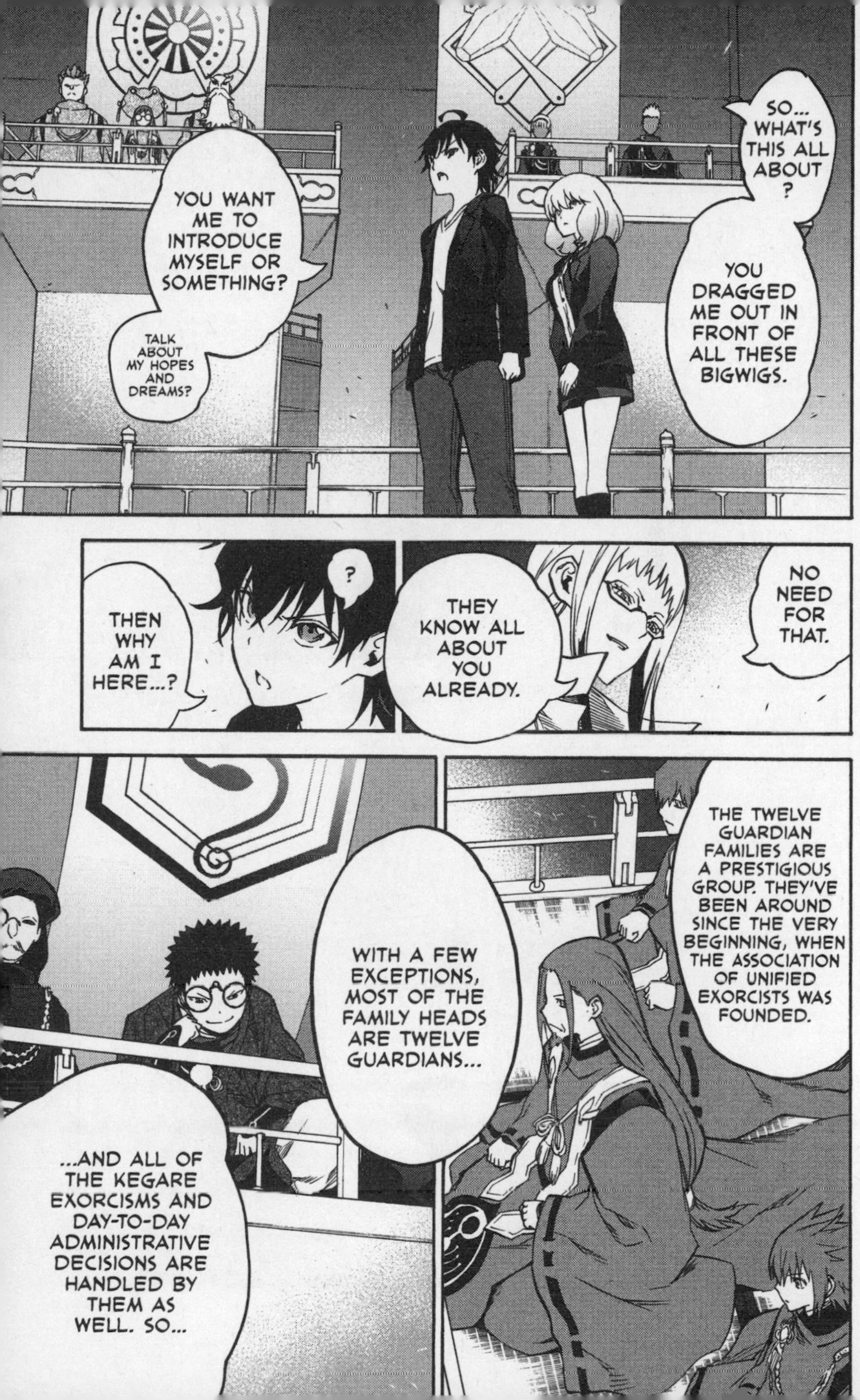
SO... WHAT'S THIS ALL ABOUT ?
YOU DRAGGED ME OUT IN FRONT OF ALL THESE BIGWIGS.
YOU WANT ME TO INTRODUCE MYSELF OR SOMETHING?
TALK ABOUT MY HOPES AND DREAMS?
NO NEED FOR THAT.
THEY KNOW ALL ABOUT YOU ALREADY.
?
THEN WHY AM I HERE...?
THE TWELVE GUARDIAN FAMILIES ARE A PRESTIGIOUS GROUP. THEY'VE BEEN AROUND SINCE THE VERY BEGINNING, WHEN THE ASSOCIATION OF UNIFIED EXORCISTS WAS FOUNDED.
WITH A FEW EXCEPTIONS, MOST OF THE FAMILY HEADS ARE TWELVE GUARDIANS...
...AND ALL OF THE KEGARE EXORCISMS AND DAY-TO-DAY ADMINISTRATIVE DECISIONS ARE HANDLED BY THEM AS WELL. SO...

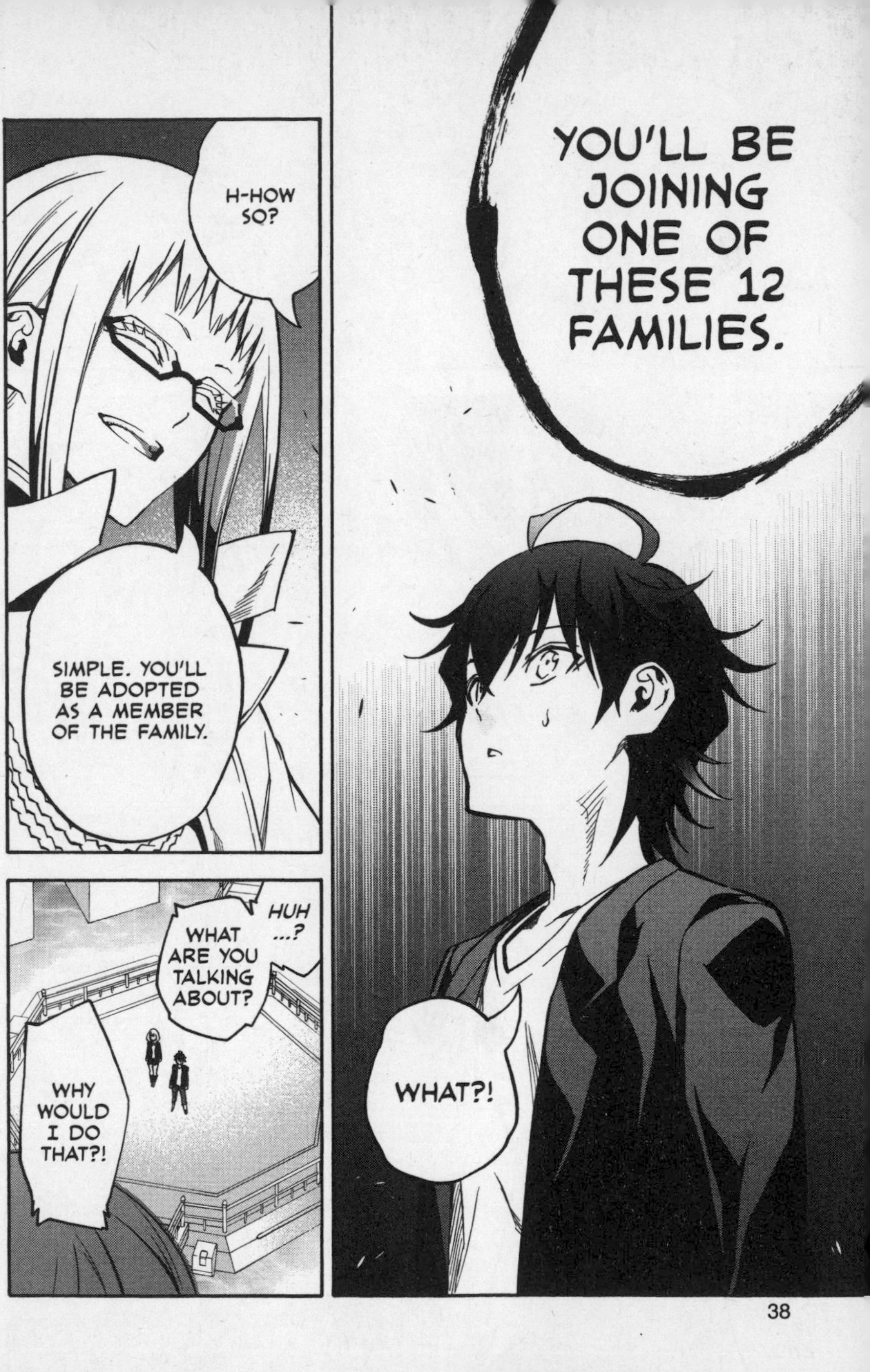
YOU'LL BE JOINING ONE OF THESE 12 FAMILIES.
WHAT?!
H-HOW SO?
SIMPLE. YOU'LL BE ADOPTED AS A MEMBER OF THE FAMILY.
HUH ...?
WHAT ARE YOU TALKING ABOUT?
WHY WOULD I DO THAT?!

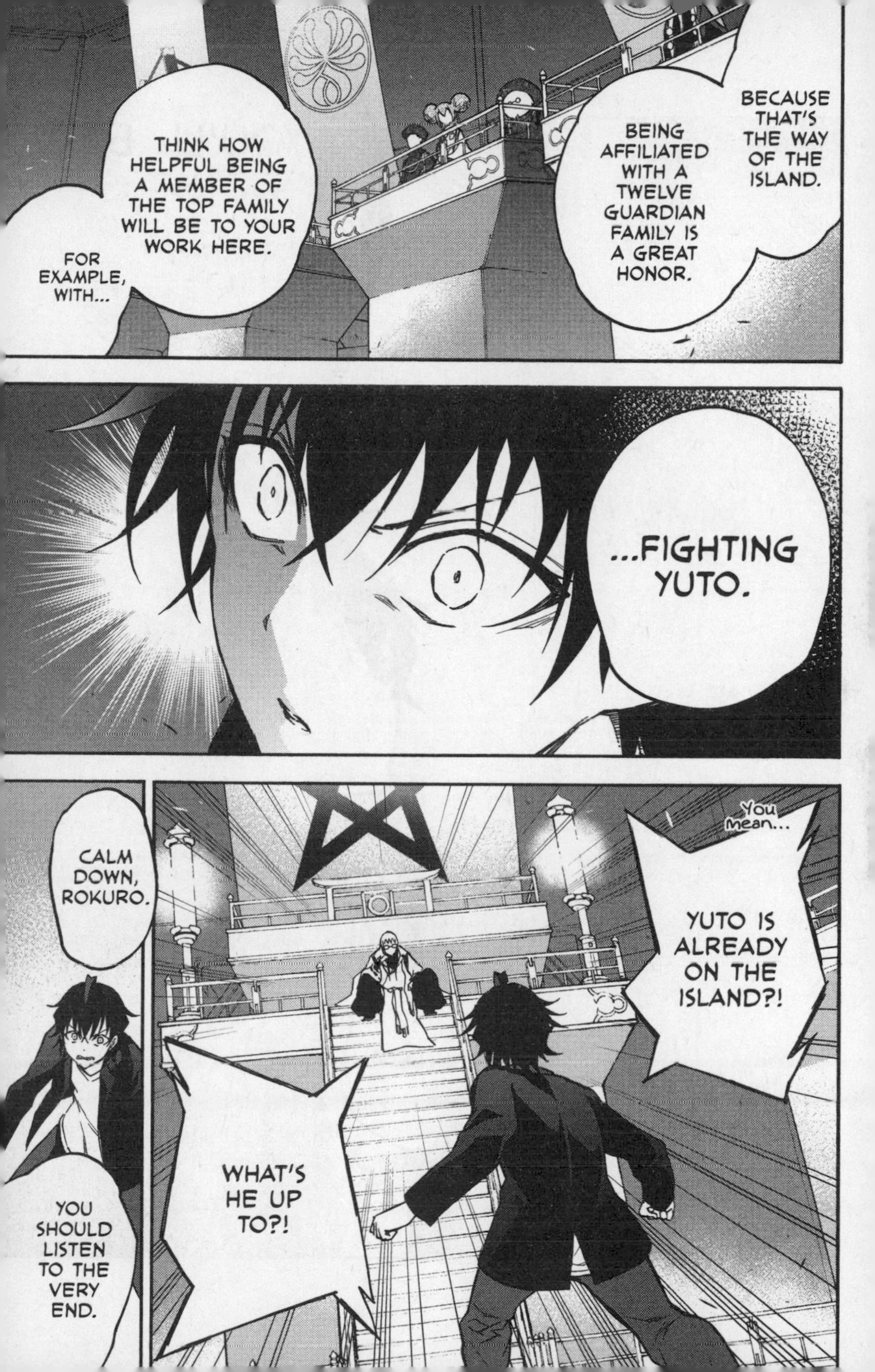
BECAUSE THAT'S THE WAY OF THE ISLAND.
BEING AFFILIATED WITH A TWELVE GUARDIAN FAMILY IS A GREAT HONOR.
THINK HOW HELPFUL BEING A MEMBER OF THE TOP FAMILY WILL BE TO YOUR WORK HERE.
FOR EXAMPLE, WITH...
...FIGHTING YUTO.
You mean...
YUTO IS ALREADY ON THE ISLAND?!
WHAT'S HE UP TO?!
CALM DOWN, ROKURO.
YOU SHOULD LISTEN TO THE VERY END.

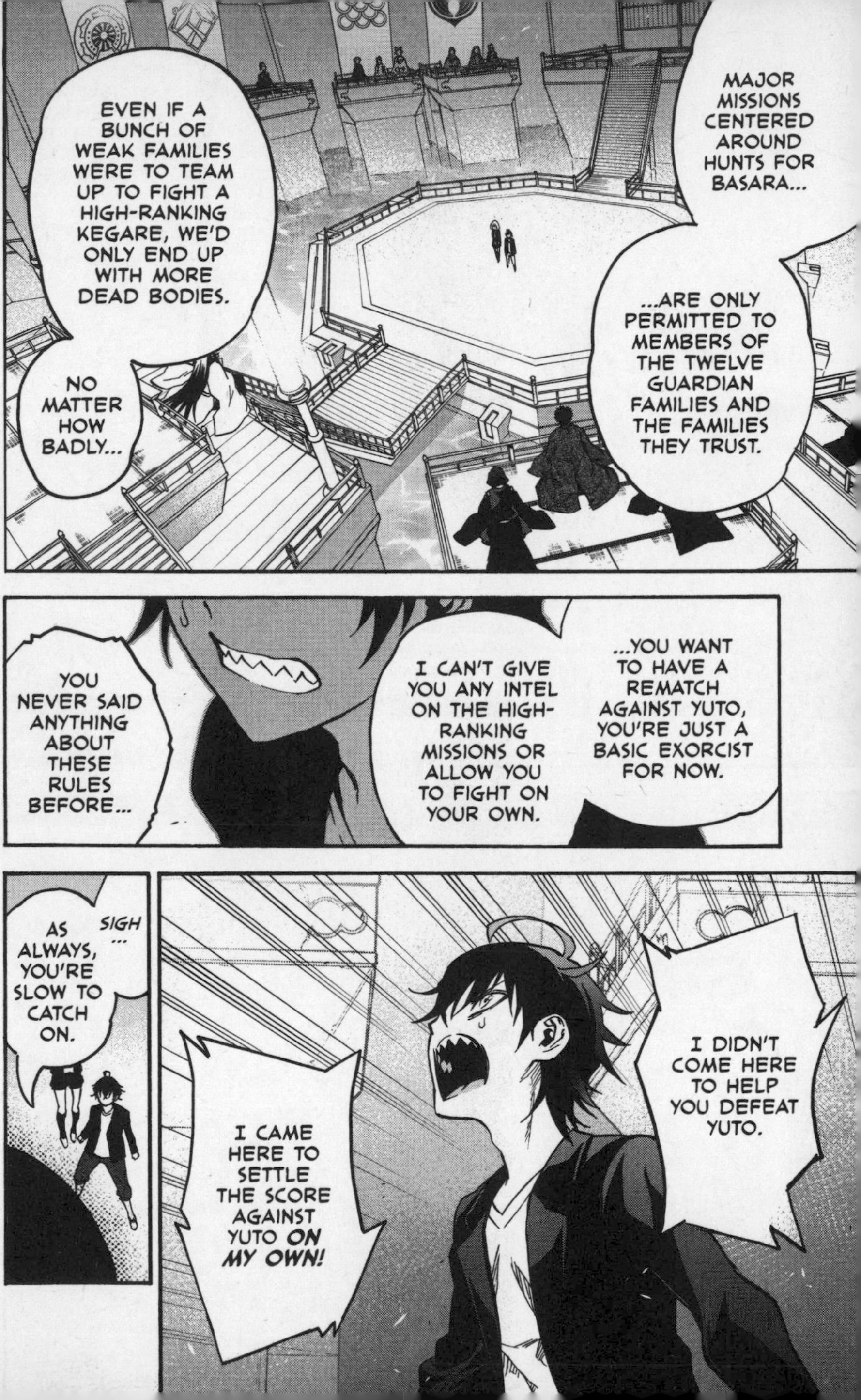
MAJOR MISSIONS CENTERED AROUND HUNTS FOR BASARA...
...ARE ONLY PERMITTED TO MEMBERS OF THE TWELVE GUARDIAN FAMILIES AND THE FAMILIES THEY TRUST.
EVEN IF A BUNCH OF WEAK FAMILIES WERE TO TEAM UP TO FIGHT A HIGH-RANKING KEGARE, WE'D ONLY END UP WITH MORE DEAD BODIES.
NO MATTER HOW BADLY...
...YOU WANT TO HAVE A REMATCH AGAINST YUTO, YOU'RE JUST A BASIC EXORCIST FOR NOW.
I CAN'T GIVE YOU ANY INTEL ON THE HIGH-RANKING MISSIONS OR ALLOW YOU TO FIGHT ON YOUR OWN.
YOU NEVER SAID ANYTHING ABOUT THESE RULES BEFORE...
I DIDN'T COME HERE TO HELP YOU DEFEAT YUTO.
I CAME HERE TO SETTLE THE SCORE AGAINST YUTO *ON MY OWN!*
SIGH...
AS ALWAYS, YOU'RE SLOW TO CATCH ON.

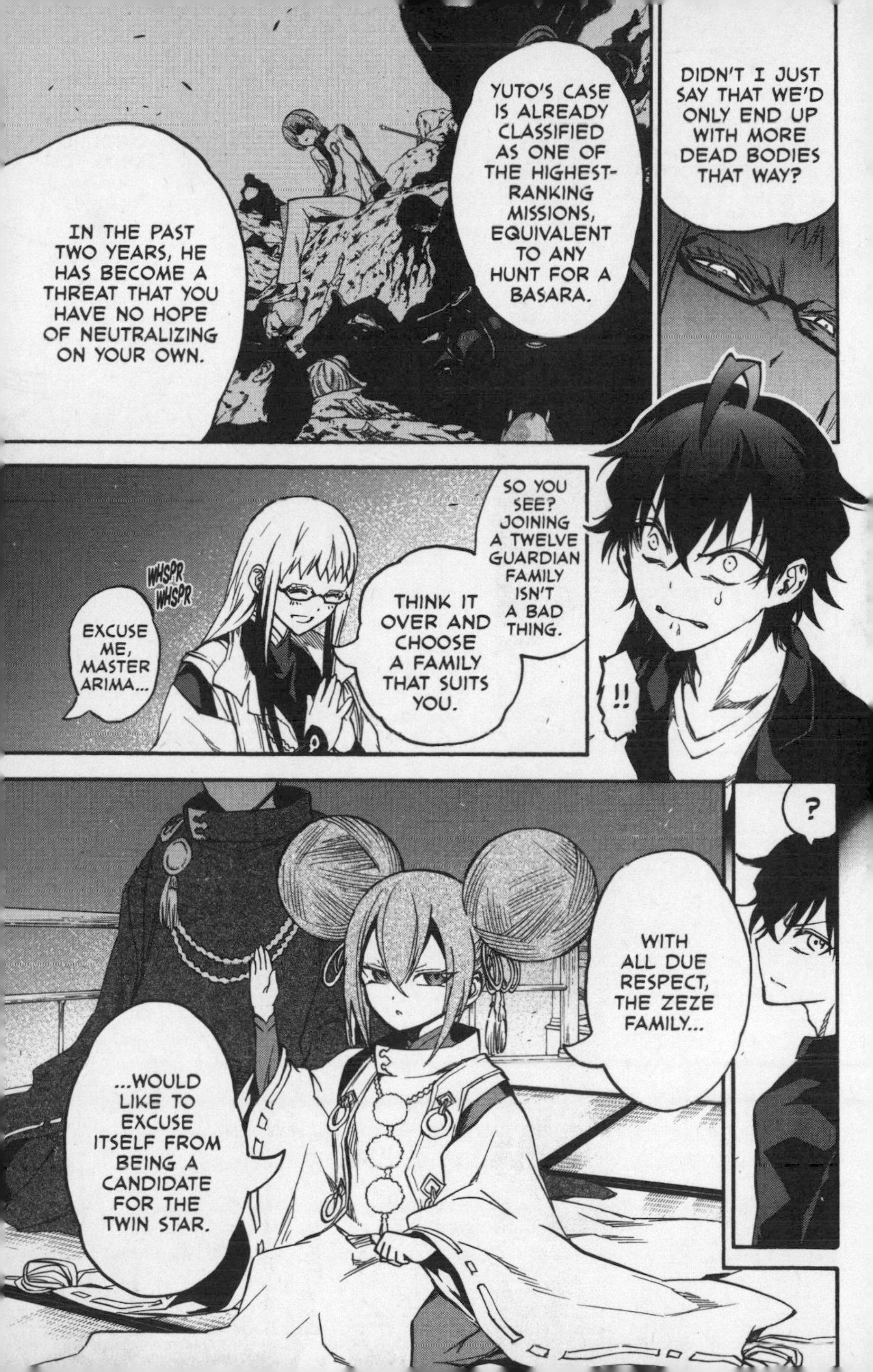
DIDN'T I JUST SAY THAT WE'D ONLY END UP WITH MORE DEAD BODIES THAT WAY?
YUTO'S CASE IS ALREADY CLASSIFIED AS ONE OF THE HIGHEST-RANKING MISSIONS, EQUIVALENT TO ANY HUNT FOR A BASARA.
IN THE PAST TWO YEARS, HE HAS BECOME A THREAT THAT YOU HAVE NO HOPE OF NEUTRALIZING ON YOUR OWN.
!!
SO YOU SEE? JOINING A TWELVE GUARDIAN FAMILY ISN'T A BAD THING.
THINK IT OVER AND CHOOSE A FAMILY THAT SUITS YOU.
WHSPR WHSPR
EXCUSE ME, MASTER ARIMA...
?
WITH ALL DUE RESPECT, THE ZEZE FAMILY...
...WOULD LIKE TO EXCUSE ITSELF FROM BEING A CANDIDATE FOR THE TWIN STAR.

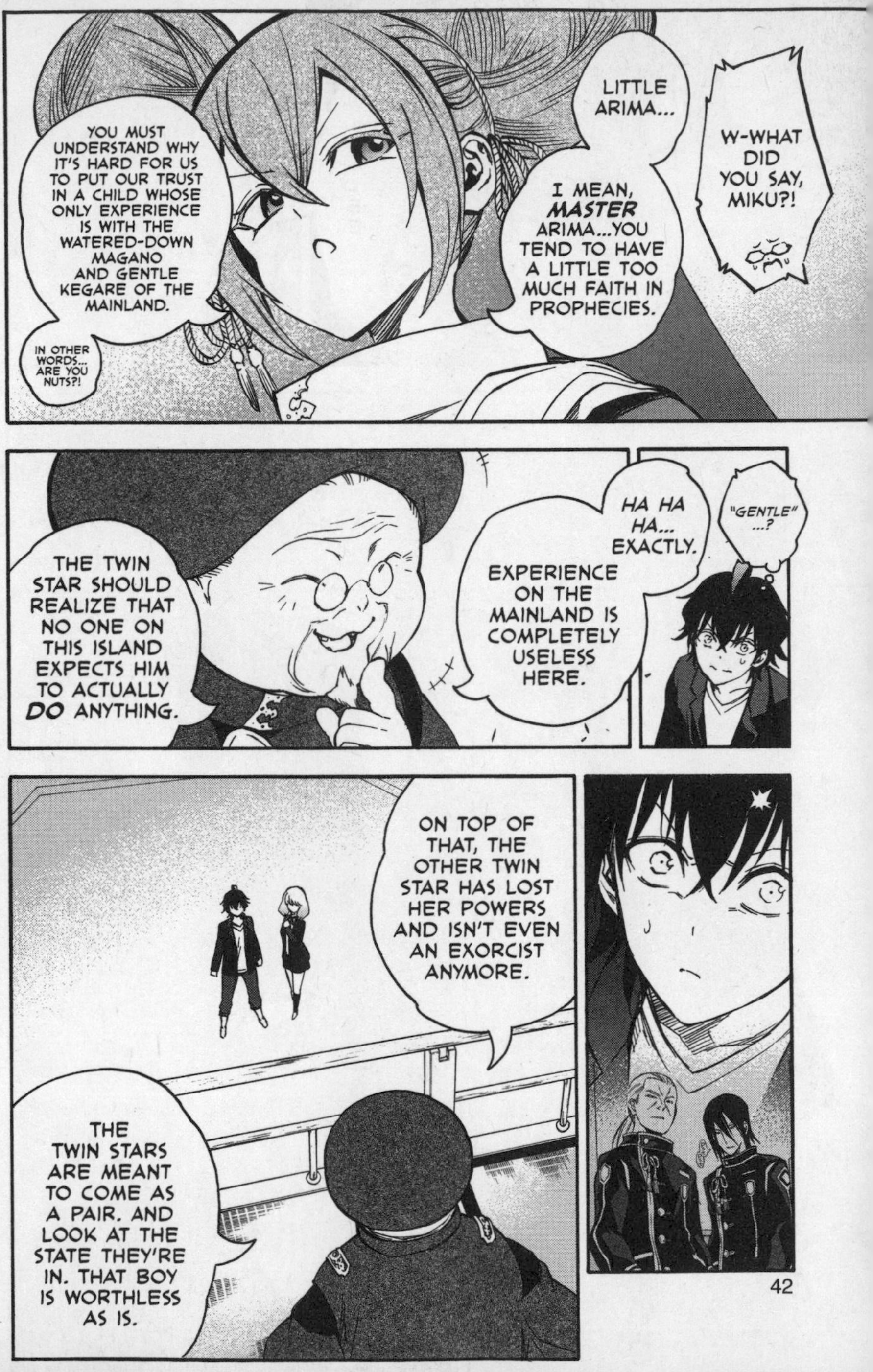
LITTLE ARIMA...
I MEAN, MASTER ARIMA...YOU TEND TO HAVE A LITTLE TOO MUCH FAITH IN PROPHECIES.
W-WHAT DID YOU SAY, MIKU?!
YOU MUST UNDERSTAND WHY IT'S HARD FOR US TO PUT OUR TRUST IN A CHILD WHOSE ONLY EXPERIENCE IS WITH THE WATERED-DOWN MAGANO AND GENTLE KEGARE OF THE MAINLAND.
IN OTHER WORDS... ARE YOU NUTS?!
"GENTLE" ...?
HA HA HA... EXACTLY.
EXPERIENCE ON THE MAINLAND IS COMPLETELY USELESS HERE.
THE TWIN STAR SHOULD REALIZE THAT NO ONE ON THIS ISLAND EXPECTS HIM TO ACTUALLY DO ANYTHING.
ON TOP OF THAT, THE OTHER TWIN STAR HAS LOST HER POWERS AND ISN'T EVEN AN EXORCIST ANYMORE.
THE TWIN STARS ARE MEANT TO COME AS A PAIR. AND LOOK AT THE STATE THEY'RE IN. THAT BOY IS WORTHLESS AS IS.

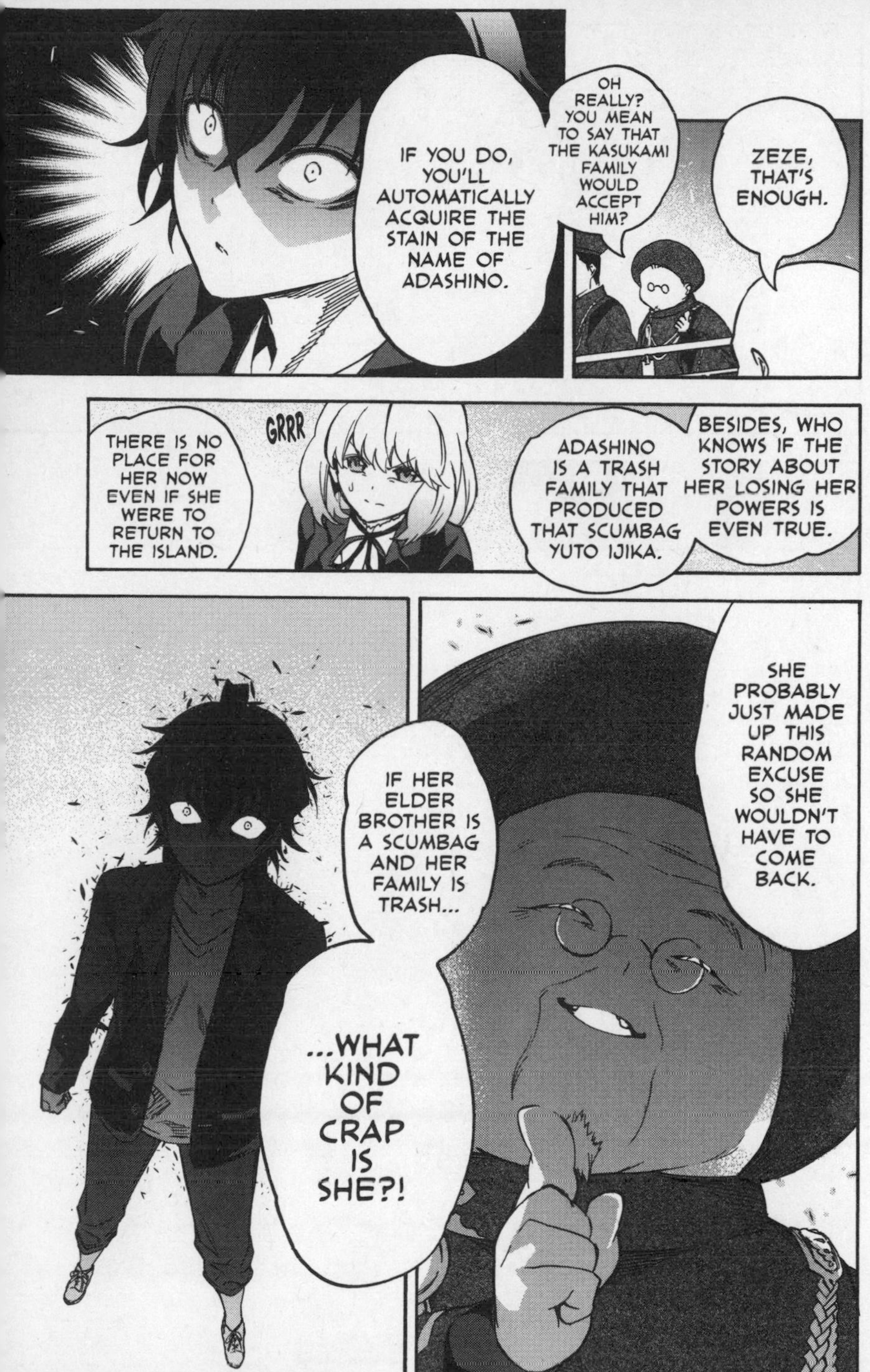
ZEZE, THAT'S ENOUGH.
OH REALLY? YOU MEAN TO SAY THAT THE KASUKAMI FAMILY WOULD ACCEPT HIM?
IF YOU DO, YOU'LL AUTOMATICALLY ACQUIRE THE STAIN OF THE NAME OF ADASHINO.
BESIDES, WHO KNOWS IF THE STORY ABOUT HER LOSING HER POWERS IS EVEN TRUE.
ADASHINO IS A TRASH FAMILY THAT PRODUCED THAT SCUMBAG YUTO IJIKA.
GRRR
THERE IS NO PLACE FOR HER NOW EVEN IF SHE WERE TO RETURN TO THE ISLAND.
SHE PROBABLY JUST MADE UP THIS RANDOM EXCUSE SO SHE WOULDN'T HAVE TO COME BACK.
IF HER ELDER BROTHER IS A SCUMBAG AND HER FAMILY IS TRASH...
...WHAT KIND OF CRAP IS SHE?!

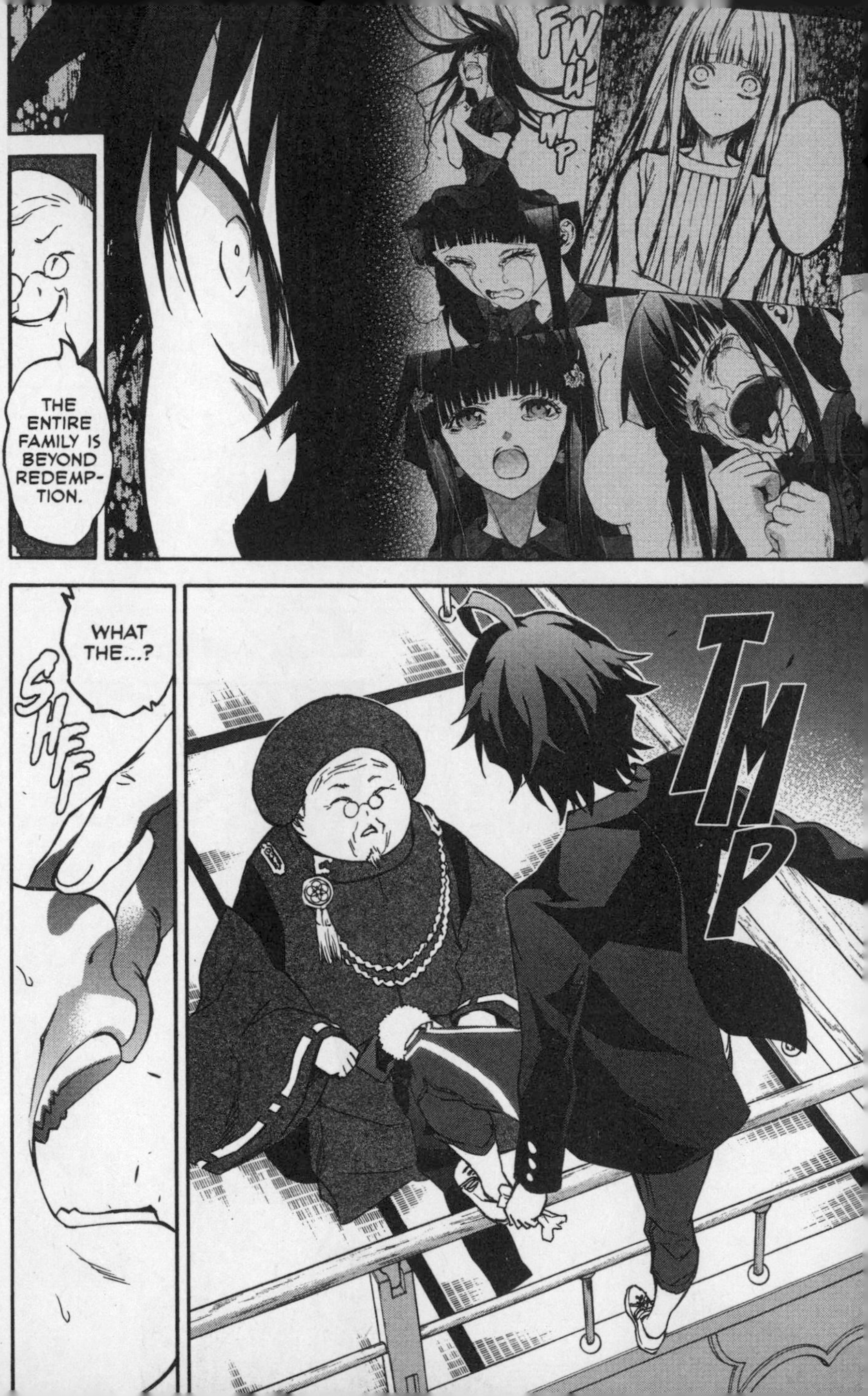
FWUMP
THE ENTIRE FAMILY IS BEYOND REDEMPTION.
TMP
WHAT THE...?
SHF

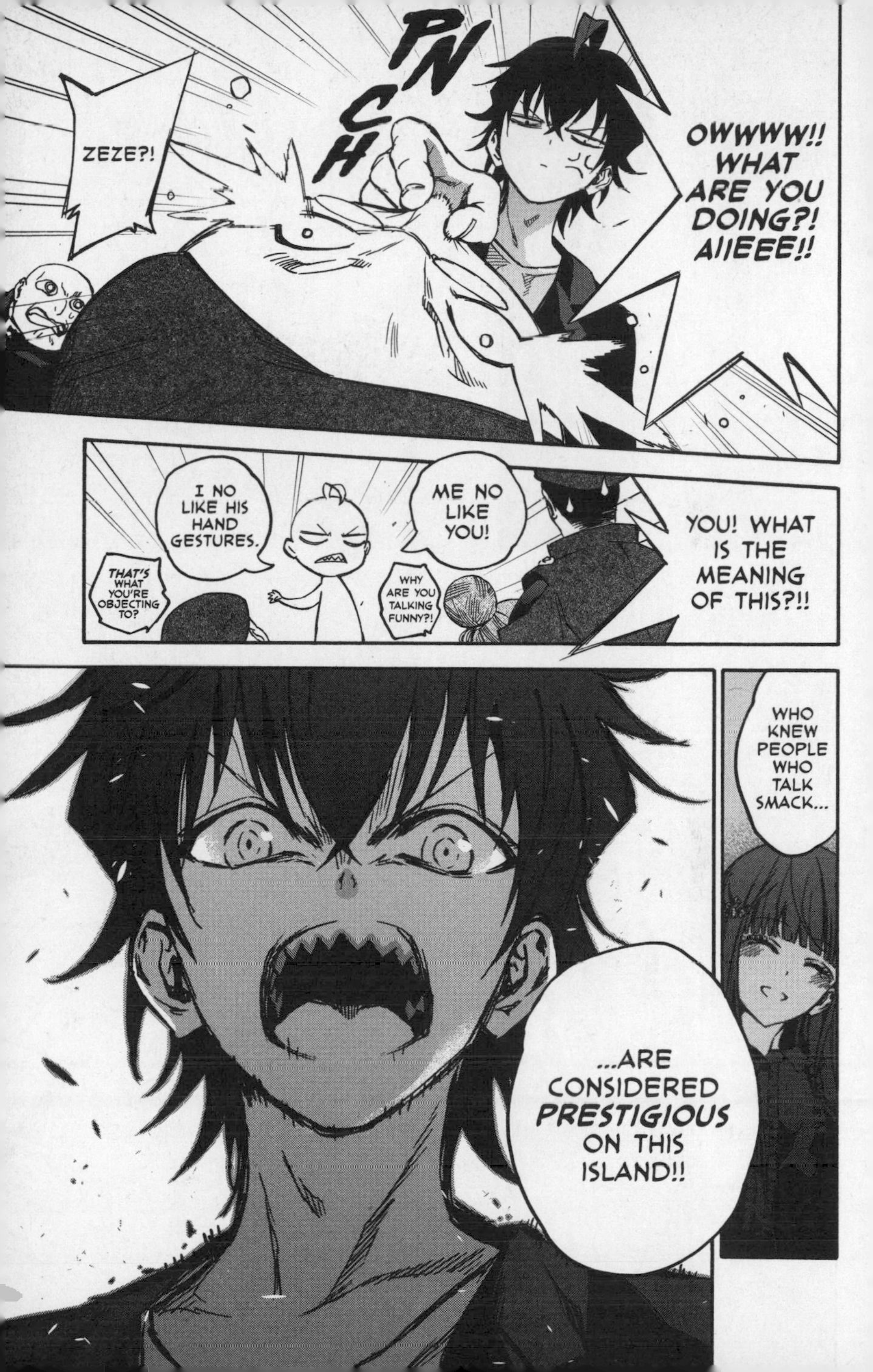
PNCH
OWWWW!! WHAT ARE YOU DOING?! AIIEEE!!
ZEZE?!
YOU! WHAT IS THE MEANING OF THIS?!!
ME NO LIKE YOU!
WHY ARE YOU TALKING FUNNY?!
I NO LIKE HIS HAND GESTURES.
THAT'S WHAT YOU'RE OBJECTING TO?
WHO KNEW PEOPLE WHO TALK SMACK...
...ARE CONSIDERED *PRESTIGIOUS* ON THIS ISLAND!!

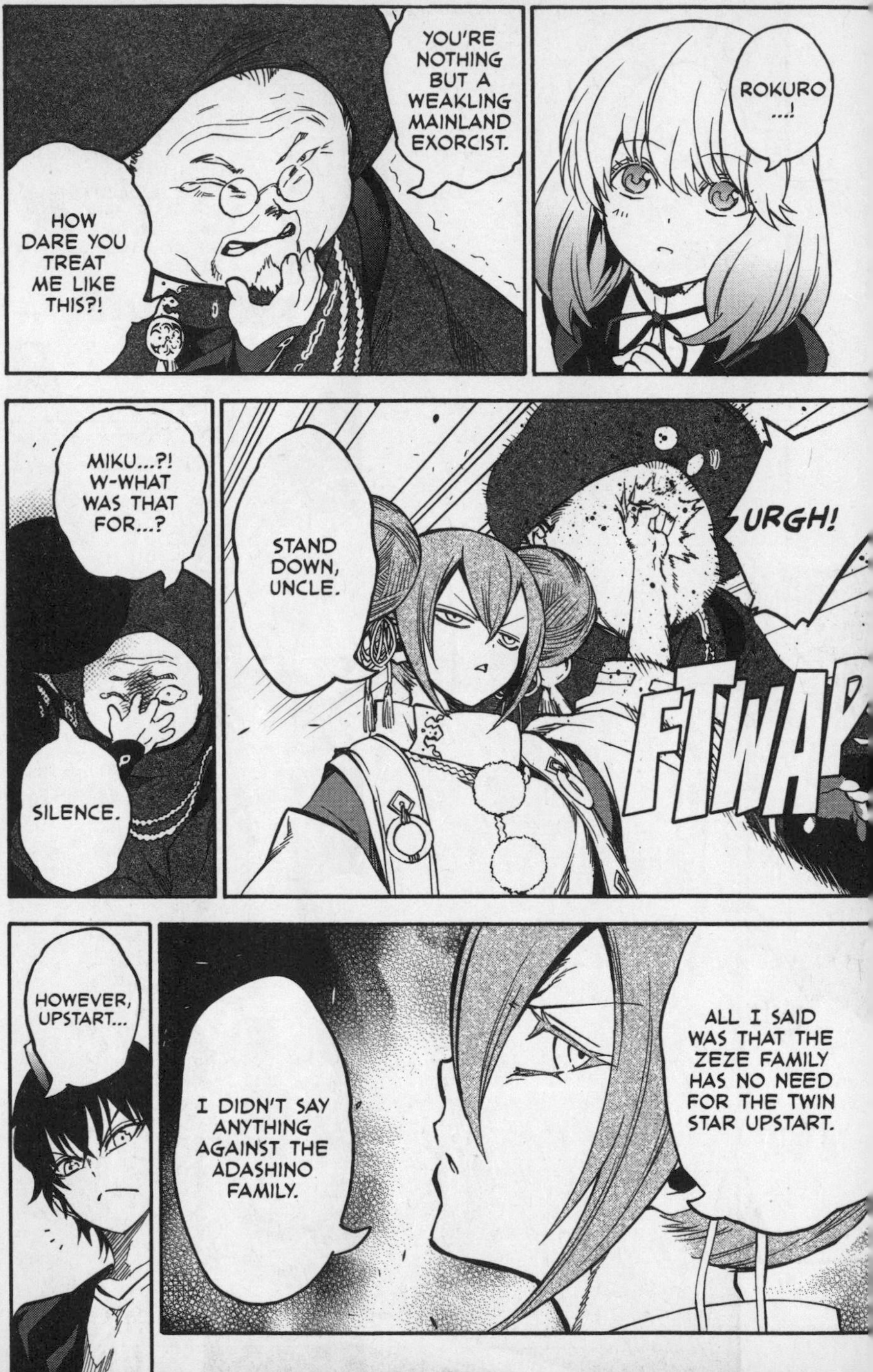
ROKURO ...!
YOU'RE NOTHING BUT A WEAKLING MAINLAND EXORCIST.
HOW DARE YOU TREAT ME LIKE THIS?!
URGH!
STAND DOWN, UNCLE.
FTWAP
MIKU...?! W-WHAT WAS THAT FOR...?
SILENCE.
ALL I SAID WAS THAT THE ZEZE FAMILY HAS NO NEED FOR THE TWIN STAR UPSTART.
I DIDN'T SAY ANYTHING AGAINST THE ADASHINO FAMILY.
HOWEVER, UPSTART...

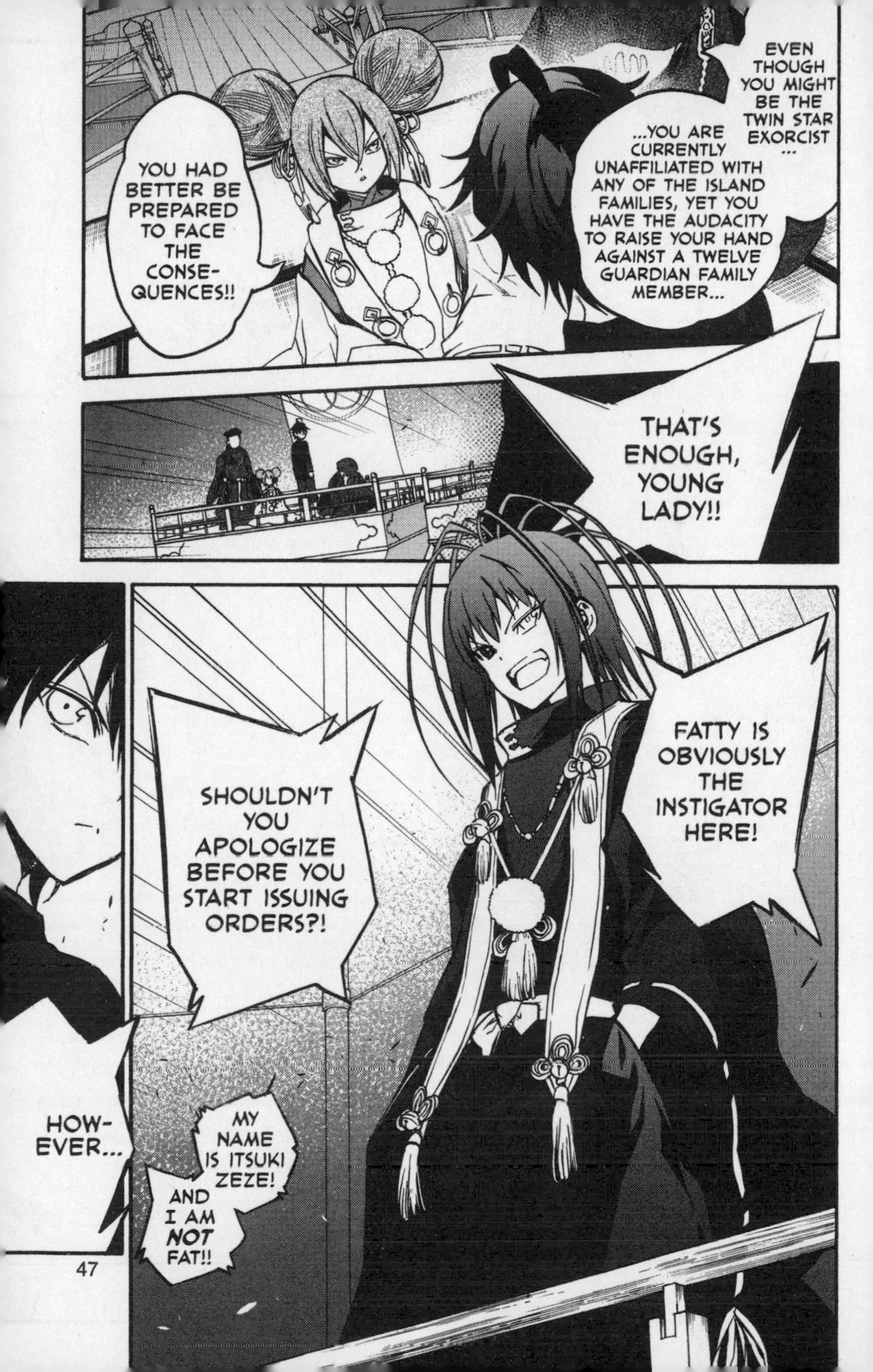
EVEN THOUGH YOU MIGHT BE THE TWIN STAR EXORCIST ...
...YOU ARE CURRENTLY UNAFFILIATED WITH ANY OF THE ISLAND FAMILIES, YET YOU HAVE THE AUDACITY TO RAISE YOUR HAND AGAINST A TWELVE GUARDIAN FAMILY MEMBER...
YOU HAD BETTER BE PREPARED TO FACE THE CONSE-QUENCES!!
THAT'S ENOUGH, YOUNG LADY!!
FATTY IS OBVIOUSLY THE INSTIGATOR HERE!
SHOULDN'T YOU APOLOGIZE BEFORE YOU START ISSUING ORDERS?!
MY NAME IS ITSUKI ZEZE!
AND I AM *NOT* FAT!!
HOW-EVER...

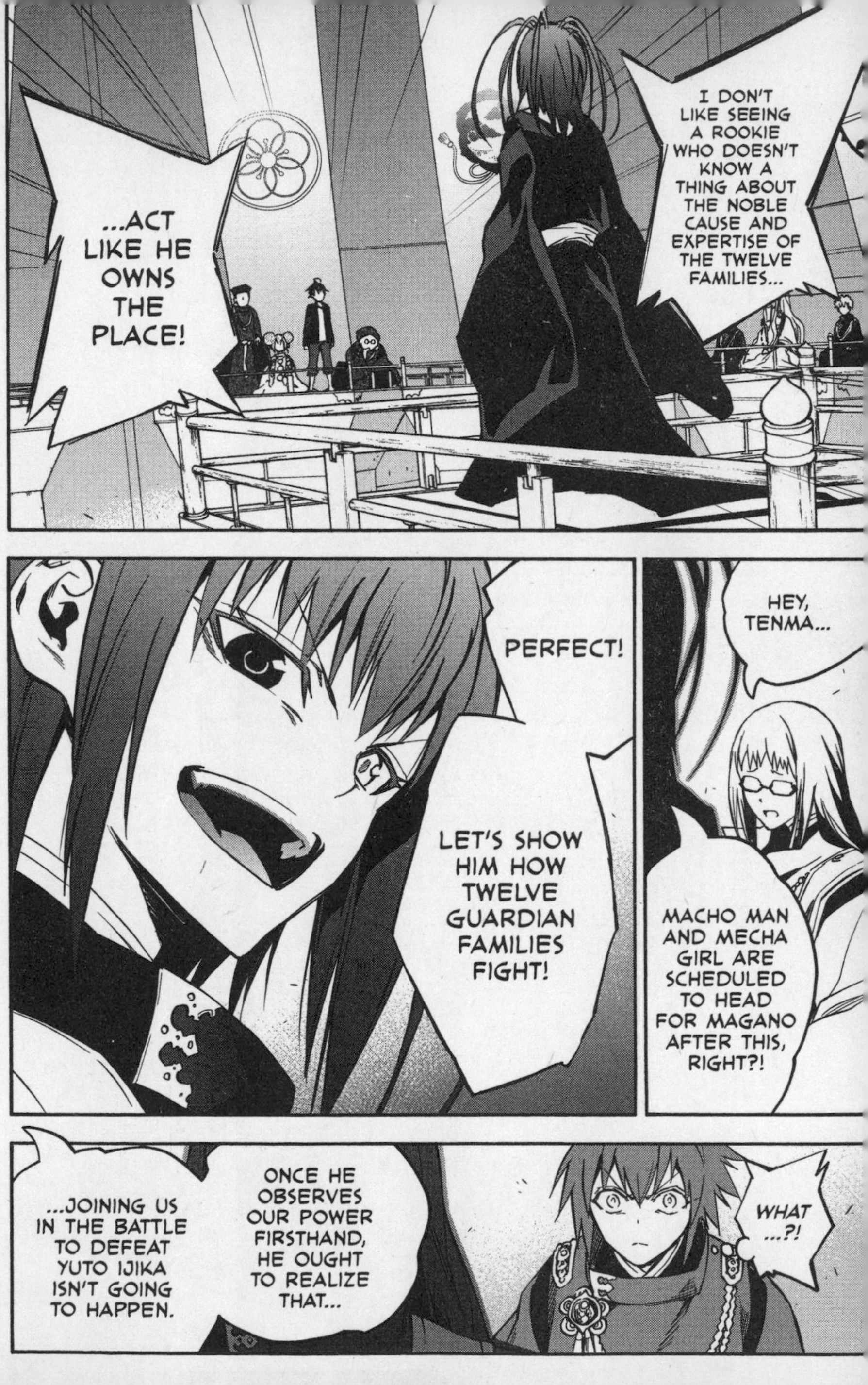
I DON'T LIKE SEEING A ROOKIE WHO DOESN'T KNOW A THING ABOUT THE NOBLE CAUSE AND EXPERTISE OF THE TWELVE FAMILIES...
...ACT LIKE HE OWNS THE PLACE!
HEY, TENMA...
MACHO MAN AND MECHA GIRL ARE SCHEDULED TO HEAD FOR MAGANO AFTER THIS, RIGHT?!
PERFECT!
LET'S SHOW HIM HOW TWELVE GUARDIAN FAMILIES FIGHT!
WHAT ...?!
ONCE HE OBSERVES OUR POWER FIRSTHAND, HE OUGHT TO REALIZE THAT...
...JOINING US IN THE BATTLE TO DEFEAT YUTO IJIKA ISN'T GOING TO HAPPEN.

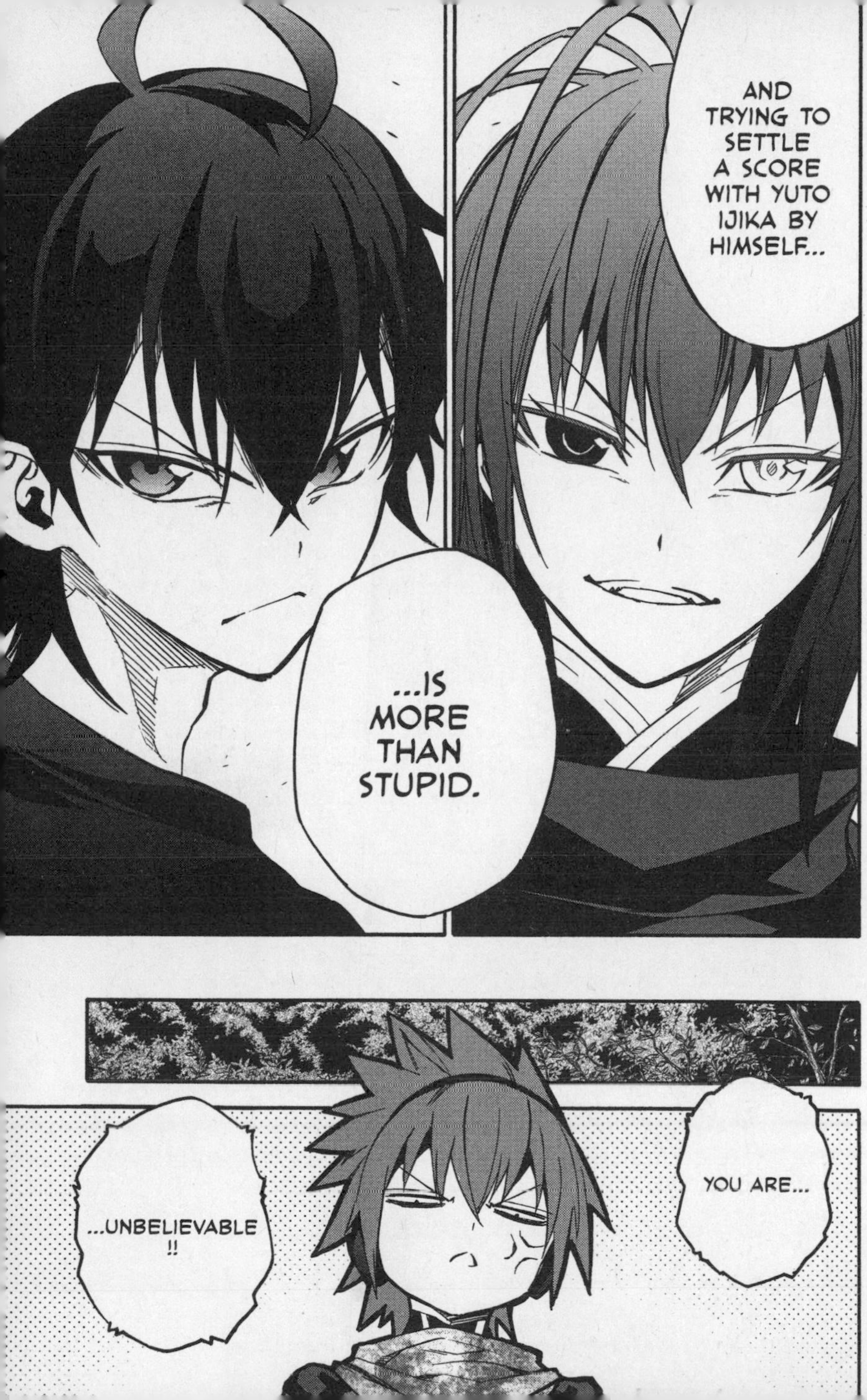
AND TRYING TO SETTLE A SCORE WITH YUTO IJIKA BY HIMSELF...
...IS MORE THAN STUPID.
YOU ARE...
...UNBELIEVABLE !!

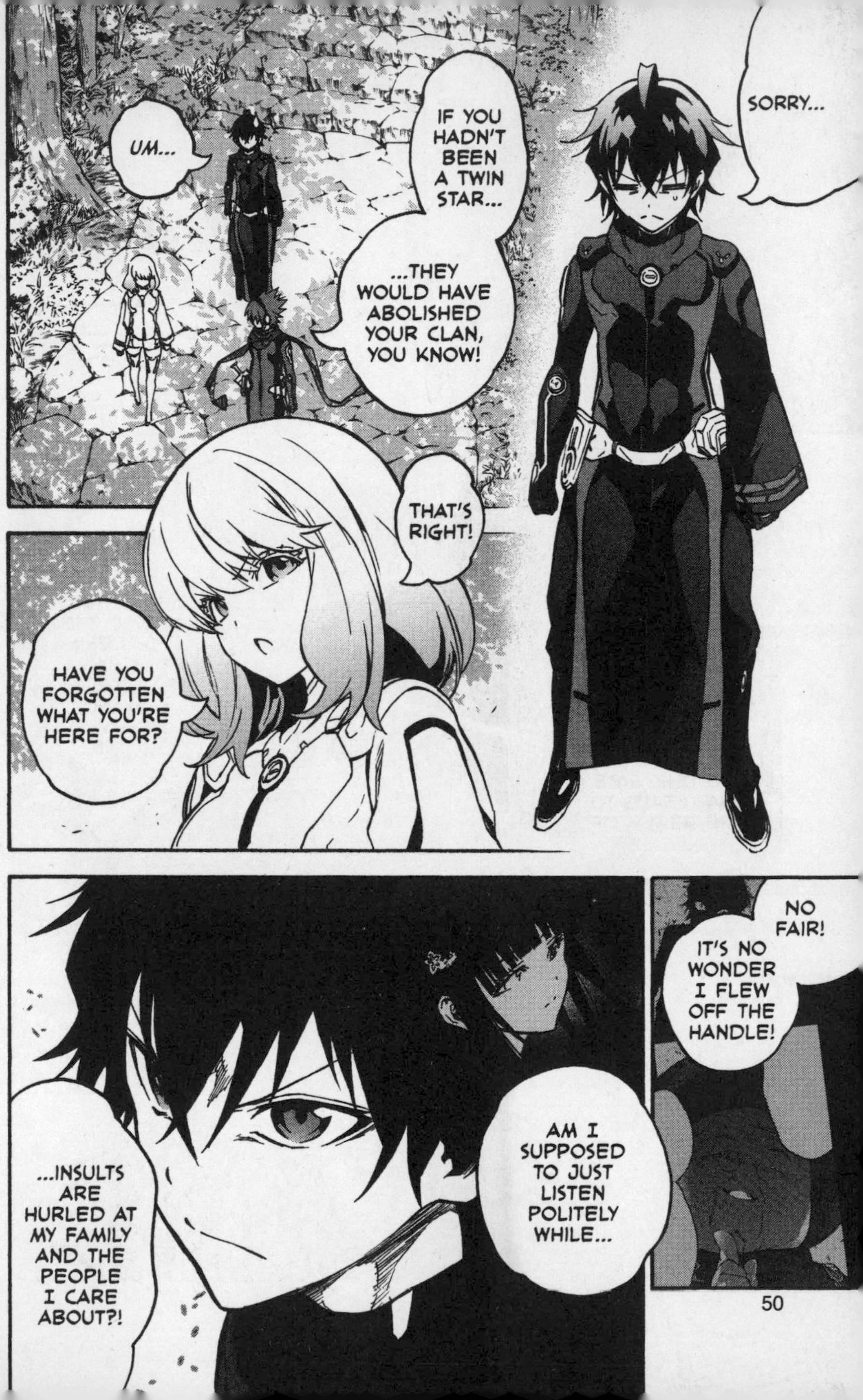
SORRY...
IF YOU HADN'T BEEN A TWIN STAR...
...THEY WOULD HAVE ABOLISHED YOUR CLAN, YOU KNOW!
UM...
THAT'S RIGHT!
HAVE YOU FORGOTTEN WHAT YOU'RE HERE FOR?
NO FAIR!
IT'S NO WONDER I FLEW OFF THE HANDLE!
AM I SUPPOSED TO JUST LISTEN POLITELY WHILE...
...INSULTS ARE HURLED AT MY FAMILY AND THE PEOPLE I CARE ABOUT?!

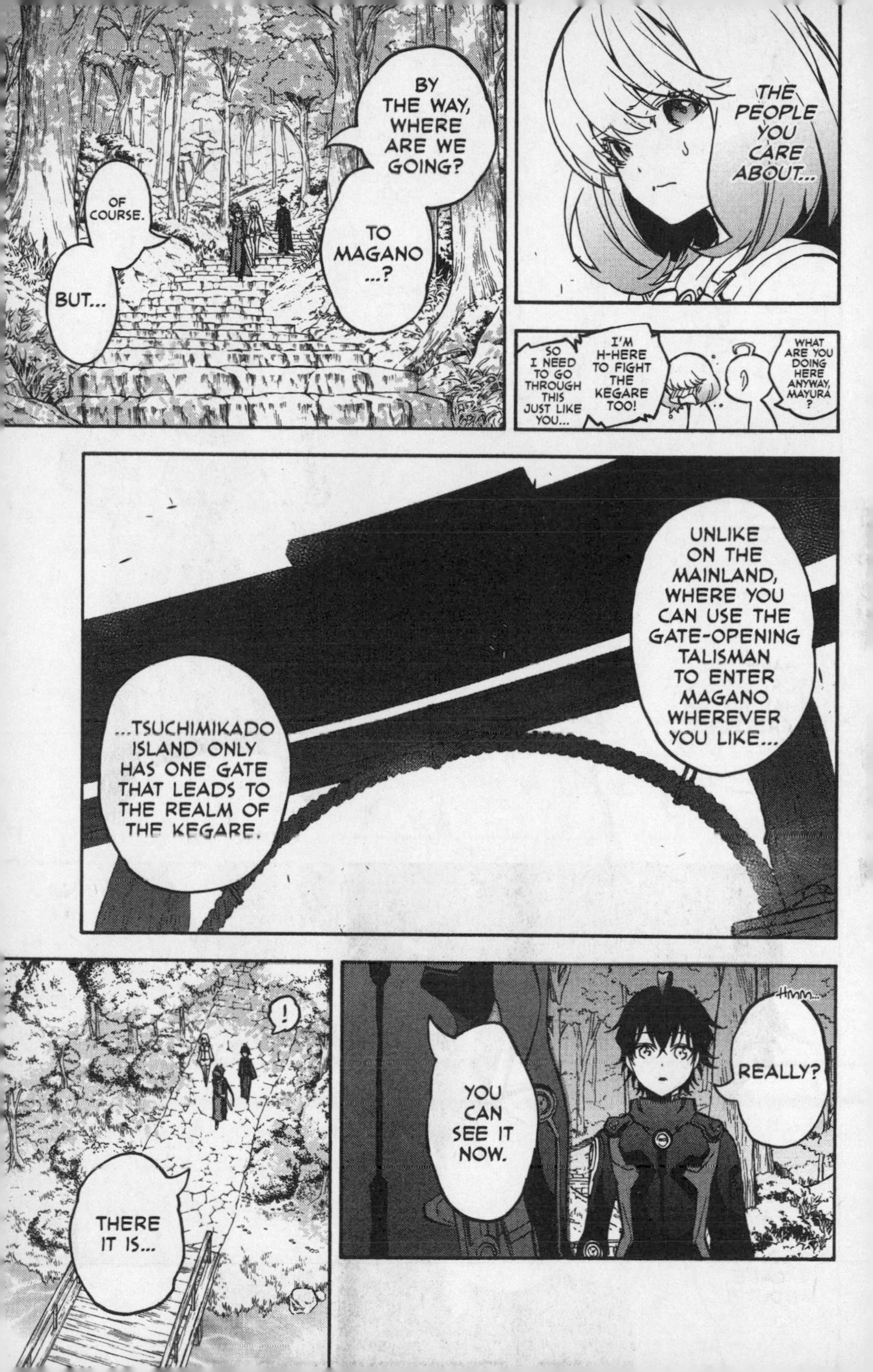
THE PEOPLE YOU CARE ABOUT...
WHAT ARE YOU DOING HERE ANYWAY, MAYURA?
I'M H-HERE TO FIGHT THE KEGARE TOO!
SO I NEED TO GO THROUGH THIS JUST LIKE YOU...
BY THE WAY, WHERE ARE WE GOING?
TO MAGANO...?
OF COURSE.
BUT...
UNLIKE ON THE MAINLAND, WHERE YOU CAN USE THE GATE-OPENING TALISMAN TO ENTER MAGANO WHEREVER YOU LIKE...
...TSUCHIMIKADO ISLAND ONLY HAS ONE GATE THAT LEADS TO THE REALM OF THE KEGARE.
Hmm...
REALLY?
YOU CAN SEE IT NOW.
!
THERE IT IS...

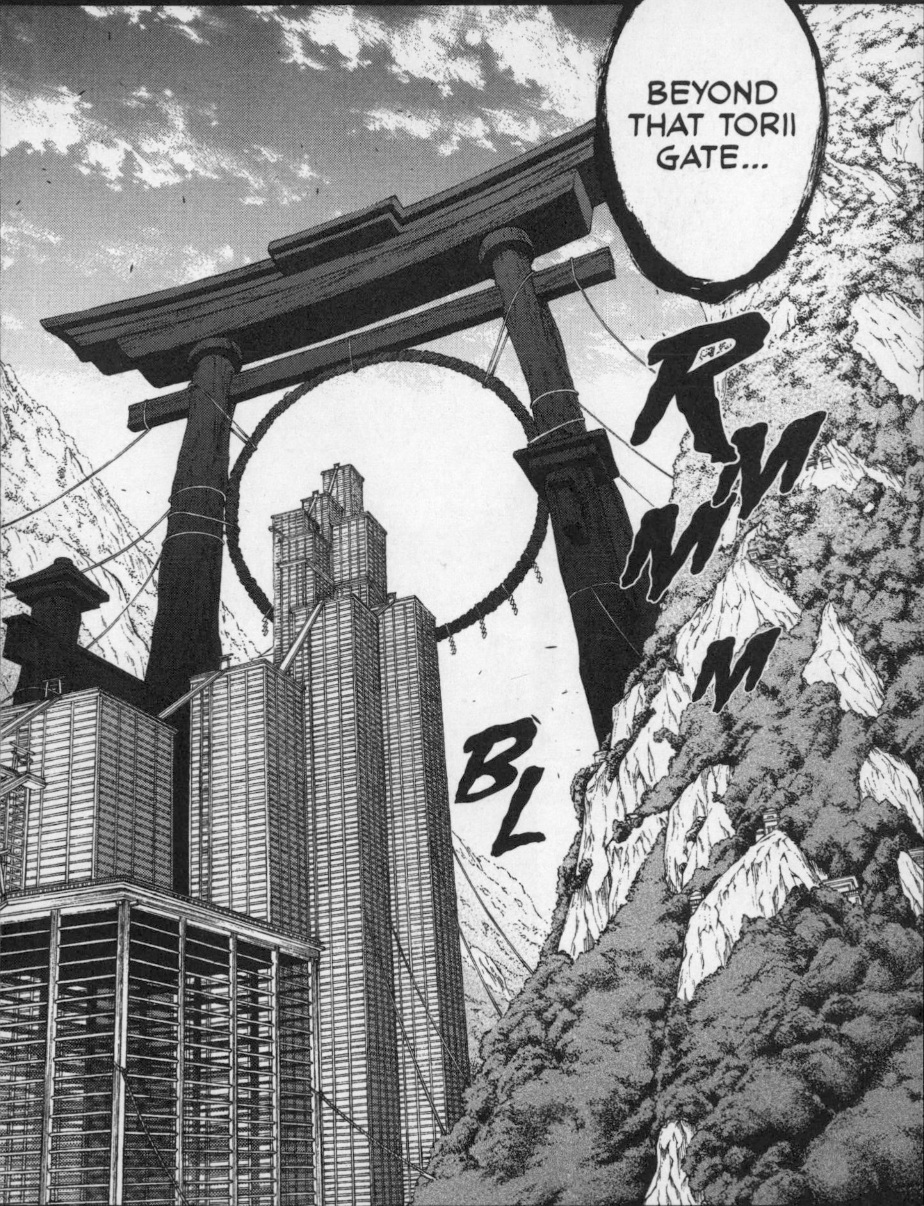
BEYOND THAT TORII GATE...
RMMM
BL

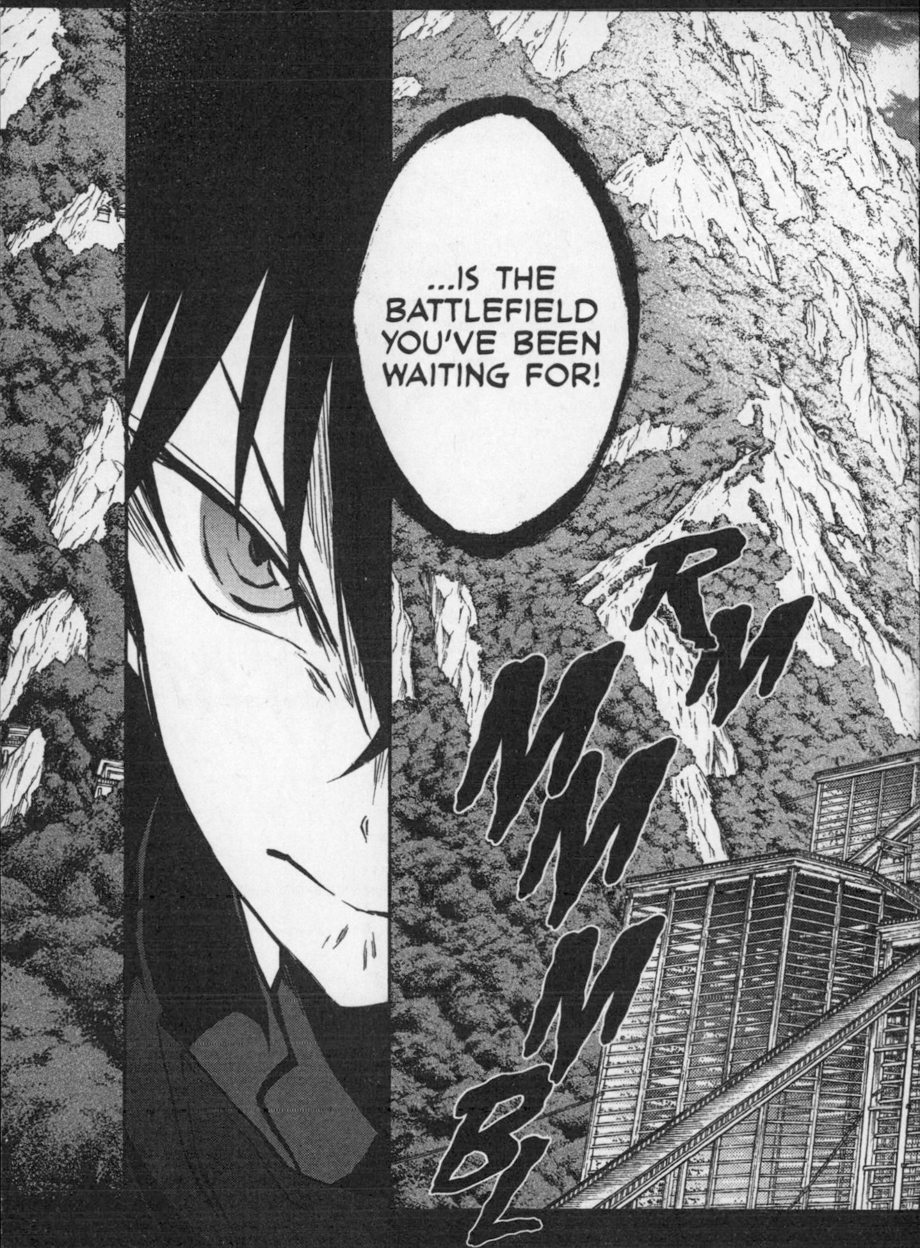
...IS THE BATTLEFIELD YOU'VE BEEN WAITING FOR!
RMMMMMBL

CHARACTER PROFILE 1

I put out a call for letters to my readers in Japan, and thankfully, I received a lot! Many of the letters asked me about the vital statistics of various characters, so I've decided to introduce them all here!

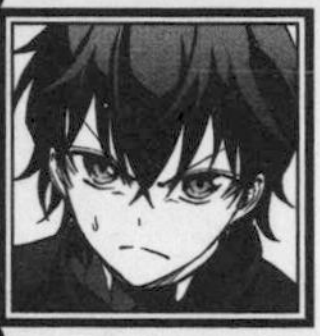

Rokuro Enmado (16 years old)

Birthday: June 6 Blood type: B Height: 5'4" Weight: 115 lbs.
(When he was 14: height: 5'2", weight: 104 lbs.)
Likes: Exorcism, curry, spicy things
Dislikes: Yuto, studies not connected to exorcism

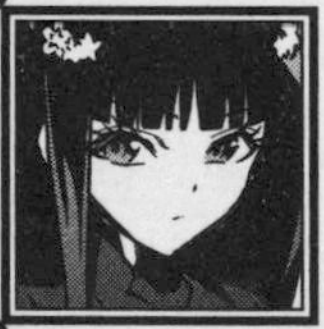

Benio Adashino (16 years old)

Birthday: April 16 Blood type: O Height: 5'3" Weight: 108 lbs.
(When she was 14: height: 5'1", weight: 99 lbs)
Likes: Exorcism, family, ohagi dumplings
Dislikes: Kamui, spicy things

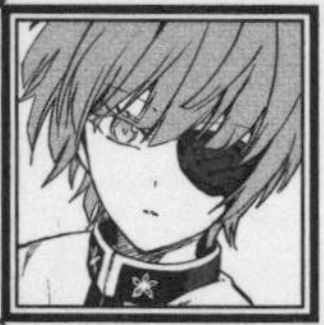

Yuto Ijika (16 years old)

Birthday: April 16 Blood type: O Height: 5'4" Weight: 112 lbs.
(When he was 14: height: 5'2", weight: 101 lbs.)
Likes: Exorcists, ohagi dumplings
Dislikes: Benio, weak exorcists

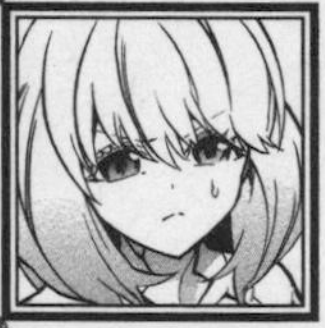

Mayura Otomi (16 years old)

Birthday: February 14 Blood type: A Height: 5'3" Weight: 119 lbs.
(When she was 14: height: 5'1", weight: 117 lbs.)
Likes: Chocolate, sweet things, dogs
Dislikes: Insects

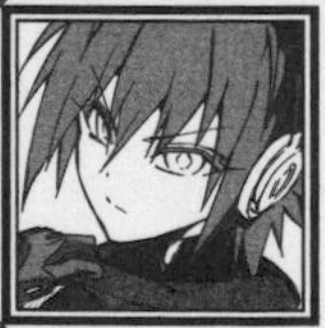

Shimon Ikaruga (18 years old)

Birthday: September 13 Blood type: O Height: 5'9" Weight: 139 lbs.
(When he was 16: height: 5'8", weight: 139 lbs.)
Likes: Family, bonsai, Seigen
Dislikes: Pickled foods

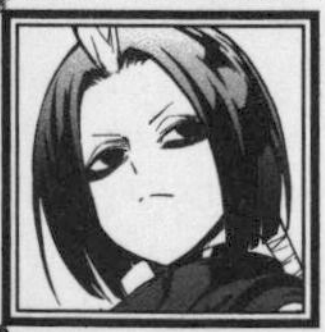

Seigen Amawaka (43 years old)

Birthday: November 29 Blood type: O Height: 5'10" Weight: 143 lbs.
Likes: Sushi
Dislikes: Children, anmitsu, television

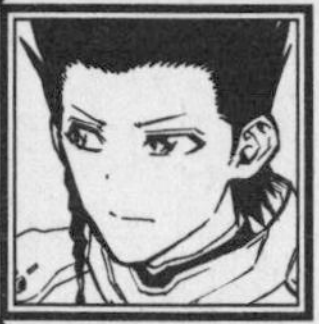

Ryogo Nagitsuji (25 years old)

Birthday: August 8 Blood type: A Height: 6'0" Weight: 159 lbs.

Likes: Curry, movies

Dislikes: Frogs, training with Seigen

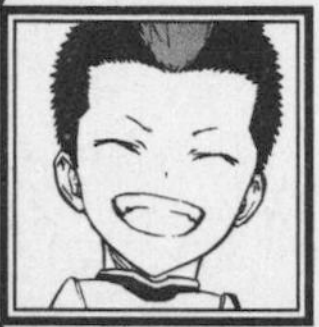

Atsushi Sukumozuka (22 years old)

Birthday: October 15 Blood type: B Height: 5'7" Weight: 132 lbs.

Likes: Shonen manga magazines, reptiles

Dislikes: Pickled scallion, training with Seigen

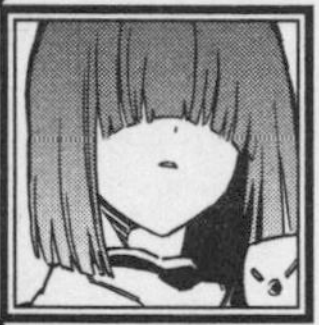

Shinnosuke Kuzaki (21 years old)

Birthday: July 3 Blood type: A Height: 5'6" Weight: 121 lbs.

Likes: Mystery novels, cooking

Dislikes: The smell of gingko nuts, training with Seigen

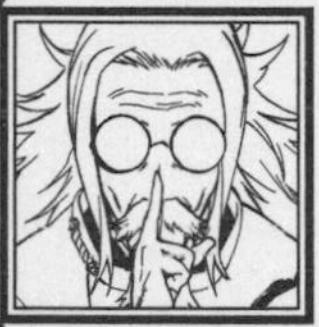

Zenkichi Otomi (70 years old)

Birthday: September 20 Blood type: AB Height: 5'8" Weight: 126 lbs.

Likes: Family (including Seigen), sushi, video games

Dislikes: Yuto, flashy music

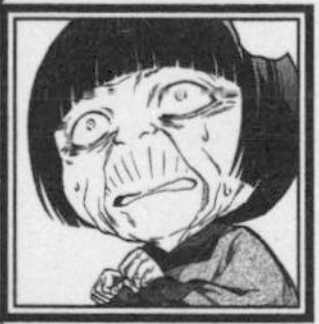

Kinu Furusato (69 years old)

Birthday: January 26 Blood type: O Height: ? Weight: ?

Likes: Benio, ohagi dumplings, video games

Dislikes: Fang Face, caterpillars

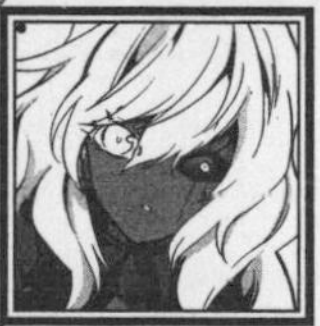

Kamui (? Years old) *8 years since he became a Basara

Birthday: ? Blood type: ? Height: 5'4" Weight: 110 lbs.

Likes: Battles, choices

Dislikes: Those who interfere with his battles (his hobby)

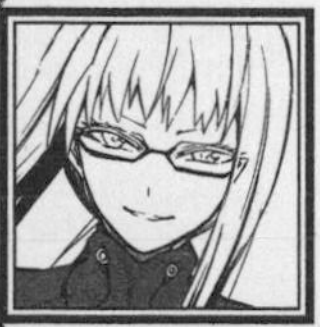

Arima Tsuchimikado (45 years old)

Birthday: December 25 Blood type: AB Height: 6'3" Weight: 156 lbs.

Likes: Women (of all ages), destroying Kegare, sweet things

Dislikes: Kegare, weak exorcists

Data 3 Twelve Guardian Family Family Crests

Every family on Tsuchimikado Island has a crest that is embroidered on the uniforms of their reserve exorcists, kimono and hunting gear worn for executive meetings and ceremonies.

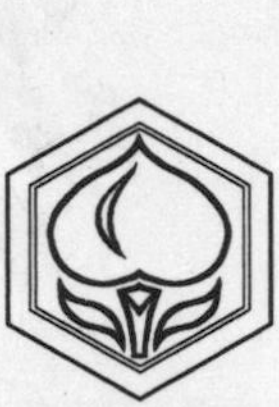

Unomiya Family
Hexagon and Peach

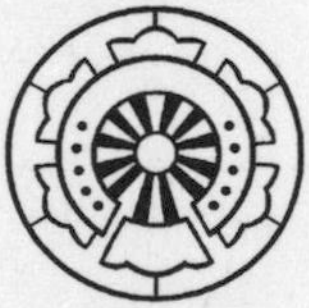

Sada Family
Horseshoe and Wheel

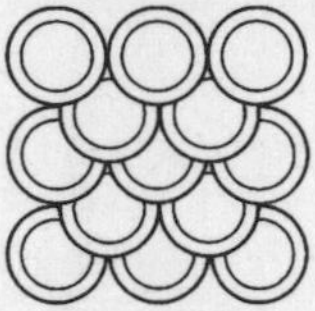

Hagusa Family (Tatara)
Serpent Pattern

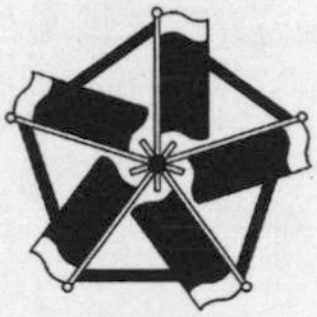

Inanaki Family
Pentagon and Banner

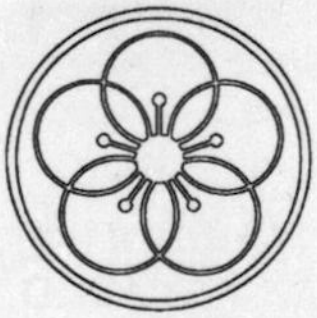

Zeze Family
Plum Flower Inside Circle

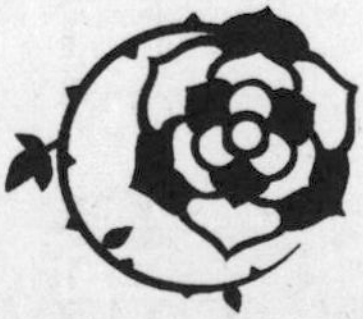

Mitejima Family
Circle and Rose

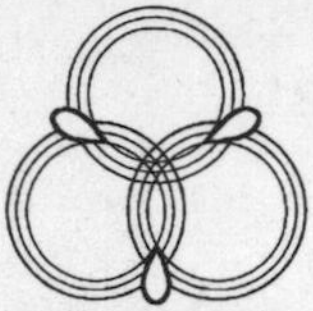

Mitosaka Family
Claw and Crystal

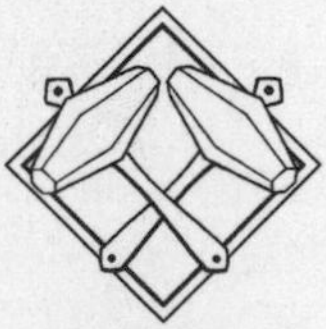

Ioroi Family
Crossed Hammer

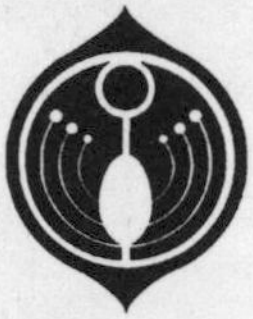

Ikaruga Family
Crimson Phoenix

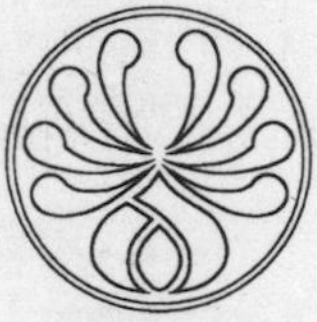

Amawaka Family
Thistle

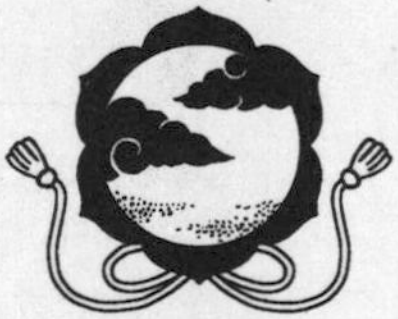

Kasukami Family
Sand and Mirror

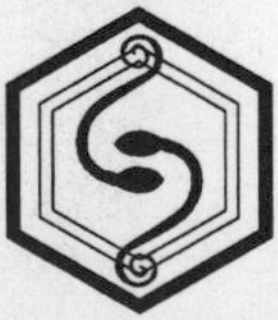

Uji Family
Tortoise-shell and Serpent

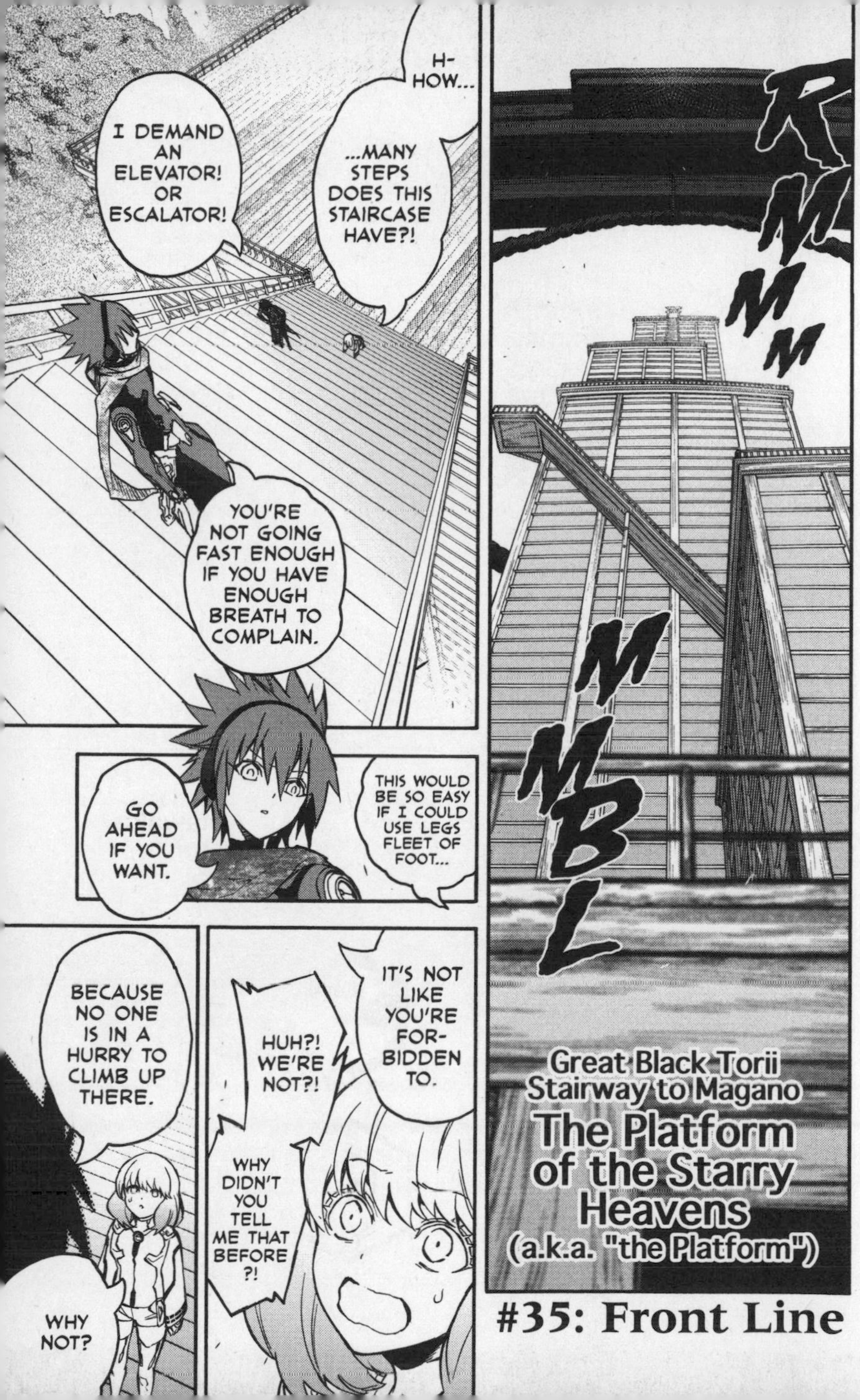
RMMM
MMBL
Great Black Torii Stairway to Magano
The Platform of the Starry Heavens
(a.k.a. "the Platform")
H-HOW...
...MANY STEPS DOES THIS STAIRCASE HAVE?!
I DEMAND AN ELEVATOR! OR ESCALATOR!
YOU'RE NOT GOING FAST ENOUGH IF YOU HAVE ENOUGH BREATH TO COMPLAIN.
THIS WOULD BE SO EASY IF I COULD USE LEGS FLEET OF FOOT...
GO AHEAD IF YOU WANT.
IT'S NOT LIKE YOU'RE FOR-BIDDEN TO.
HUH?! WE'RE NOT?!
WHY DIDN'T YOU TELL ME THAT BEFORE?!
BECAUSE NO ONE IS IN A HURRY TO CLIMB UP THERE.
WHY NOT?

#35: Front Line

WELL, DEPENDING ON HOW DANGEROUS YOUR MISSION IS...

...THERE'S A CHANCE YOU'LL NEVER COME BACK DOWN THIS STAIRCASE.

SO EVERY-ONE...

...TAKES THEIR TIME AS THEY GO UP... TO THINK THINGS OVER...

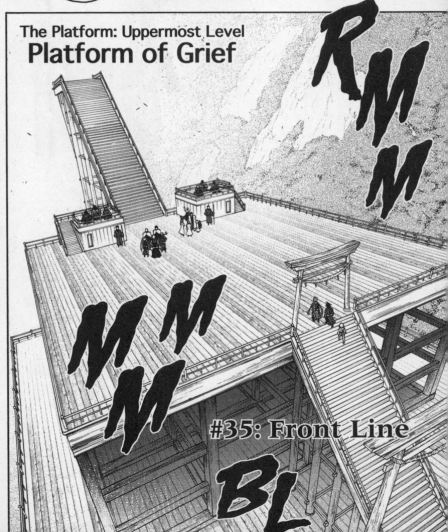

The Platform: Uppermost Level
Platform of Grief

RMM

MMM

BL

#35: Front Line

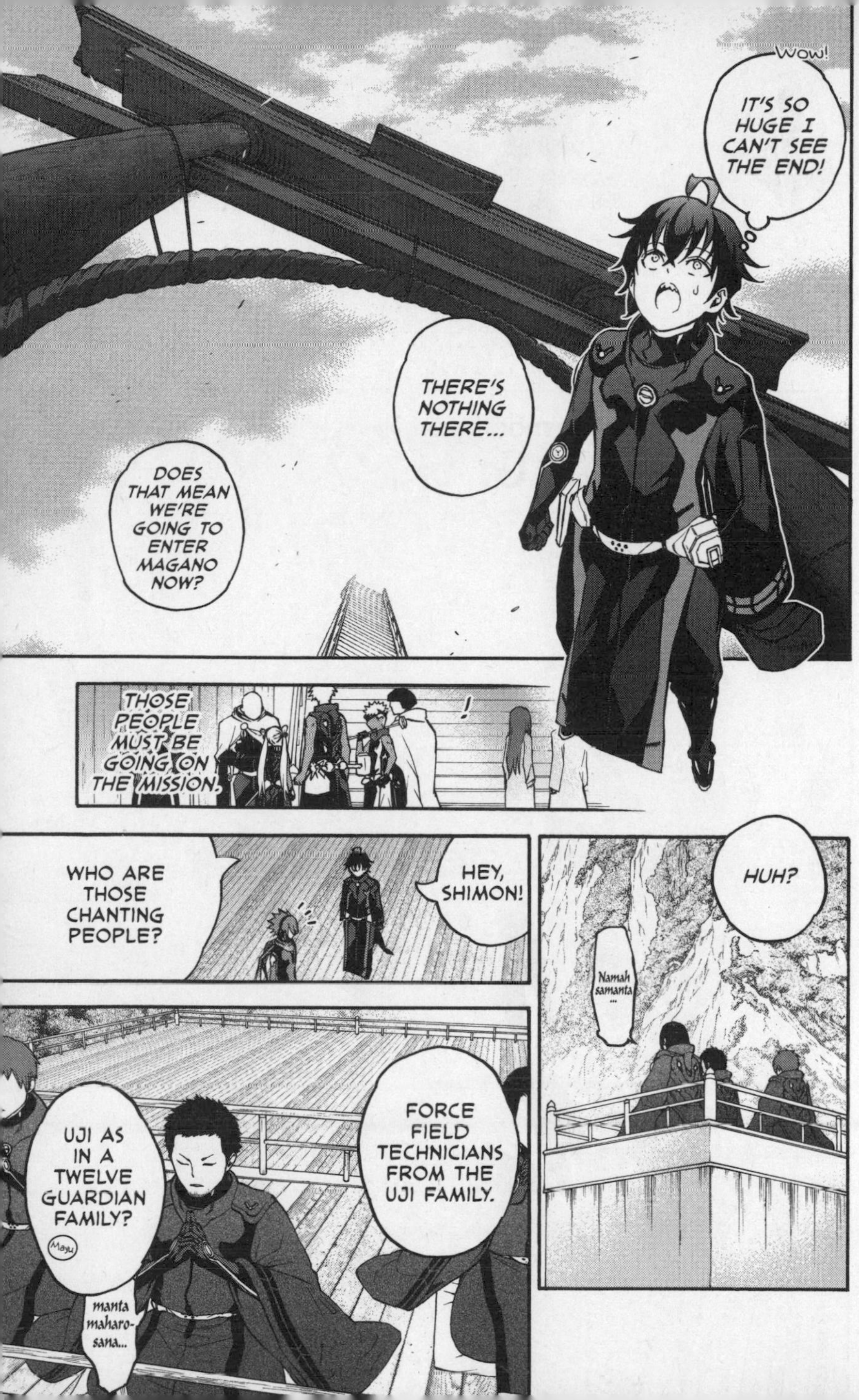
WOW!
IT'S SO HUGE I CAN'T SEE THE END!
THERE'S NOTHING THERE...
DOES THAT MEAN WE'RE GOING TO ENTER MAGANO NOW?
THOSE PEOPLE MUST BE GOING ON THE MISSION.
!
HUH?
Namah samanta...
HEY, SHIMON!
WHO ARE THOSE CHANTING PEOPLE?
FORCE FIELD TECHNICIANS FROM THE UJI FAMILY.
UJI AS IN A TWELVE GUARDIAN FAMILY?
Mayu
manta maharo-sana...

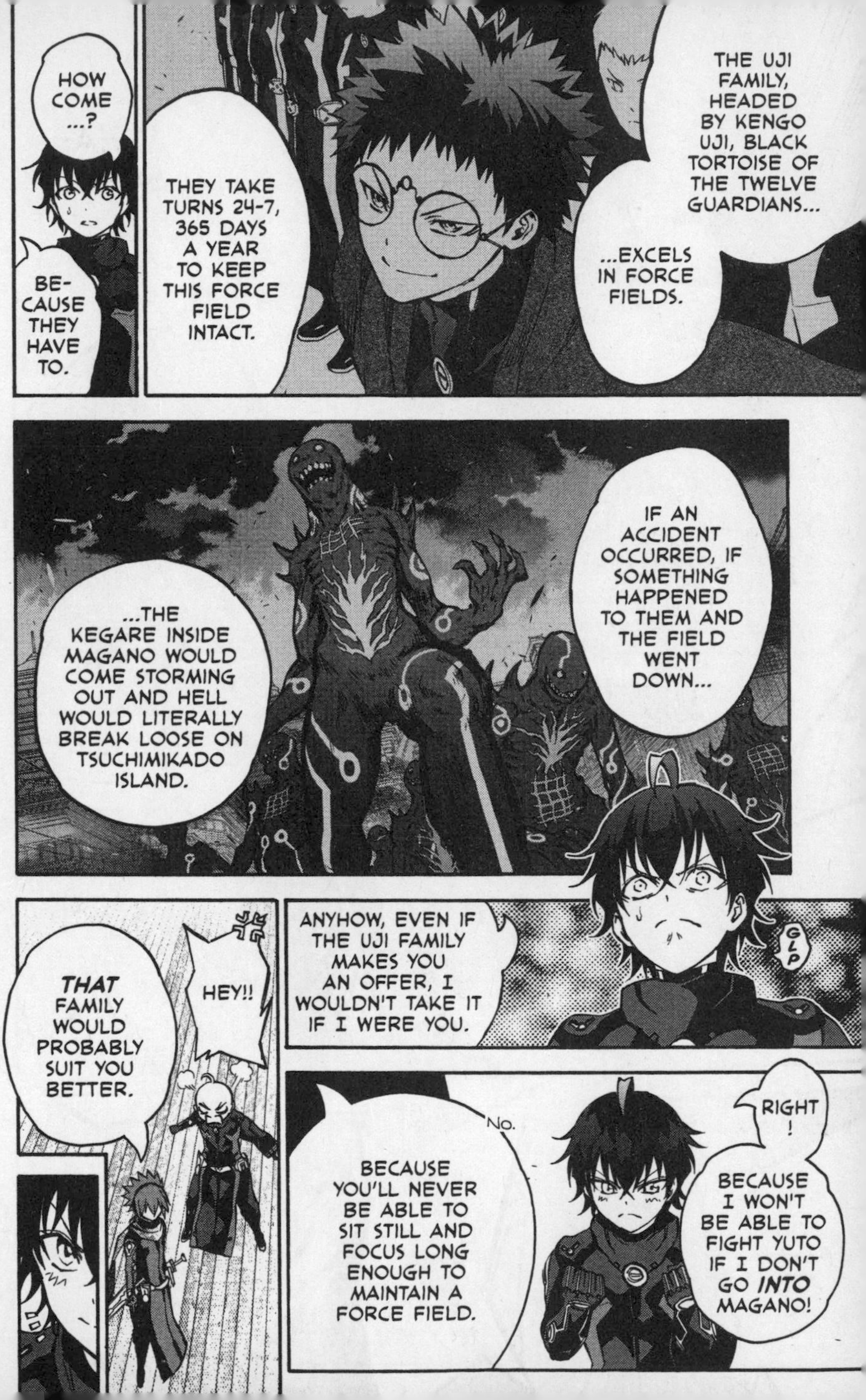
THE UJI FAMILY, HEADED BY KENGO UJI, BLACK TORTOISE OF THE TWELVE GUARDIANS...
...EXCELS IN FORCE FIELDS.
THEY TAKE TURNS 24-7, 365 DAYS A YEAR TO KEEP THIS FORCE FIELD INTACT.
HOW COME ...?
BE-CAUSE THEY HAVE TO.
IF AN ACCIDENT OCCURRED, IF SOMETHING HAPPENED TO THEM AND THE FIELD WENT DOWN...
...THE KEGARE INSIDE MAGANO WOULD COME STORMING OUT AND HELL WOULD LITERALLY BREAK LOOSE ON TSUCHIMIKADO ISLAND.
GLP
ANYHOW, EVEN IF THE UJI FAMILY MAKES YOU AN OFFER, I WOULDN'T TAKE IT IF I WERE YOU.
RIGHT!
BECAUSE I WON'T BE ABLE TO FIGHT YUTO IF I DON'T GO *INTO* MAGANO!
No.
BECAUSE YOU'LL NEVER BE ABLE TO SIT STILL AND FOCUS LONG ENOUGH TO MAINTAIN A FORCE FIELD.
THAT FAMILY WOULD PROBABLY SUIT YOU BETTER.
HEY!!

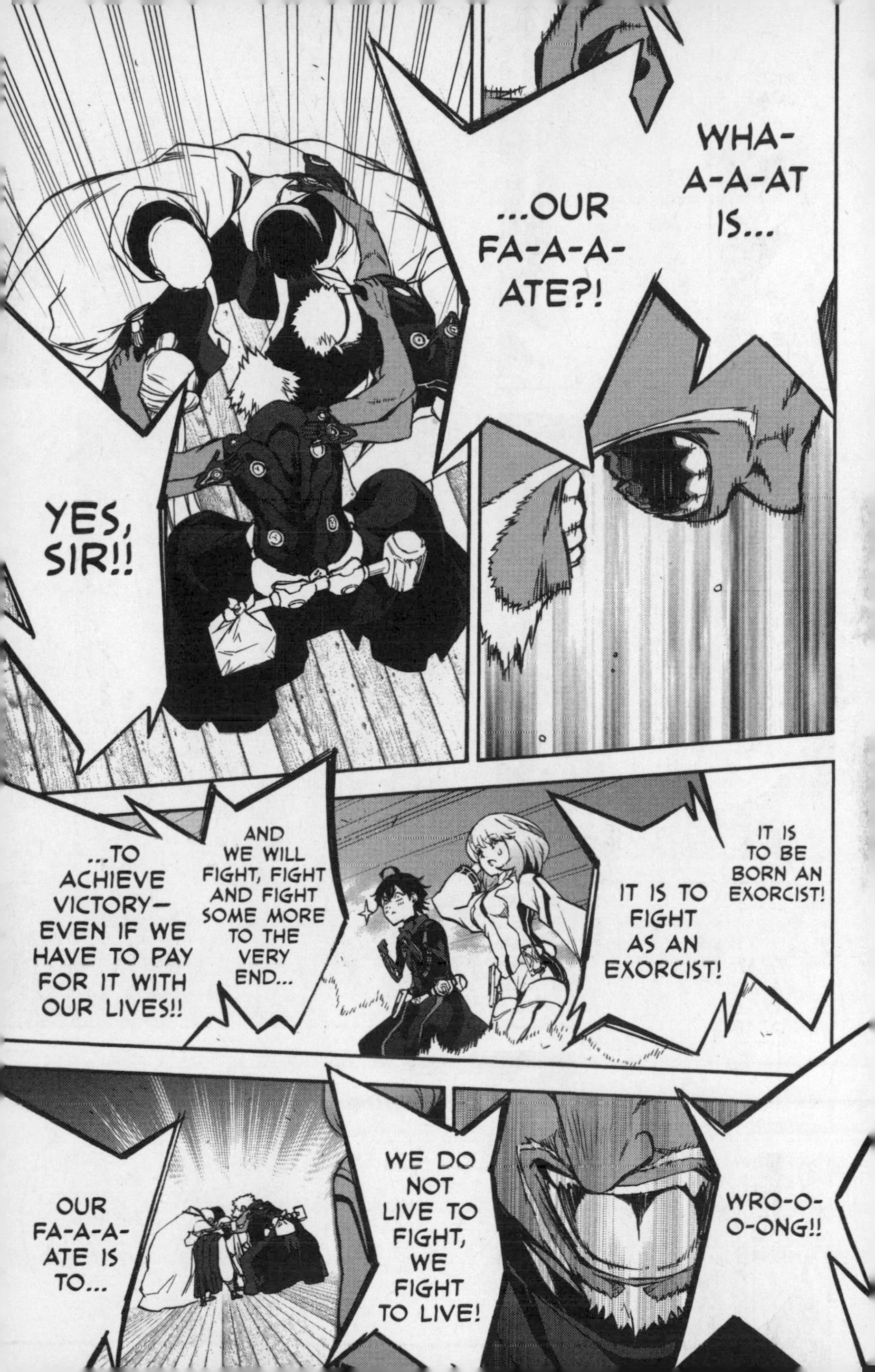
WHA-A-A-AT IS...
...OUR FA-A-A-ATE?!
YES, SIR!!
IT IS TO BE BORN AN EXORCIST!
IT IS TO FIGHT AS AN EXORCIST!
AND WE WILL FIGHT, FIGHT AND FIGHT SOME MORE TO THE VERY END...
...TO ACHIEVE VICTORY—EVEN IF WE HAVE TO PAY FOR IT WITH OUR LIVES!!
WRO-O-O-ONG!!
WE DO NOT LIVE TO FIGHT, WE FIGHT TO LIVE!
OUR FA-A-A-ATE IS TO...

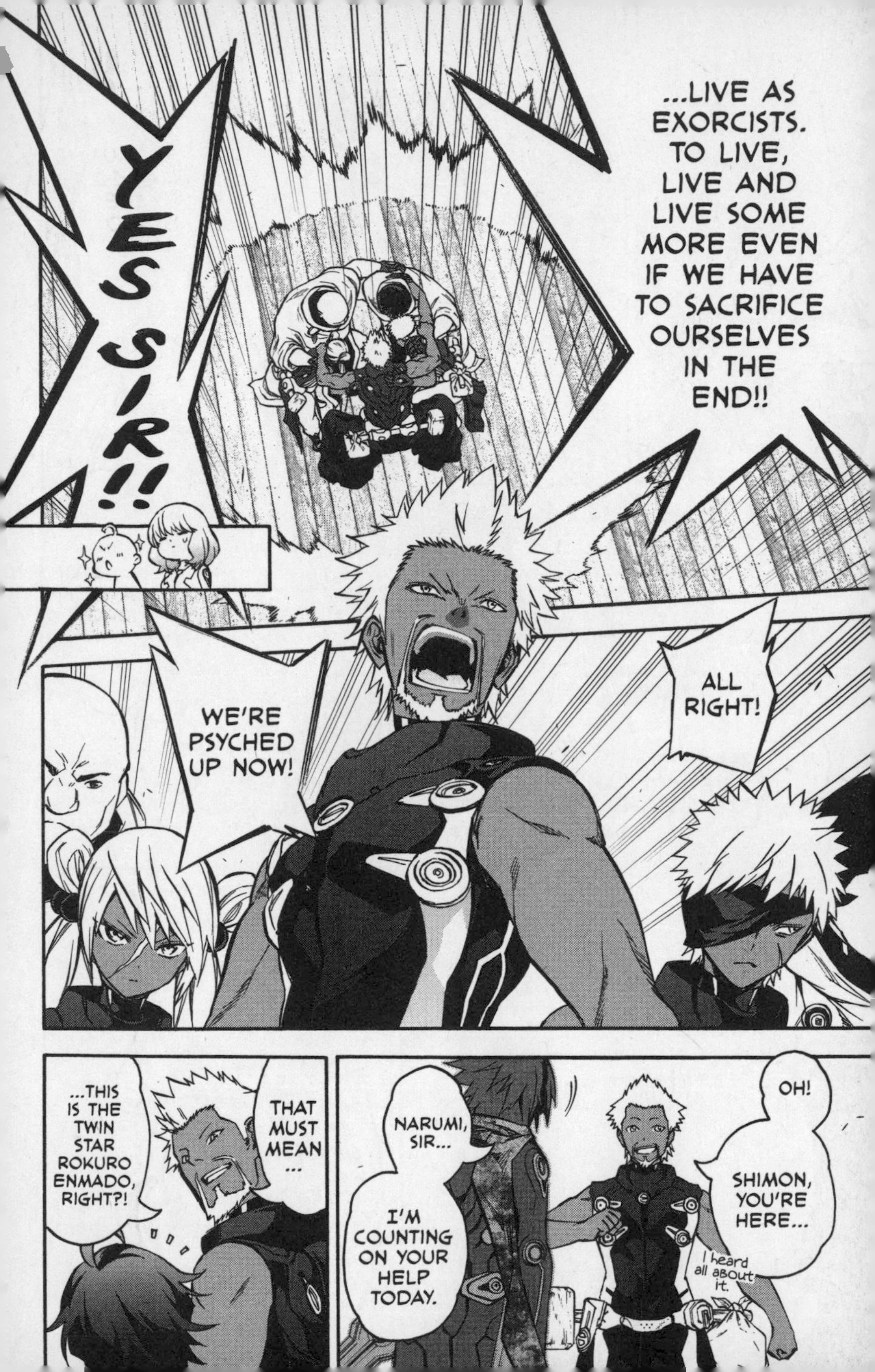
...LIVE AS EXORCISTS. TO LIVE, LIVE AND LIVE SOME MORE EVEN IF WE HAVE TO SACRIFICE OURSELVES IN THE END!!
YES SIR!!
ALL RIGHT!
WE'RE PSYCHED UP NOW!
OH!
SHIMON, YOU'RE HERE...
I heard all about it.
NARUMI, SIR...
I'M COUNTING ON YOUR HELP TODAY.
THAT MUST MEAN...
...THIS IS THE TWIN STAR ROKURO ENMADO, RIGHT?!

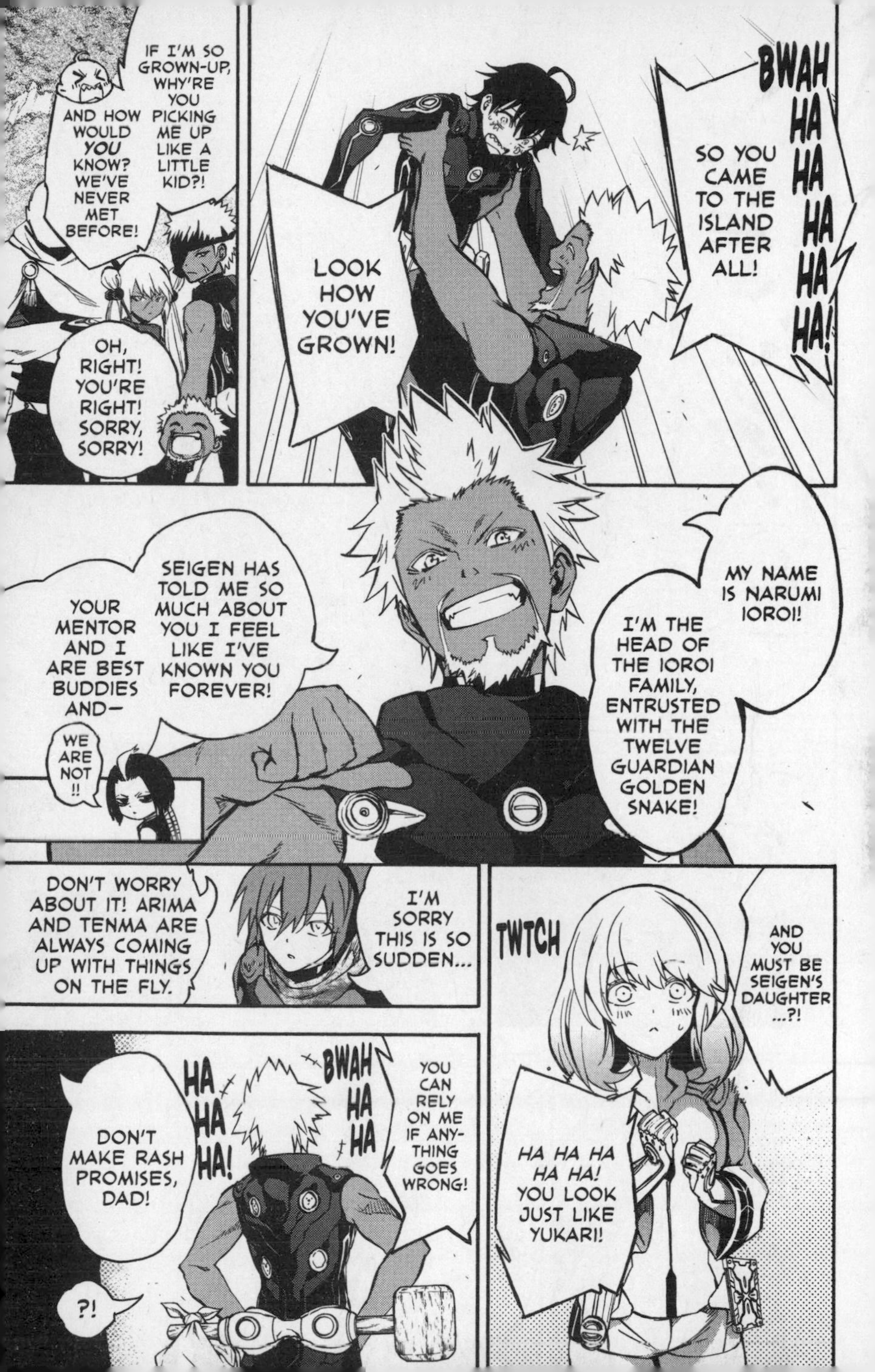
BWAH HA HA HA HA HA!
SO YOU CAME TO THE ISLAND AFTER ALL!
LOOK HOW YOU'VE GROWN!
IF I'M SO GROWN-UP, WHY'RE YOU PICKING ME UP LIKE A LITTLE KID?!
AND HOW WOULD *YOU* KNOW? WE'VE NEVER MET BEFORE!
OH, RIGHT! YOU'RE RIGHT! SORRY, SORRY!
MY NAME IS NARUMI IOROI!
I'M THE HEAD OF THE IOROI FAMILY, ENTRUSTED WITH THE TWELVE GUARDIAN GOLDEN SNAKE!
SEIGEN HAS TOLD ME SO MUCH ABOUT YOU I FEEL LIKE I'VE KNOWN YOU FOREVER!
YOUR MENTOR AND I ARE BEST BUDDIES AND—
WE ARE NOT !!
AND YOU MUST BE SEIGEN'S DAUGHTER ...?!
TWTCH
HA HA HA HA HA! YOU LOOK JUST LIKE YUKARI!
I'M SORRY THIS IS SO SUDDEN...
DON'T WORRY ABOUT IT! ARIMA AND TENMA ARE ALWAYS COMING UP WITH THINGS ON THE FLY.
YOU CAN RELY ON ME IF ANYTHING GOES WRONG!
BWAH HA HA
HA HA HA!
DON'T MAKE RASH PROMISES, DAD!
?!

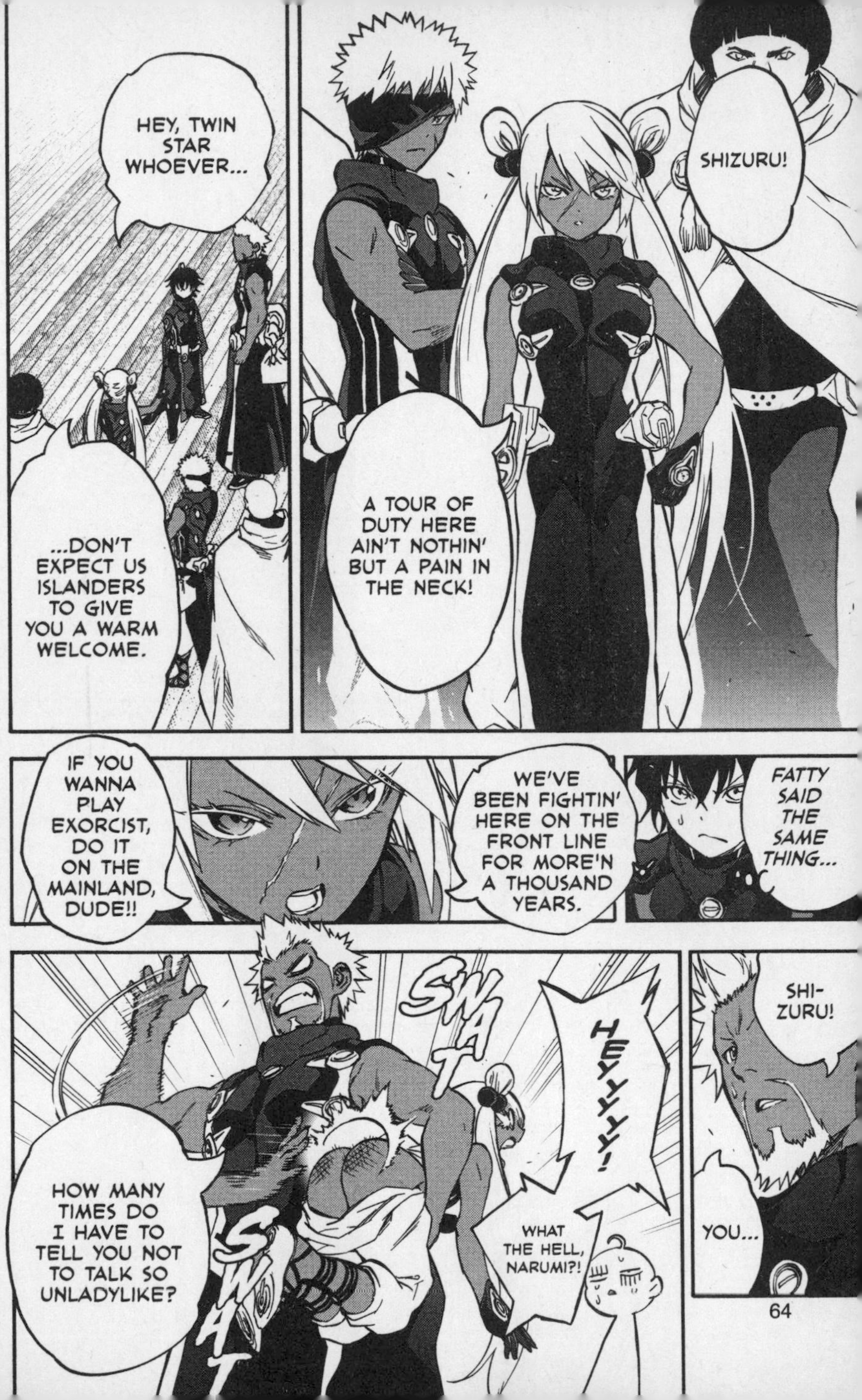
SHIZURU!
A TOUR OF DUTY HERE AIN'T NOTHIN' BUT A PAIN IN THE NECK!
HEY, TWIN STAR WHOEVER...
...DON'T EXPECT US ISLANDERS TO GIVE YOU A WARM WELCOME.
FATTY SAID THE SAME THING...
WE'VE BEEN FIGHTIN' HERE ON THE FRONT LINE FOR MORE'N A THOUSAND YEARS.
IF YOU WANNA PLAY EXORCIST, DO IT ON THE MAINLAND, DUDE!!
SHI-ZURU!
YOU...
HEYYYYY!
SWAT
WHAT THE HELL, NARUMI?!
HOW MANY TIMES DO I HAVE TO TELL YOU NOT TO TALK SO UNLADYLIKE?
SWAT

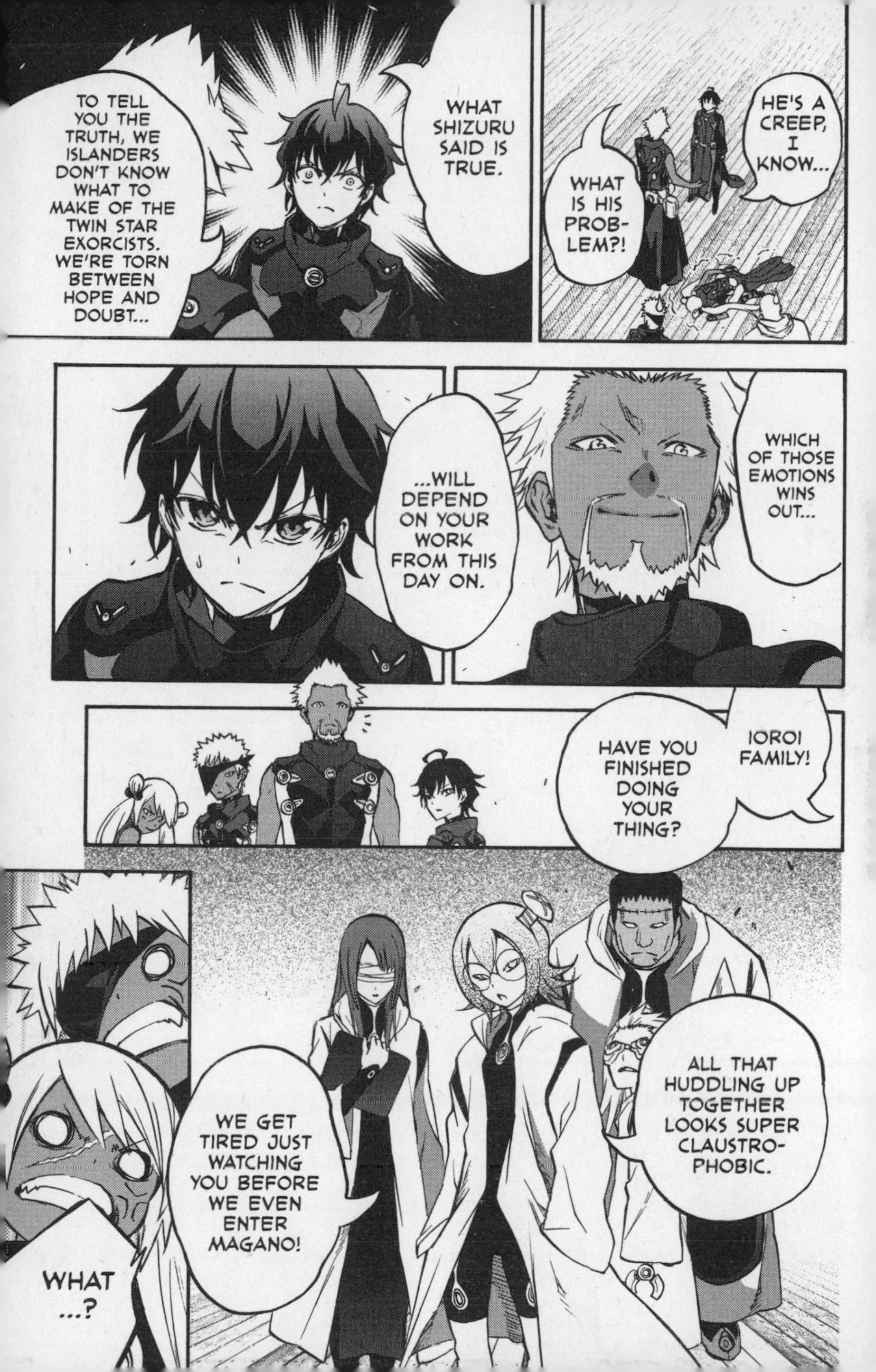
HE'S A CREEP, I KNOW...
WHAT IS HIS PROBLEM?!
WHAT SHIZURU SAID IS TRUE.
TO TELL YOU THE TRUTH, WE ISLANDERS DON'T KNOW WHAT TO MAKE OF THE TWIN STAR EXORCISTS. WE'RE TORN BETWEEN HOPE AND DOUBT...
WHICH OF THOSE EMOTIONS WINS OUT...
...WILL DEPEND ON YOUR WORK FROM THIS DAY ON.
IOROI FAMILY!
HAVE YOU FINISHED DOING YOUR THING?
ALL THAT HUDDLING UP TOGETHER LOOKS SUPER CLAUSTROPHOBIC.
WE GET TIRED JUST WATCHING YOU BEFORE WE EVEN ENTER MAGANO!
WHAT ...?

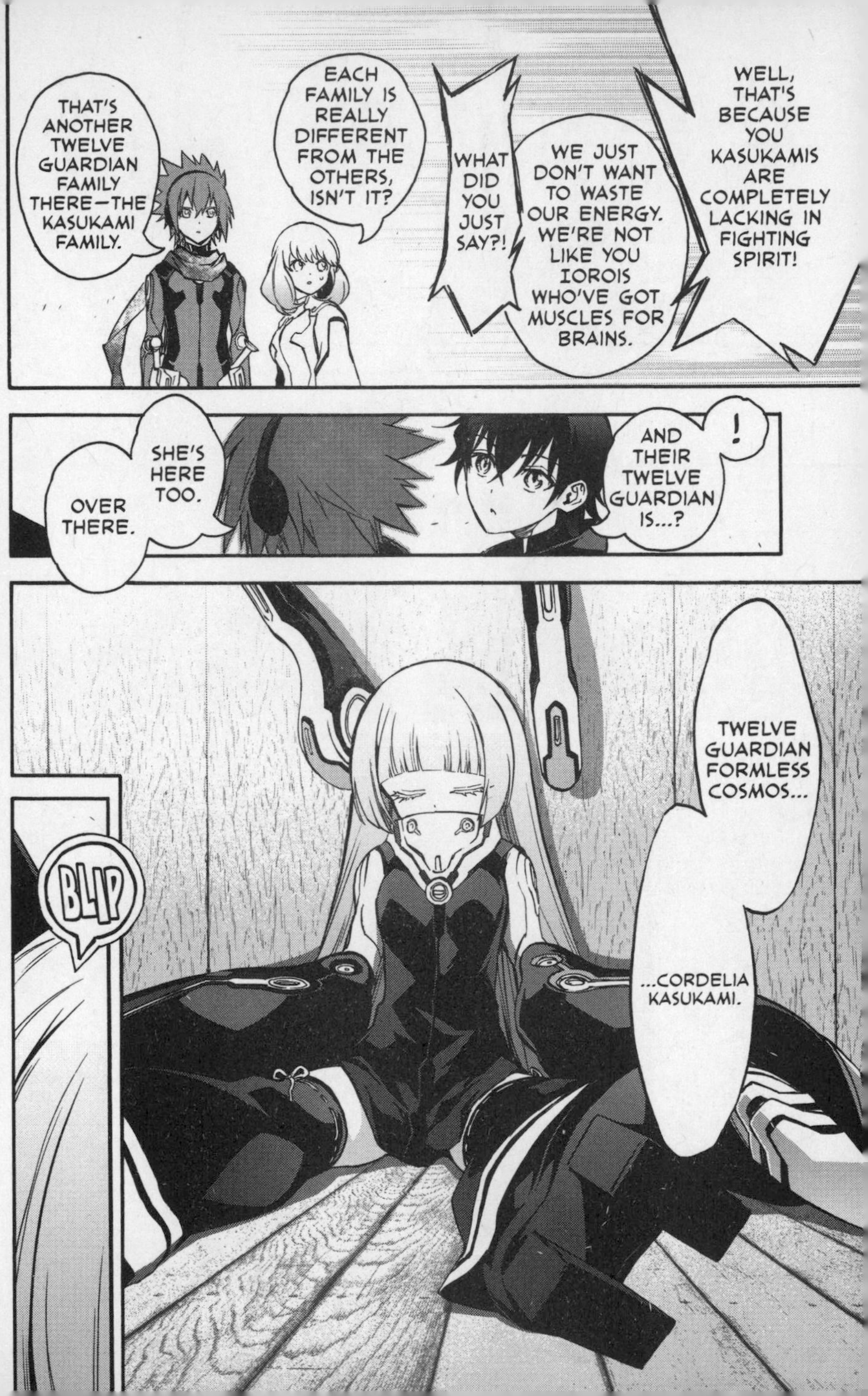
WELL, THAT'S BECAUSE YOU KASUKAMIS ARE COMPLETELY LACKING IN FIGHTING SPIRIT!
WE JUST DON'T WANT TO WASTE OUR ENERGY. WE'RE NOT LIKE YOU IOROIS WHO'VE GOT MUSCLES FOR BRAINS.
WHAT DID YOU JUST SAY?!
EACH FAMILY IS REALLY DIFFERENT FROM THE OTHERS, ISN'T IT?
THAT'S ANOTHER TWELVE GUARDIAN FAMILY THERE—THE KASUKAMI FAMILY.
!
AND THEIR TWELVE GUARDIAN IS...?
SHE'S HERE TOO.
OVER THERE.
TWELVE GUARDIAN FORMLESS COSMOS...
...CORDELIA KASUKAMI.
BLIP

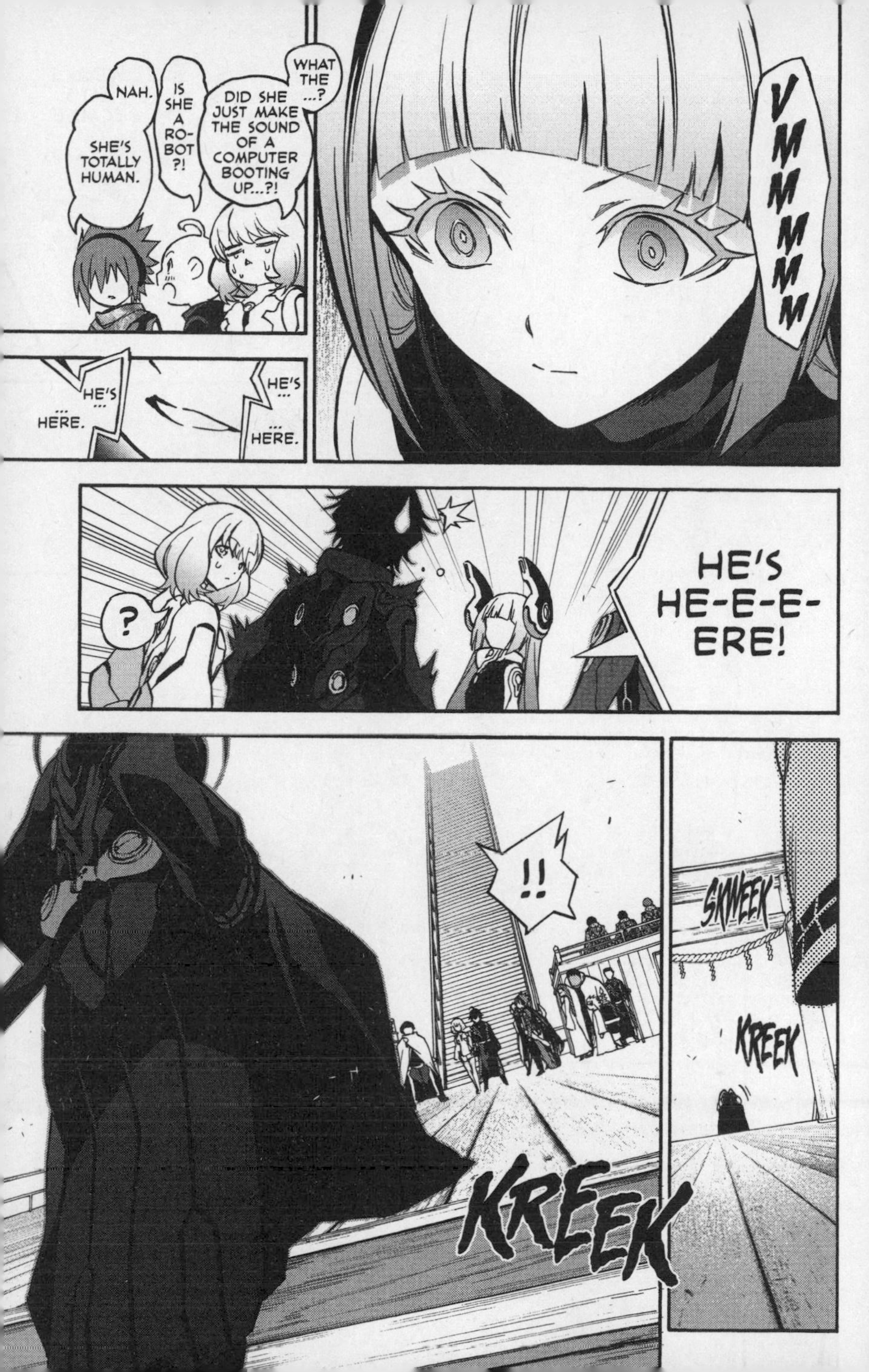
VMMMMMM
WHAT THE ...?
DID SHE JUST MAKE THE SOUND OF A COMPUTER BOOTING UP...?!
IS SHE A RO-BOT?!
NAH.
SHE'S TOTALLY HUMAN.
HE'S ... ... HERE.
HE'S ... ... HERE.
HE'S HE-E-E-ERE!
?
SKWEEK
KREEK
!!
KREEK

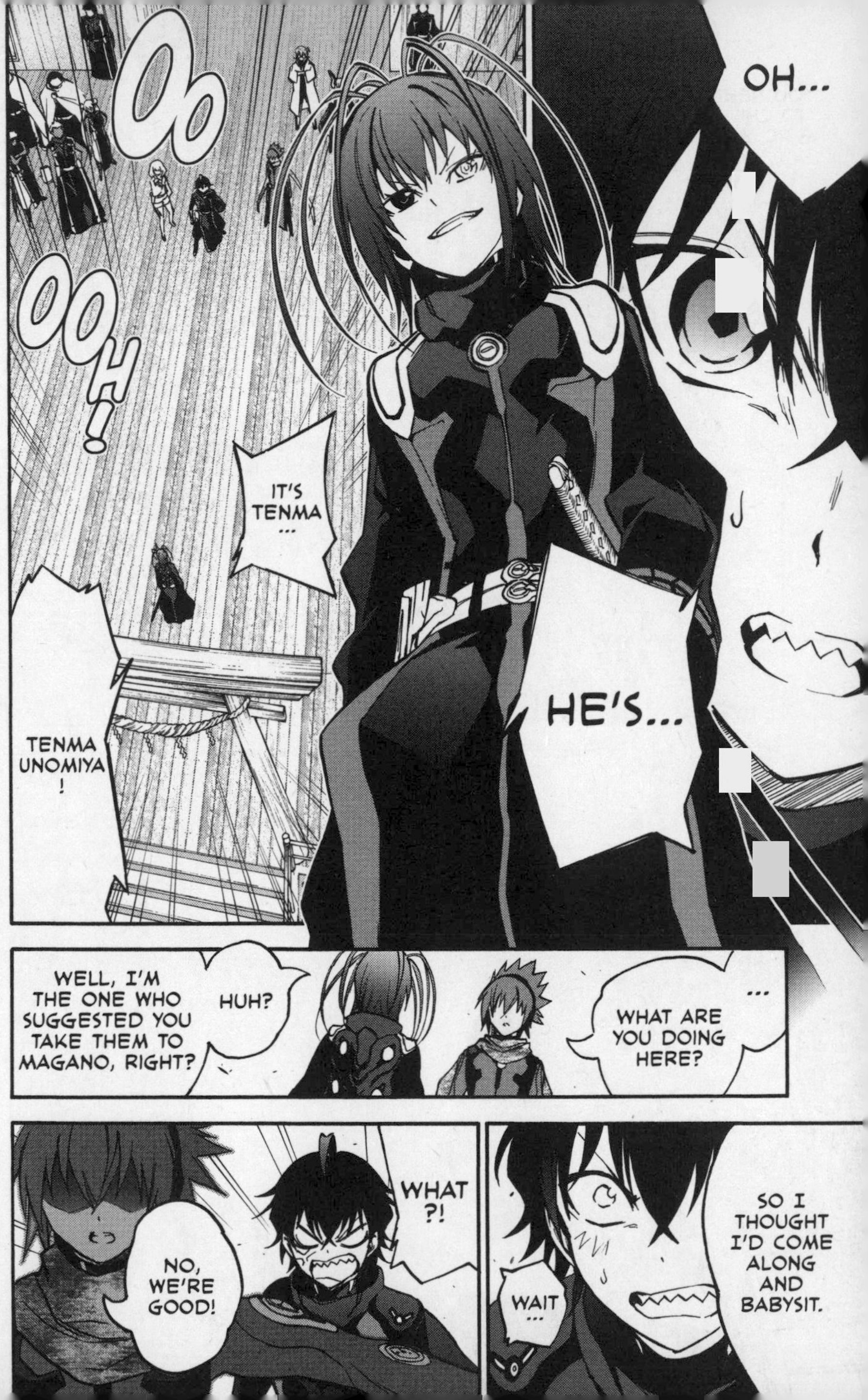
OH...
HE'S...
OoOOH!
IT'S TENMA...
TENMA UNOMIYA!
...
WHAT ARE YOU DOING HERE?
HUH?
WELL, I'M THE ONE WHO SUGGESTED YOU TAKE THEM TO MAGANO, RIGHT?
SO I THOUGHT I'D COME ALONG AND BABYSIT.
WAIT...
WHAT?!
NO, WE'RE GOOD!

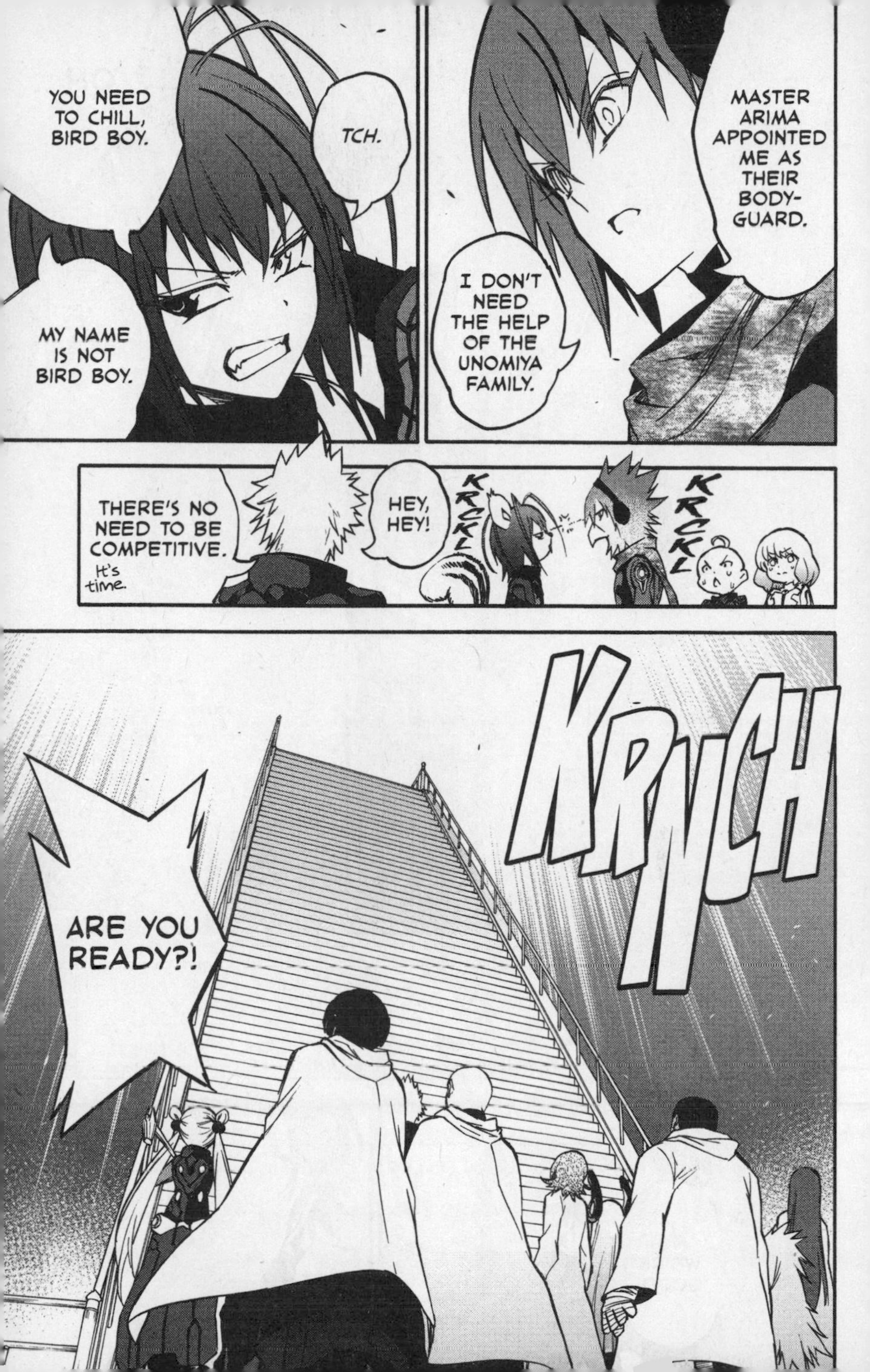
MASTER ARIMA APPOINTED ME AS THEIR BODY-GUARD.
I DON'T NEED THE HELP OF THE UNOMIYA FAMILY.
TCH.
YOU NEED TO CHILL, BIRD BOY.
MY NAME IS NOT BIRD BOY.
KRCKL
KRCKL
HEY, HEY!
THERE'S NO NEED TO BE COMPETITIVE.
It's time.
KRNCH
ARE YOU READY?!

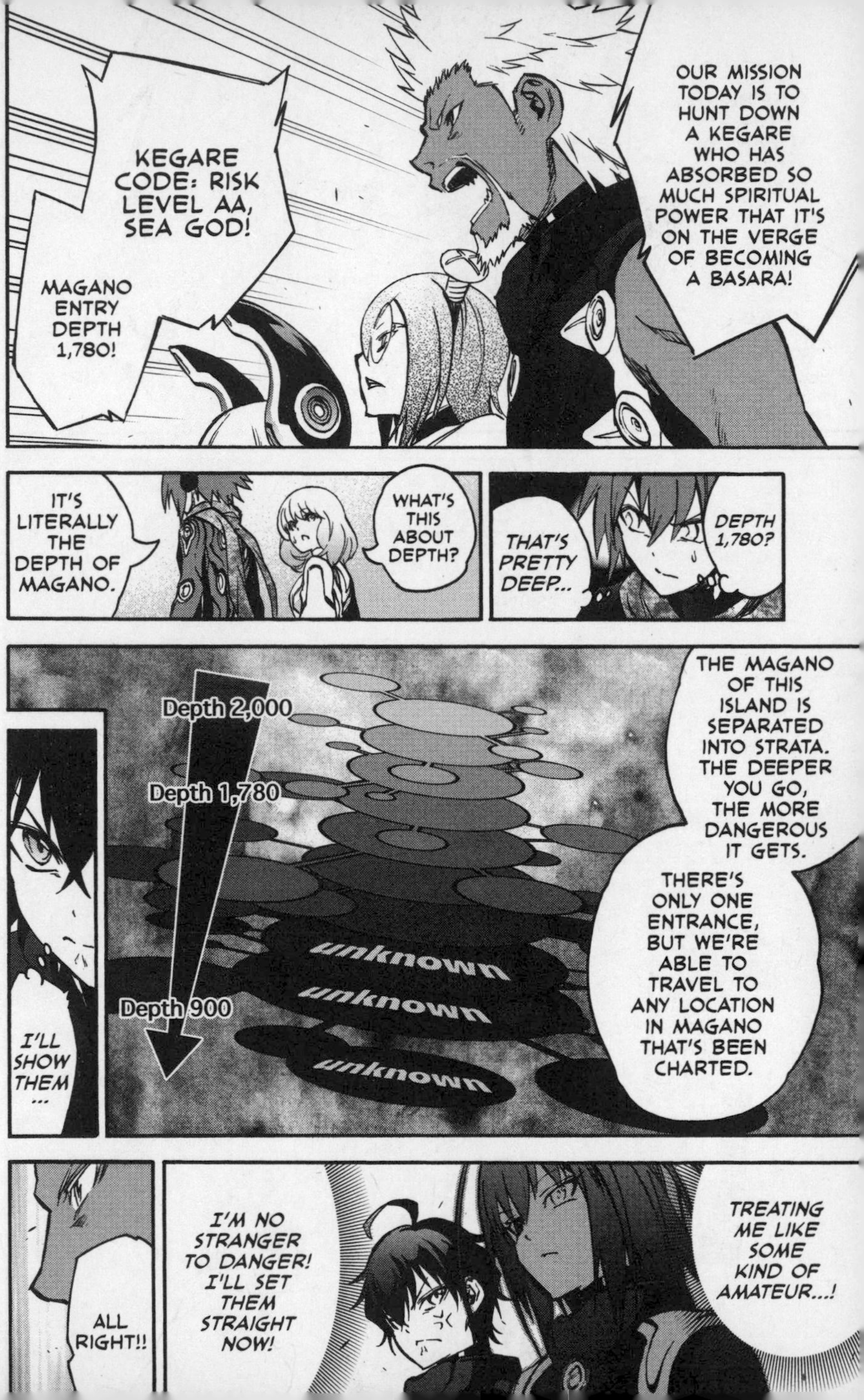
OUR MISSION TODAY IS TO HUNT DOWN A KEGARE WHO HAS ABSORBED SO MUCH SPIRITUAL POWER THAT IT'S ON THE VERGE OF BECOMING A BASARA!
KEGARE CODE: RISK LEVEL AA, SEA GOD!
MAGANO ENTRY DEPTH 1,780!
DEPTH 1,780?
THAT'S PRETTY DEEP...
WHAT'S THIS ABOUT DEPTH?
IT'S LITERALLY THE DEPTH OF MAGANO.
THE MAGANO OF THIS ISLAND IS SEPARATED INTO STRATA. THE DEEPER YOU GO, THE MORE DANGEROUS IT GETS.
THERE'S ONLY ONE ENTRANCE, BUT WE'RE ABLE TO TRAVEL TO ANY LOCATION IN MAGANO THAT'S BEEN CHARTED.
Depth 2,000
Depth 1,780
Depth 900
unknown
unknown
unknown
I'LL SHOW THEM...
TREATING ME LIKE SOME KIND OF AMATEUR...!
I'M NO STRANGER TO DANGER! I'LL SET THEM STRAIGHT NOW!
ALL RIGHT!!

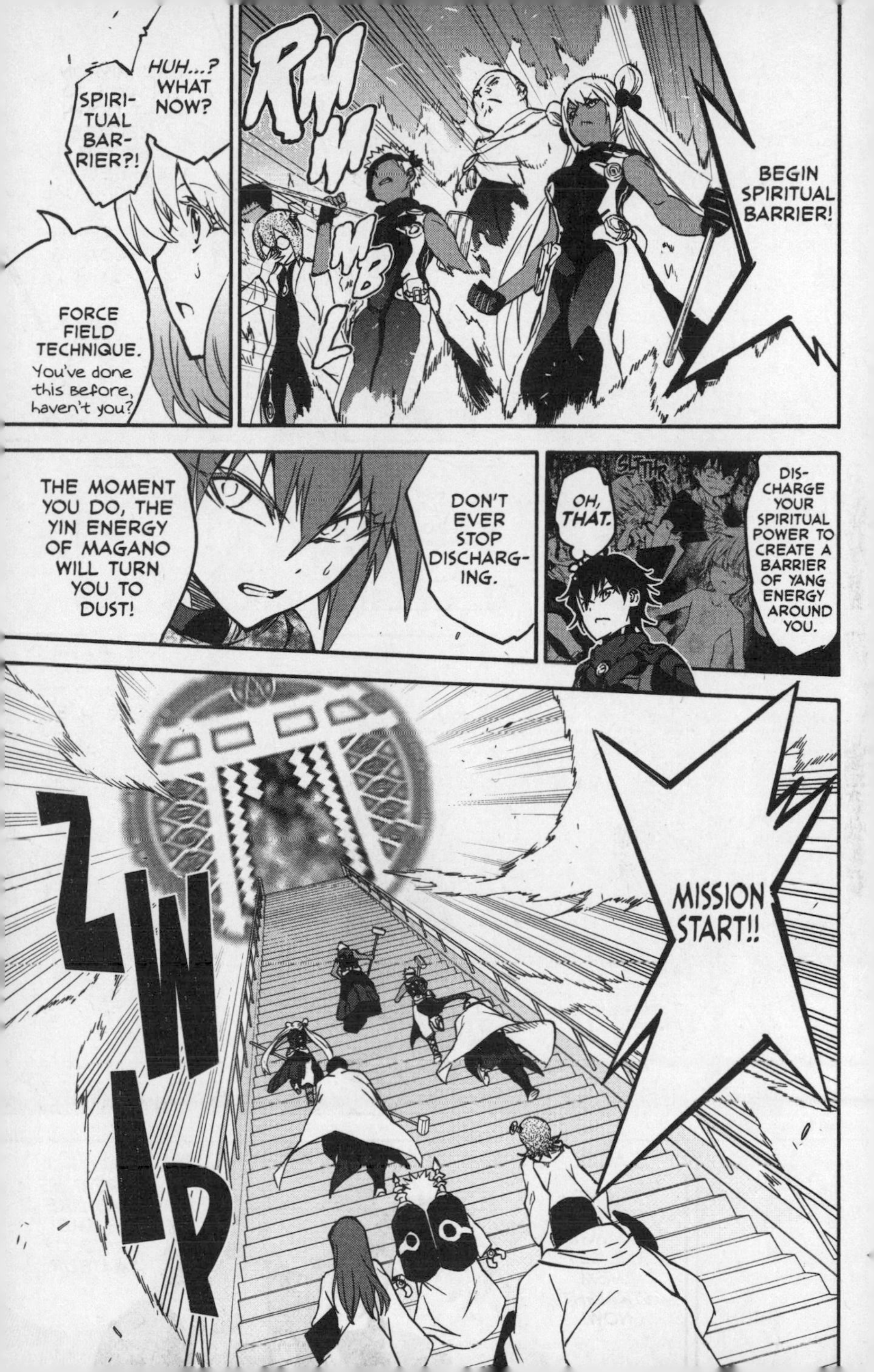
BEGIN SPIRITUAL BARRIER!
RMMMBL
HUH...? WHAT NOW?
SPIRITUAL BARRIER?!
FORCE FIELD TECHNIQUE. You've done this before, haven't you?
DISCHARGE YOUR SPIRITUAL POWER TO CREATE A BARRIER OF YANG ENERGY AROUND YOU.
OH, THAT.
DON'T EVER STOP DISCHARGING.
THE MOMENT YOU DO, THE YIN ENERGY OF MAGANO WILL TURN YOU TO DUST!
MISSION START!!
ZWIP

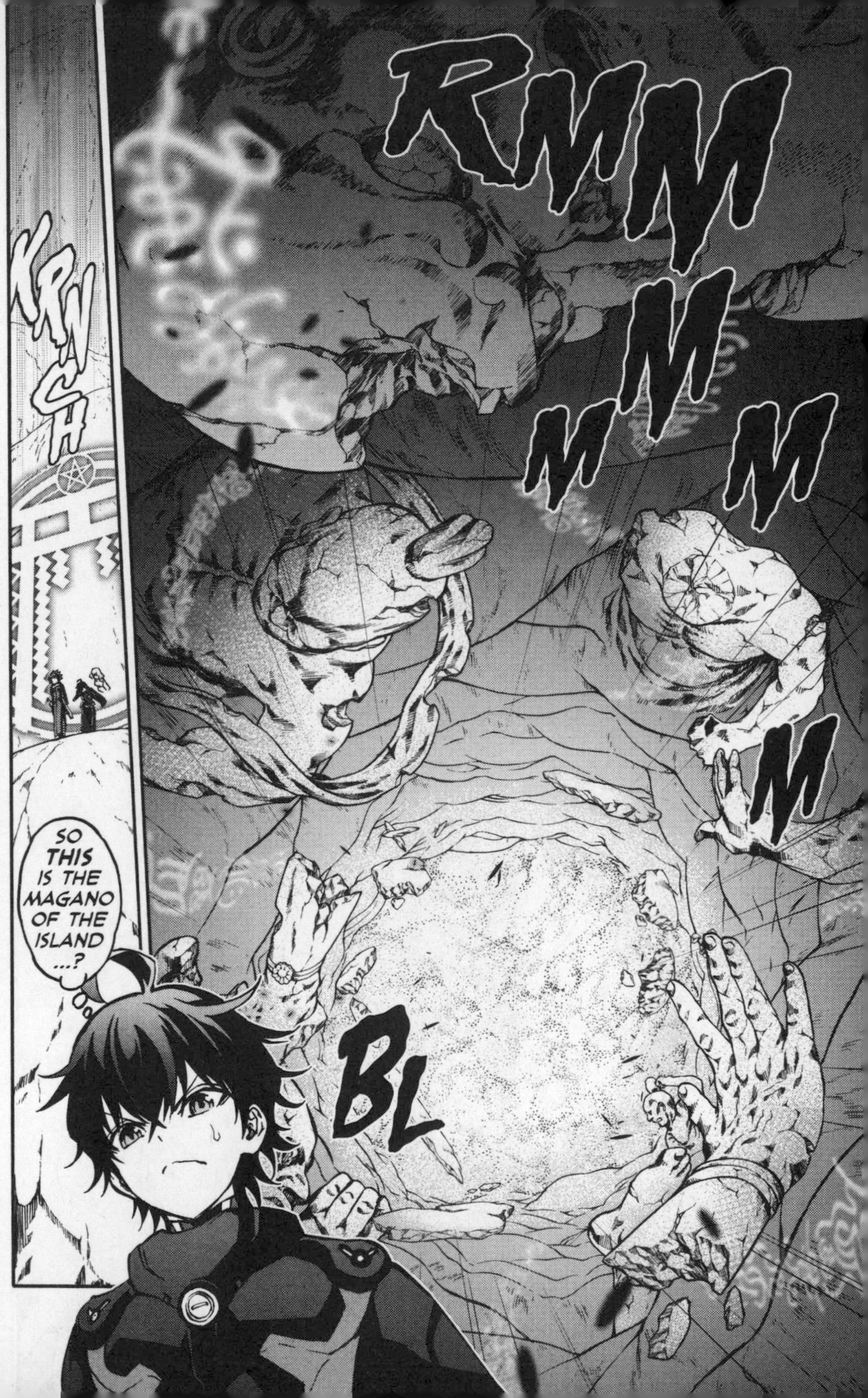
RMMMMMMMM
SO THIS IS THE MAGANO OF THE ISLAND ...?
BL
KRNCH

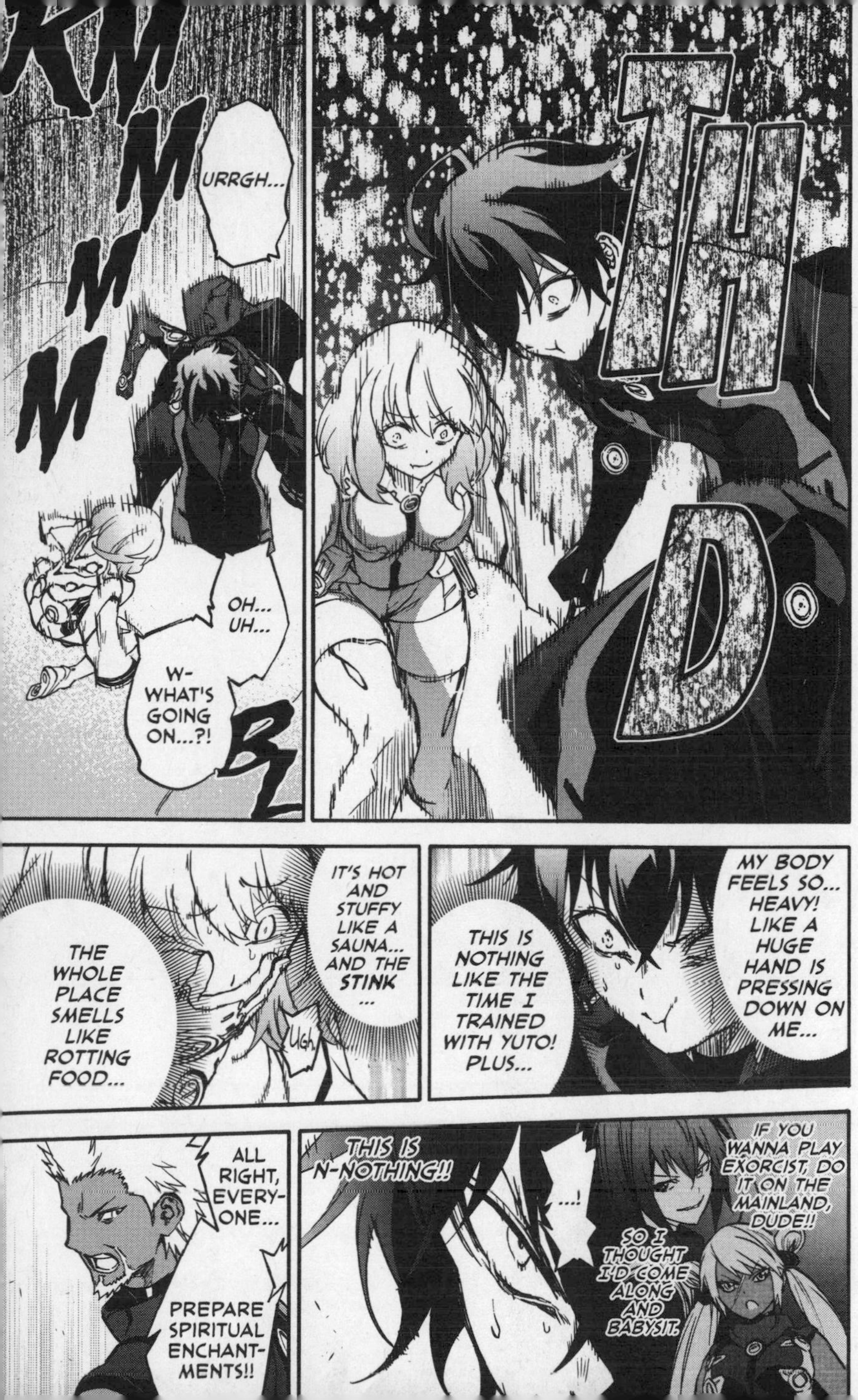
THD
KWMMMM
URRGH...
OH... UH...
W-WHAT'S GOING ON...?!
MY BODY FEELS SO... HEAVY! LIKE A HUGE HAND IS PRESSING DOWN ON ME...
THIS IS NOTHING LIKE THE TIME I TRAINED WITH YUTO! PLUS...
IT'S HOT AND STUFFY LIKE A SAUNA... AND THE STINK...
UGH
THE WHOLE PLACE SMELLS LIKE ROTTING FOOD...
IF YOU WANNA PLAY EXORCIST, DO IT ON THE MAINLAND, DUDE!!
SO I THOUGHT I'D COME ALONG AND BABYSIT.
...!
THIS IS N-NOTHING!!
ALL RIGHT, EVERYONE...
PREPARE SPIRITUAL ENCHANTMENTS!!

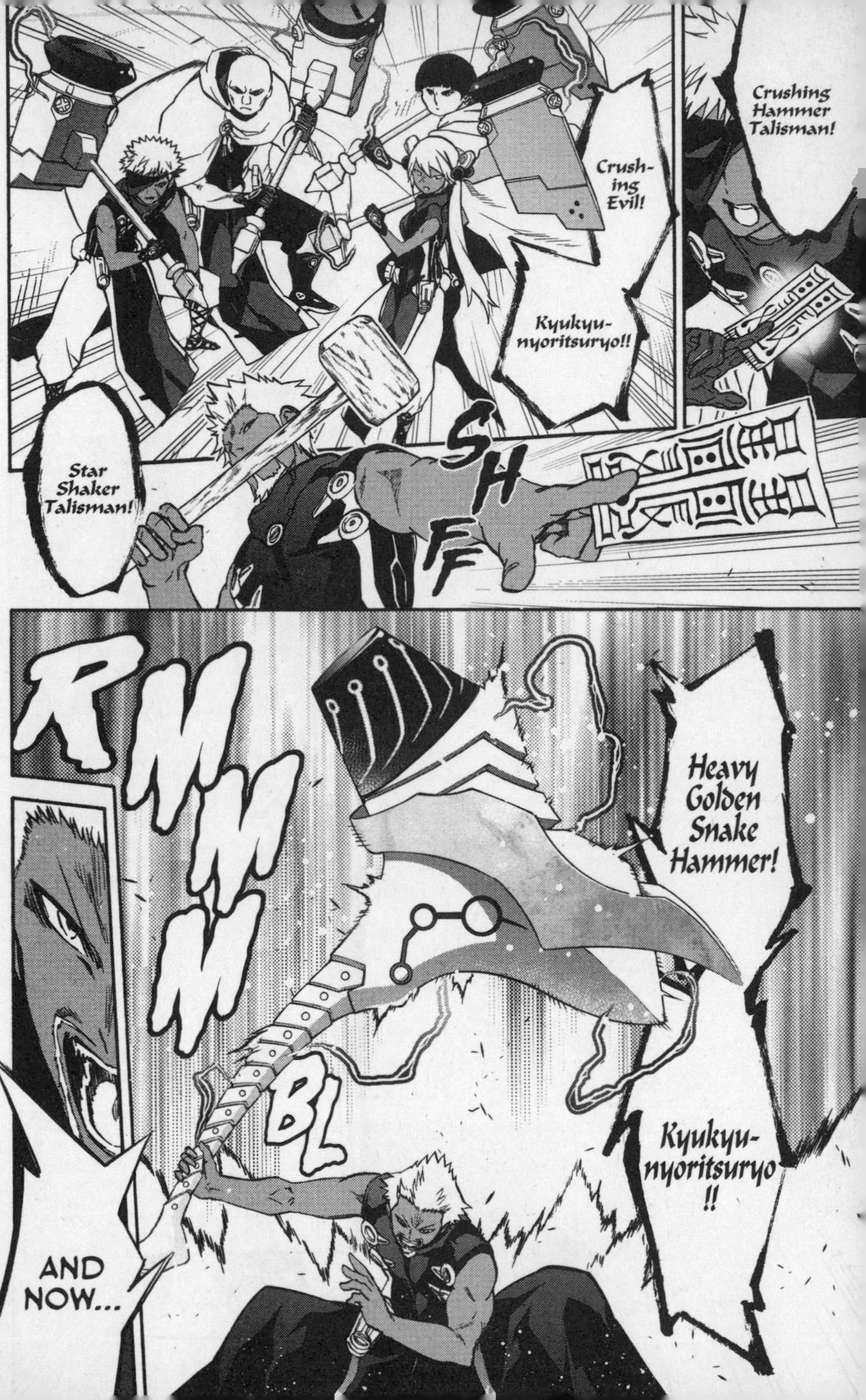
Crushing Hammer Talisman!
Crushing Evil!
Kyukyu-nyoritsuryo!!
SHFF
Star Shaker Talisman!
Heavy Golden Snake Hammer!
RMMMBL
Kyukyu-nyoritsuryo!!
AND NOW...

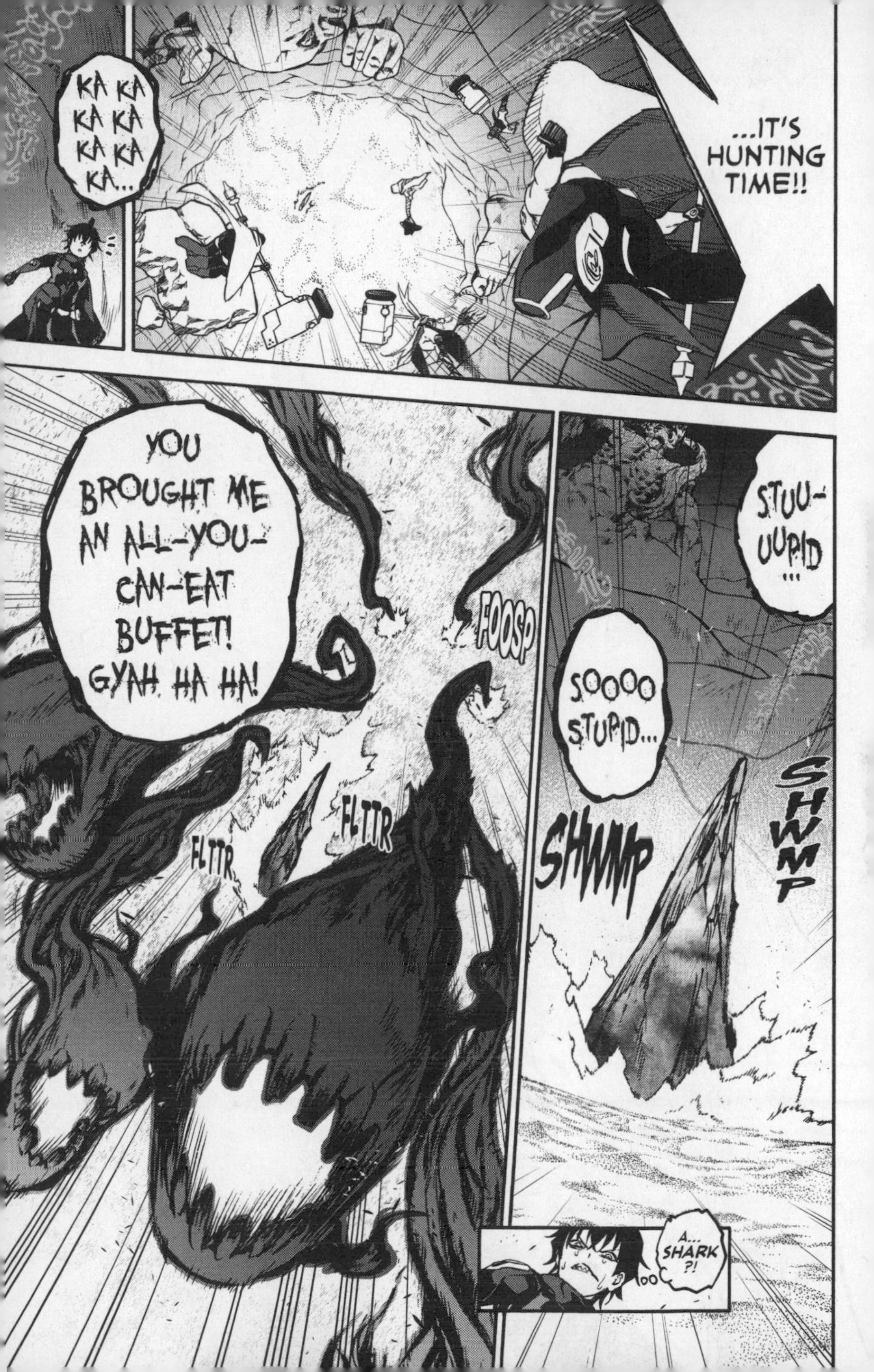
...IT'S HUNTING TIME!!
KA KA KA KA KA KA KA...
STUU-UUPID...
SOOOO STUPID...
SHWMP
SHWMP
YOU BROUGHT ME AN ALL-YOU-CAN-EAT BUFFET! GYAH HA HA!
FOOSP
FLTTR
FLTTR
A... SHARK?!

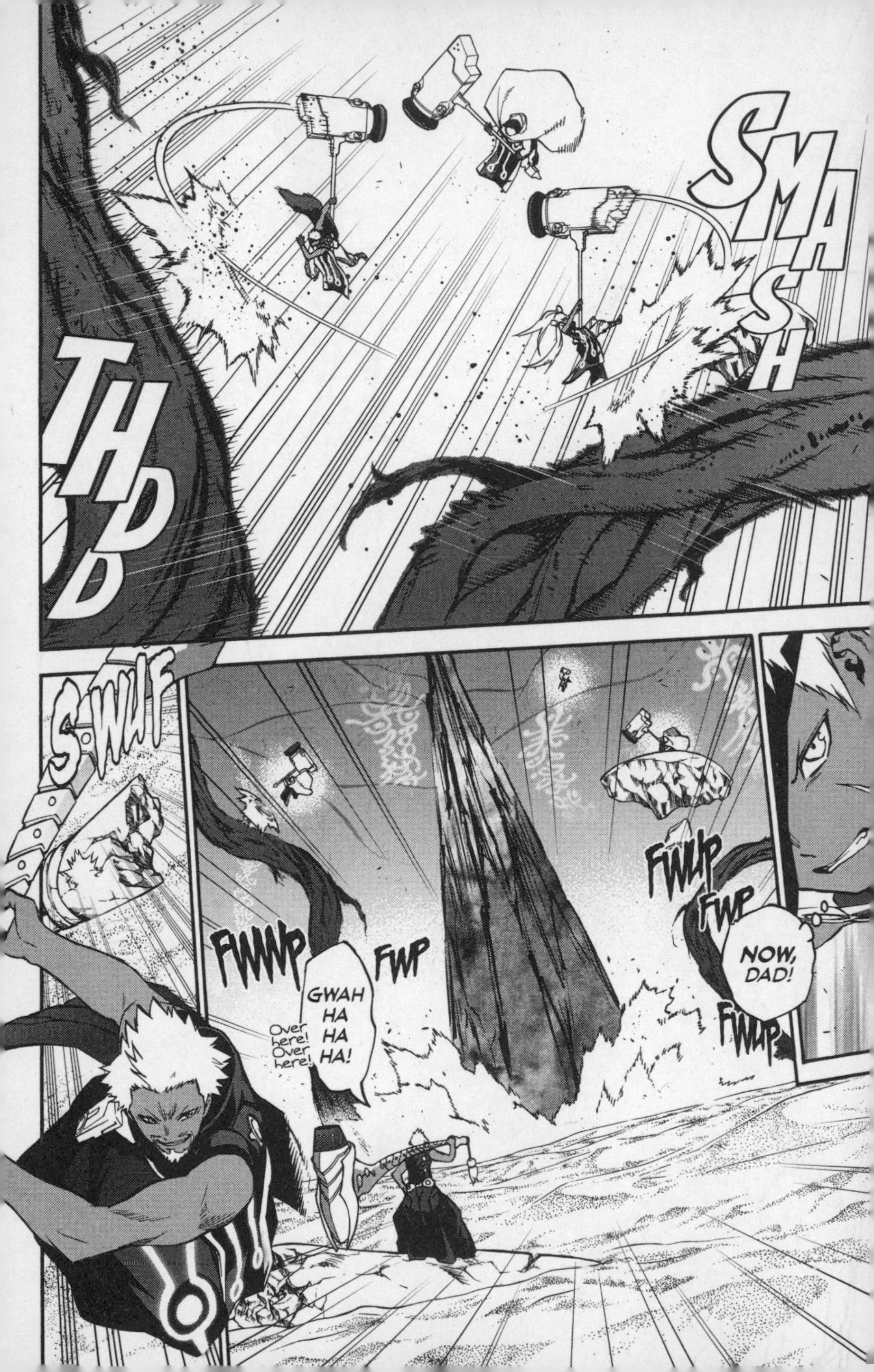
SMASH
THDD
FWUP
FWP
NOW, DAD!
FWUP
FWP
GWAH HA HA HA!
FWNP
Over here! Over here!
SWUF

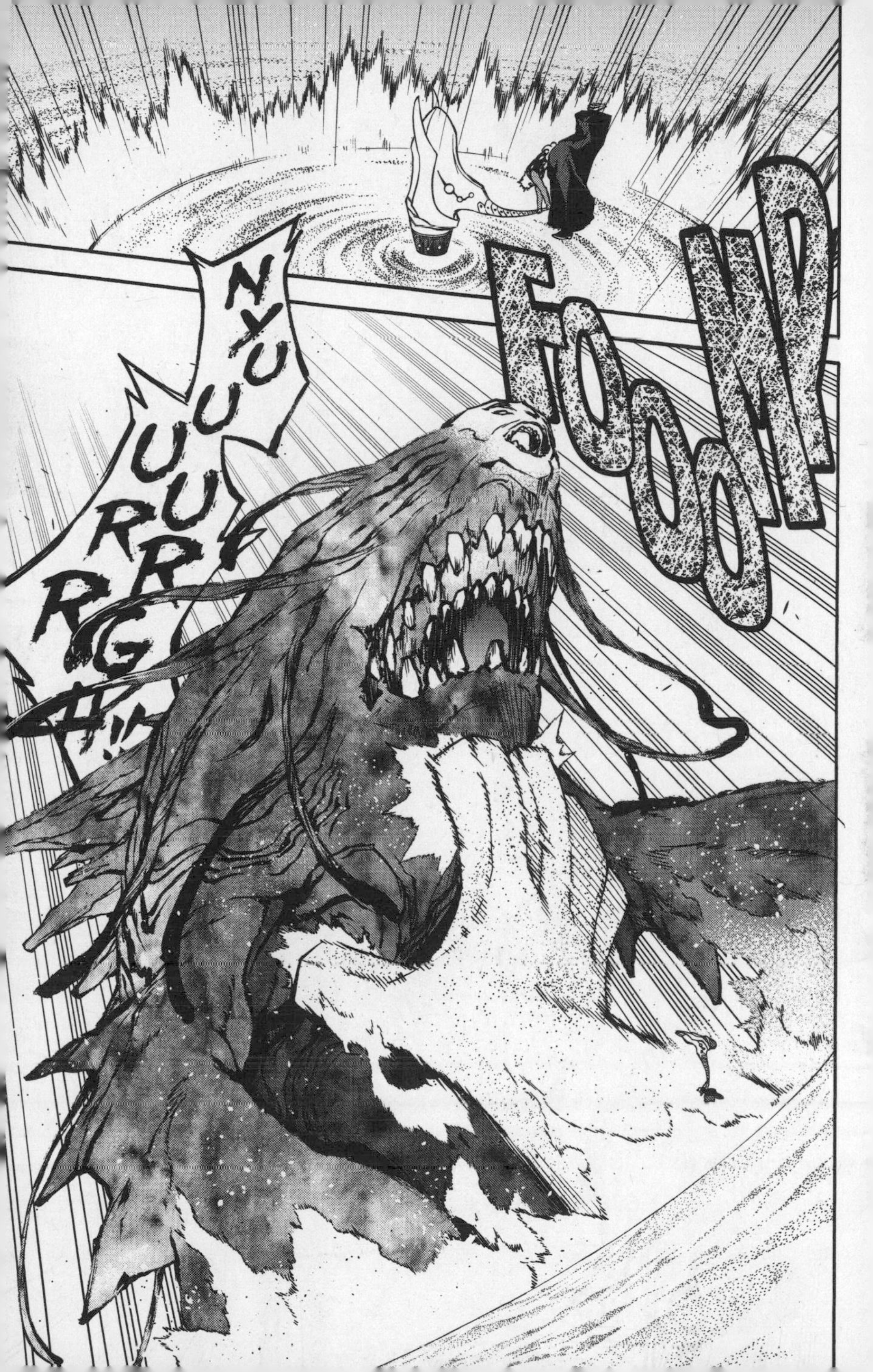
FOOOMP!
NYUUUURRRGH!!

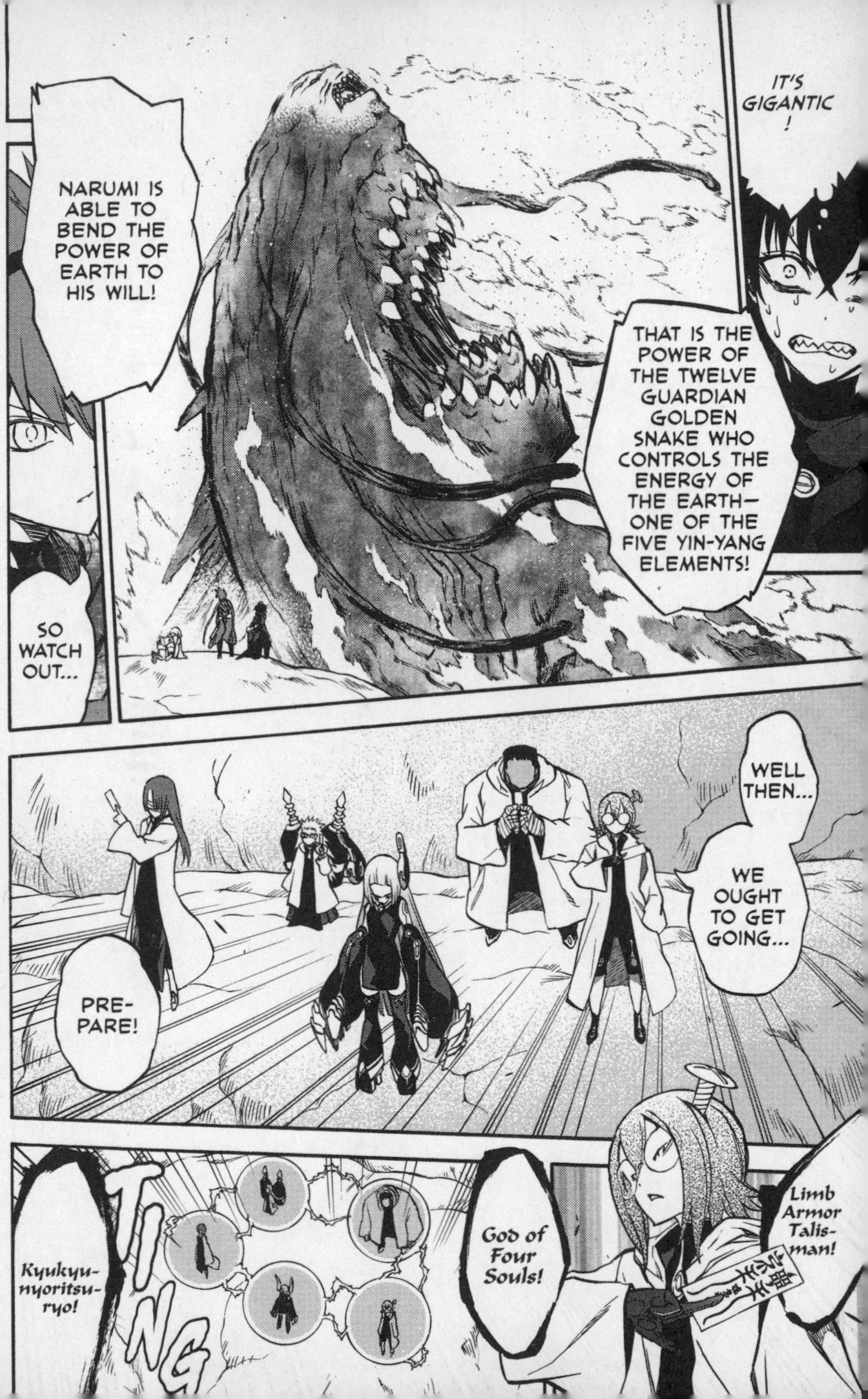
IT'S GIGANTIC!
THAT IS THE POWER OF THE TWELVE GUARDIAN GOLDEN SNAKE WHO CONTROLS THE ENERGY OF THE EARTH—ONE OF THE FIVE YIN-YANG ELEMENTS!
NARUMI IS ABLE TO BEND THE POWER OF EARTH TO HIS WILL!
SO WATCH OUT...
WELL THEN...
WE OUGHT TO GET GOING...
PRE-PARE!
Limb Armor Talis-man!
God of Four Souls!
Kyukyu-nyoritsu-ryo!
TING

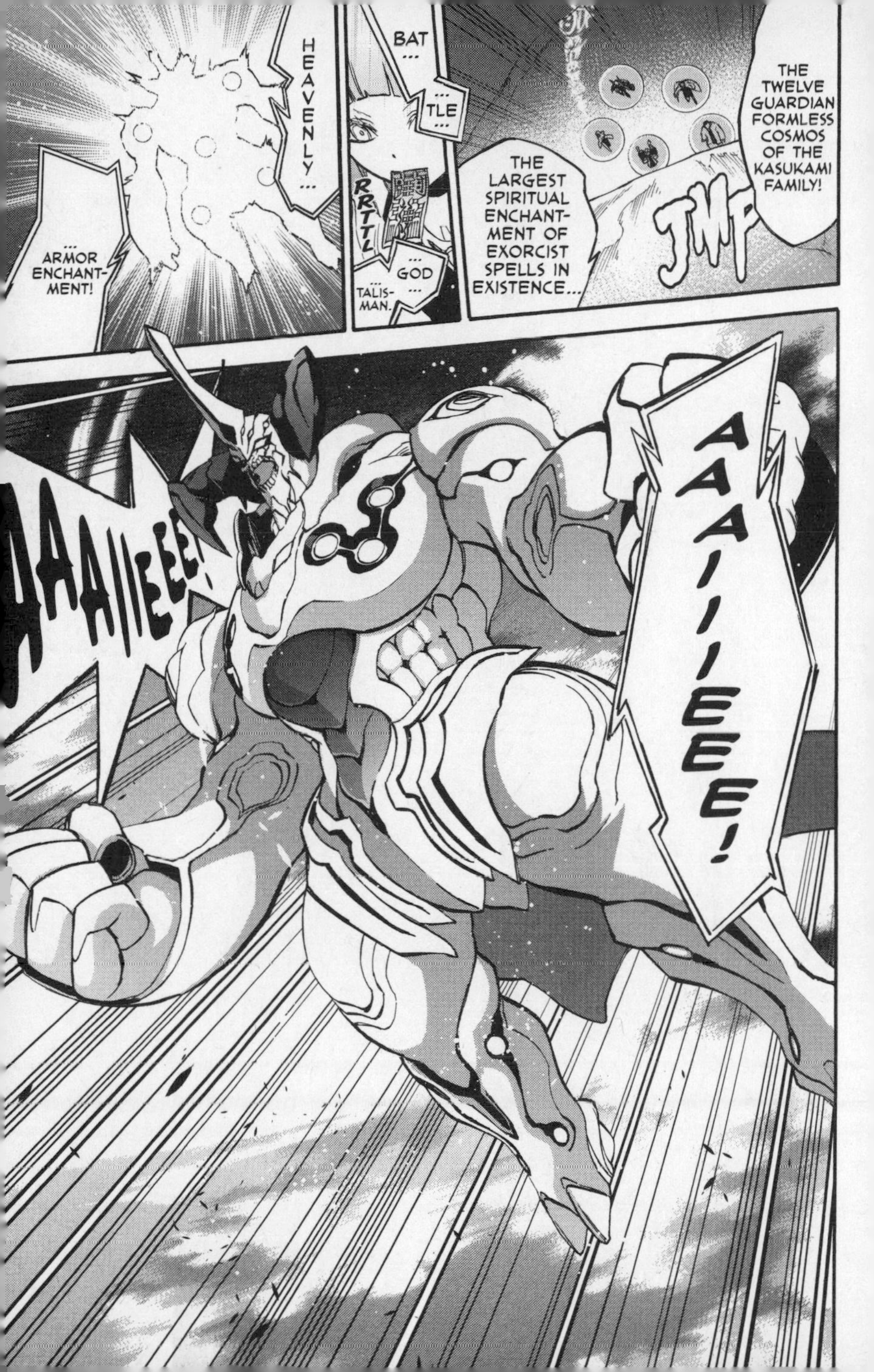
THE TWELVE GUARDIAN FORMLESS COSMOS OF THE KASUKAMI FAMILY!
JMP
THE LARGEST SPIRITUAL ENCHANTMENT OF EXORCIST SPELLS IN EXISTENCE...
BAT...
...TLE...
RRTTL
...GOD...
...TALISMAN.
HEAVENLY...
...ARMOR ENCHANTMENT!
AAAIIIEEEE!
AAAIIIEEE!

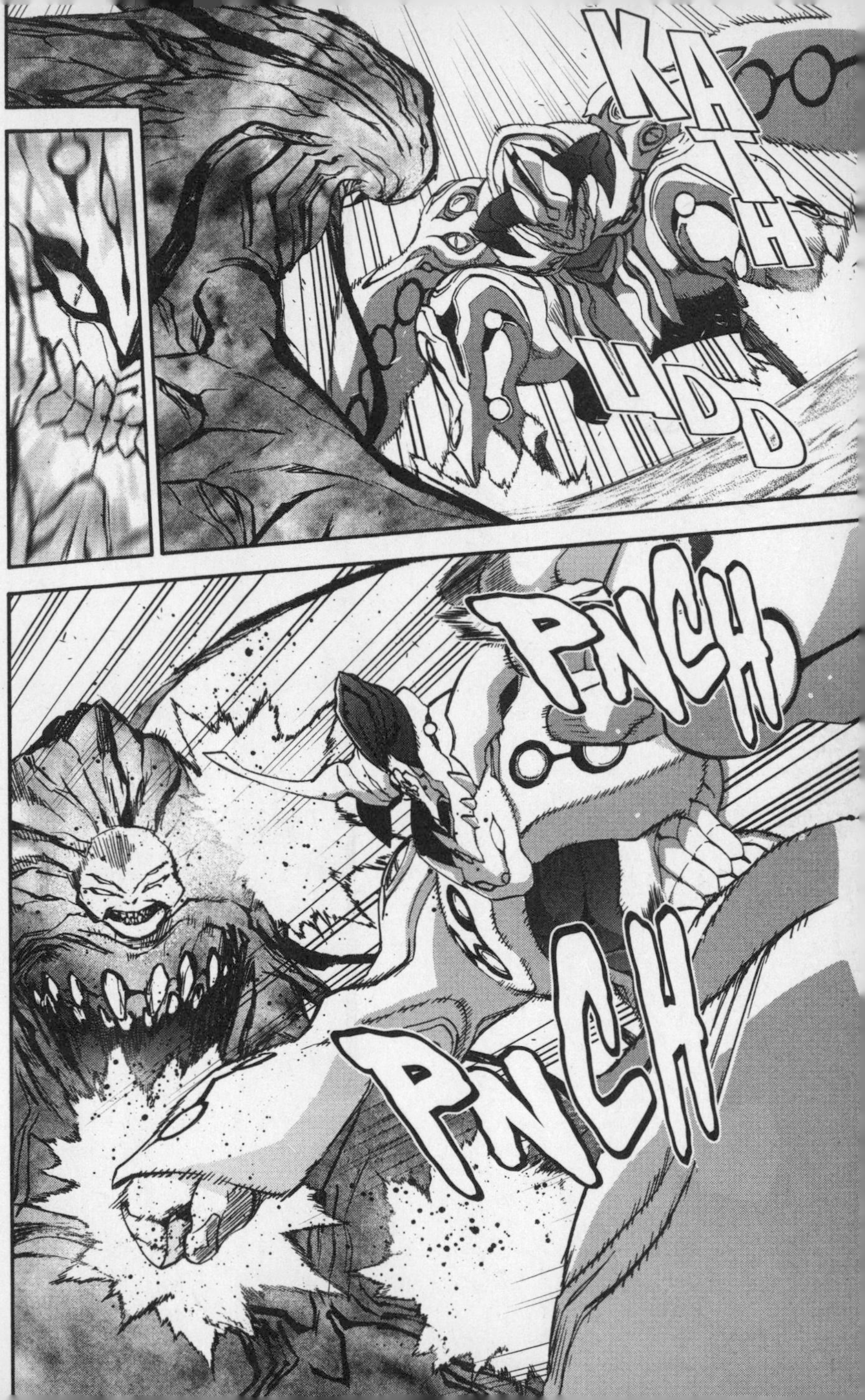
KATCH
UDD
PUNCH
PUNCH

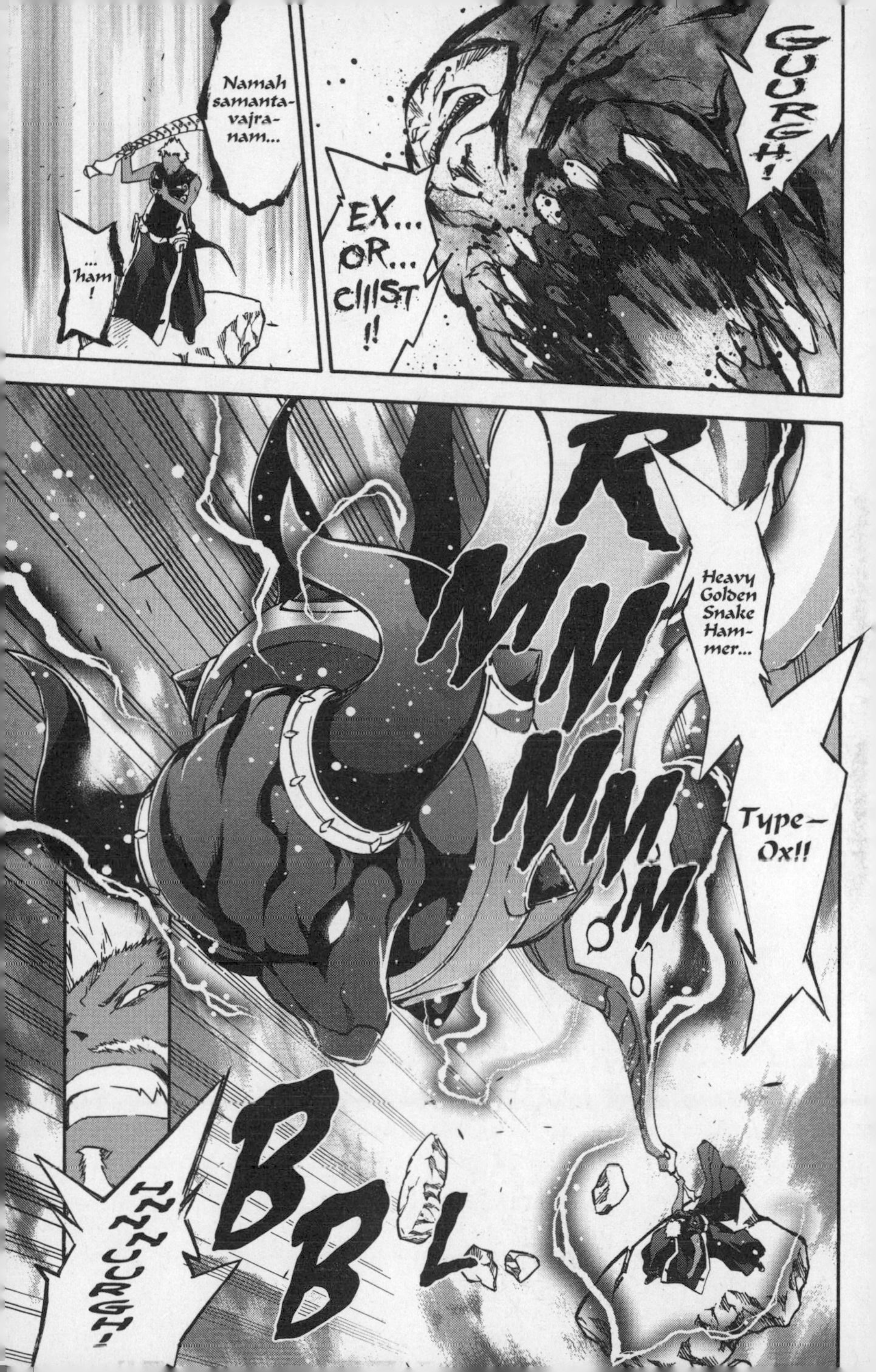
GUURGH!
EX... OR... CIIIST!!
Namah samanta-vajra-nam...
...ham!
RMMMMMM
Heavy Golden Snake Ham-mer...
Type-Ox!!
BBL...
HNNUURGH-

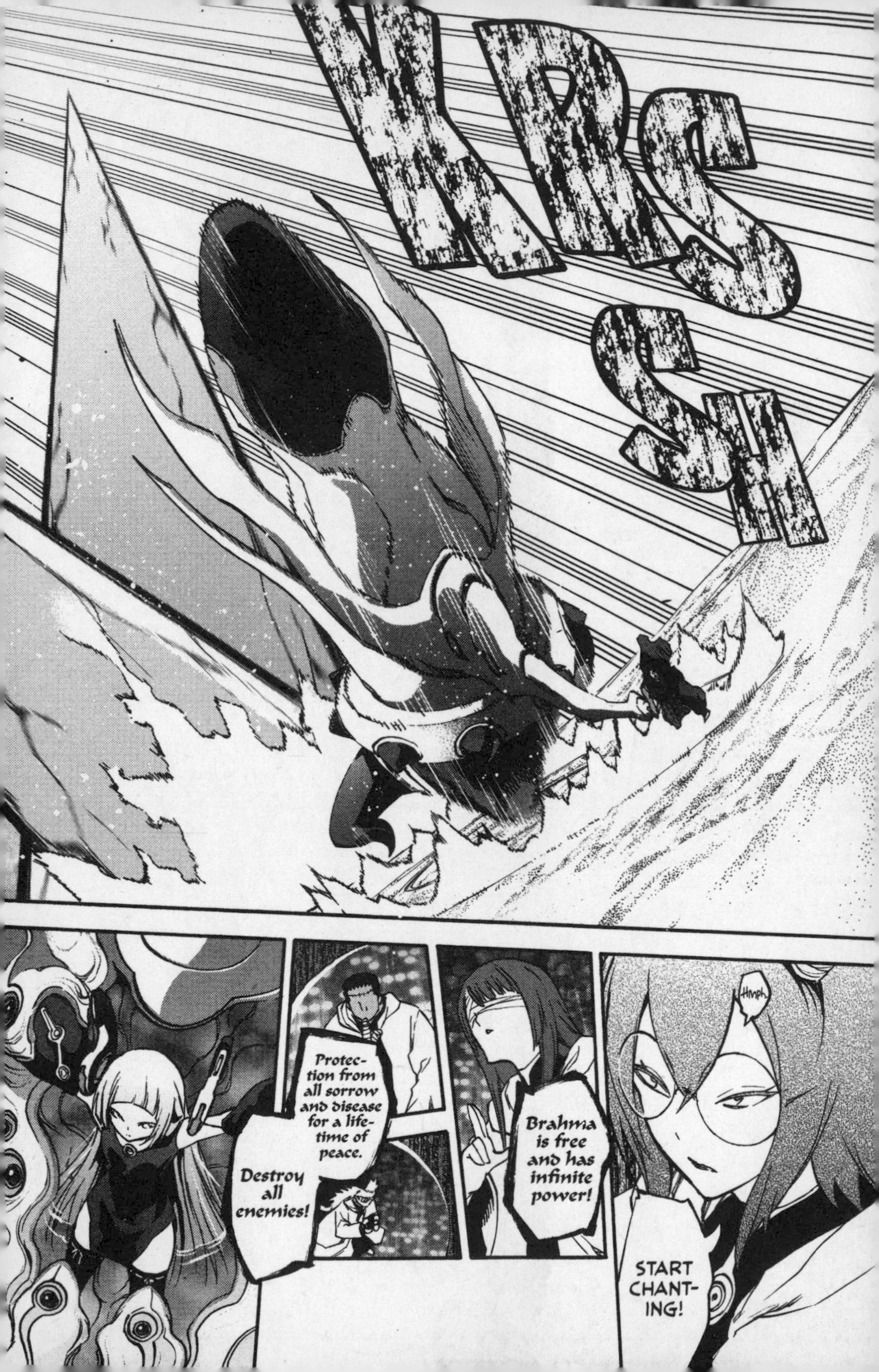
KRSSH
Hmph
START CHANT-ING!
Brahma is free and has infinite power!
Protec-tion from all sorrow and disease for a life-time of peace.
Destroy all enemies!

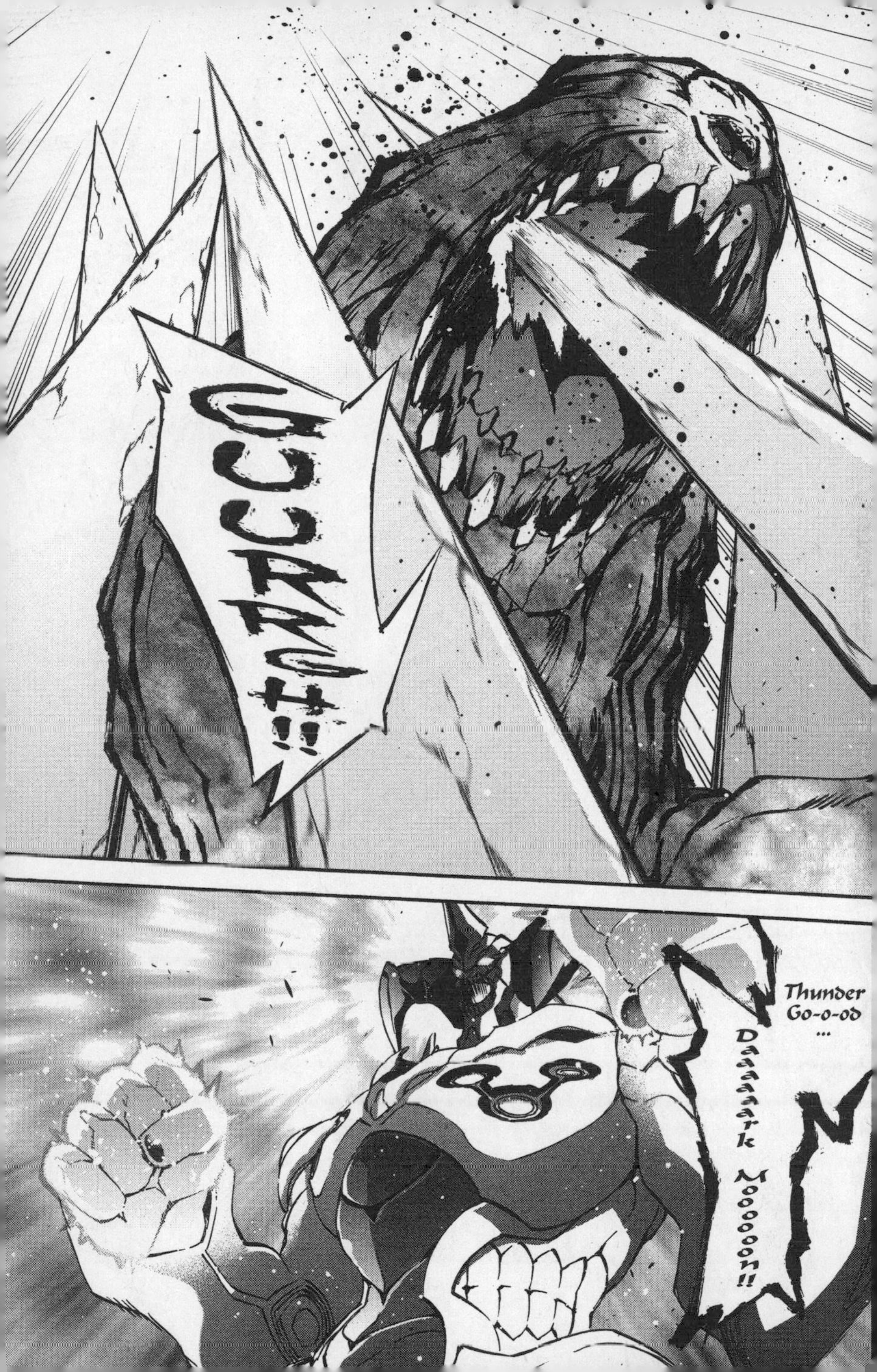
GURRGH!!
Thunder Go-o-od ...
Daaaaaark Moooooon!!

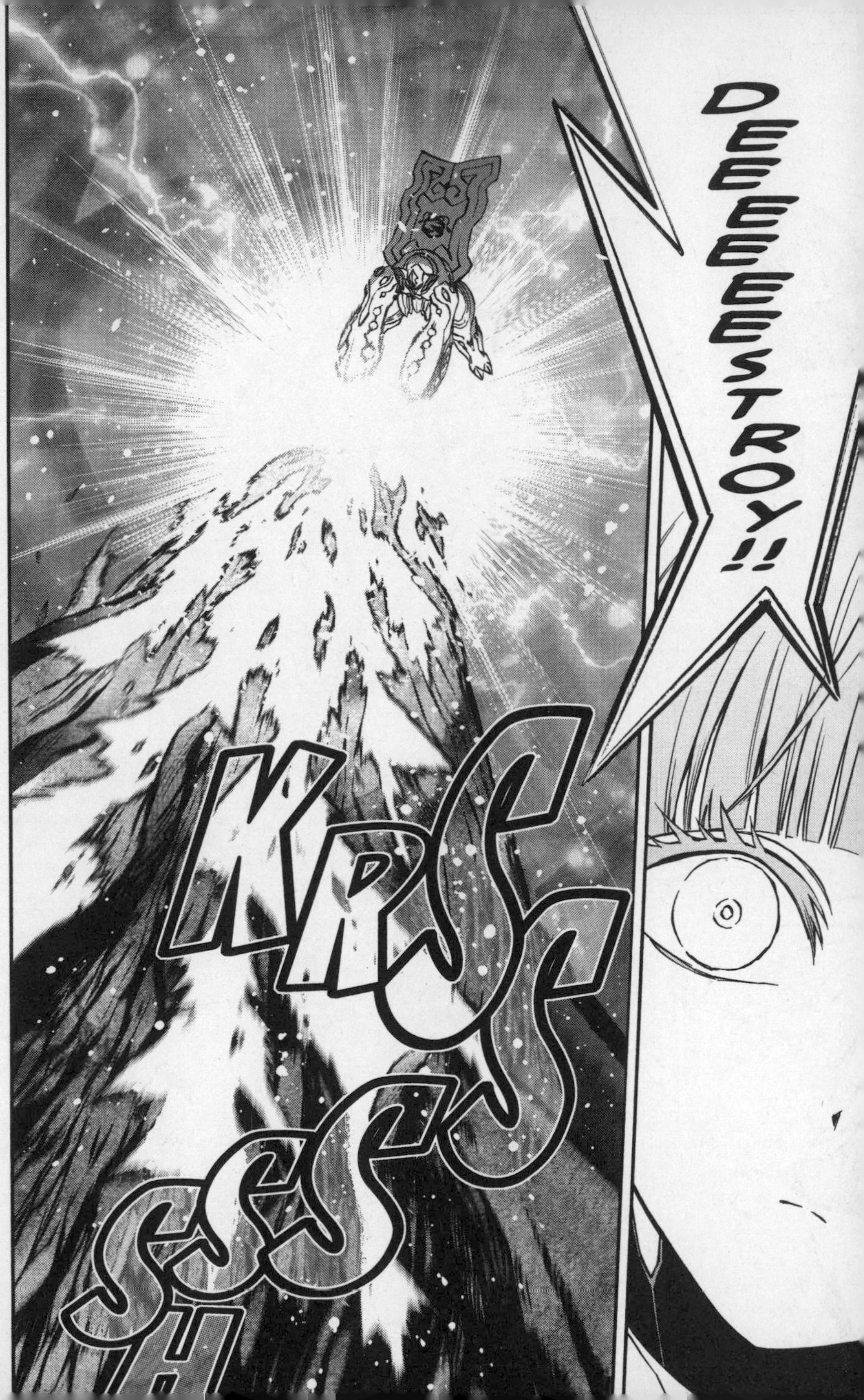
DEEEEEESTROY!!
KRSSSSSH

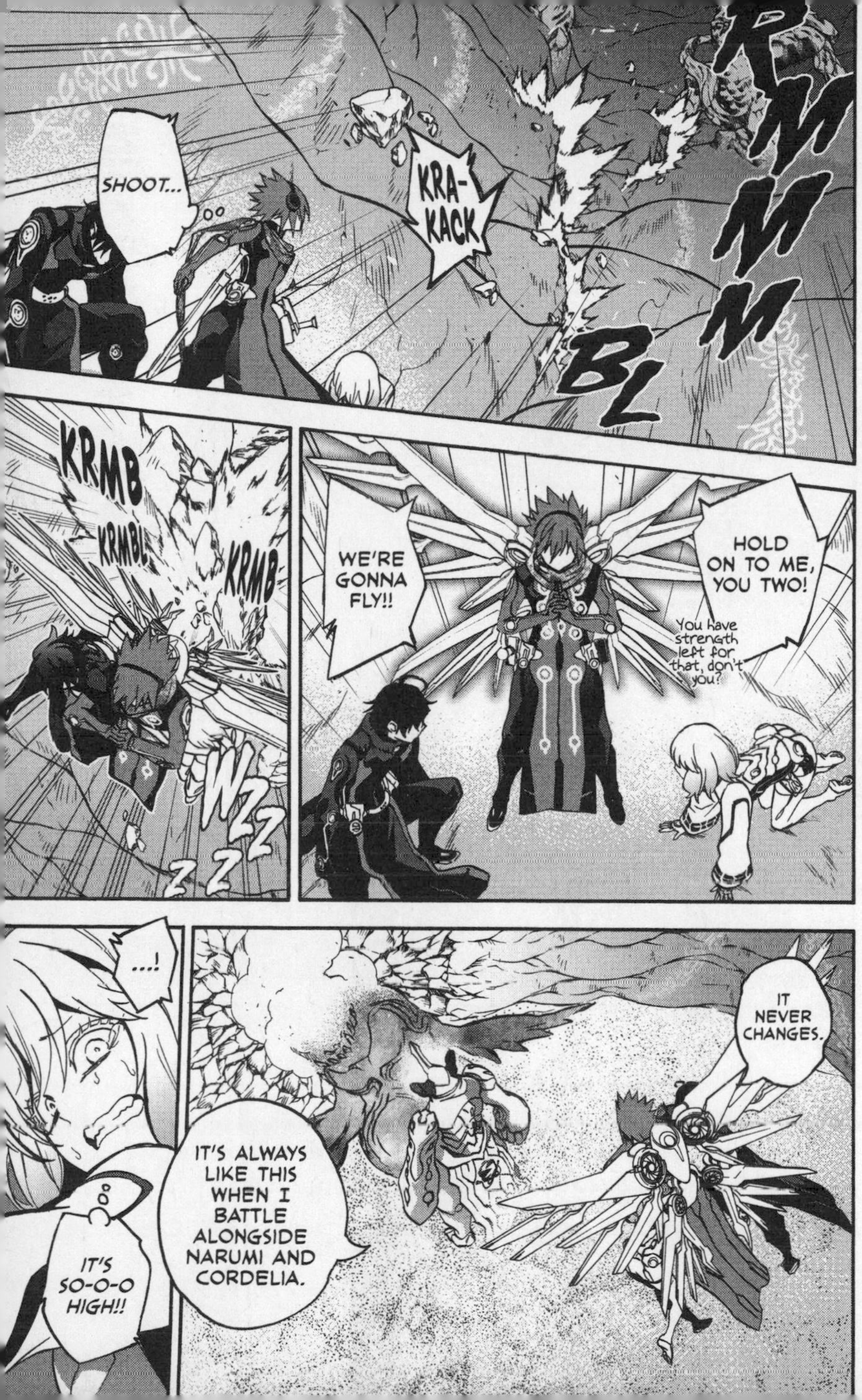
RMMMBL
KRA-KACK
SHOOT...
HOLD ON TO ME, YOU TWO!
You have strength left for that, don't you?
WE'RE GONNA FLY!!
KRMB
KRMBL
KRMB
WZZZZ
IT NEVER CHANGES.
IT'S ALWAYS LIKE THIS WHEN I BATTLE ALONGSIDE NARUMI AND CORDELIA.
...!
IT'S SO-O-O HIGH!!

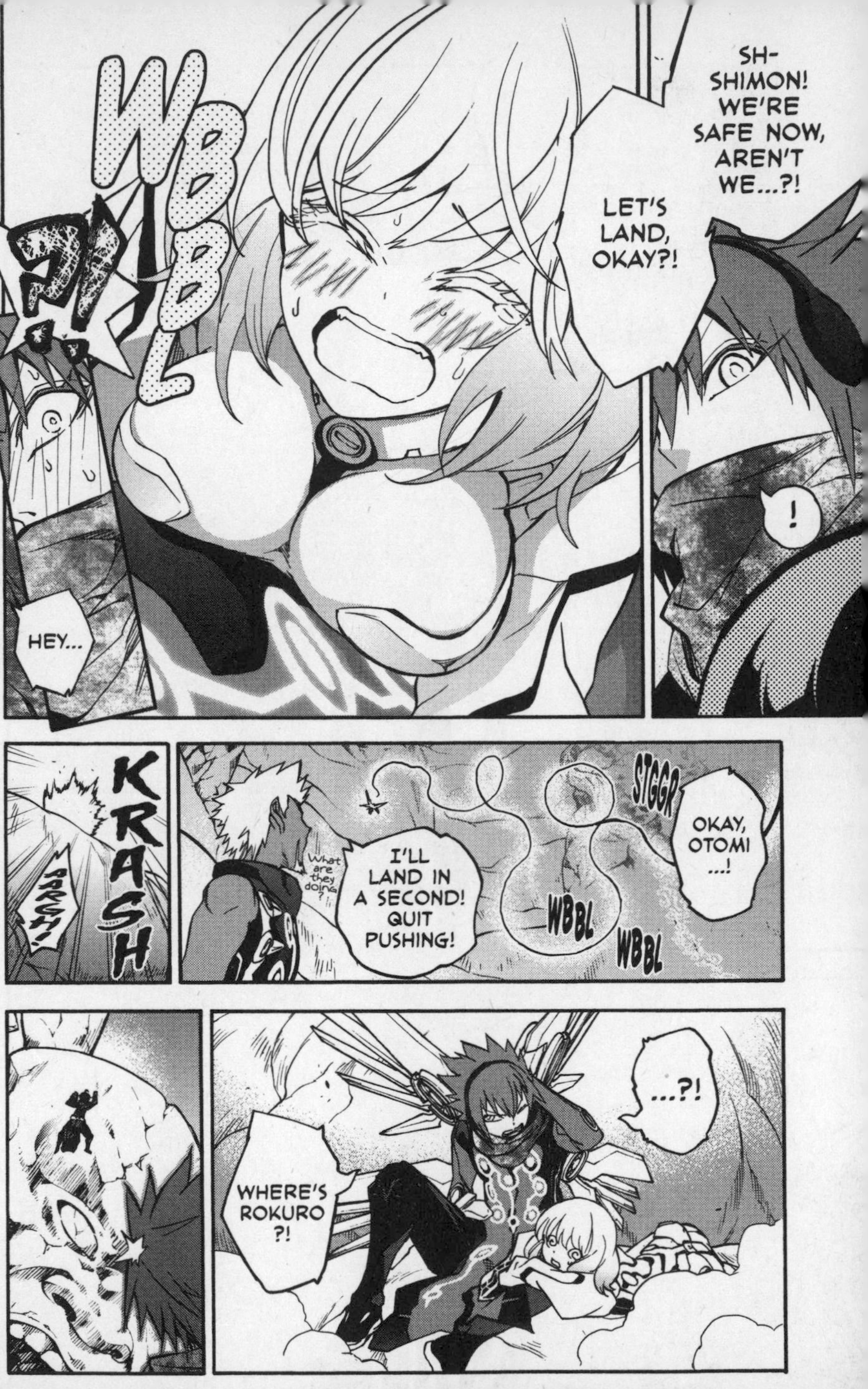
SH-SHIMON! WE'RE SAFE NOW, AREN'T WE...?!
LET'S LAND, OKAY?!
!
WBBL
PI!
HEY...
STGGR
OKAY, OTOMI ...!
WBBL
WBBL
I'LL LAND IN A SECOND! QUIT PUSHING!
What are they doing?
KRASH
SPRSH!
...?!
WHERE'S ROKURO?!

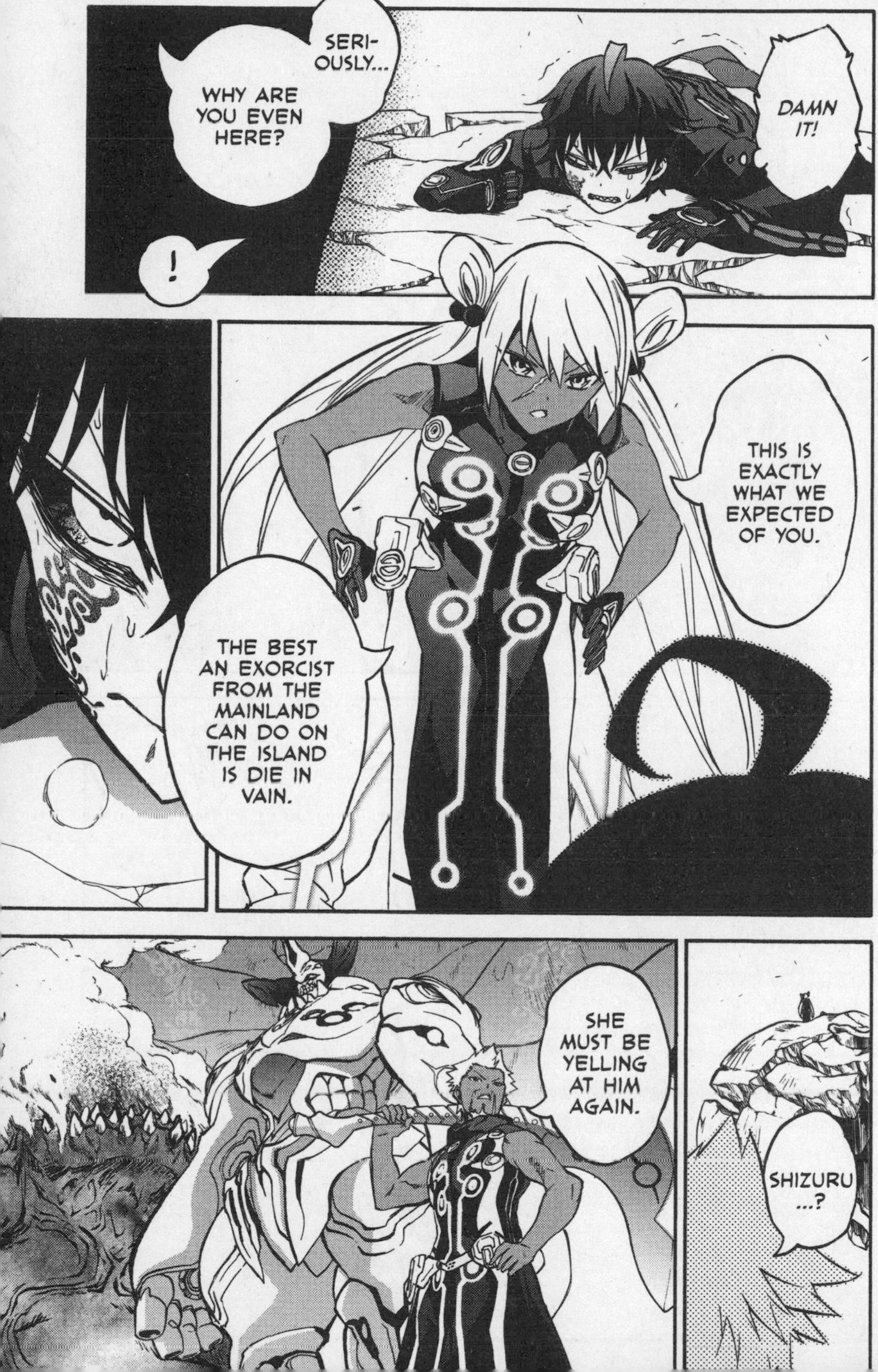
DAMN IT!
SERI-OUSLY... WHY ARE YOU EVEN HERE?
!
THIS IS EXACTLY WHAT WE EXPECTED OF YOU.
THE BEST AN EXORCIST FROM THE MAINLAND CAN DO ON THE ISLAND IS DIE IN VAIN.
SHIZURU ...?
SHE MUST BE YELLING AT HIM AGAIN.

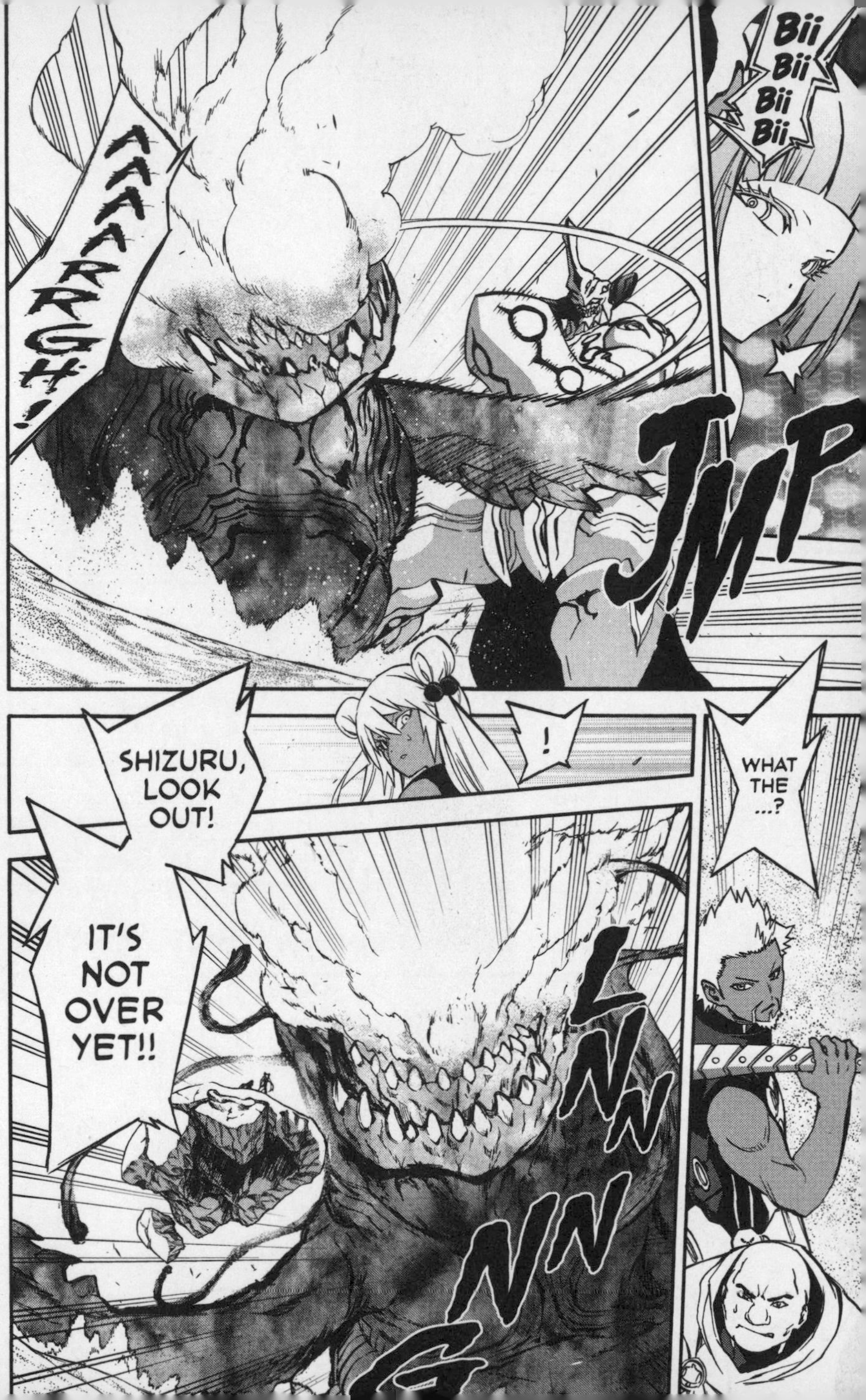
Bii Bii Bii Bii
JMP
AAAARRGH!!
WHAT THE ...?
!
SHIZURU, LOOK OUT!
IT'S NOT OVER YET!!

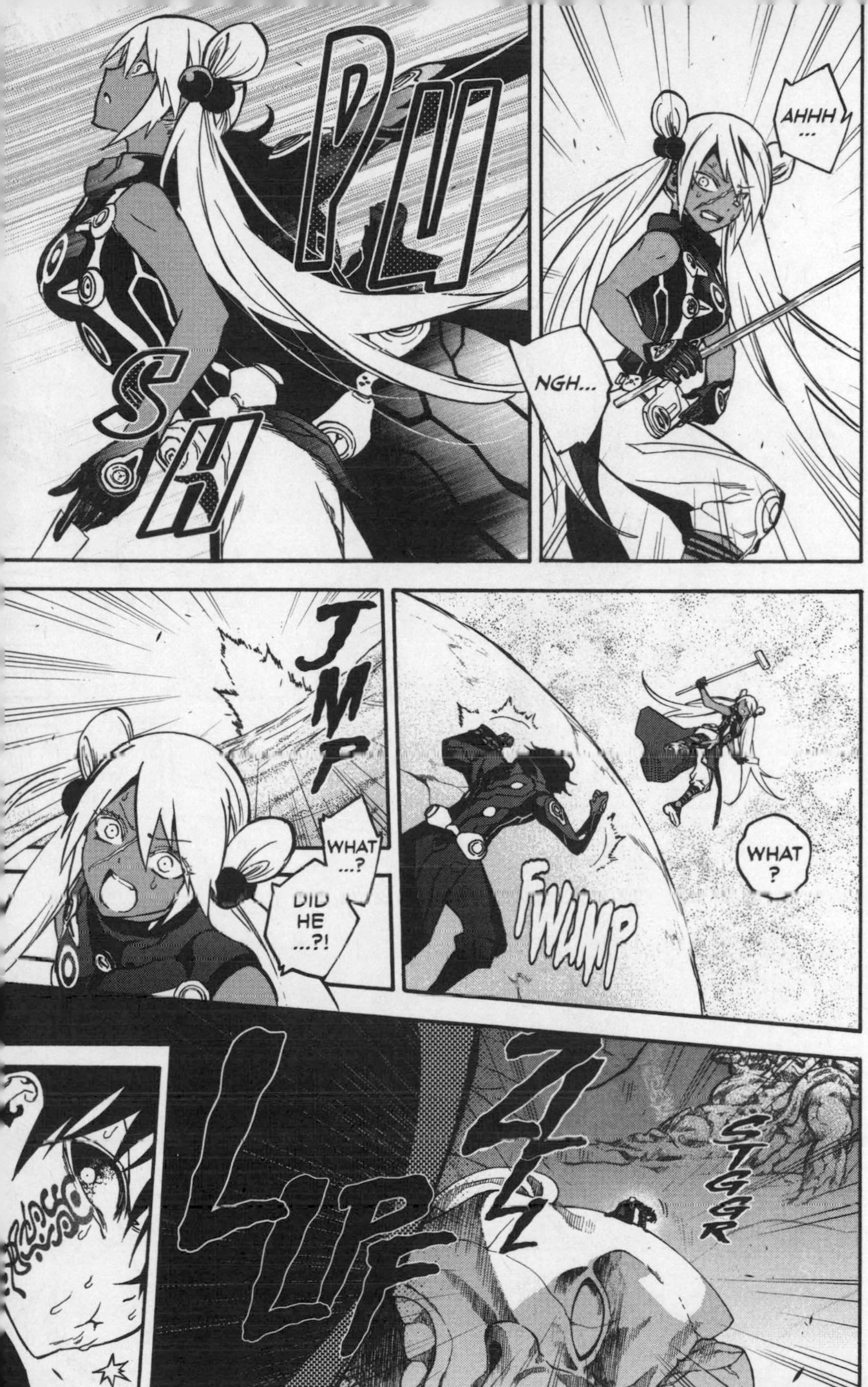
AHHH ...
NGH...
PUSH
WHAT ?
FWUMP
JMP
WHAT ...?
DID HE ...?!
STGGR

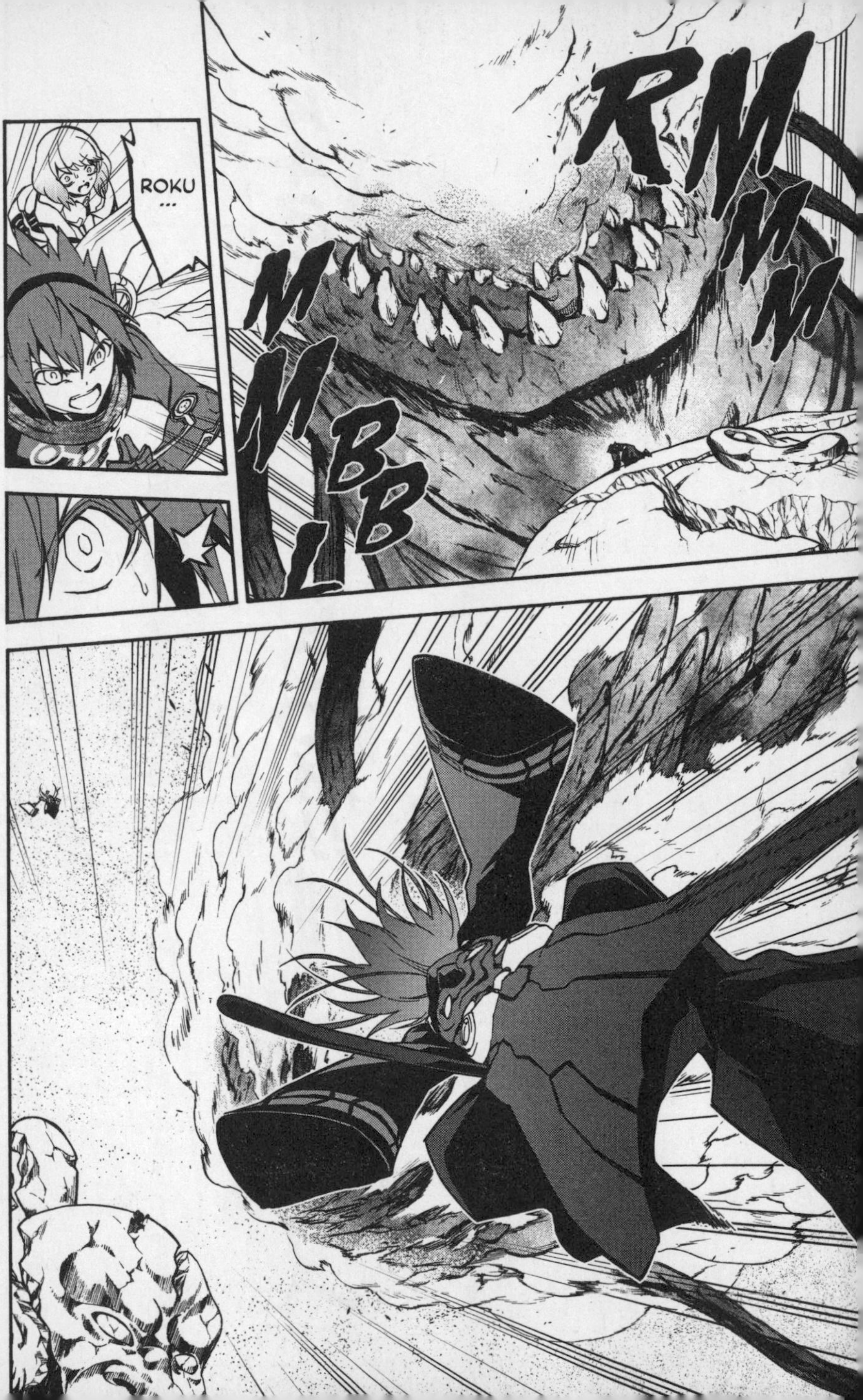
RMMMMMBBL
ROKU...

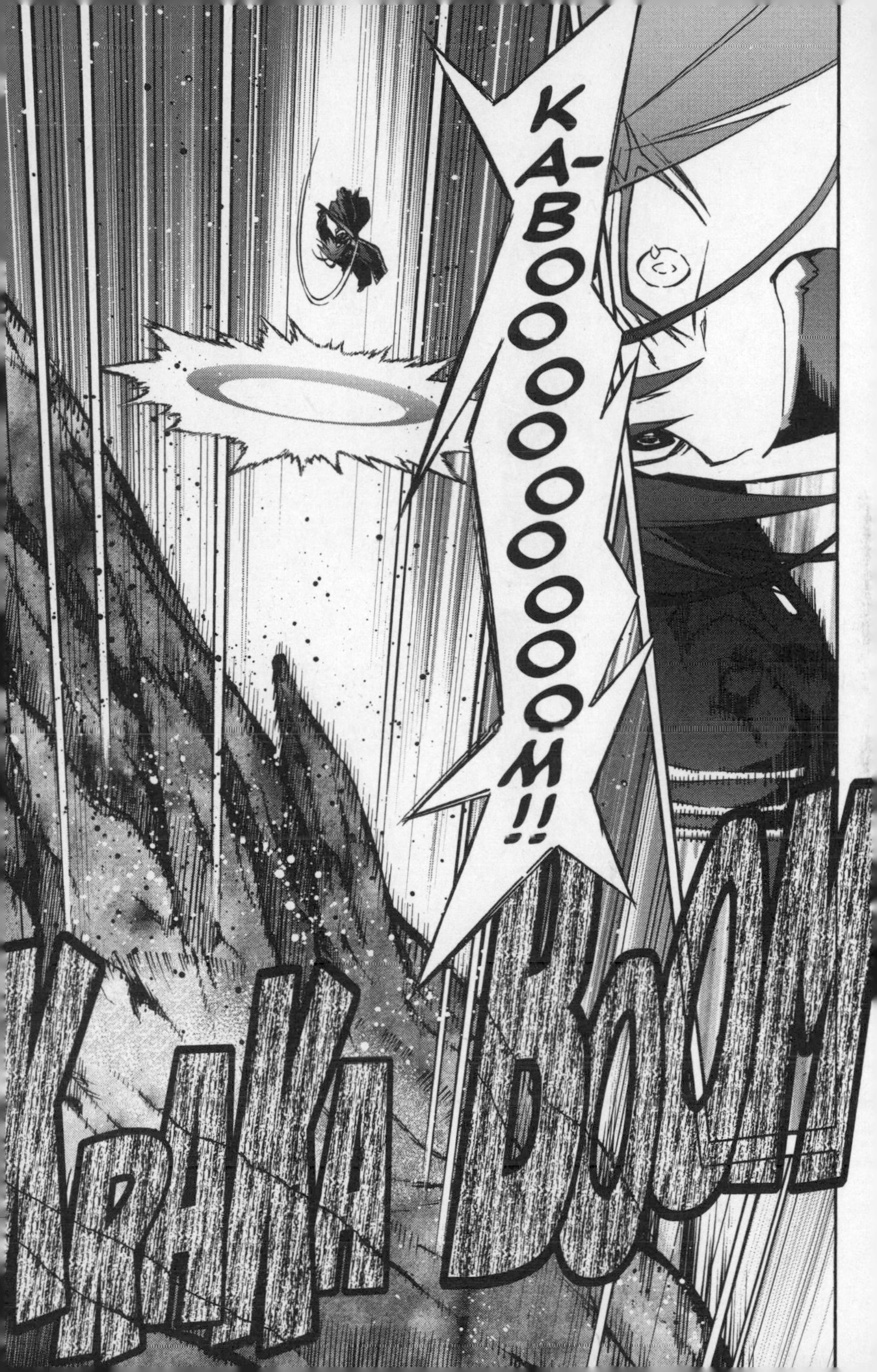
KA-BOOOOOOOOOOM!!
KRAKA DOOM

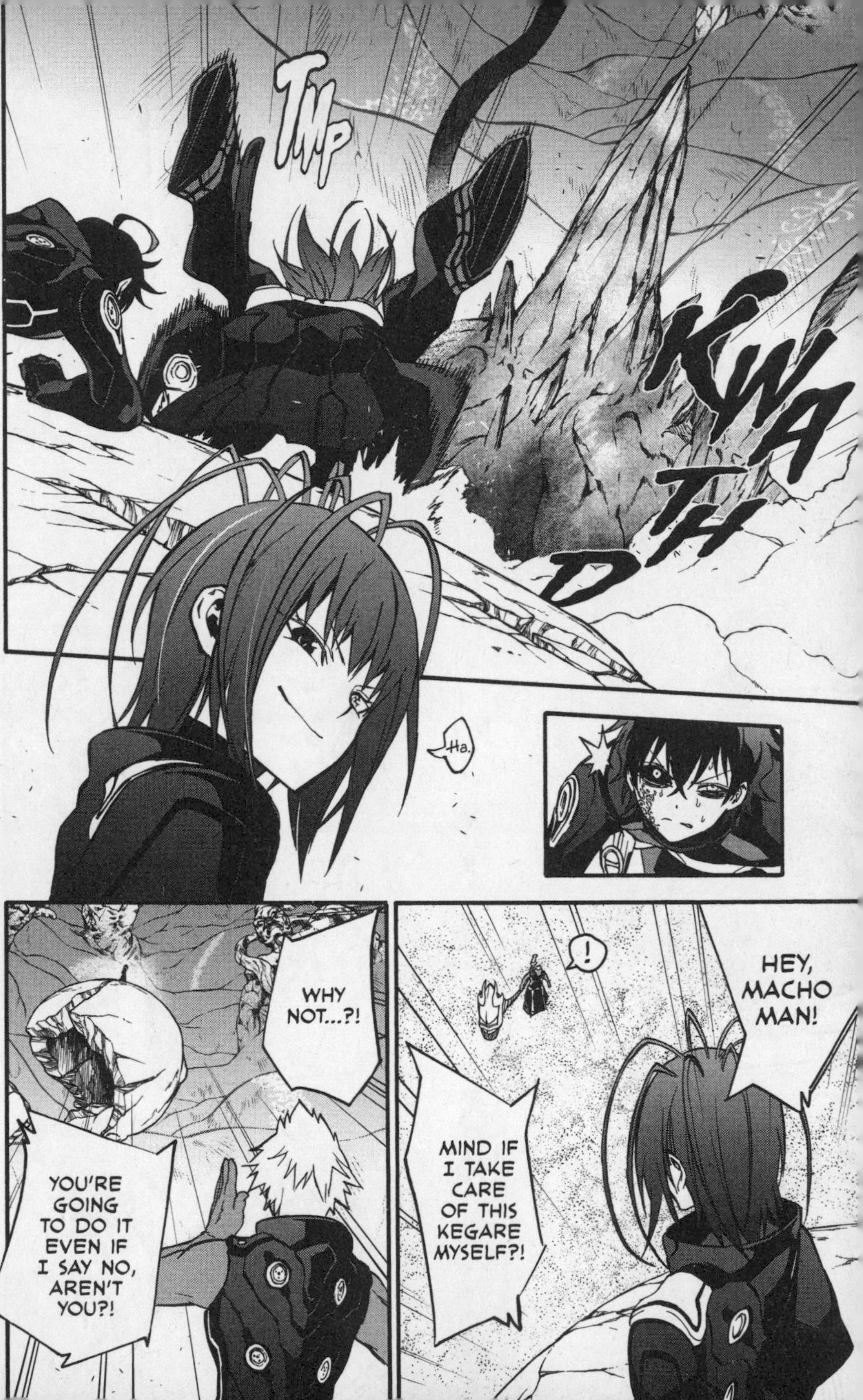
TMP
KWATHD
Ha.
!
HEY, MACHO MAN!
MIND IF I TAKE CARE OF THIS KEGARE MYSELF?!
WHY NOT...?!
YOU'RE GOING TO DO IT EVEN IF I SAY NO, AREN'T YOU?!

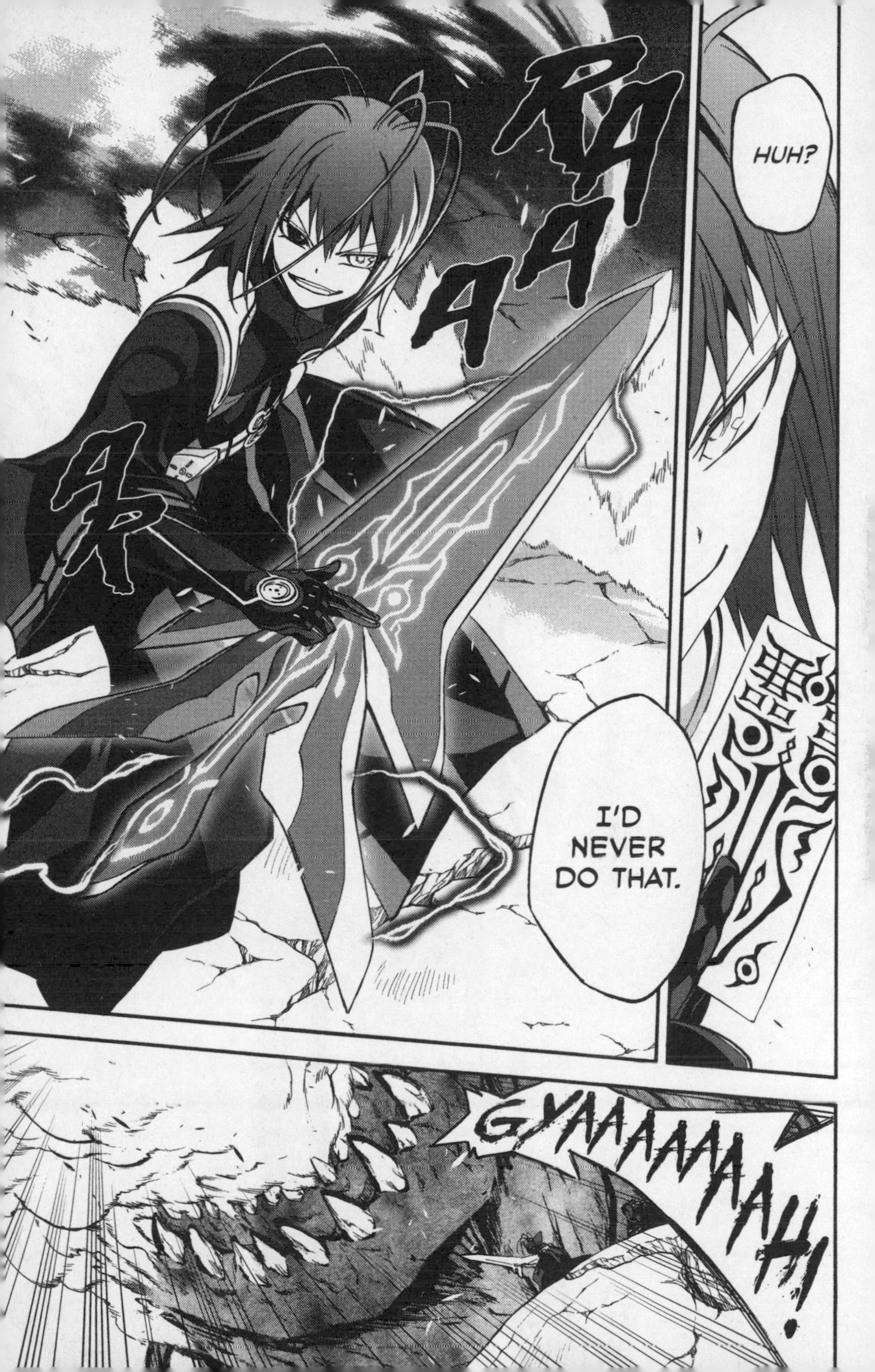
HUH?
I'D NEVER DO THAT.
RAAA
GYAAAAAAAH!

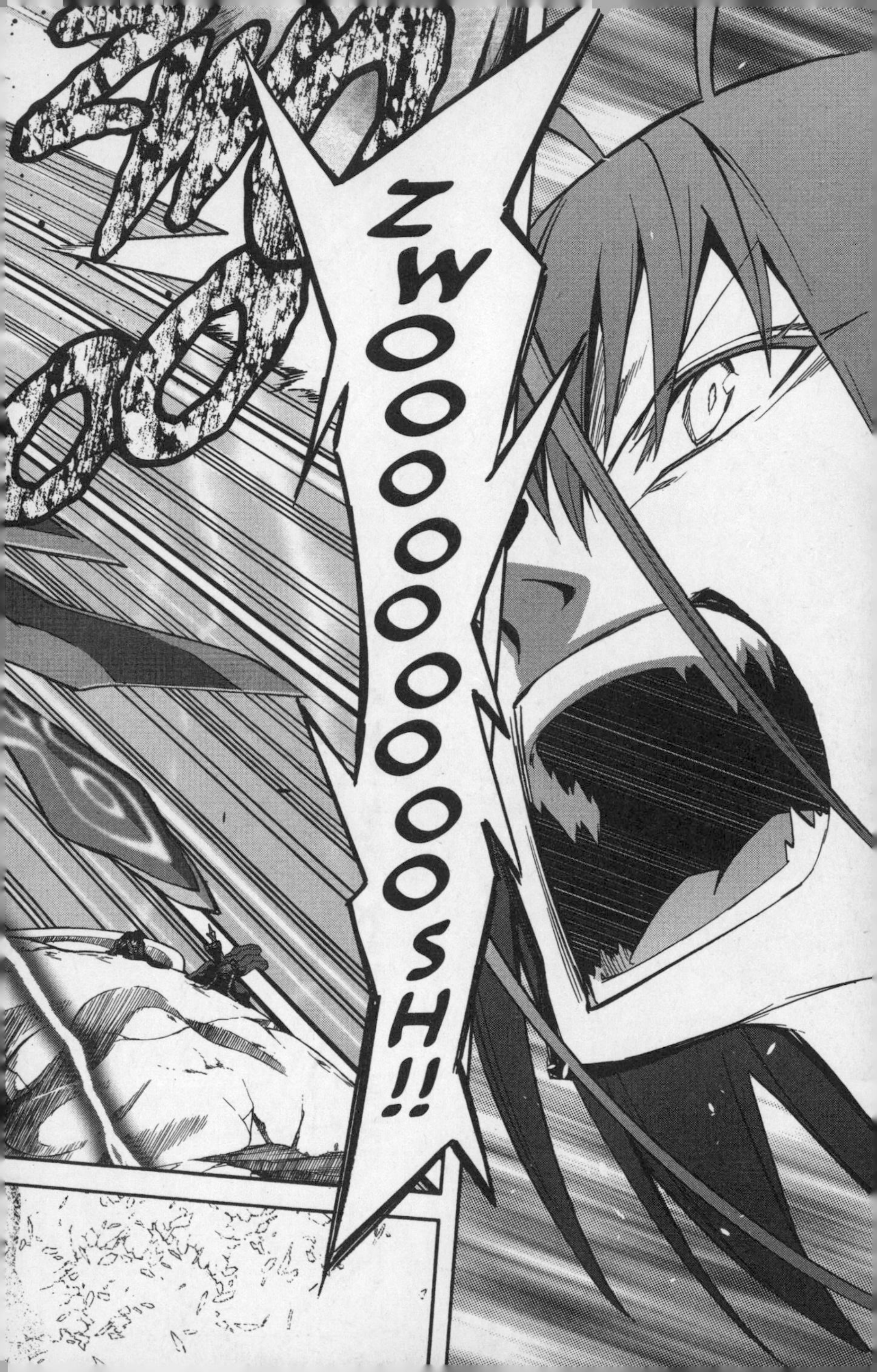
ZWOOOOOOOOOOSH!!

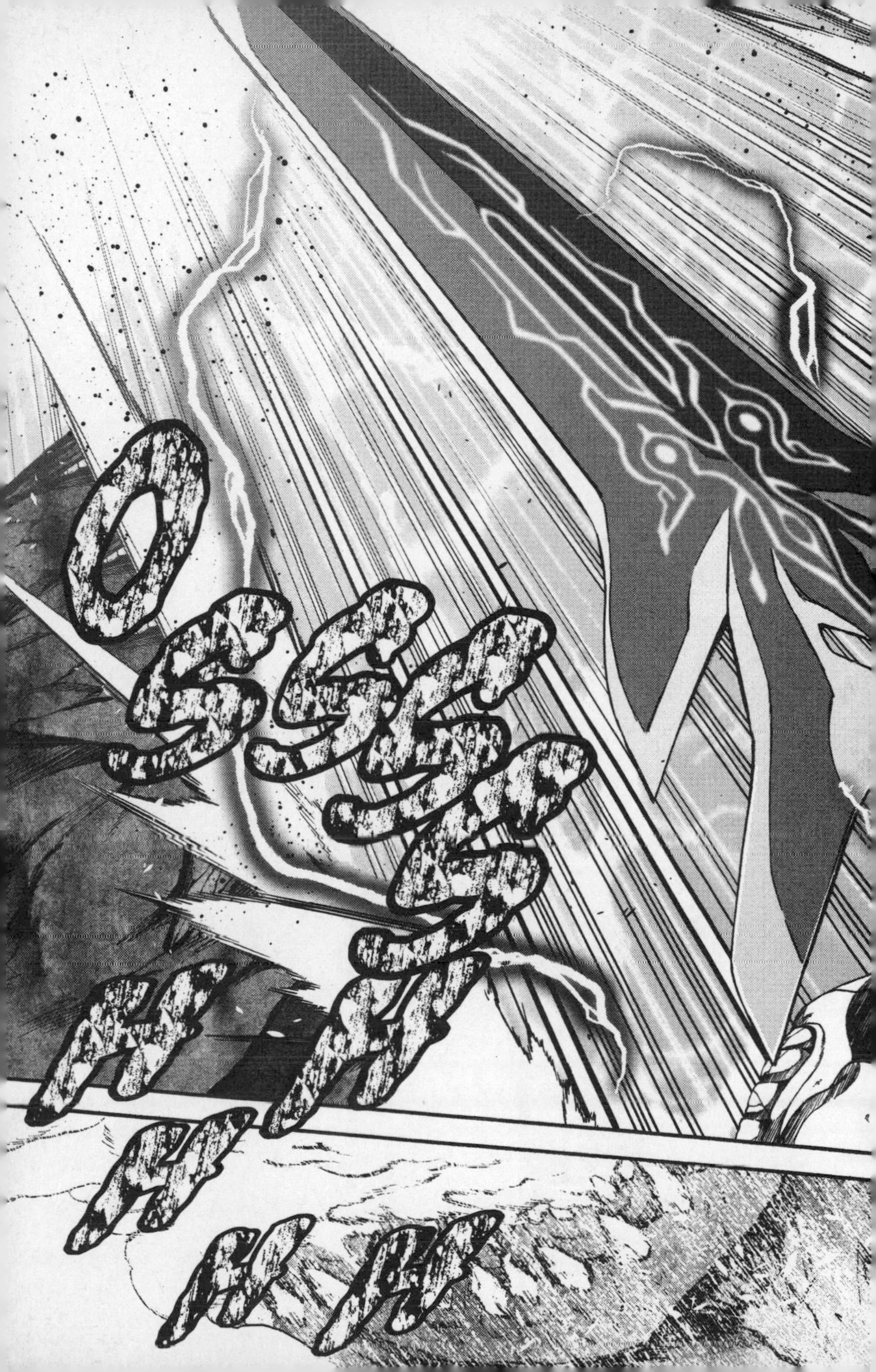
OSSSSHHHHH

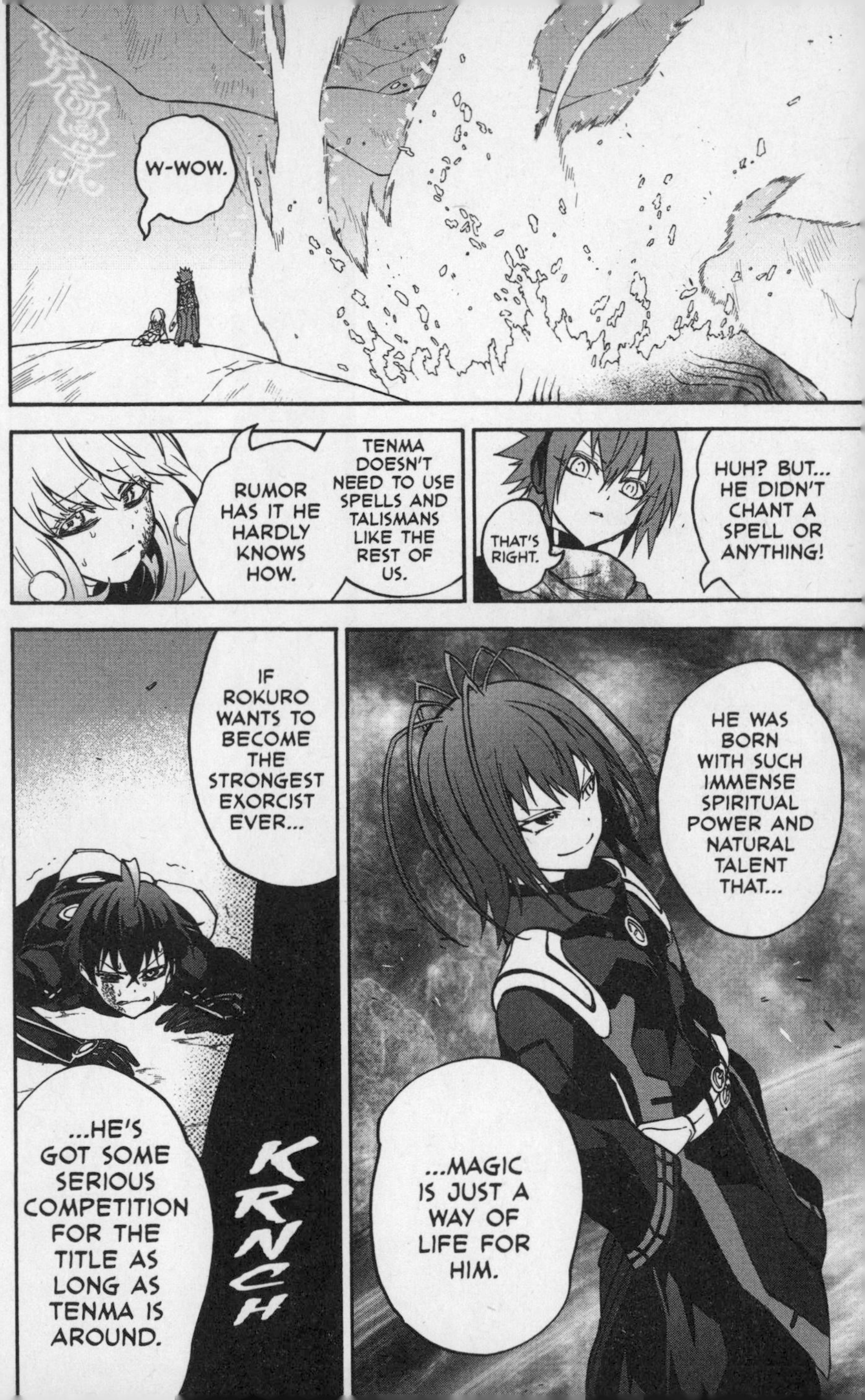
W-WOW.
HUH? BUT... HE DIDN'T CHANT A SPELL OR ANYTHING!
THAT'S RIGHT.
TENMA DOESN'T NEED TO USE SPELLS AND TALISMANS LIKE THE REST OF US.
RUMOR HAS IT HE HARDLY KNOWS HOW.
HE WAS BORN WITH SUCH IMMENSE SPIRITUAL POWER AND NATURAL TALENT THAT...
...MAGIC IS JUST A WAY OF LIFE FOR HIM.
IF ROKURO WANTS TO BECOME THE STRONGEST EXORCIST EVER...
KRNCH
...HE'S GOT SOME SERIOUS COMPETITION FOR THE TITLE AS LONG AS TENMA IS AROUND.

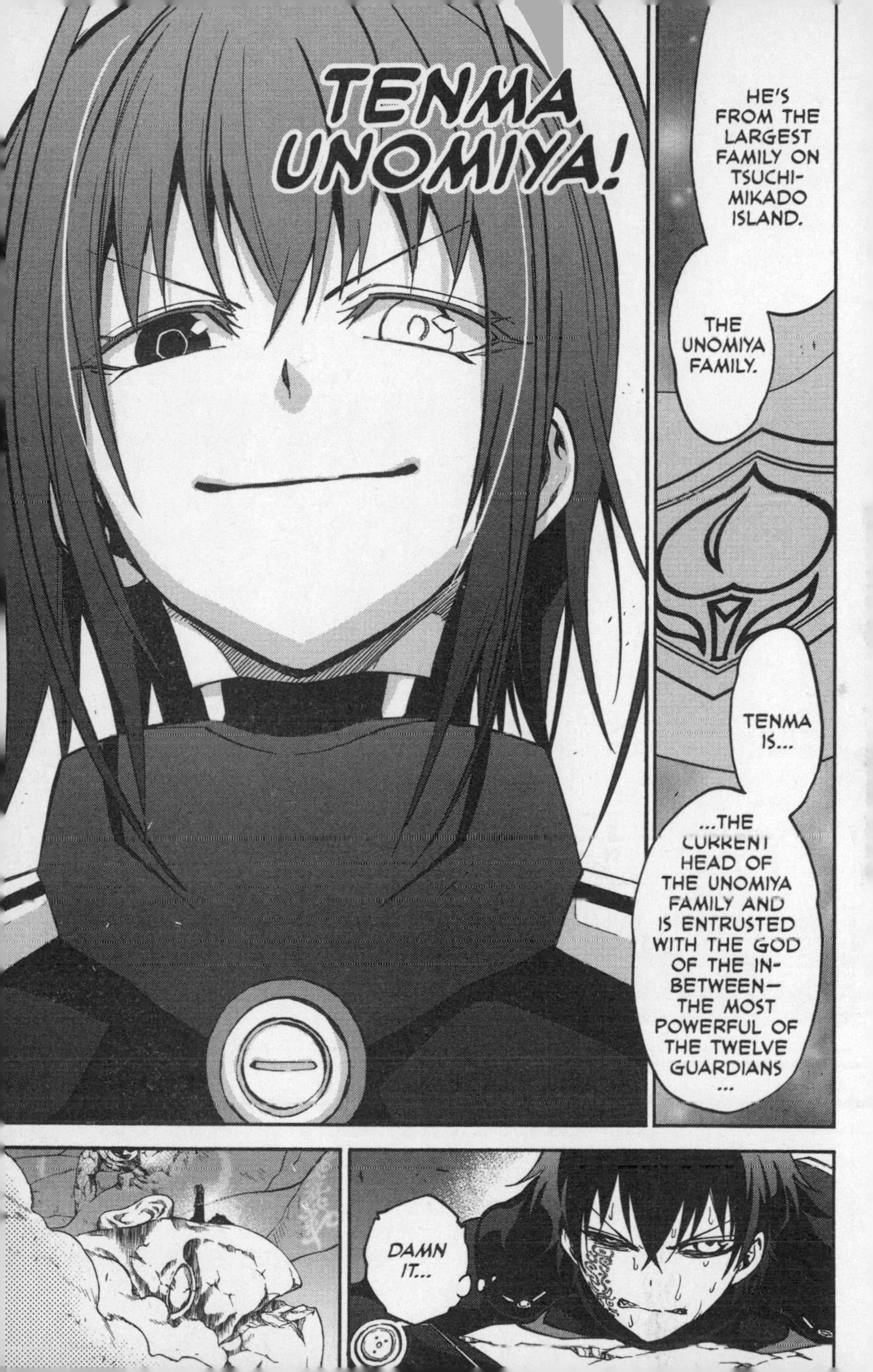
HE'S FROM THE LARGEST FAMILY ON TSUCHI-MIKADO ISLAND.
THE UNOMIYA FAMILY.
TENMA IS...
...THE CURRENT HEAD OF THE UNOMIYA FAMILY AND IS ENTRUSTED WITH THE GOD OF THE IN-BETWEEN—THE MOST POWERFUL OF THE TWELVE GUARDIANS...
TENMA UNOMIYA!
DAMN IT...

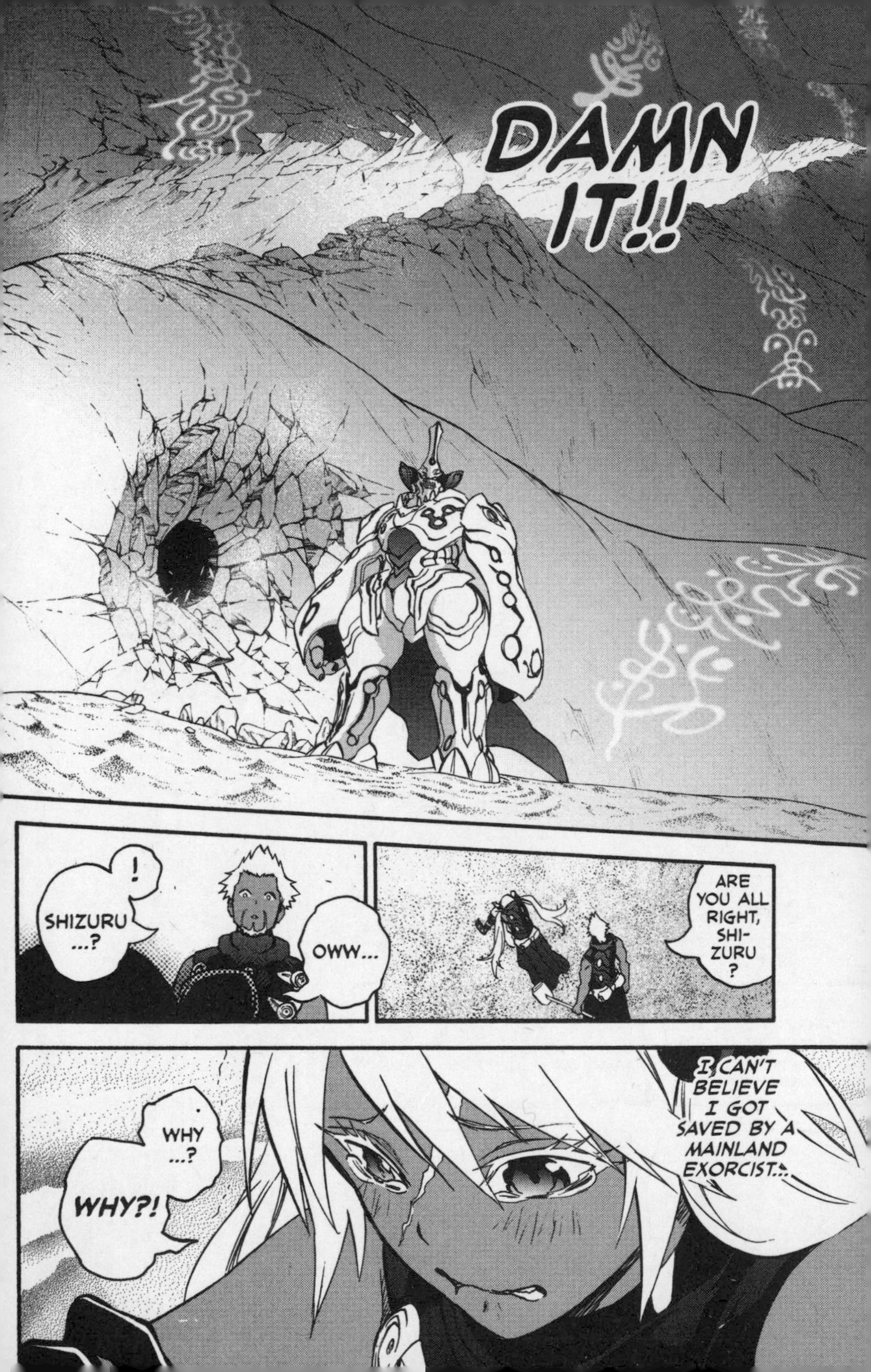
DAMN IT!!
ARE YOU ALL RIGHT, SHI-ZURU?
!
SHIZURU...?
OWW...
I CAN'T BELIEVE I GOT SAVED BY A MAINLAND EXORCIST...
WHY...?
WHY?!

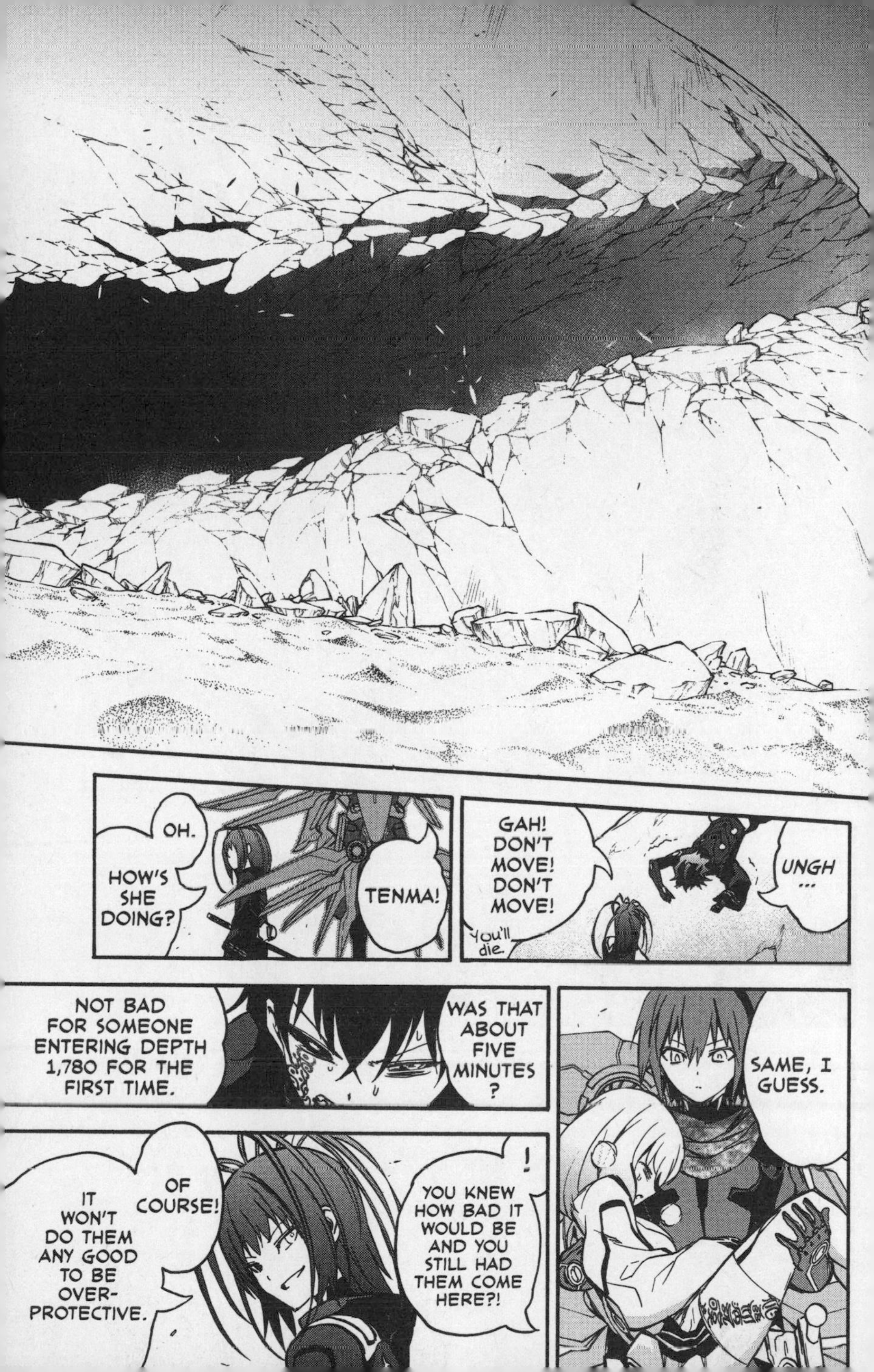
UNGH ...
GAH! DON'T MOVE! DON'T MOVE!
You'll die.
TENMA!
OH.
HOW'S SHE DOING?
SAME, I GUESS.
WAS THAT ABOUT FIVE MINUTES?
NOT BAD FOR SOMEONE ENTERING DEPTH 1,780 FOR THE FIRST TIME.
!
YOU KNEW HOW BAD IT WOULD BE AND YOU STILL HAD THEM COME HERE?!
OF COURSE!
IT WON'T DO THEM ANY GOOD TO BE OVER-PROTECTIVE.

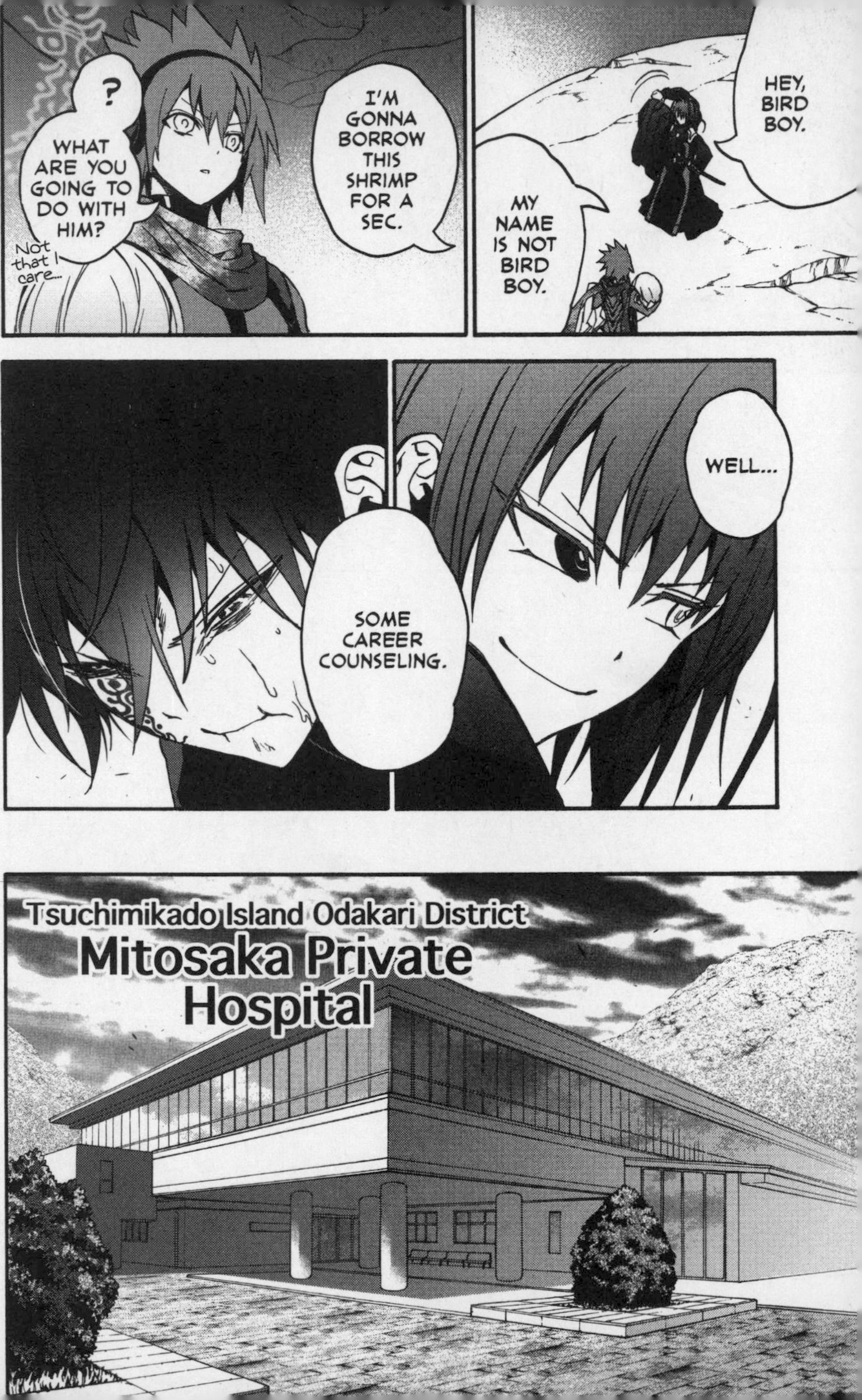
HEY, BIRD BOY.
MY NAME IS NOT BIRD BOY.
I'M GONNA BORROW THIS SHRIMP FOR A SEC.
?
WHAT ARE YOU GOING TO DO WITH HIM?
Not that I care...
WELL...
SOME CAREER COUNSELING.
Tsuchimikado Island Odakari District
Mitosaka Private Hospital

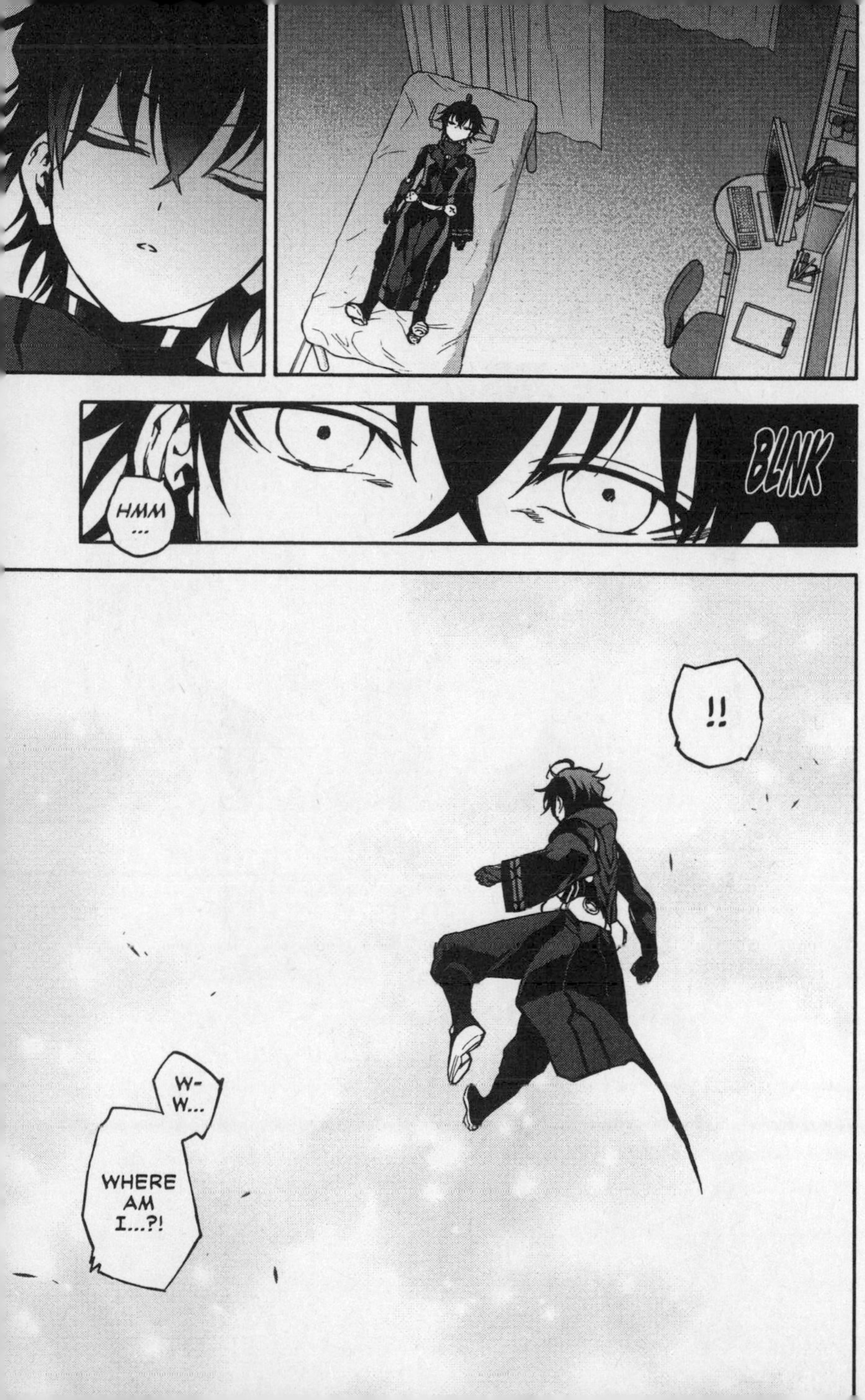
BLINK
HMM...
!!
W-W...
WHERE AM I...?!

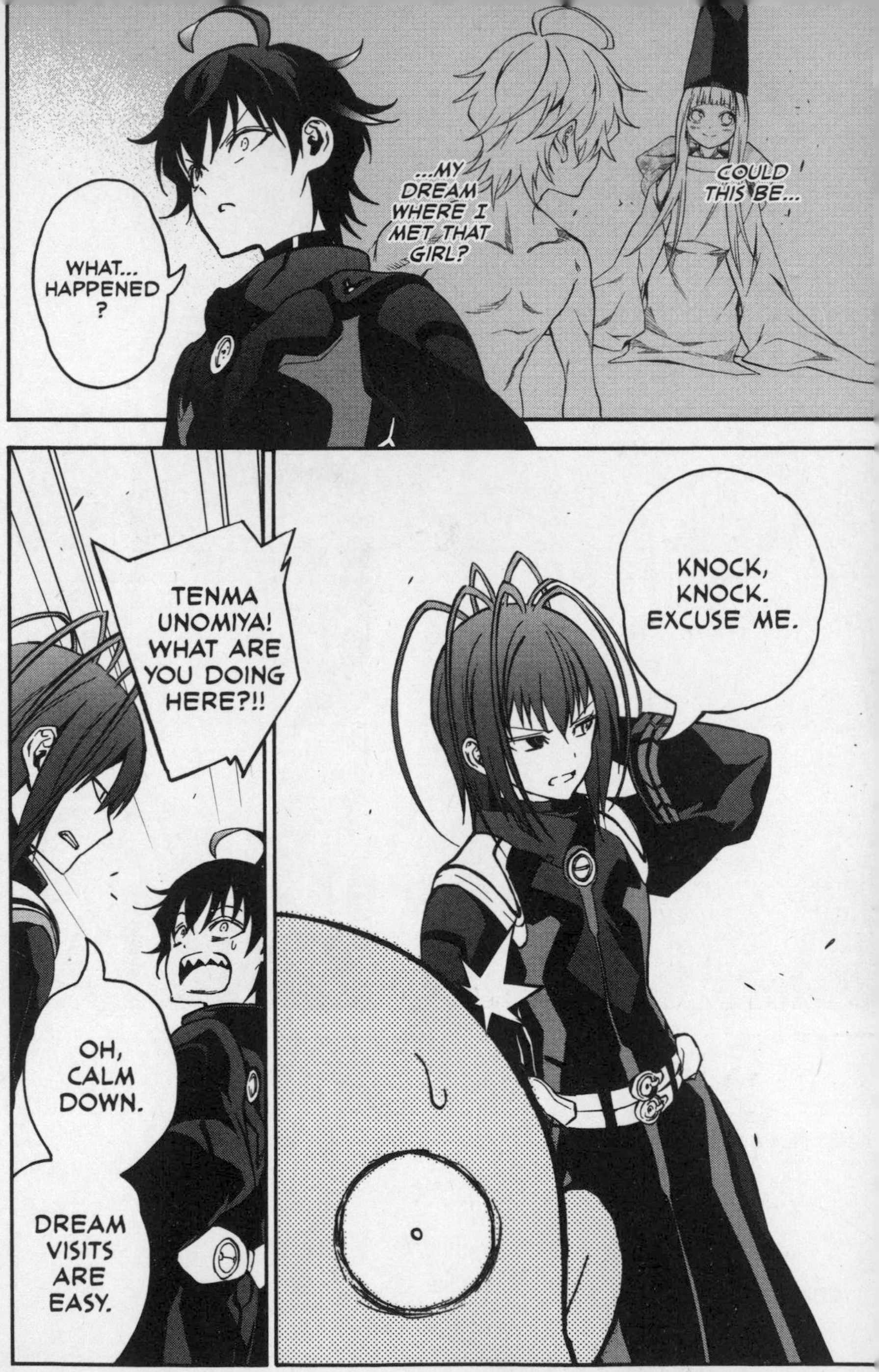
COULD THIS BE...
...MY DREAM WHERE I MET THAT GIRL?
WHAT... HAPPENED?
KNOCK, KNOCK. EXCUSE ME.
TENMA UNOMIYA! WHAT ARE YOU DOING HERE?!!
OH, CALM DOWN.
DREAM VISITS ARE EASY.

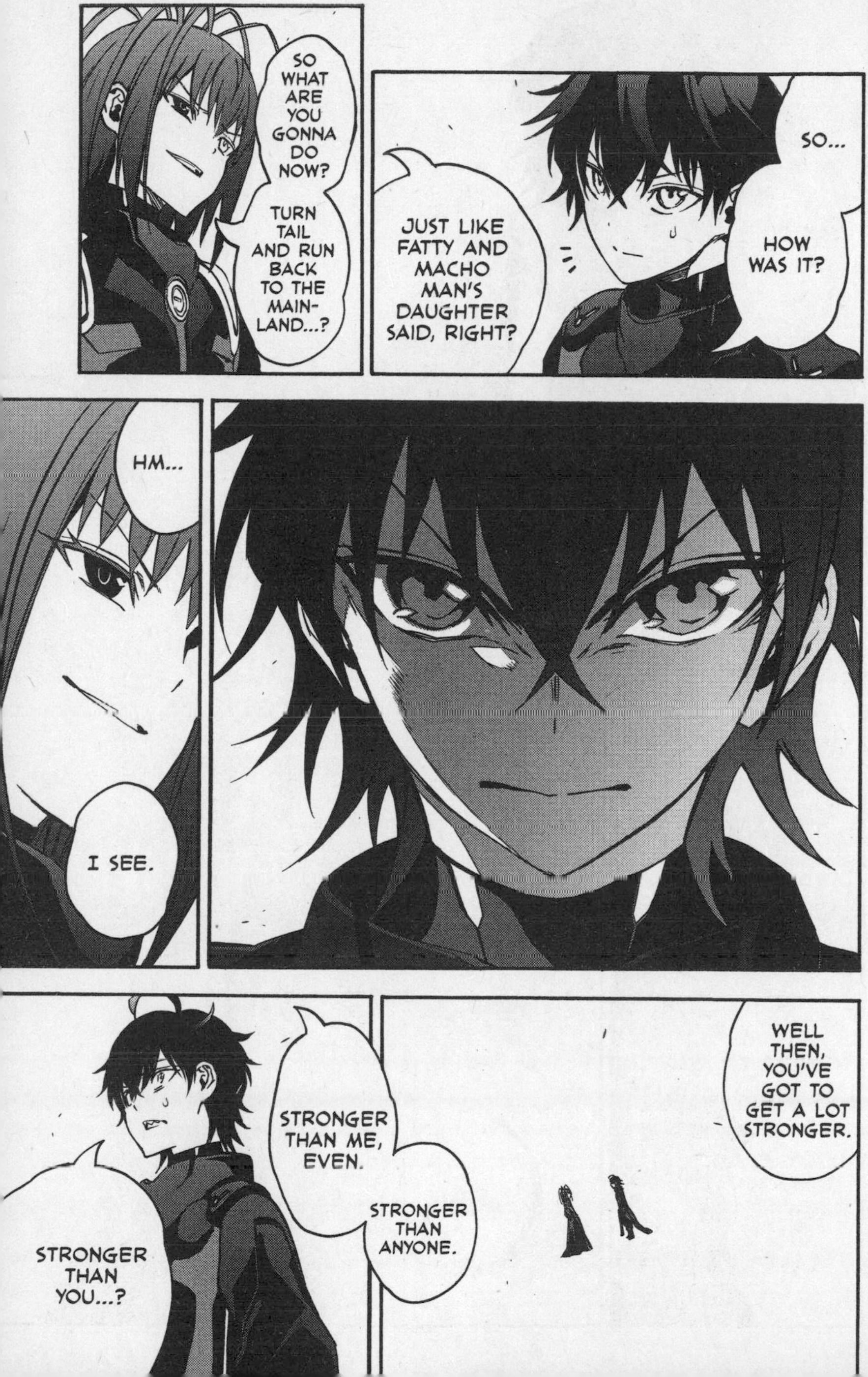
SO...
HOW WAS IT?
JUST LIKE FATTY AND MACHO MAN'S DAUGHTER SAID, RIGHT?
SO WHAT ARE YOU GONNA DO NOW?
TURN TAIL AND RUN BACK TO THE MAIN-LAND...?
HM...
I SEE.
WELL THEN, YOU'VE GOT TO GET A LOT STRONGER.
STRONGER THAN ME, EVEN.
STRONGER THAN ANYONE.
STRONGER THAN YOU...?

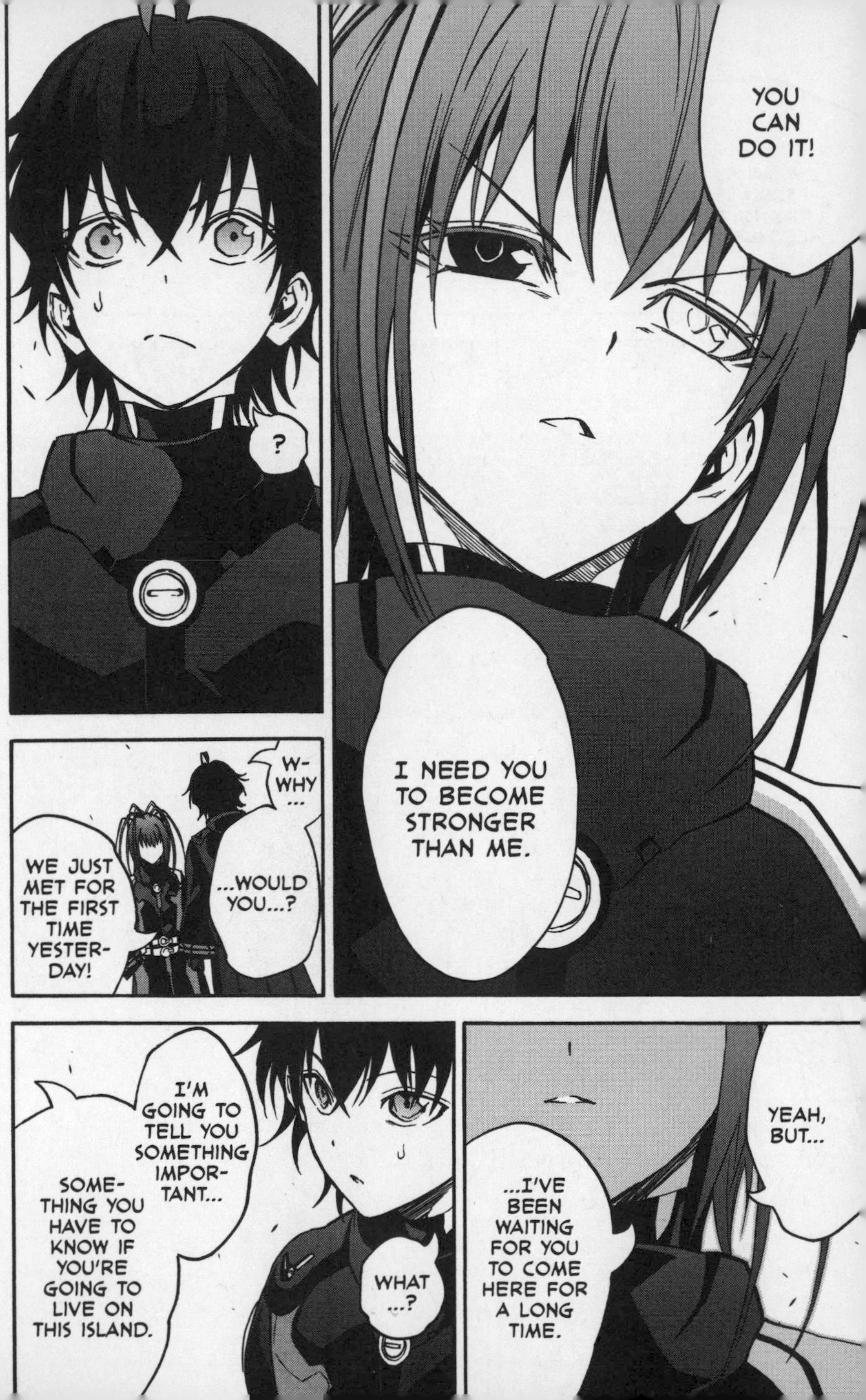

YOU CAN DO IT!
I NEED YOU TO BECOME STRONGER THAN ME.
?
W-WHY ...
...WOULD YOU...?
WE JUST MET FOR THE FIRST TIME YESTER-DAY!
YEAH, BUT...
...I'VE BEEN WAITING FOR YOU TO COME HERE FOR A LONG TIME.
WHAT ...?
I'M GOING TO TELL YOU SOMETHING IMPOR-TANT...
SOME-THING YOU HAVE TO KNOW IF YOU'RE GOING TO LIVE ON THIS ISLAND.

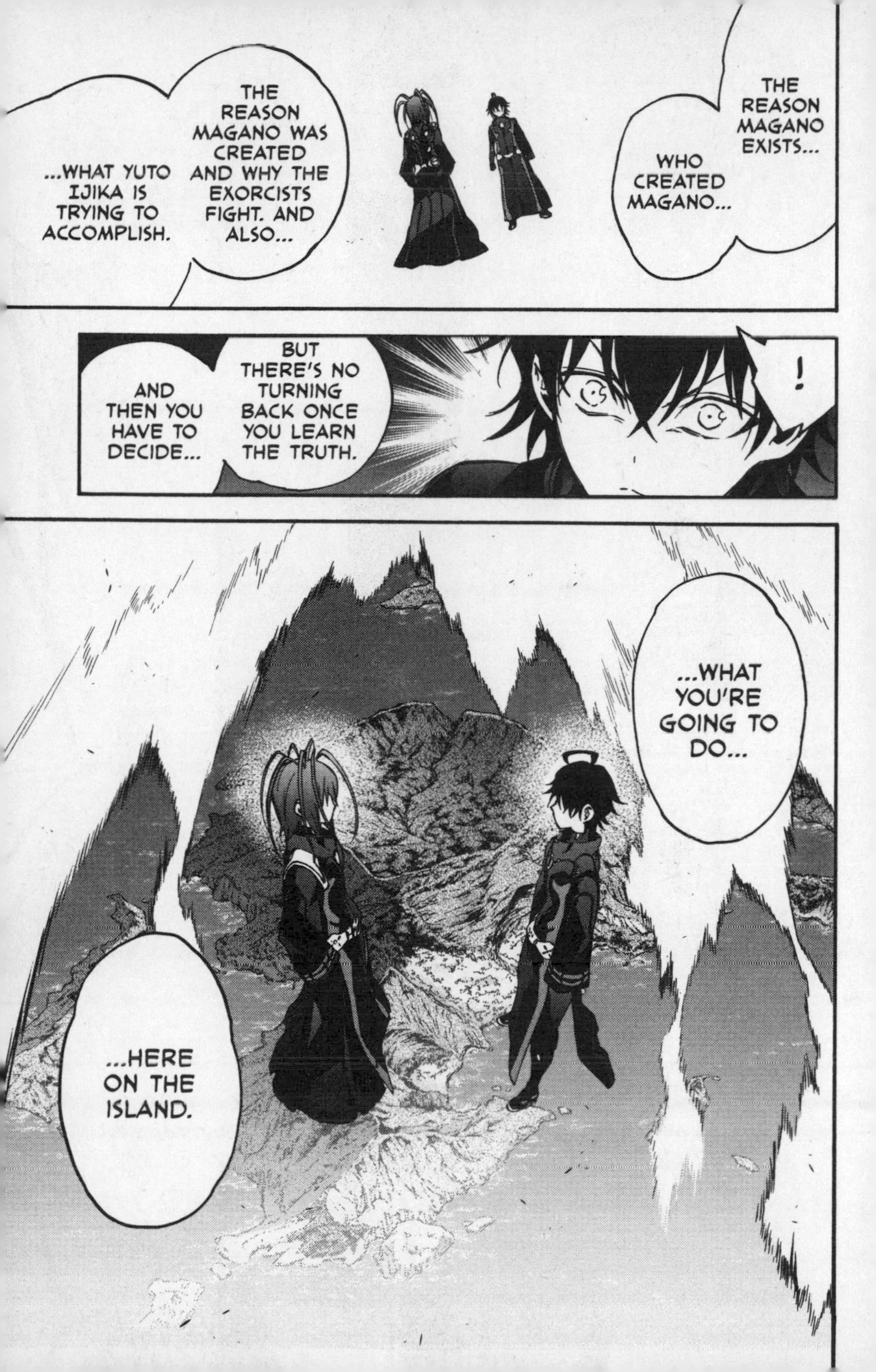
THE REASON MAGANO EXISTS...
WHO CREATED MAGANO...
THE REASON MAGANO WAS CREATED AND WHY THE EXORCISTS FIGHT. AND ALSO...
...WHAT YUTO IJIKA IS TRYING TO ACCOMPLISH.
!
BUT THERE'S NO TURNING BACK ONCE YOU LEARN THE TRUTH.
AND THEN YOU HAVE TO DECIDE...
...WHAT YOU'RE GOING TO DO...
...HERE ON THE ISLAND.

CHARACTER PROFILE 2

Part 2 of the character profiles, continued from pages 54 and 55! Some of these characters have already appeared in the anime. Their likes and dislikes are very different.

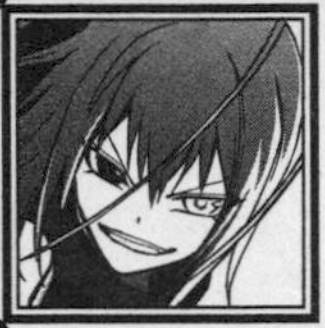

Tenma Unomiya (19 years old)

Birthday: August 20 Blood type: AB Height: 5'3" Weight: 110 lbs.
Likes: Soba noodles, mainland TV shows
Dislikes: Training, waiting

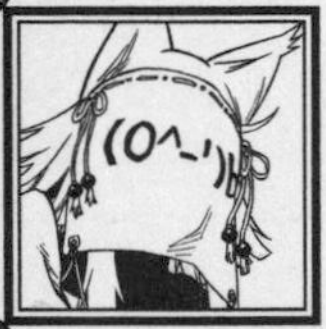

Tatara (? years old)

Birthday: ? Blood type: ? Height: 6'5" Weight: 154 lbs.
Likes: The heels of bread
Dislikes: Jam, margarine

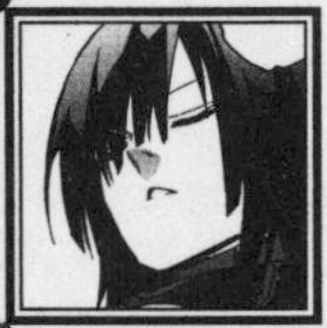

Arata Inanaki (42 years old)

Birthday: January 3 Blood type: A Height: 6'3" Weight: 170 lbs.
Likes: Otaku culture on the mainland (anime, video games, music)
Dislikes: Anmitsu. His catchphrase is "In the name of the moon, I will punish all those who look down upon otaku culture."

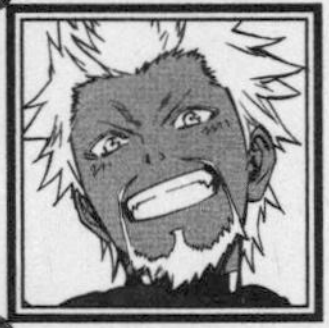

Narumi Ioroi (45 years old)

Birthday: May 5 Blood type: O Height: 6'9" Weight: 209 lbs.
(When he was 14: height: 5'1", weight: 117 lbs.)
Likes: Family, all of his wife's cooking, summer
Dislikes: Anmitsu, winter

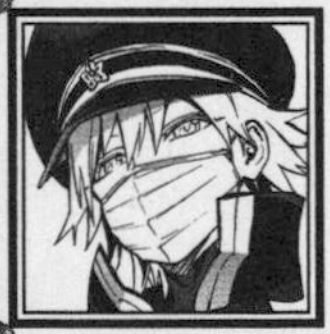

Kankuro Mitosaka (27 years old)

Birthday: December 1 Blood type: O Height: 5'10" Weight: 137 lbs.
Likes: Human experiments, the Kengo family, fish dishes
Dislikes: Red meat

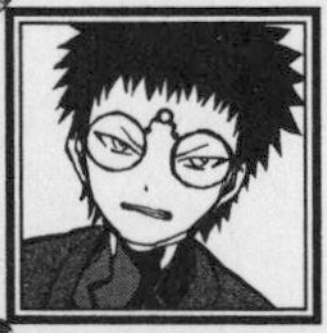

Kengo Uji (26 years old)

Birthday: February 3 Blood type: A Height: 5'10" Weight: 143 lbs.
Likes: Money, sukiyaki
Dislikes: Hospitals, doctors, operations, medical examinations, hospital stays, hospital visits, injections, hospital rooms, medical checkups

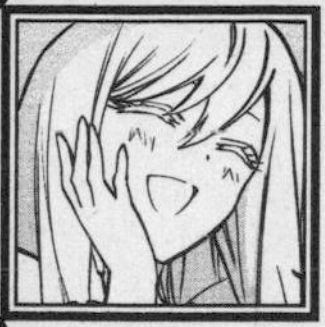

Subaru Mitejima (35 years old)

Birthday: November 13 Blood type: A Height: 5'6" Weight: 119 lbs.
Likes: Handsome men, ohagi dumplings, udon
Dislikes: To be somewhere without handsome men, summer

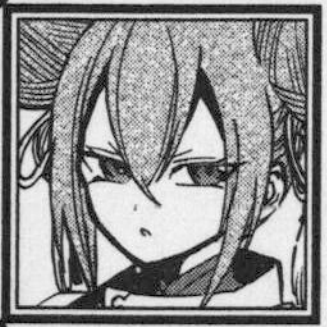

Zeze Miku (56 years old)

Birthday: October 9 Blood type: A Height: 5'1" Weight: 90 lbs.
Likes: Stuffed animals, Gothic Lolita fashion, macarons
Dislikes: Otaku, noisy people, dairy products

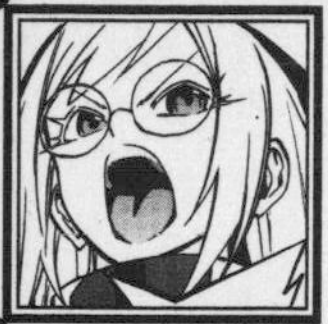

Sakura Sada (23 years old)

Birthday: June 30 Blood type: B Height: 5'8" Weight: 128 lbs.
Likes: Training, rice-bowl dishes
Dislikes: TV shows on the mainland, vegetables

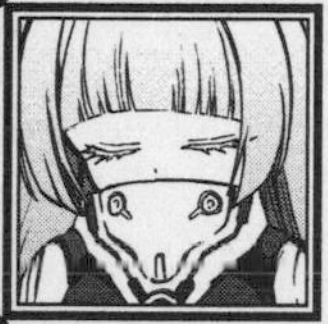

Cordelia Kasukami

Birthday: April 2 Blood type: ? Height: 5'3" Weight: ? (3 digits for sure)
Likes: Cute things, dorayaki
Dislikes: Water, heat, mice (a mouse bit her on the ear once)

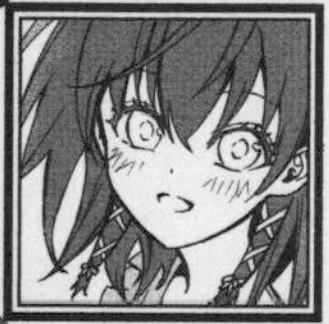

Sayo Ikaruga (11 years old)

Birthday: March 3 Blood type: B Height: 4'8" Weight: 79 lbs.
Likes: Roku ♡, family, cake, ramen
Dislikes: Green peppers, insects, Kuzu no Ha

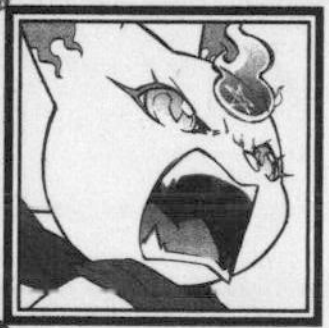

Kinako (11 years old)

Birthday: March 19 Blood type: ? Height: 1'8" Weight: 9.48 lbs.
Likes: Benio, ohagi dumplings
Dislikes: Spoiled brats, anyone who says bad things about the Adashino family

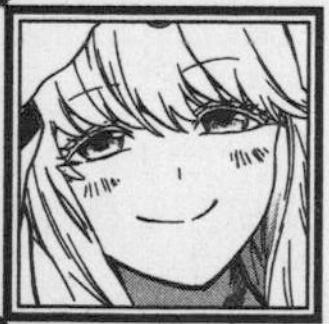

Yukari Otomi (45 years old)

Birthday: September 2 Blood type: A Height: 5'4" Weight: 117 lbs.
Likes: Family, anmitsu, plants
Dislikes: Thunder

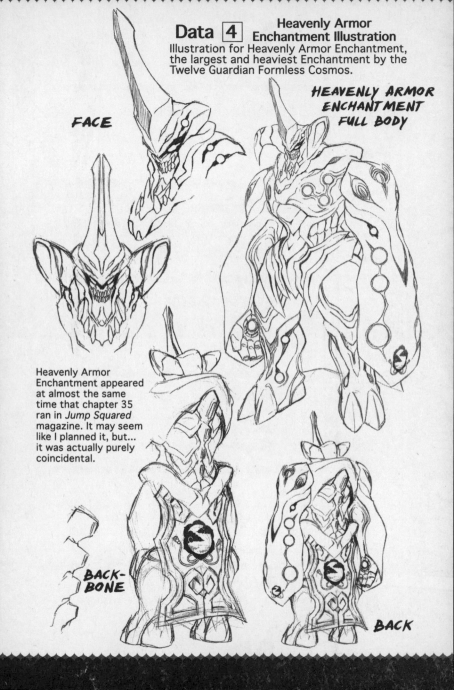

Data 4 — Heavenly Armor Enchantment Illustration

Illustration for Heavenly Armor Enchantment, the largest and heaviest Enchantment by the Twelve Guardian Formless Cosmos.

FACE

HEAVENLY ARMOR ENCHANTMENT FULL BODY

Heavenly Armor Enchantment appeared at almost the same time that chapter 35 ran in *Jump Squared* magazine. It may seem like I planned it, but... it was actually purely coincidental.

BACK-BONE

BACK

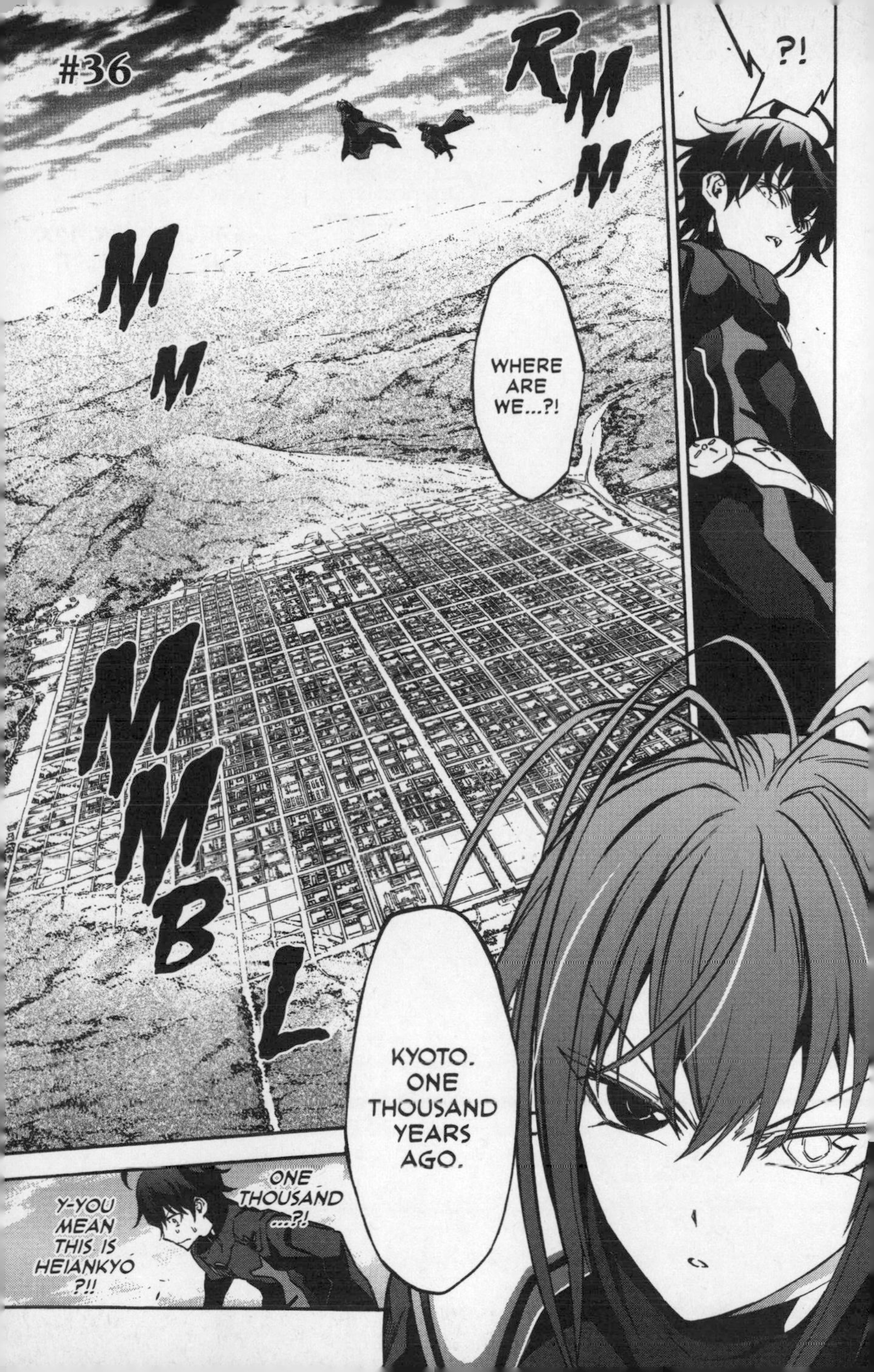
#36
?!
RMMMMMMMBL
WHERE ARE WE...?!
KYOTO. ONE THOUSAND YEARS AGO.
ONE THOUSAND ...?!
Y-YOU MEAN THIS IS HEIANKYO ?!!

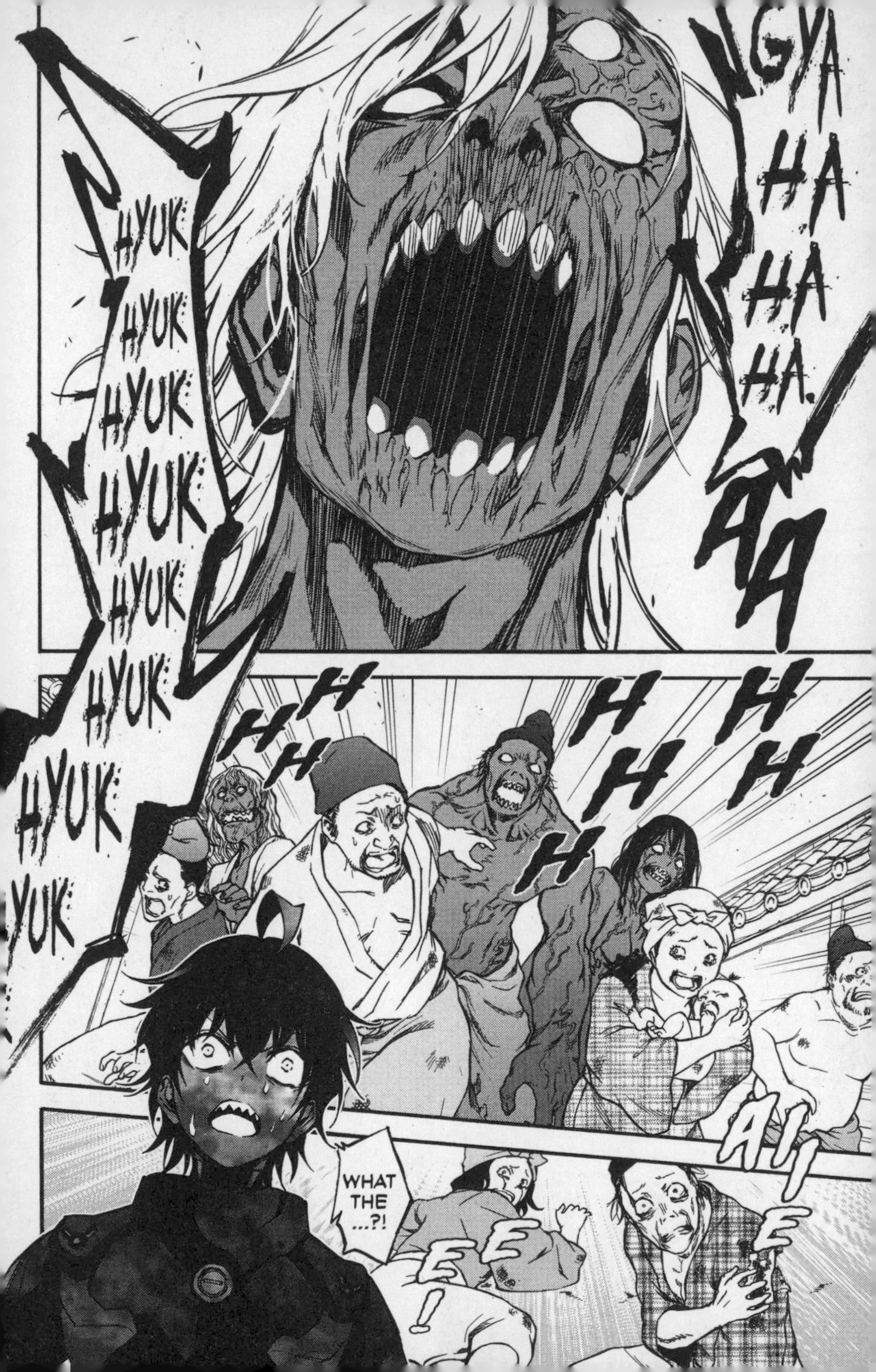
NGYA HA HA HA.
HYUK HYUK HYUK HYUK HYUK HYUK HYUK HYUK YUK
HHHHHHHHHHH
AIIEE!
WHAT THE ...?!

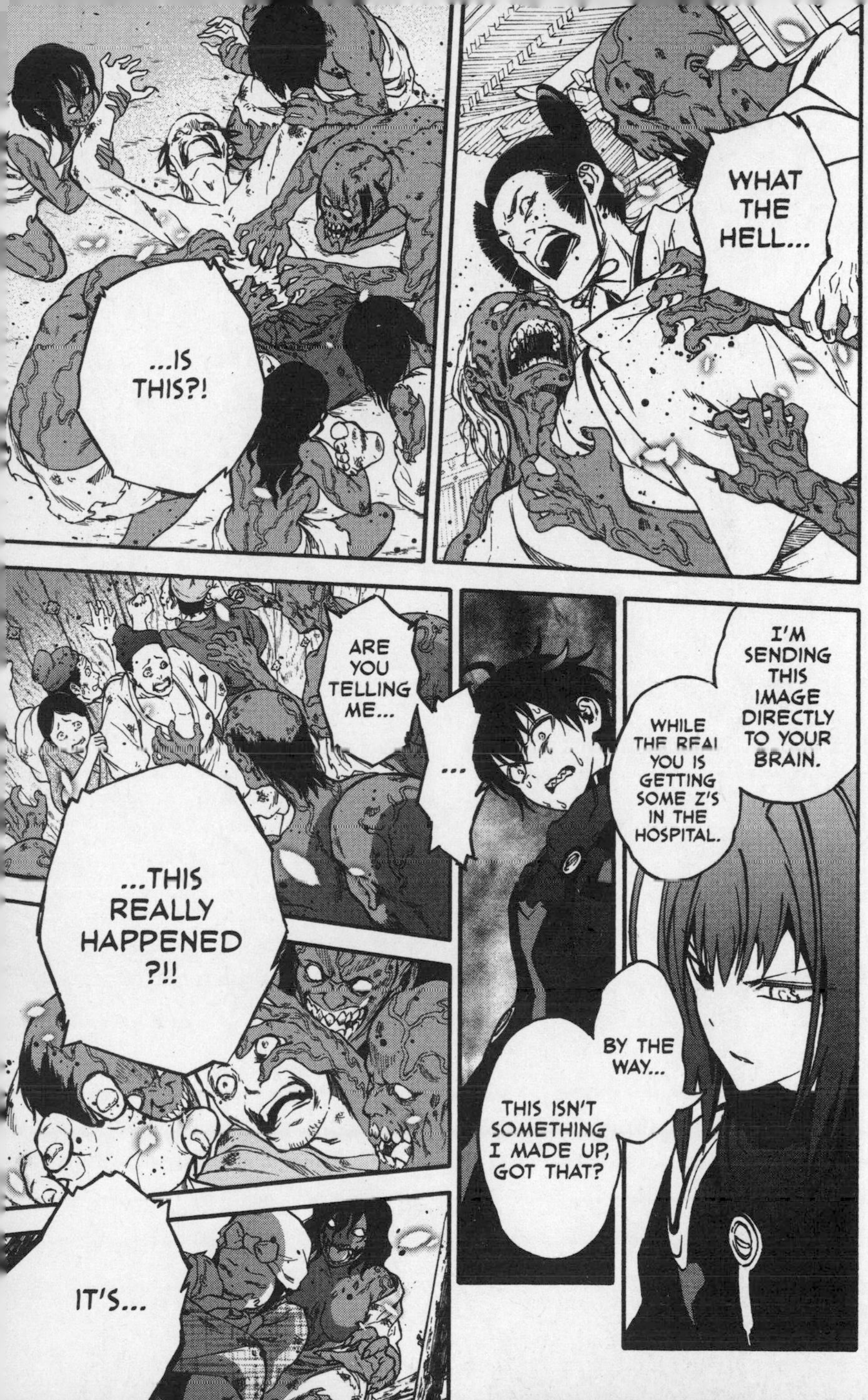
WHAT THE HELL...
...IS THIS?!
I'M SENDING THIS IMAGE DIRECTLY TO YOUR BRAIN.
WHILE THE REAL YOU IS GETTING SOME Z'S IN THE HOSPITAL.
BY THE WAY...
THIS ISN'T SOMETHING I MADE UP, GOT THAT?
...
ARE YOU TELLING ME...
...THIS REALLY HAPPENED ?!!
IT'S...

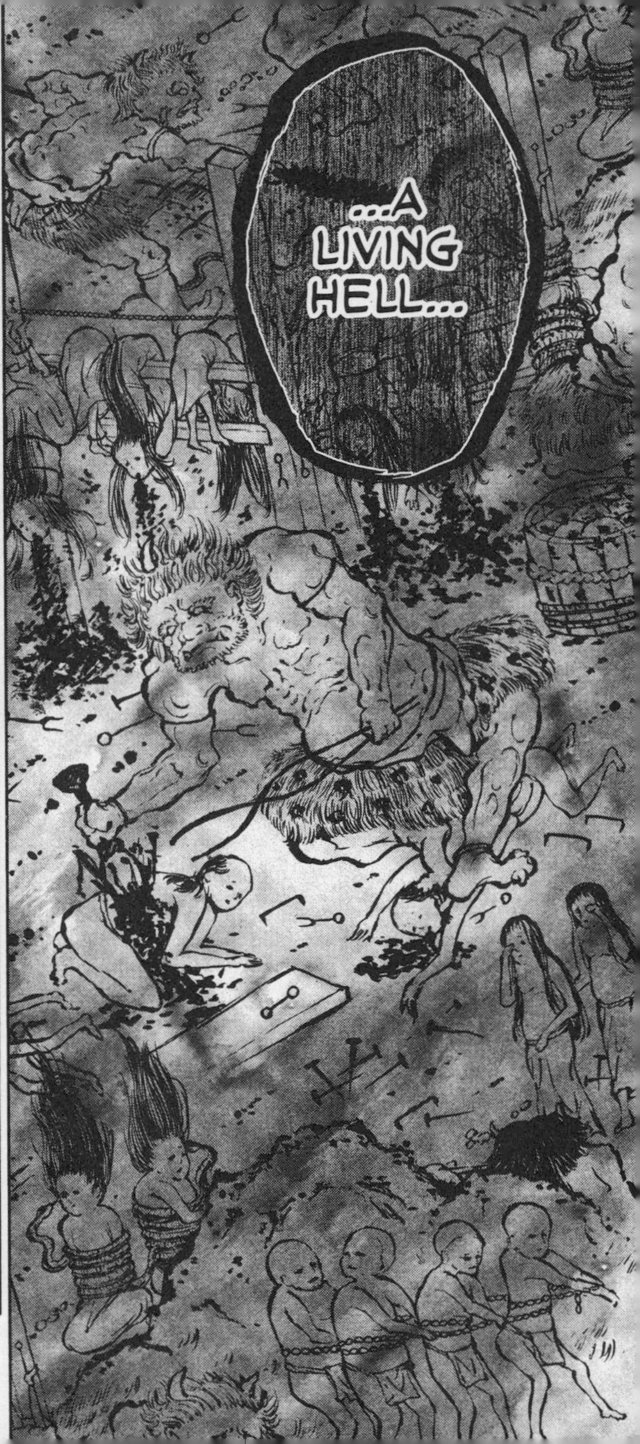
...A LIVING HELL...

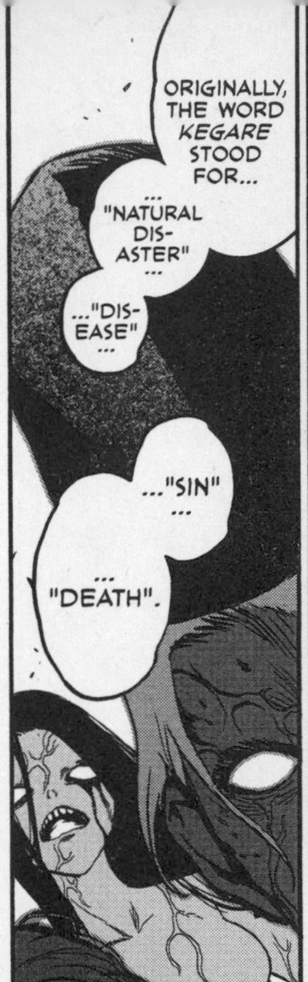
ORIGINALLY, THE WORD *KEGARE* STOOD FOR...
..."NATURAL DIS-ASTER"...
..."DIS-EASE"...
..."SIN"...
..."DEATH".
ANYTHING TERRIBLE AND UNCOMMON.

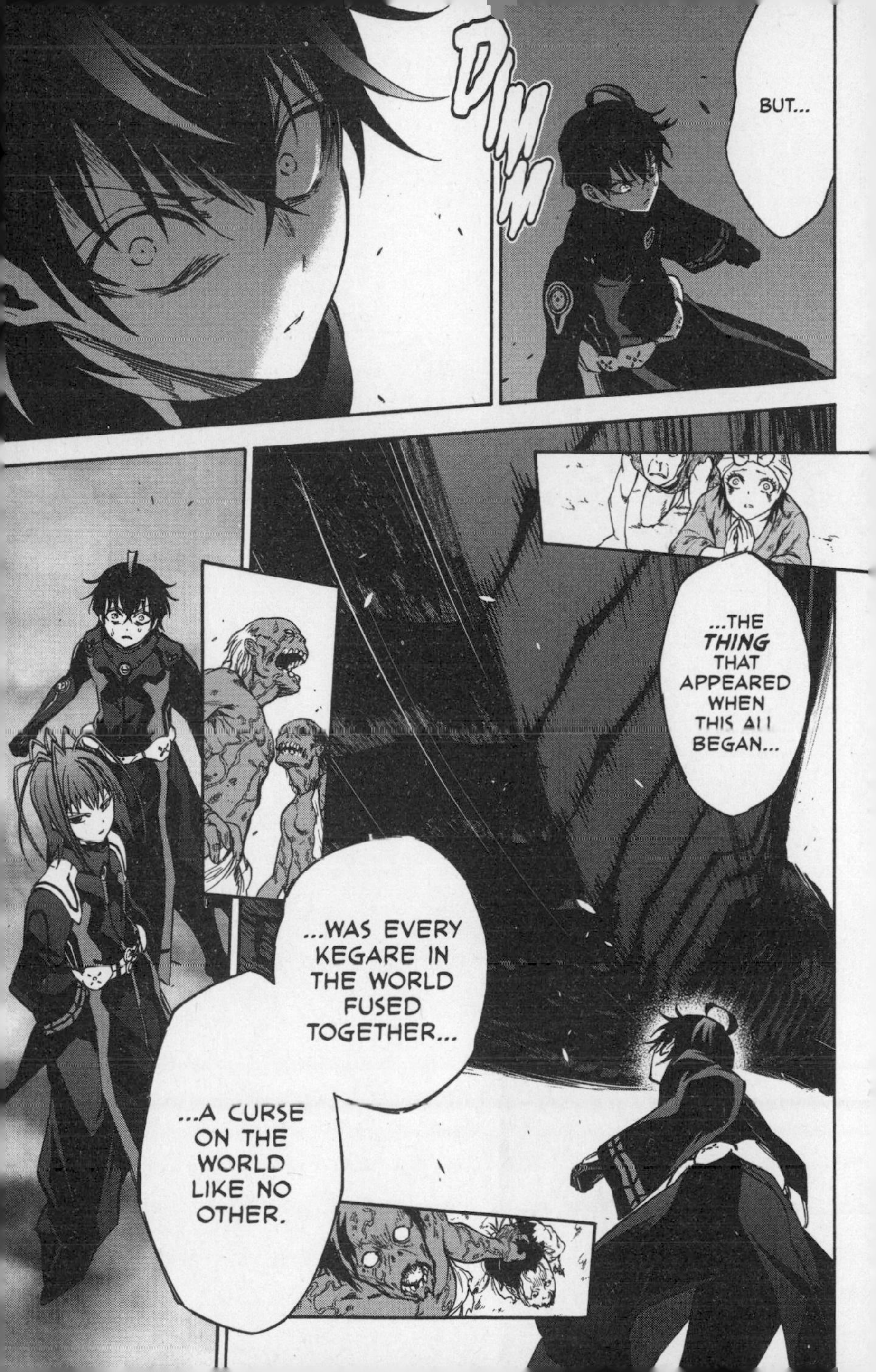
BUT...
DIMM
...THE *THING* THAT APPEARED WHEN THIS ALL BEGAN...
...WAS EVERY KEGARE IN THE WORLD FUSED TOGETHER...
...A CURSE ON THE WORLD LIKE NO OTHER.

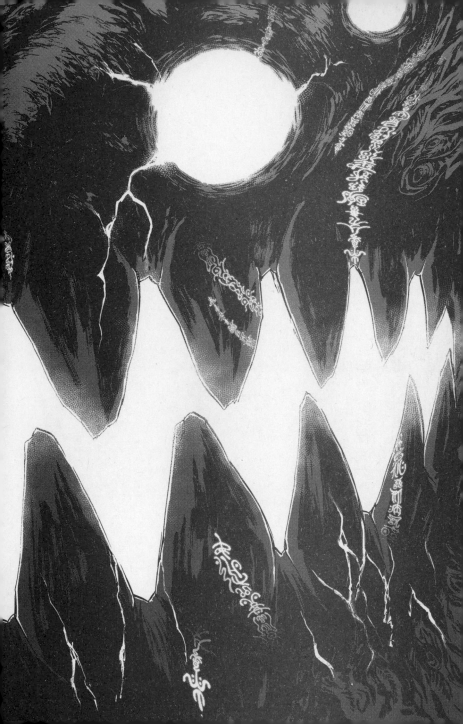

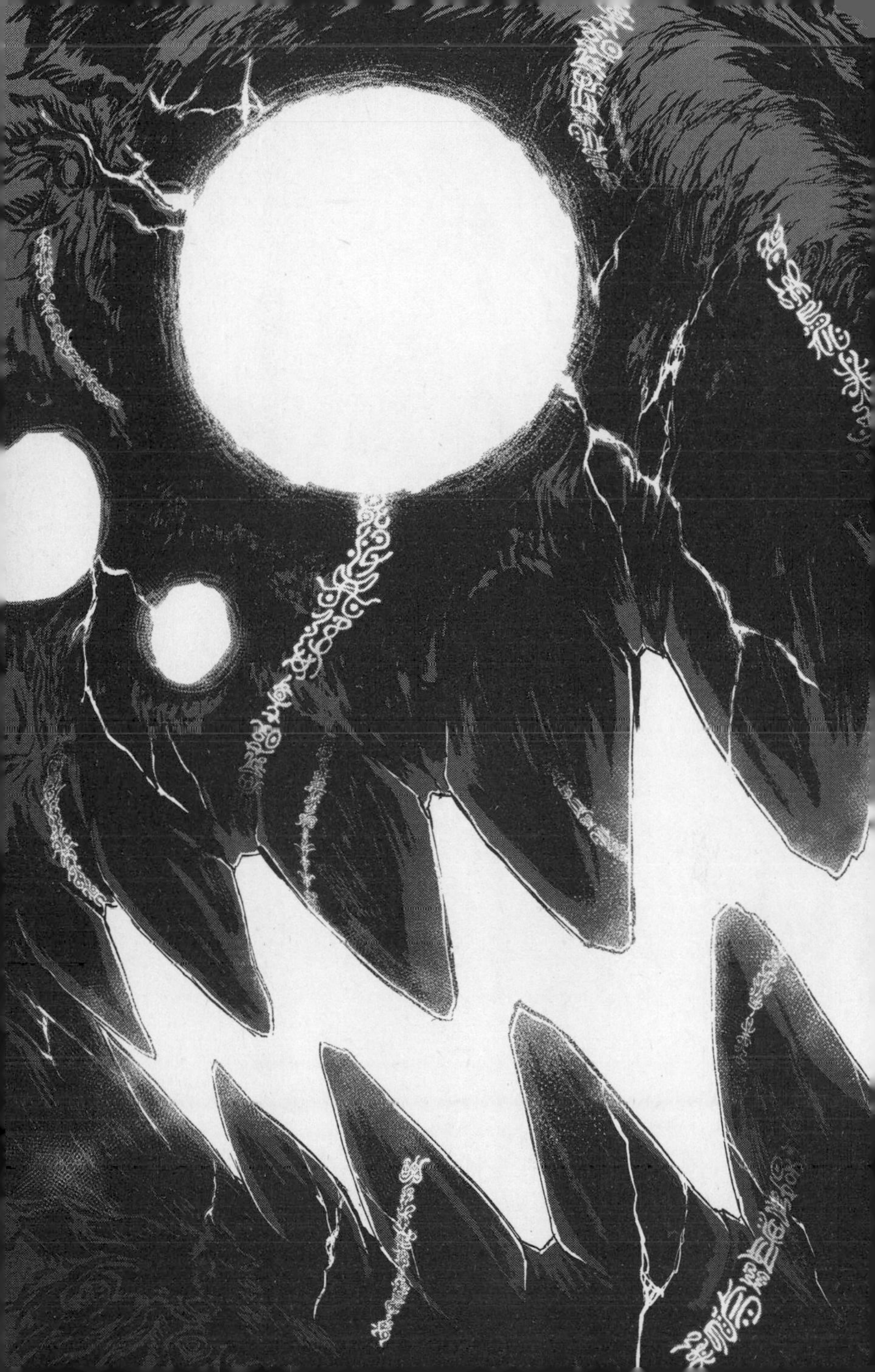

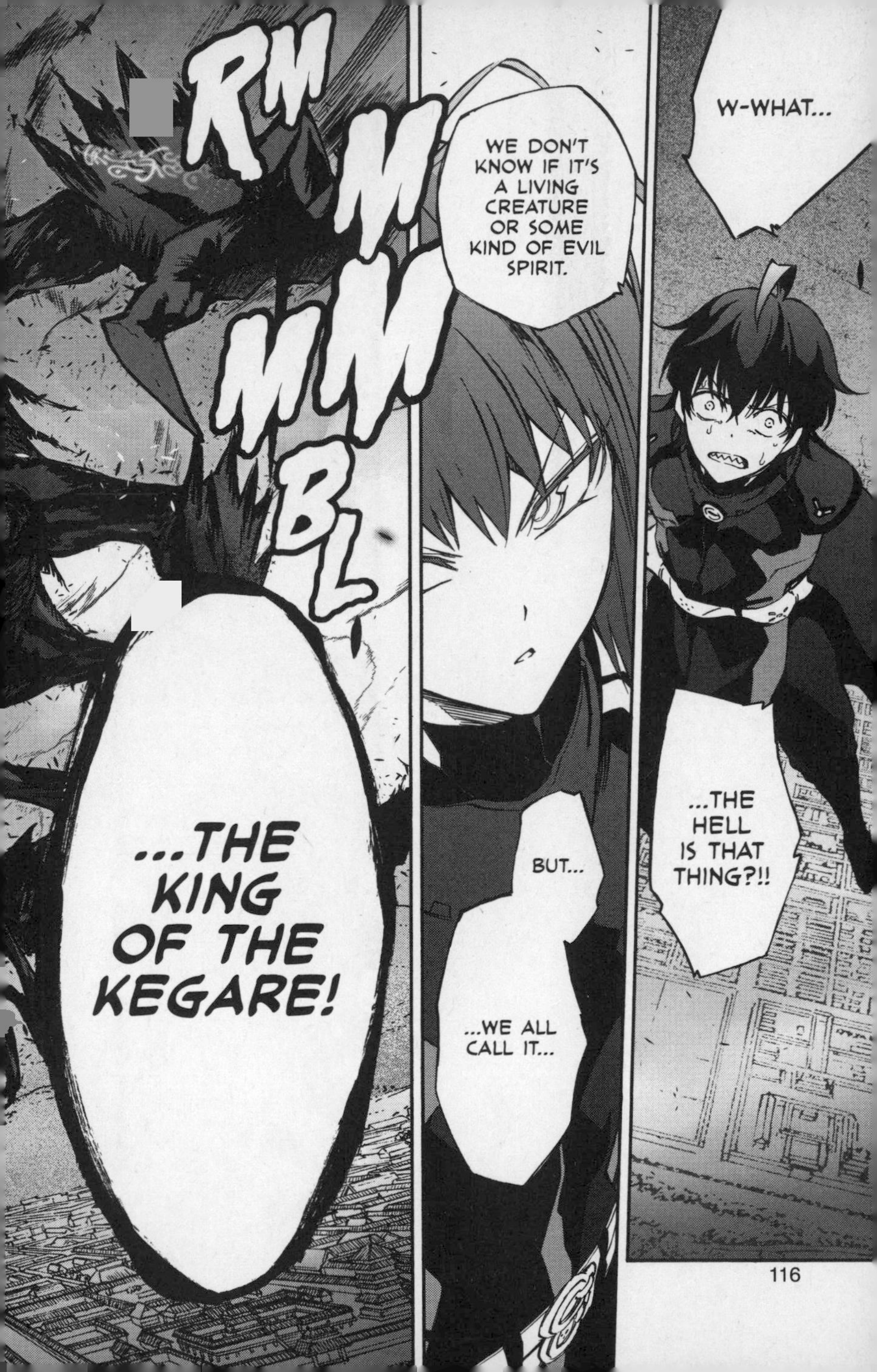
W-WHAT...
...THE HELL IS THAT THING?!!
WE DON'T KNOW IF IT'S A LIVING CREATURE OR SOME KIND OF EVIL SPIRIT.
BUT...
...WE ALL CALL IT...
RMMMMBL
...THE KING OF THE KEGARE!

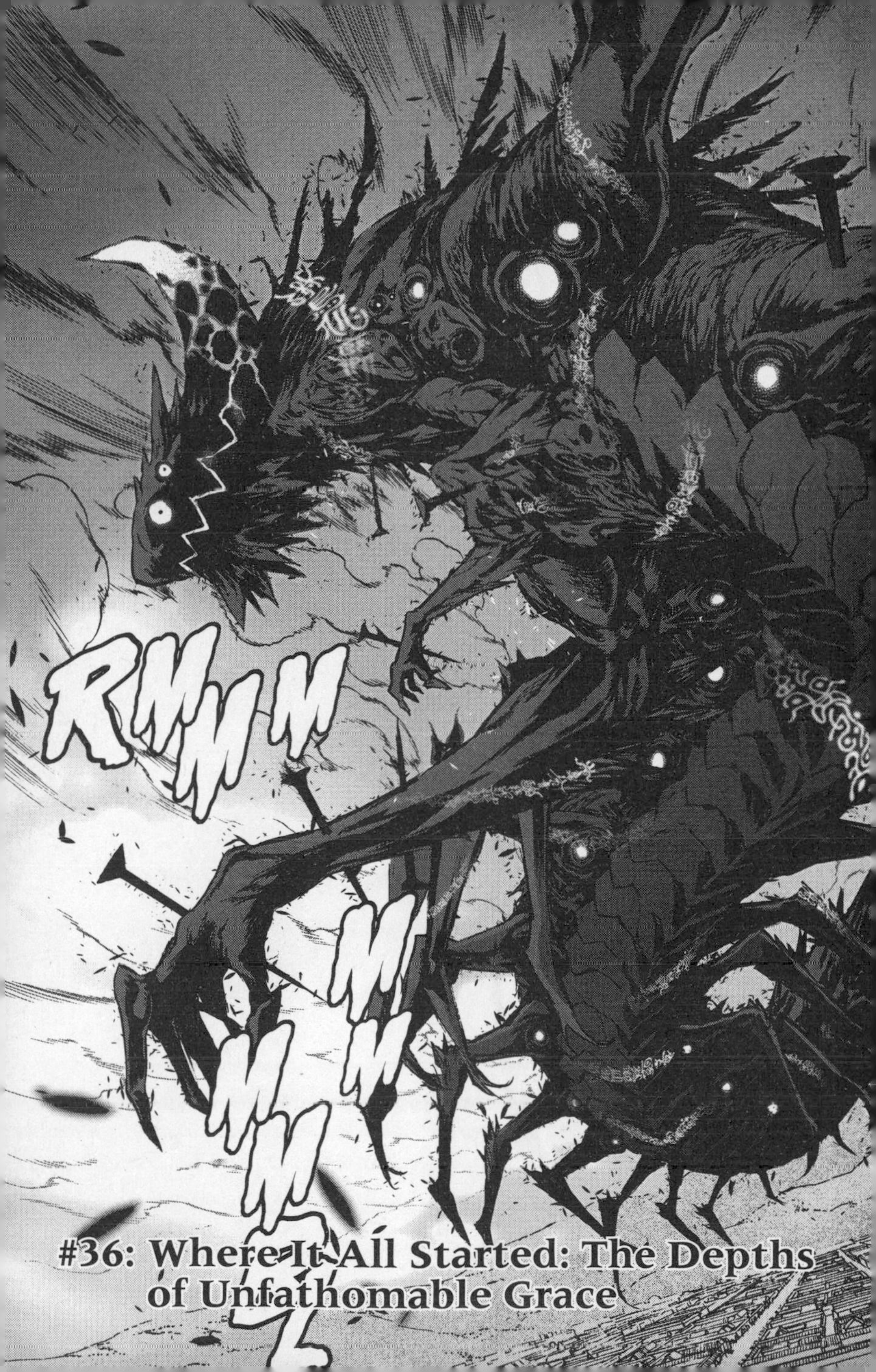
RMMM
MMMM

#36: Where It All Started: The Depths of Unfathomable Grace

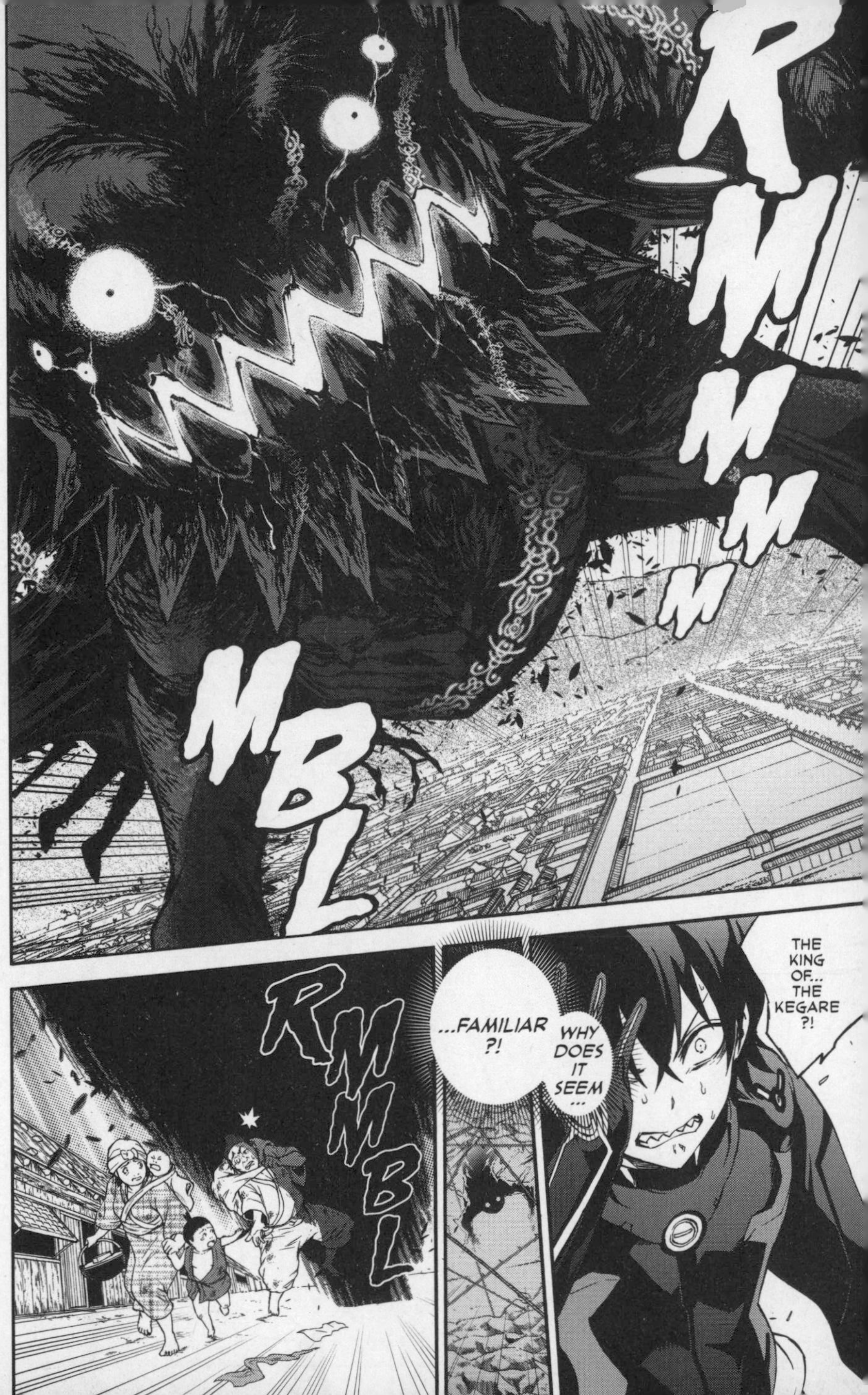
RMMMMM
MBL
THE KING OF... THE KEGARE ?!
WHY DOES IT SEEM ...
...FAMILIAR ?!
RMMBL

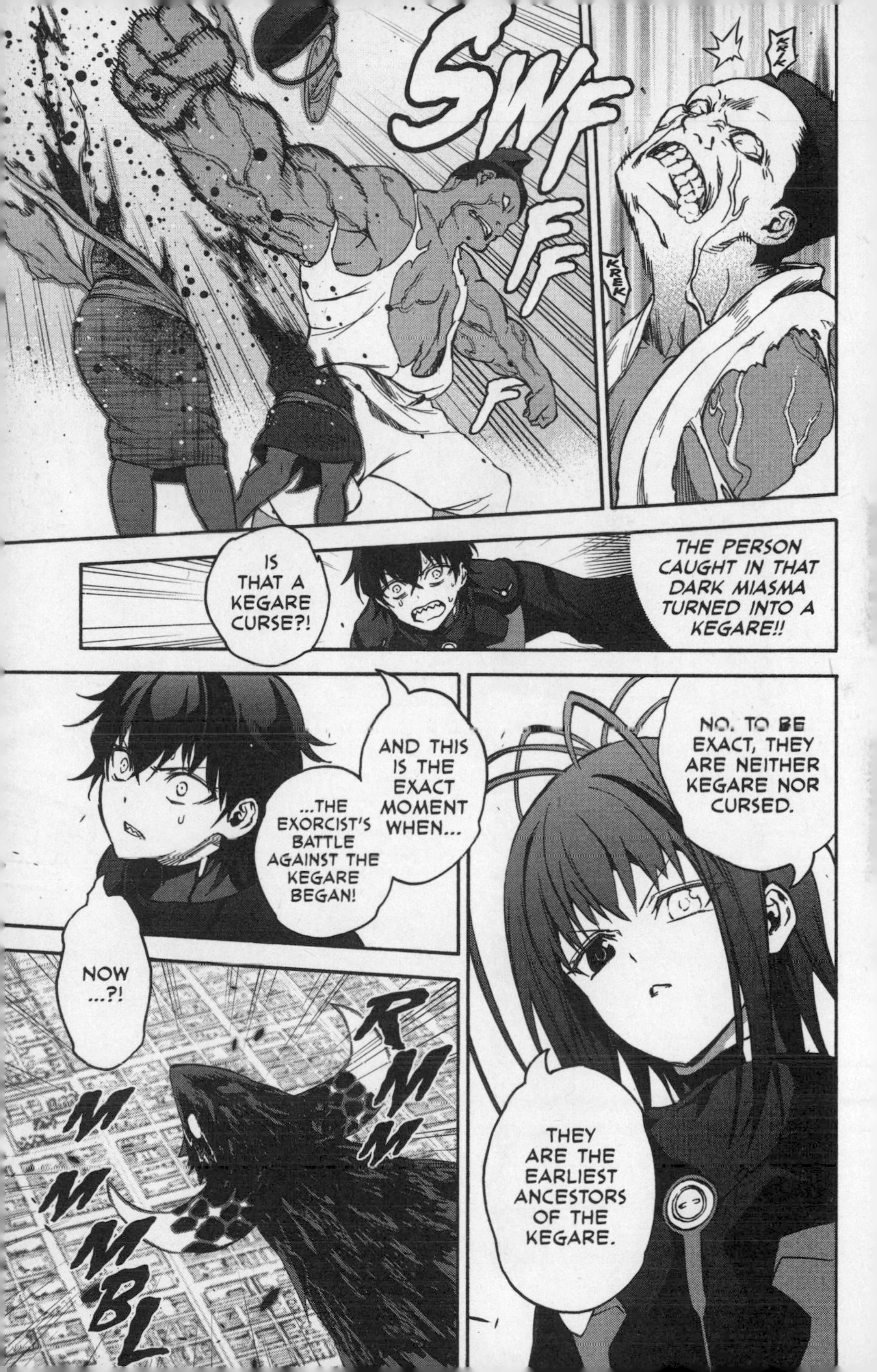
KRK
KREK
SWFF
THE PERSON CAUGHT IN THAT DARK MIASMA TURNED INTO A KEGARE!!
IS THAT A KEGARE CURSE?!
NO. TO BE EXACT, THEY ARE NEITHER KEGARE NOR CURSED.
THEY ARE THE EARLIEST ANCESTORS OF THE KEGARE.
AND THIS IS THE EXACT MOMENT WHEN...
...THE EXORCIST'S BATTLE AGAINST THE KEGARE BEGAN!
NOW ...?!
RMM
MMMMBL

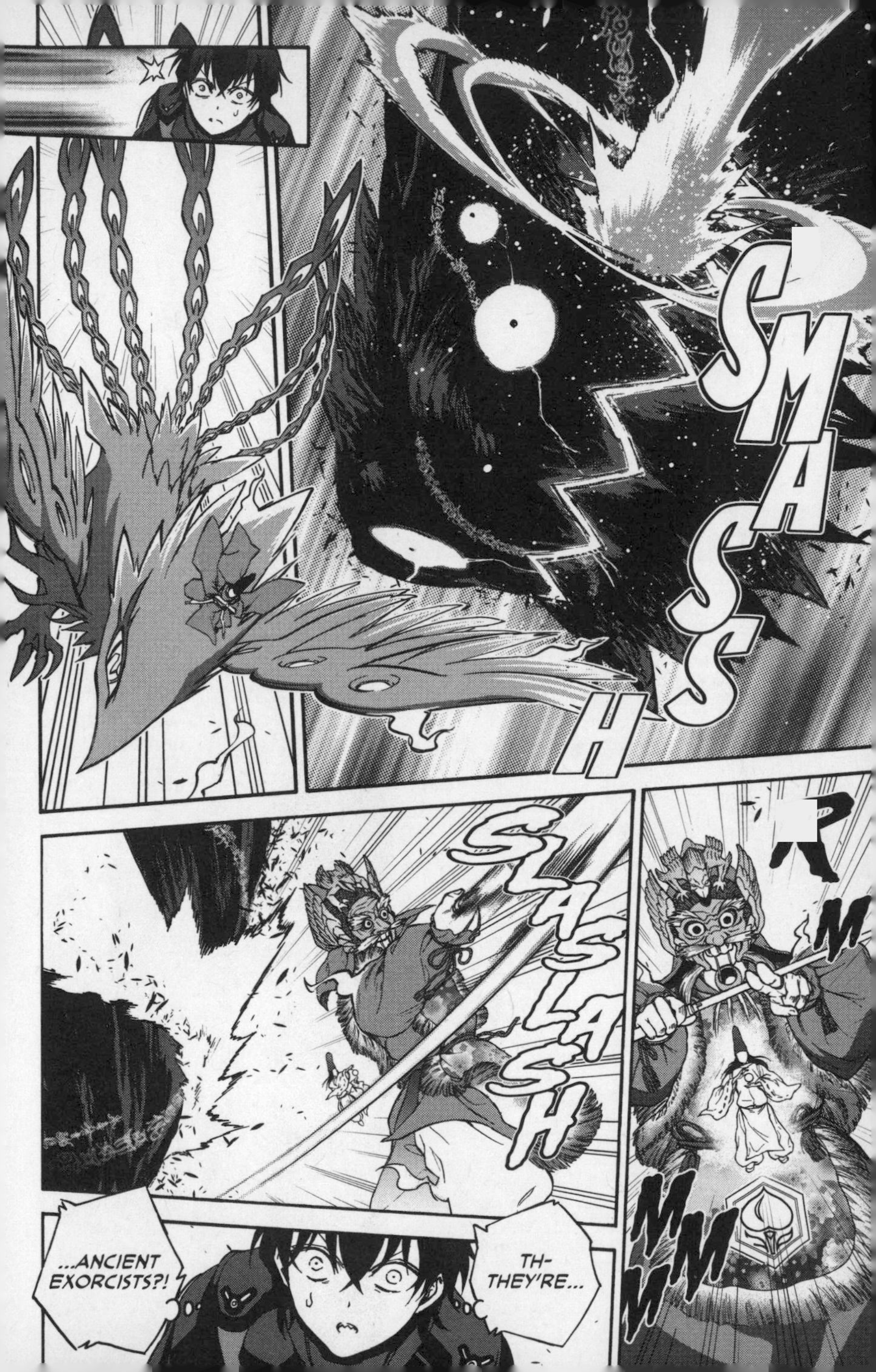
SMASSSH
RMMMMM
SLASH
TH-THEY'RE...
...ANCIENT EXORCISTS?!

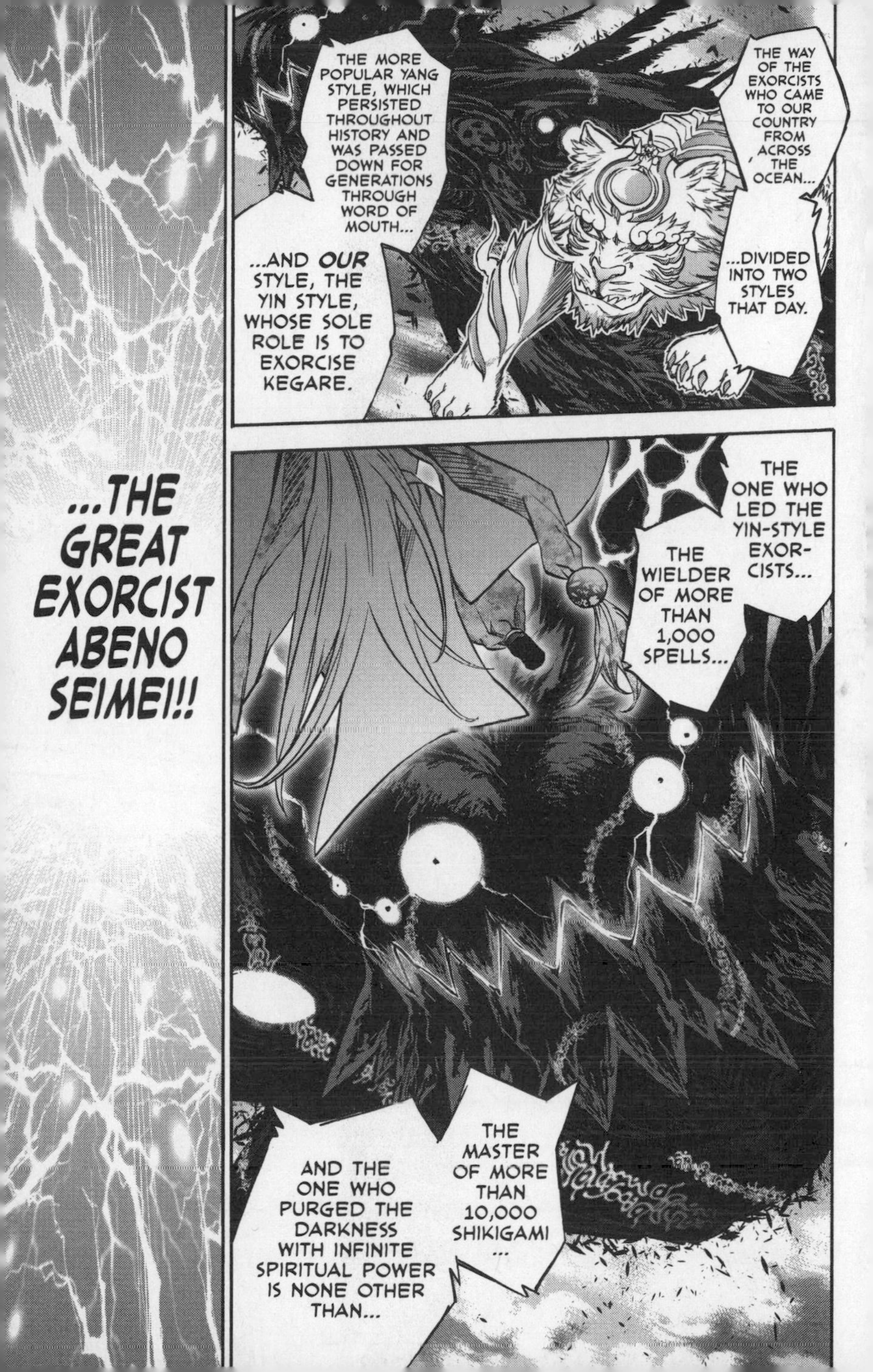
THE WAY OF THE EXORCISTS WHO CAME TO OUR COUNTRY FROM ACROSS THE OCEAN...
...DIVIDED INTO TWO STYLES THAT DAY.
THE MORE POPULAR YANG STYLE, WHICH PERSISTED THROUGHOUT HISTORY AND WAS PASSED DOWN FOR GENERATIONS THROUGH WORD OF MOUTH...
...AND *OUR* STYLE, THE YIN STYLE, WHOSE SOLE ROLE IS TO EXORCISE KEGARE.
THE ONE WHO LED THE YIN-STYLE EXOR-CISTS...
THE WIELDER OF MORE THAN 1,000 SPELLS...
THE MASTER OF MORE THAN 10,000 SHIKIGAMI ...
AND THE ONE WHO PURGED THE DARKNESS WITH INFINITE SPIRITUAL POWER IS NONE OTHER THAN...
...THE GREAT EXORCIST ABENO SEIMEI!!

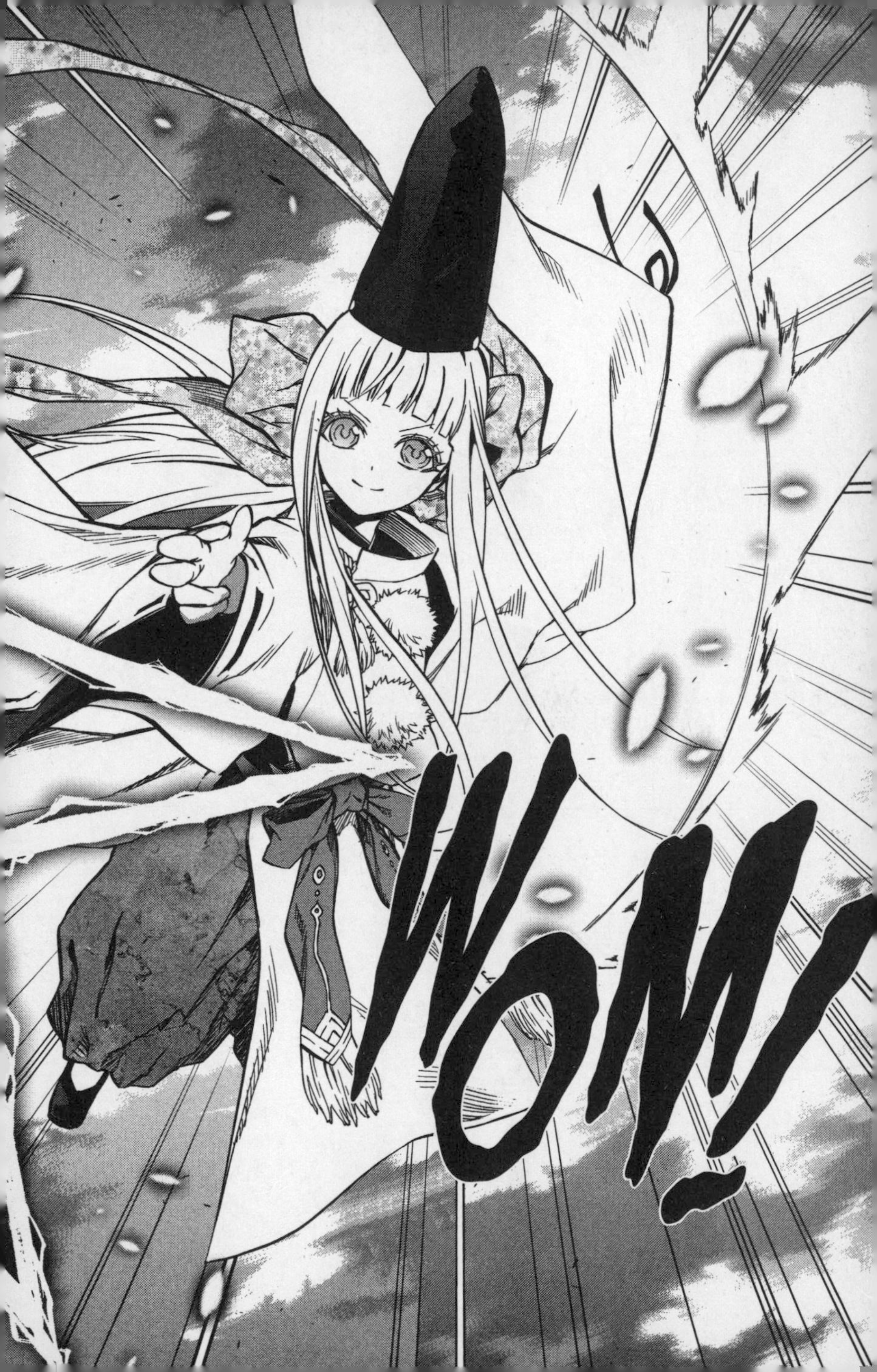
WOMP!

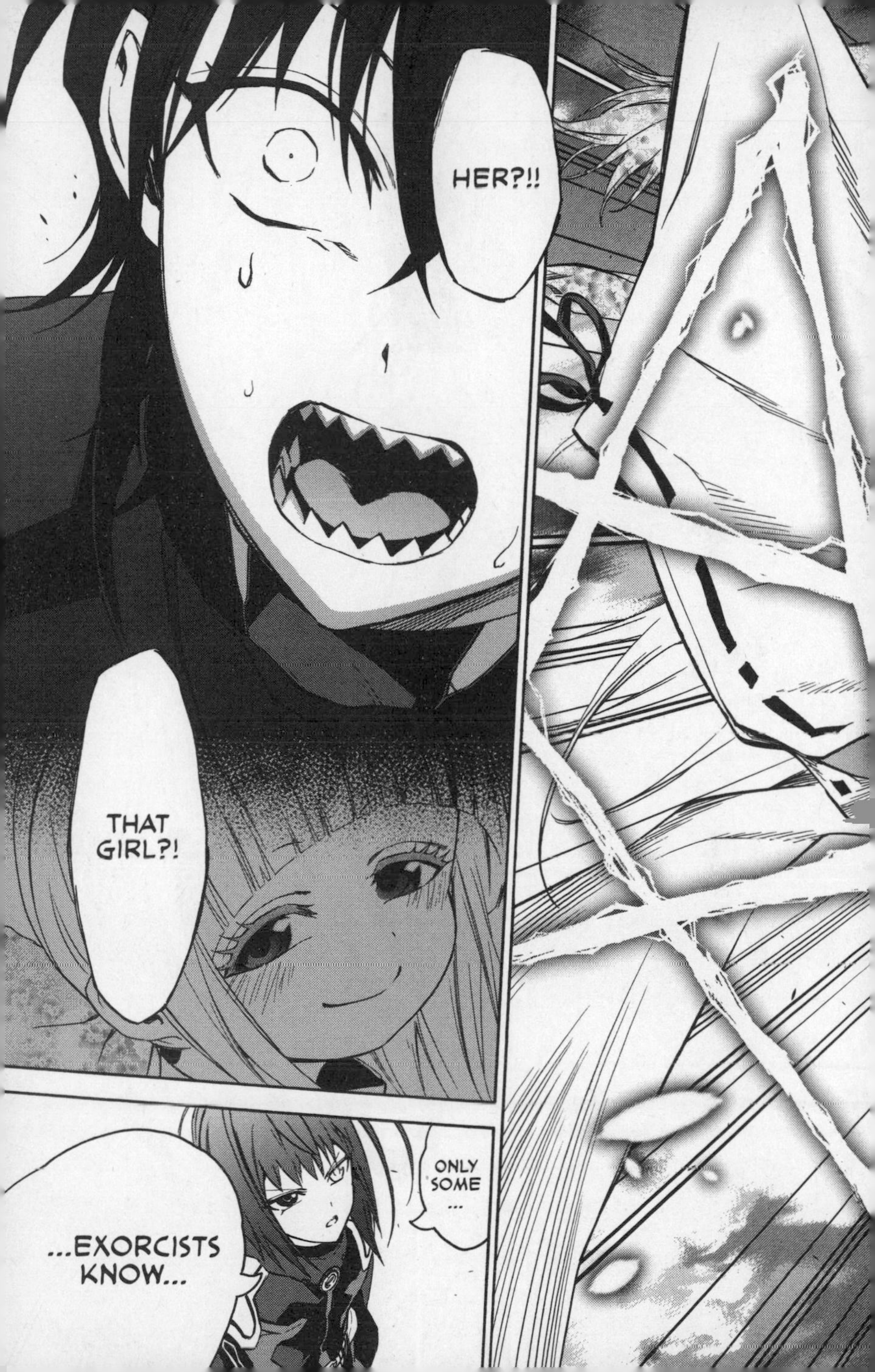
HER?!!
THAT GIRL?!
ONLY SOME ...
...EXORCISTS KNOW...

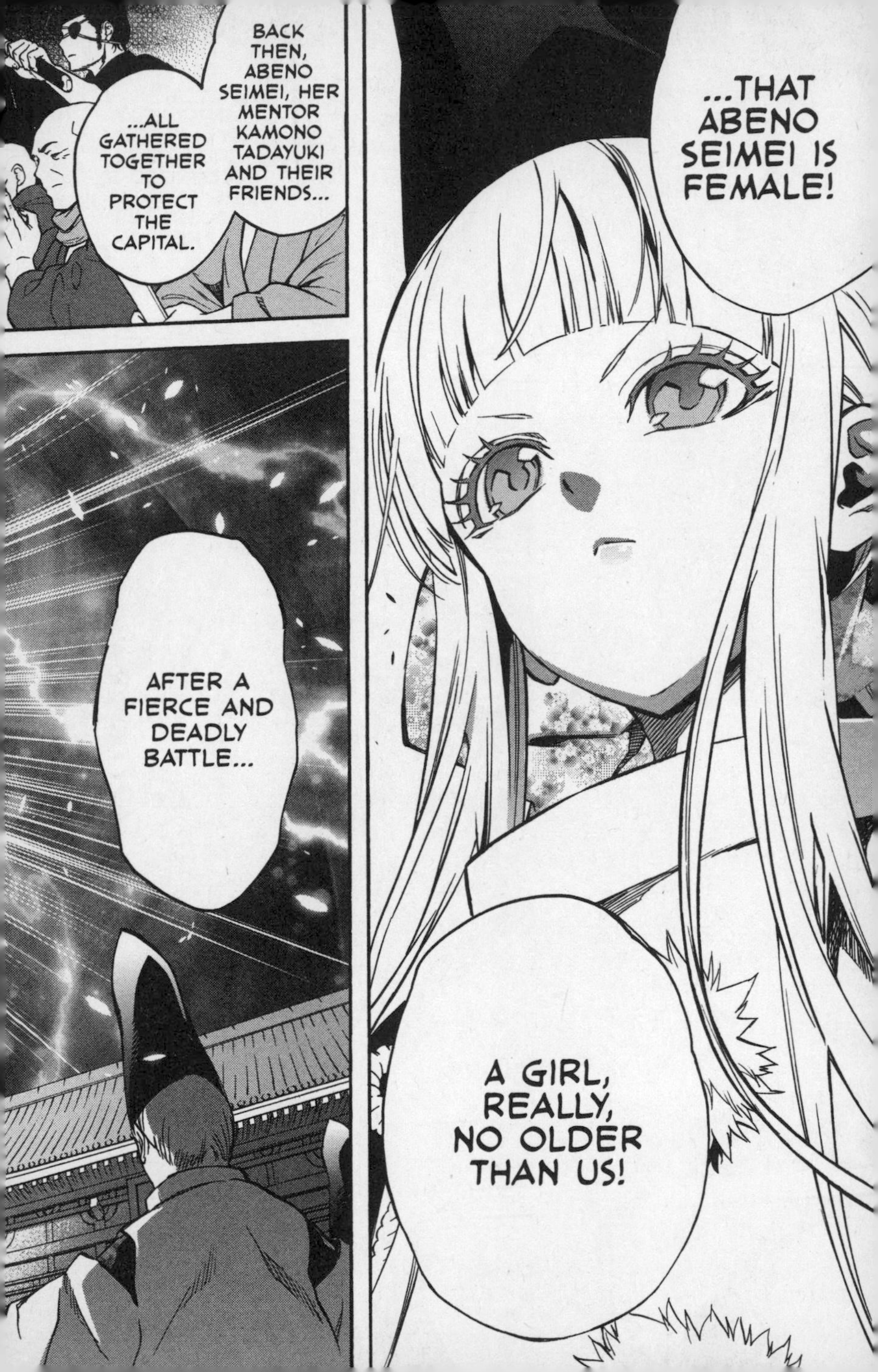
...THAT ABENO SEIMEI IS FEMALE!
A GIRL, REALLY, NO OLDER THAN US!
BACK THEN, ABENO SEIMEI, HER MENTOR KAMONO TADAYUKI AND THEIR FRIENDS...
...ALL GATHERED TOGETHER TO PROTECT THE CAPITAL.
AFTER A FIERCE AND DEADLY BATTLE...

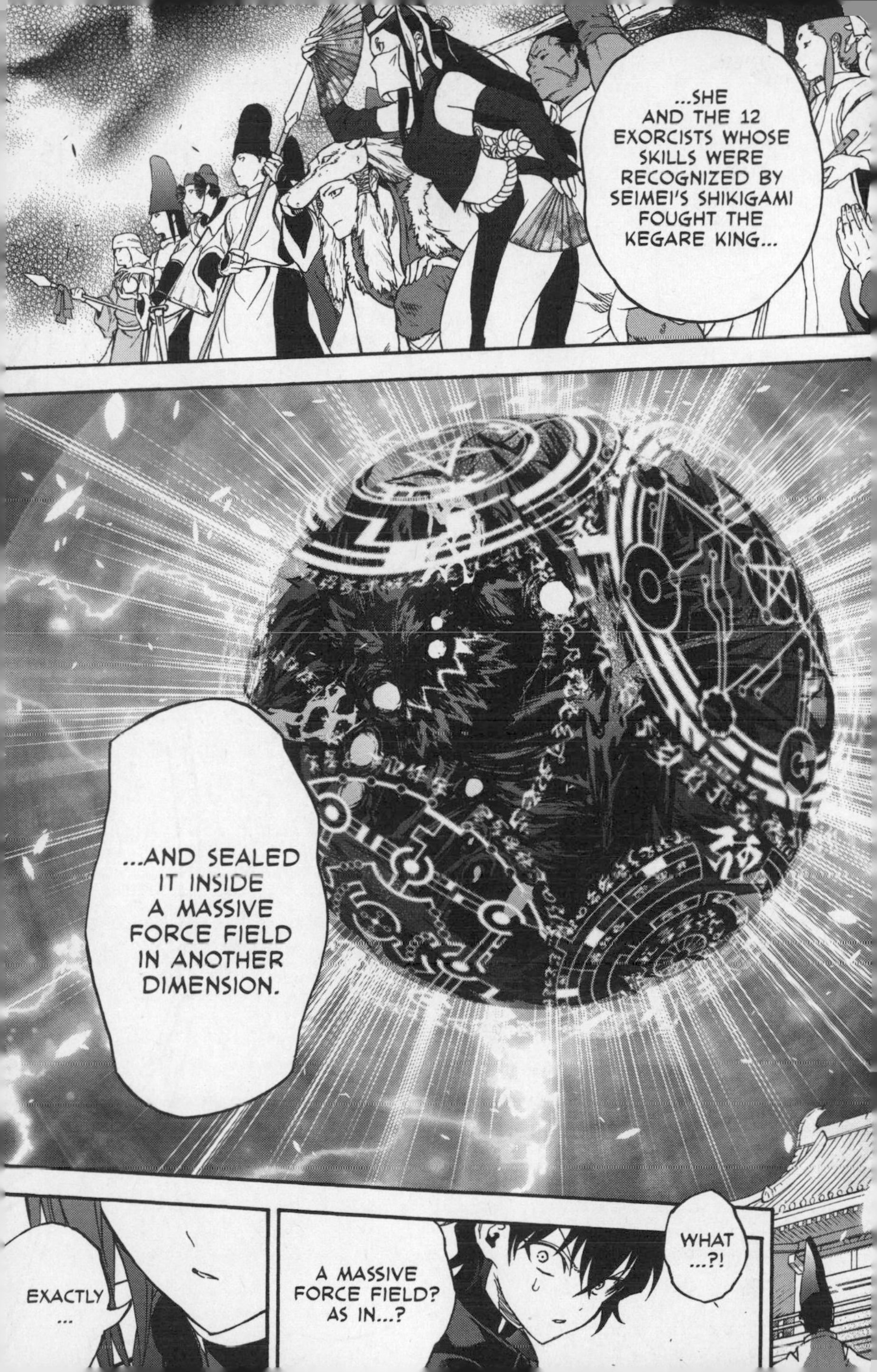
...SHE AND THE 12 EXORCISTS WHOSE SKILLS WERE RECOGNIZED BY SEIMEI'S SHIKIGAMI FOUGHT THE KEGARE KING...
...AND SEALED IT INSIDE A MASSIVE FORCE FIELD IN ANOTHER DIMENSION.
WHAT ...?!
A MASSIVE FORCE FIELD? AS IN...?
EXACTLY ...

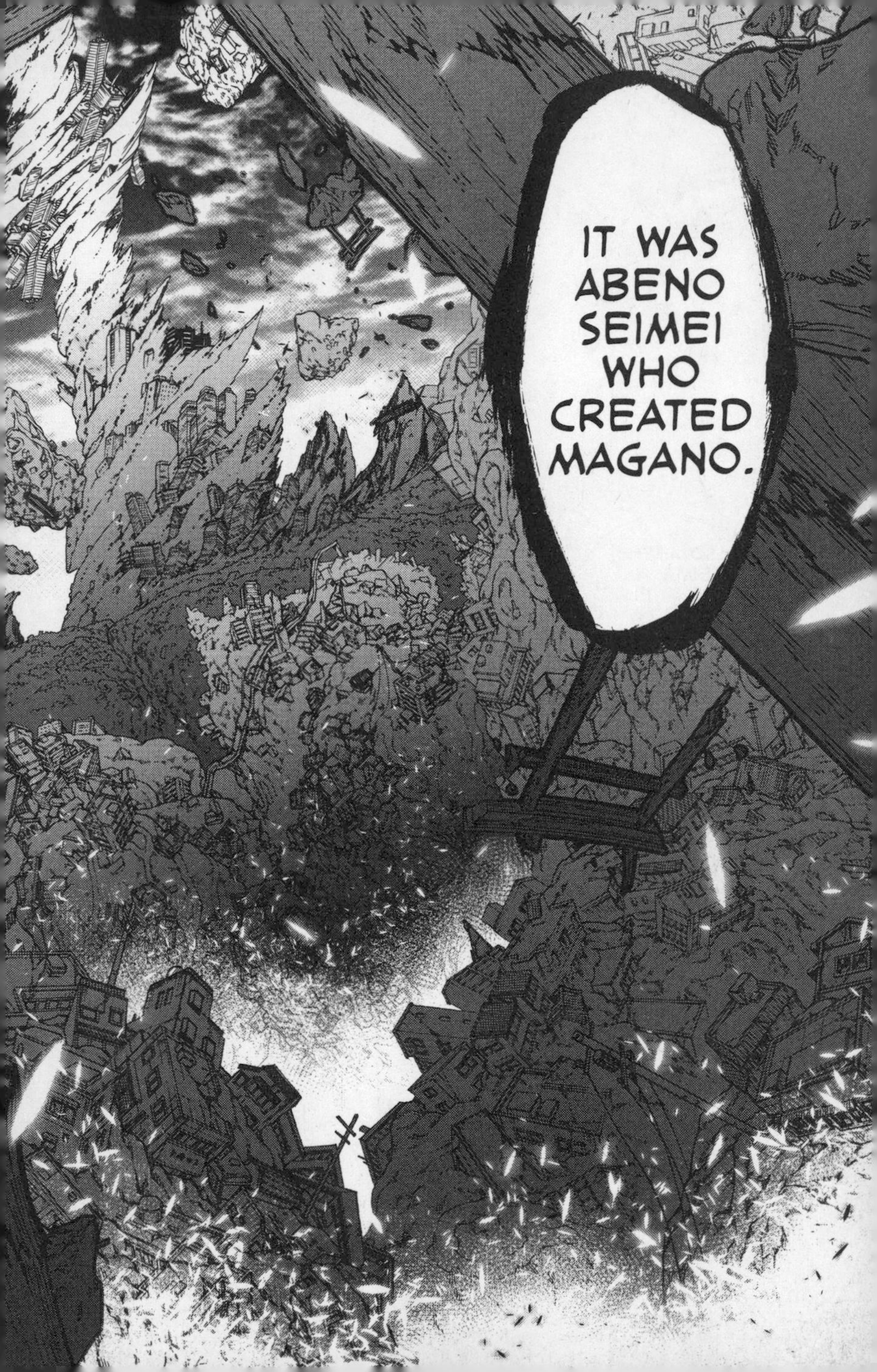
IT WAS ABENO SEIMEI WHO CREATED MAGANO.

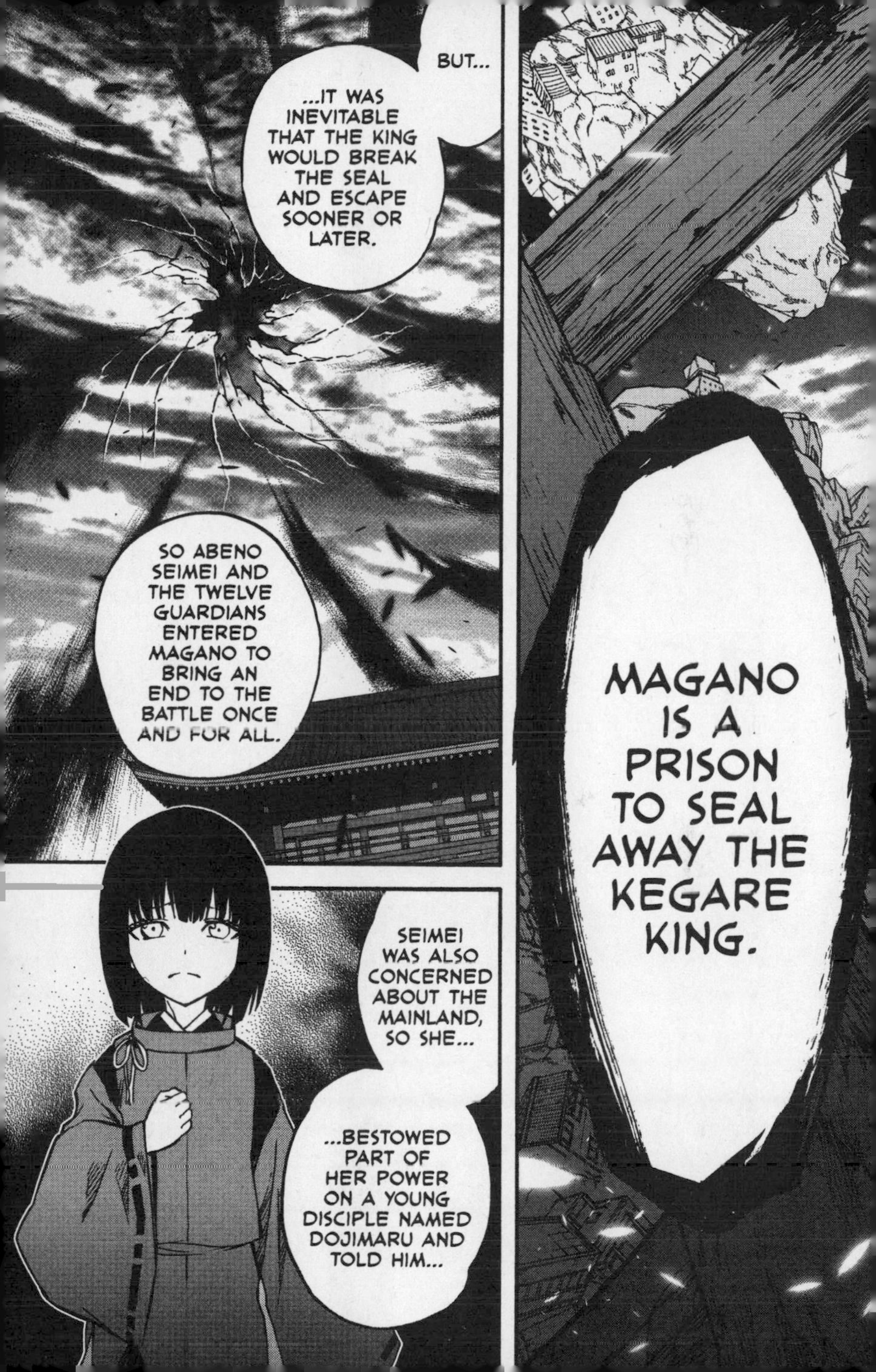
MAGANO IS A PRISON TO SEAL AWAY THE KEGARE KING.
BUT...
...IT WAS INEVITABLE THAT THE KING WOULD BREAK THE SEAL AND ESCAPE SOONER OR LATER.
SO ABENO SEIMEI AND THE TWELVE GUARDIANS ENTERED MAGANO TO BRING AN END TO THE BATTLE ONCE AND FOR ALL.
SEIMEI WAS ALSO CONCERNED ABOUT THE MAINLAND, SO SHE...
...BESTOWED PART OF HER POWER ON A YOUNG DISCIPLE NAMED DOJIMARU AND TOLD HIM...

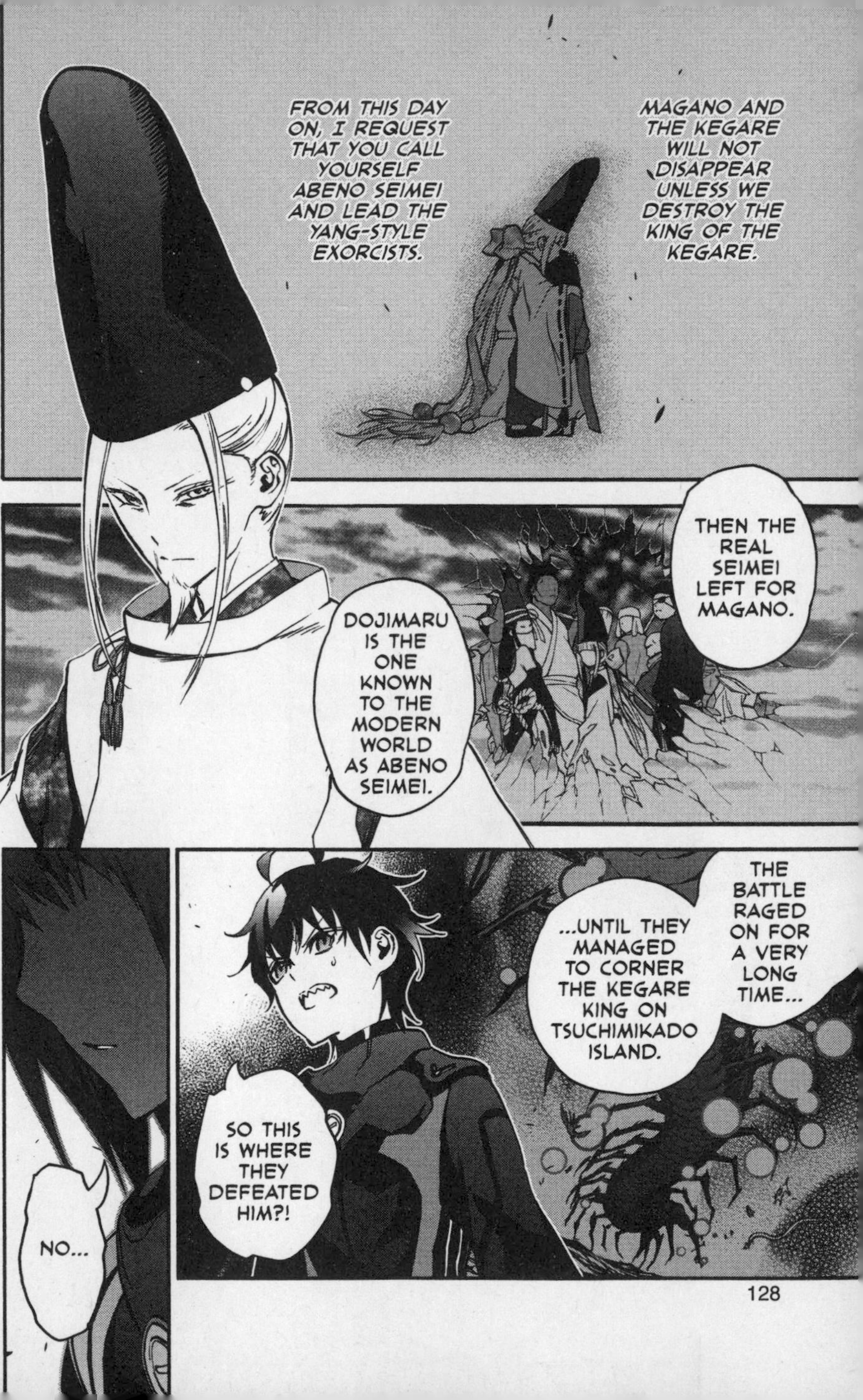
MAGANO AND THE KEGARE WILL NOT DISAPPEAR UNLESS WE DESTROY THE KING OF THE KEGARE.
FROM THIS DAY ON, I REQUEST THAT YOU CALL YOURSELF ABENO SEIMEI AND LEAD THE YANG-STYLE EXORCISTS.
THEN THE REAL SEIMEI LEFT FOR MAGANO.
DOJIMARU IS THE ONE KNOWN TO THE MODERN WORLD AS ABENO SEIMEI.
THE BATTLE RAGED ON FOR A VERY LONG TIME...
...UNTIL THEY MANAGED TO CORNER THE KEGARE KING ON TSUCHIMIKADO ISLAND.
SO THIS IS WHERE THEY DEFEATED HIM?!
NO...

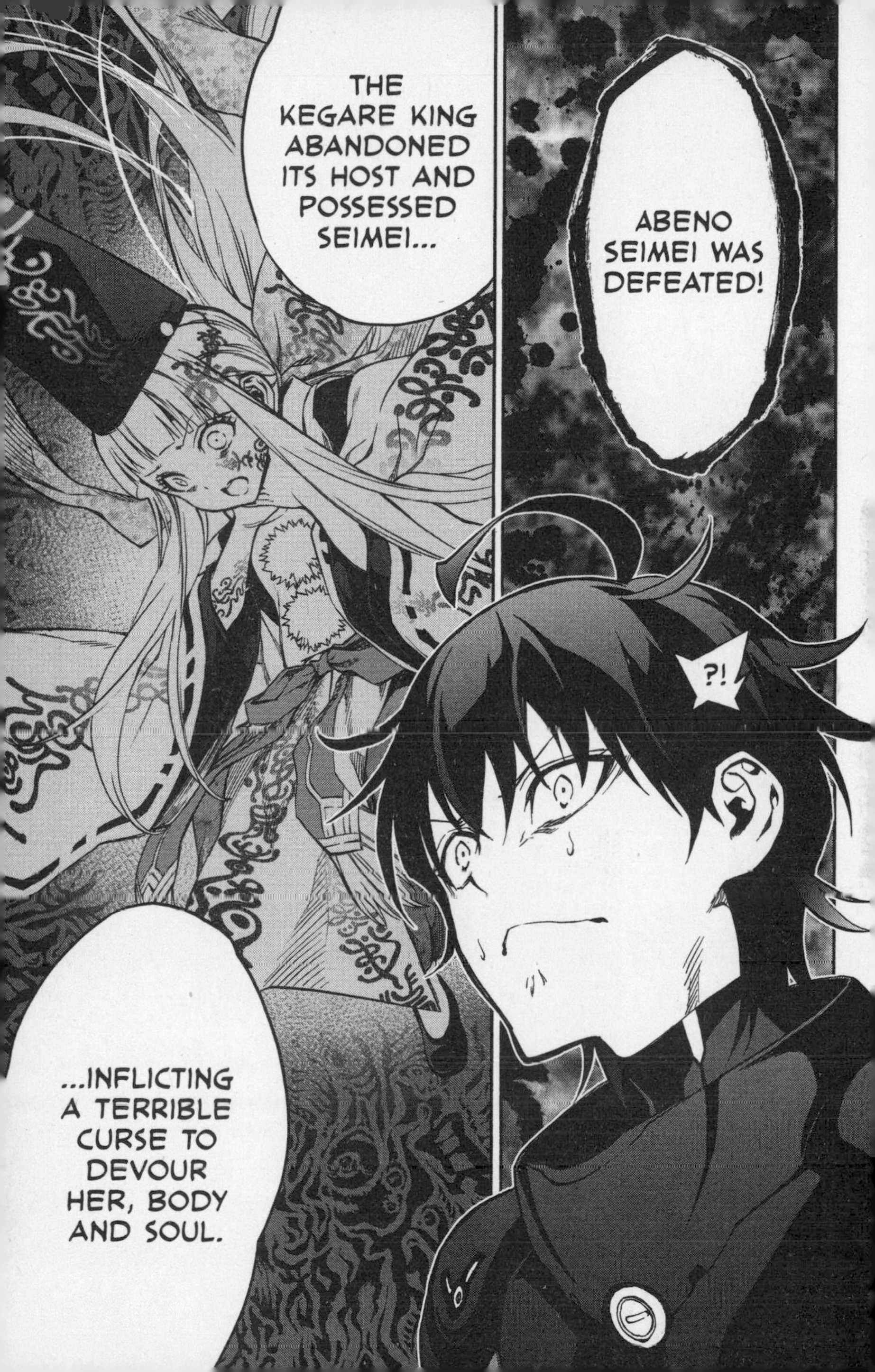
ABENO SEIMEI WAS DEFEATED!
?!
THE KEGARE KING ABANDONED ITS HOST AND POSSESSED SEIMEI...
...INFLICTING A TERRIBLE CURSE TO DEVOUR HER, BODY AND SOUL.

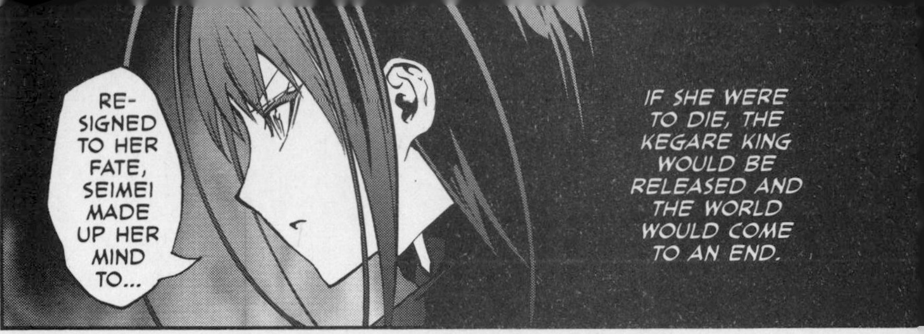
IF SHE WERE TO DIE, THE KEGARE KING WOULD BE RELEASED AND THE WORLD WOULD COME TO AN END.
RE-SIGNED TO HER FATE, SEIMEI MADE UP HER MIND TO...

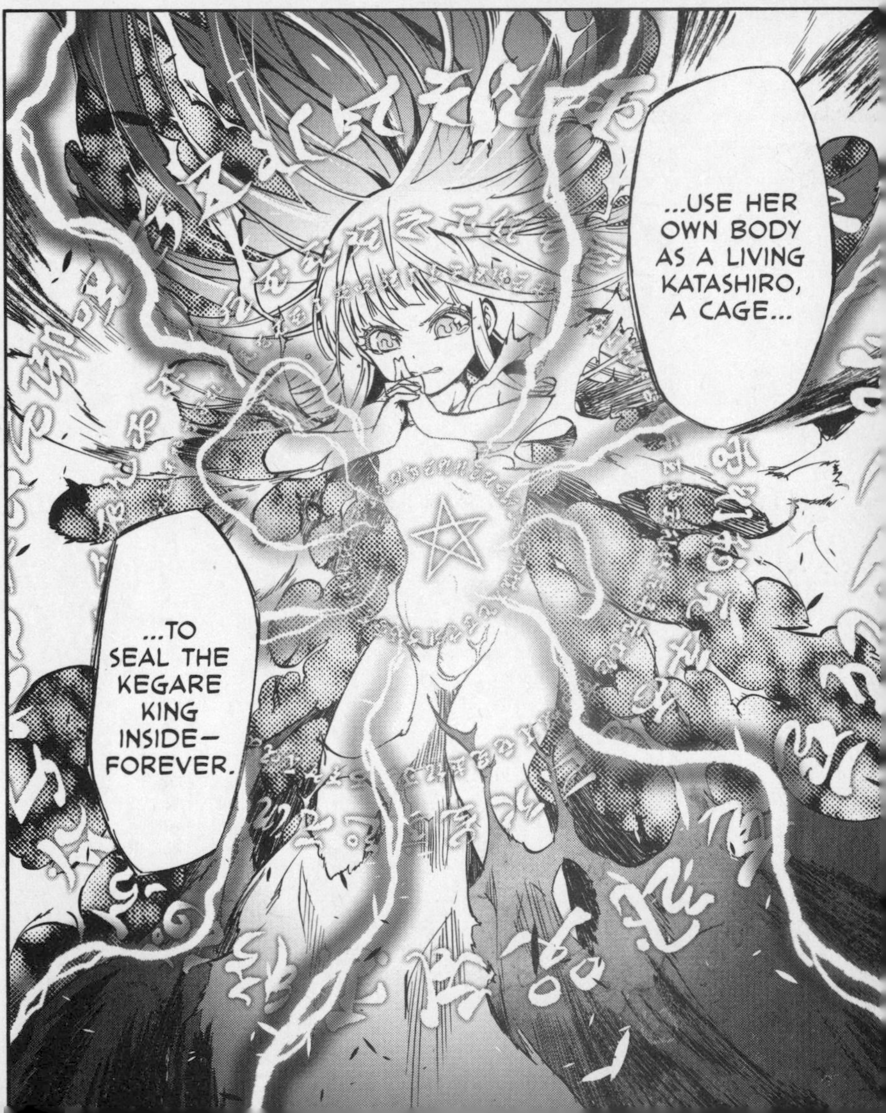
...USE HER OWN BODY AS A LIVING KATASHIRO, A CAGE...
...TO SEAL THE KEGARE KING INSIDE—FOREVER.

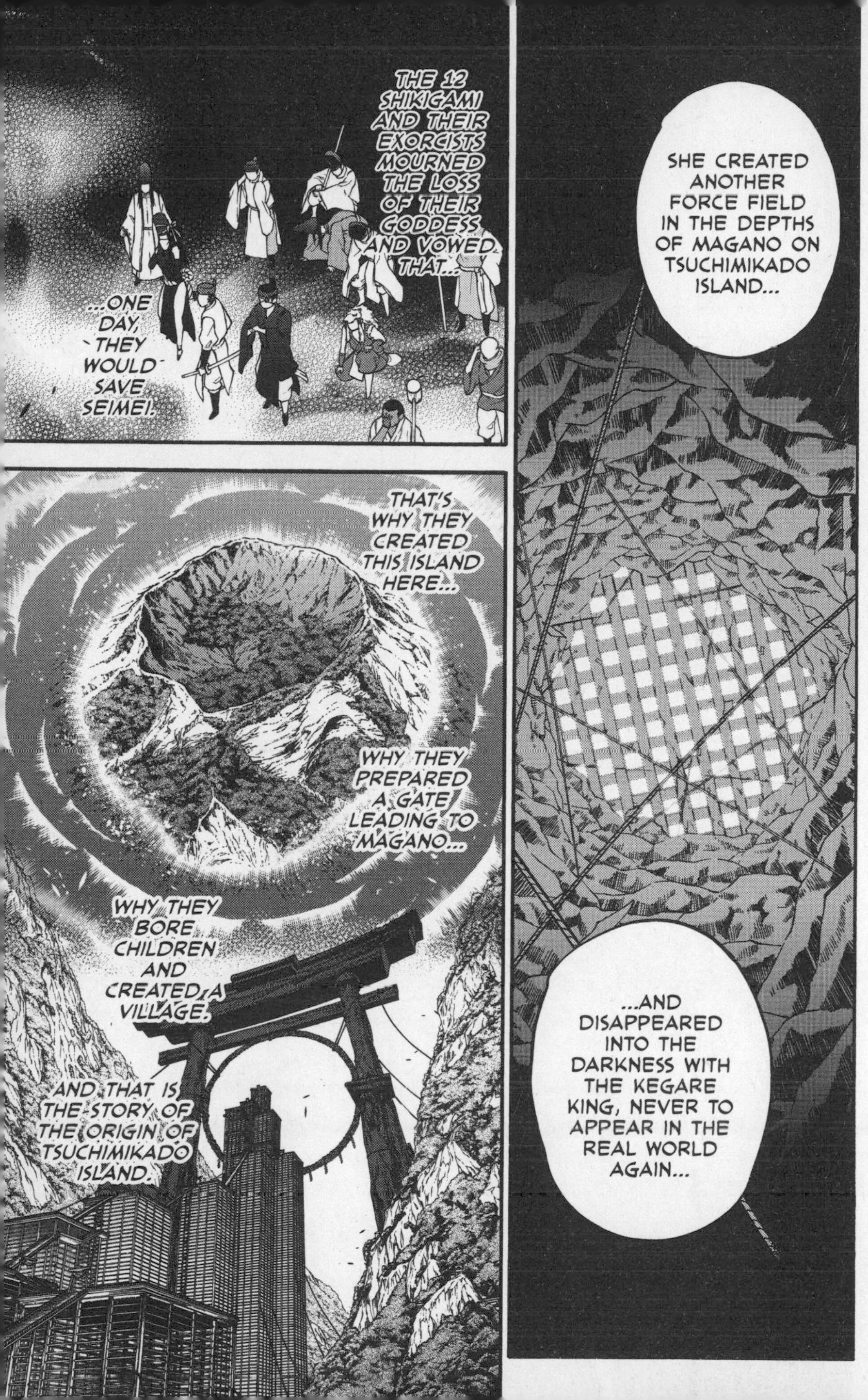
SHE CREATED ANOTHER FORCE FIELD IN THE DEPTHS OF MAGANO ON TSUCHIMIKADO ISLAND...
...AND DISAPPEARED INTO THE DARKNESS WITH THE KEGARE KING, NEVER TO APPEAR IN THE REAL WORLD AGAIN...
THE 12 SHIKIGAMI AND THEIR EXORCISTS MOURNED THE LOSS OF THEIR GODDESS AND VOWED THAT...
...ONE DAY, THEY WOULD SAVE SEIMEI.
THAT'S WHY THEY CREATED THIS ISLAND HERE...
WHY THEY PREPARED A GATE LEADING TO MAGANO...
WHY THEY BORE CHILDREN AND CREATED A VILLAGE.
AND THAT IS THE STORY OF THE ORIGIN OF TSUCHIMIKADO ISLAND.

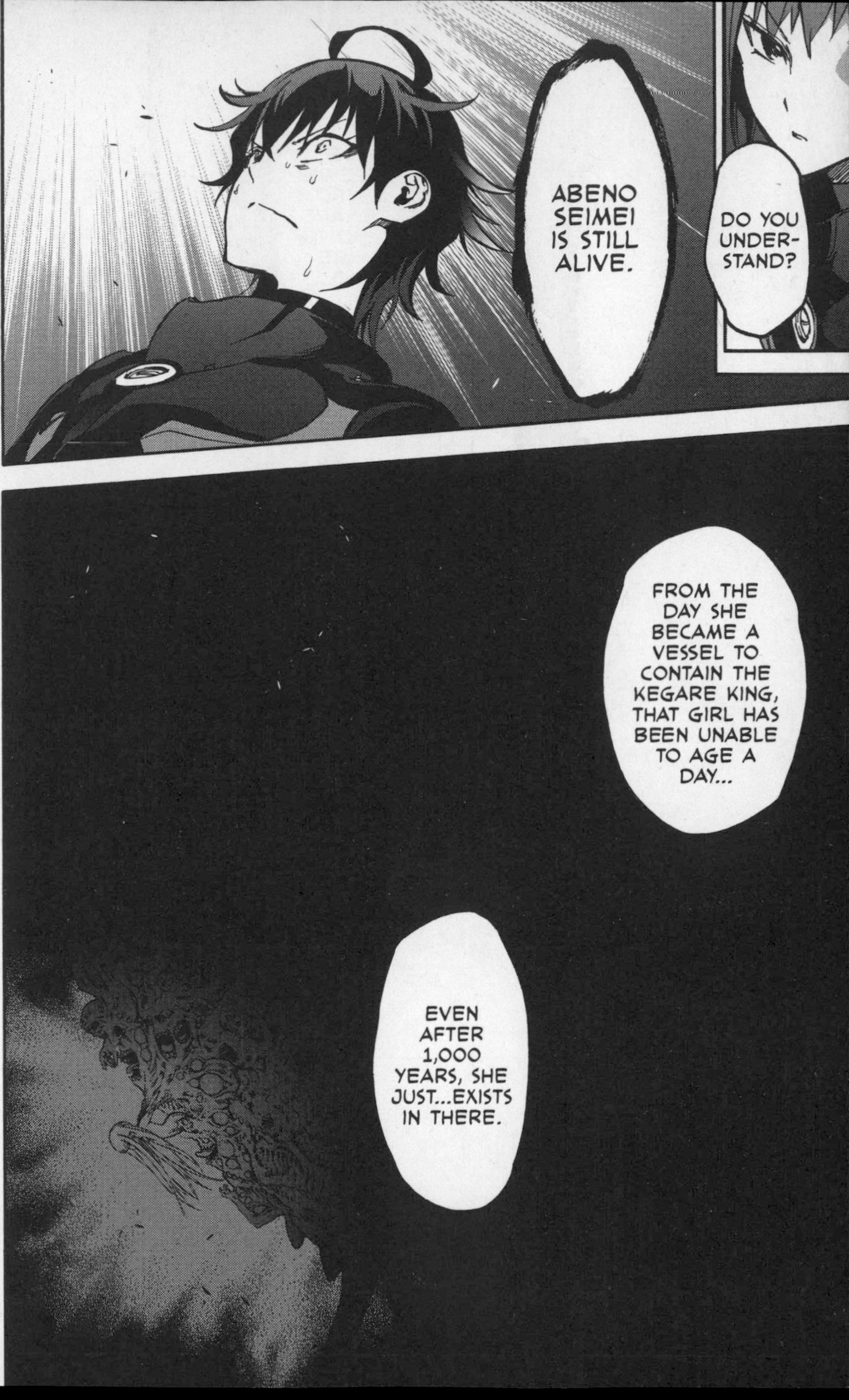
DO YOU UNDER-STAND?
ABENO SEIMEI IS STILL ALIVE.
FROM THE DAY SHE BECAME A VESSEL TO CONTAIN THE KEGARE KING, THAT GIRL HAS BEEN UNABLE TO AGE A DAY...
EVEN AFTER 1,000 YEARS, SHE JUST...EXISTS IN THERE.

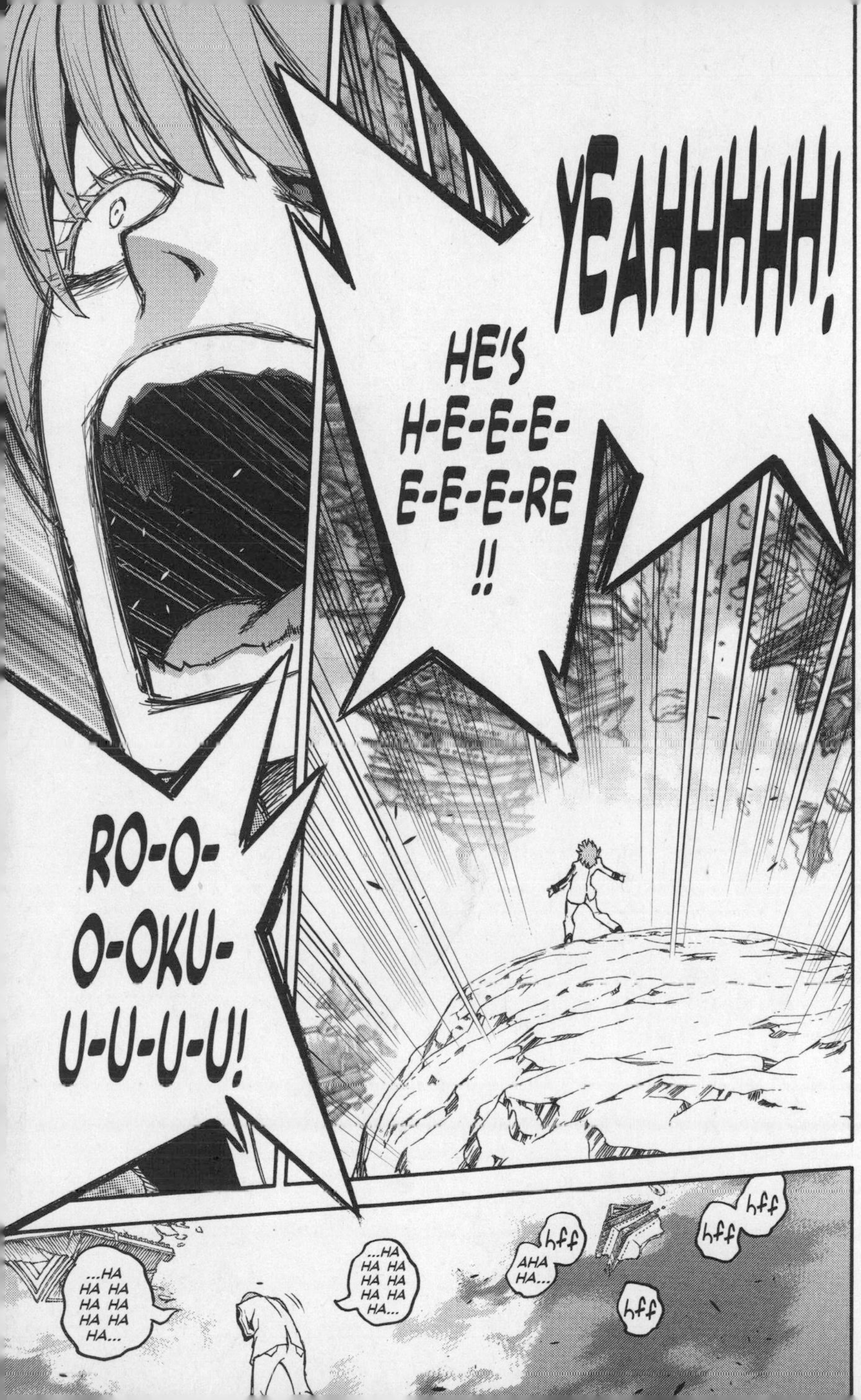
YEAHHHHH!
HE'S H-E-E-E-E-E-E-RE!!
RO-O-O-OKU-U-U-U-U!
hff
hff
hff
hff
AHA HA...
...HA HA HA HA HA HA HA HA...
...HA HA HA HA HA HA HA HA...

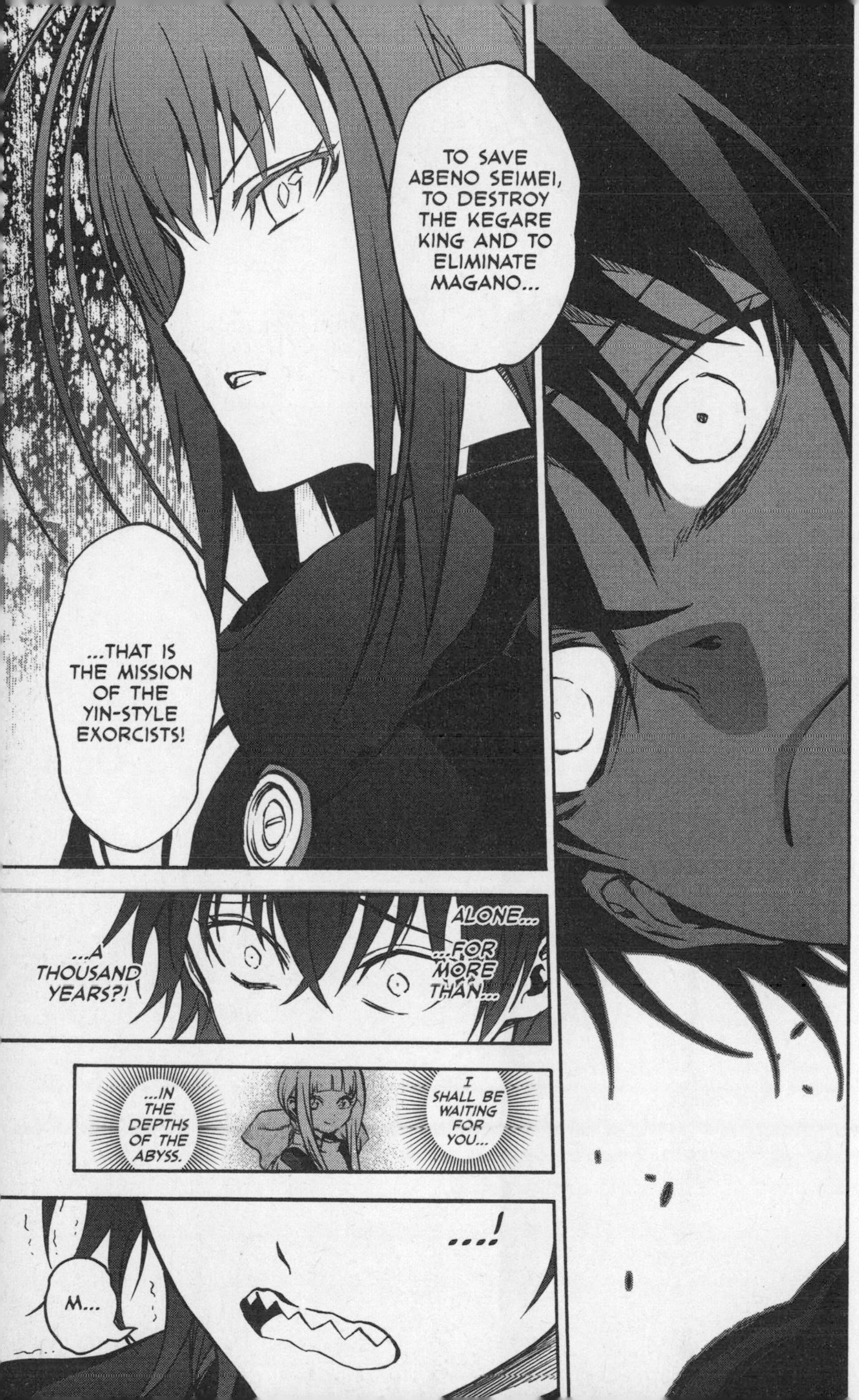
TO SAVE ABENO SEIMEI, TO DESTROY THE KEGARE KING AND TO ELIMINATE MAGANO...
...THAT IS THE MISSION OF THE YIN-STYLE EXORCISTS!
ALONE...
...FOR MORE THAN...
...A THOUSAND YEARS?!
I SHALL BE WAITING FOR YOU...
...IN THE DEPTHS OF THE ABYSS.
...!
M...

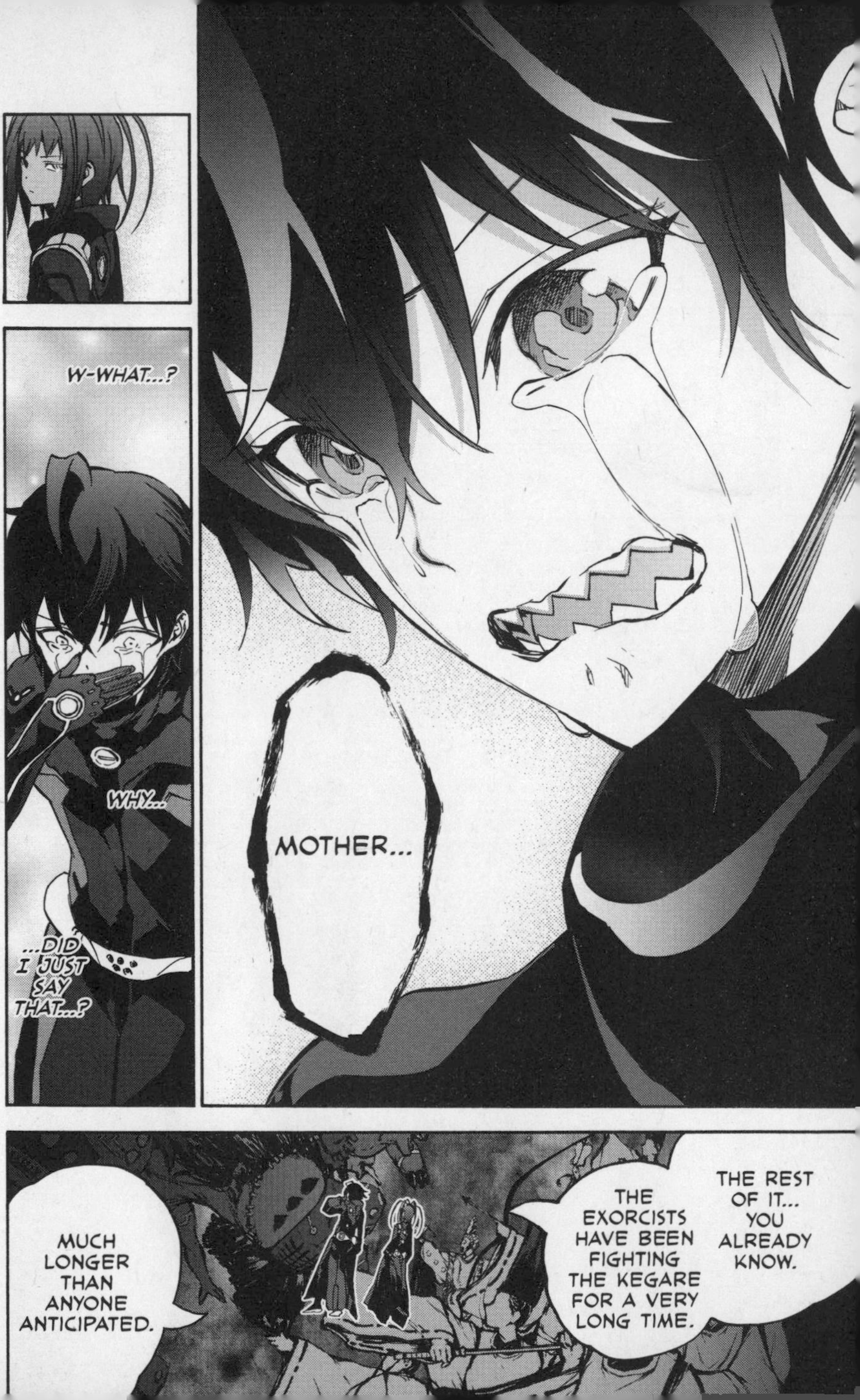
MOTHER...
W-WHAT...?
WHY...
...DID I JUST SAY THAT...?
THE REST OF IT... YOU ALREADY KNOW.
THE EXORCISTS HAVE BEEN FIGHTING THE KEGARE FOR A VERY LONG TIME.
MUCH LONGER THAN ANYONE ANTICIPATED.

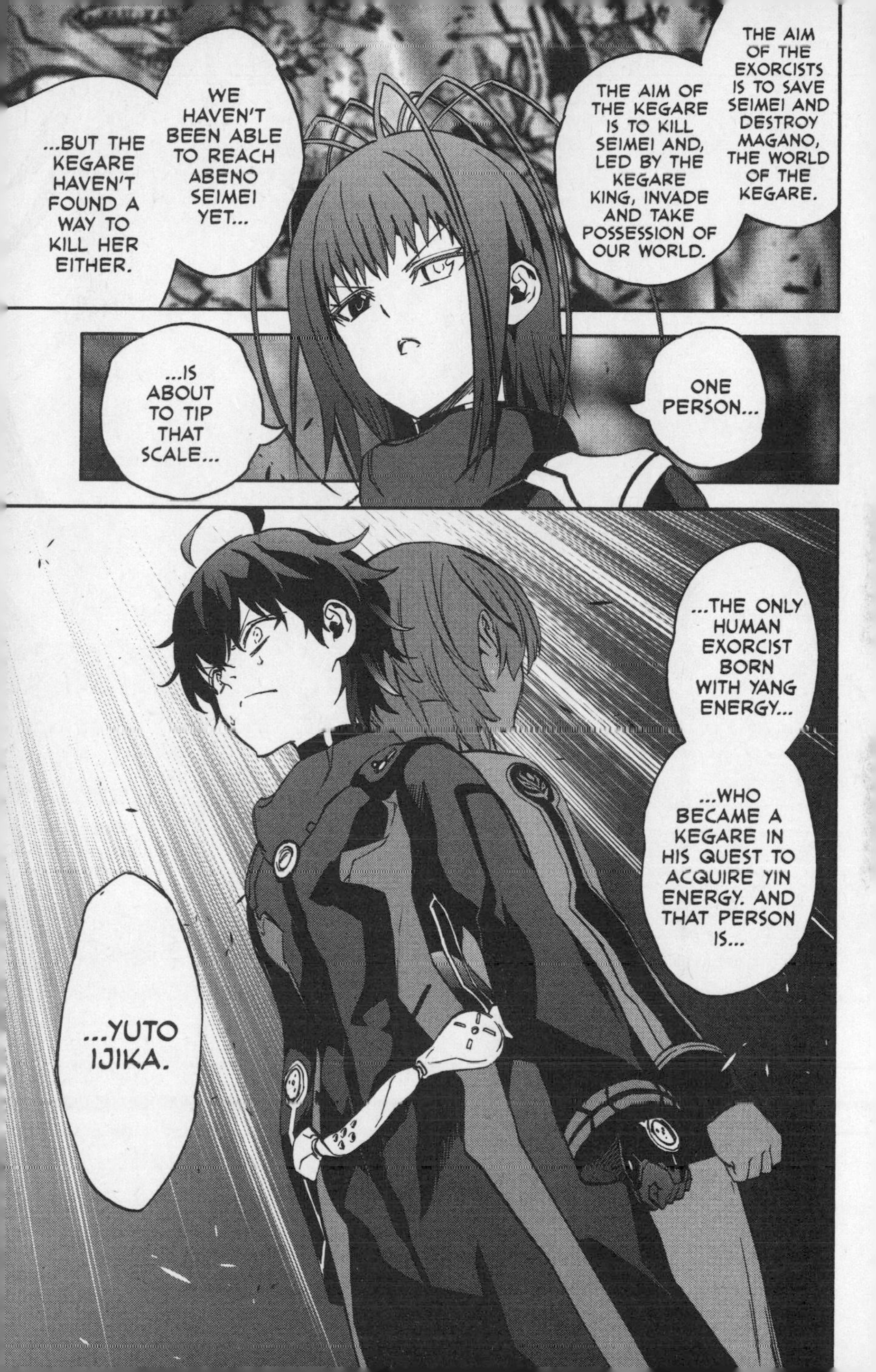
THE AIM OF THE EXORCISTS IS TO SAVE SEIMEI AND DESTROY MAGANO, THE WORLD OF THE KEGARE.
THE AIM OF THE KEGARE IS TO KILL SEIMEI AND, LED BY THE KEGARE KING, INVADE AND TAKE POSSESSION OF OUR WORLD.
WE HAVEN'T BEEN ABLE TO REACH ABENO SEIMEI YET...
...BUT THE KEGARE HAVEN'T FOUND A WAY TO KILL HER EITHER.
ONE PERSON...
...IS ABOUT TO TIP THAT SCALE...
...THE ONLY HUMAN EXORCIST BORN WITH YANG ENERGY...
...WHO BECAME A KEGARE IN HIS QUEST TO ACQUIRE YIN ENERGY. AND THAT PERSON IS...
...YUTO IJIKA.

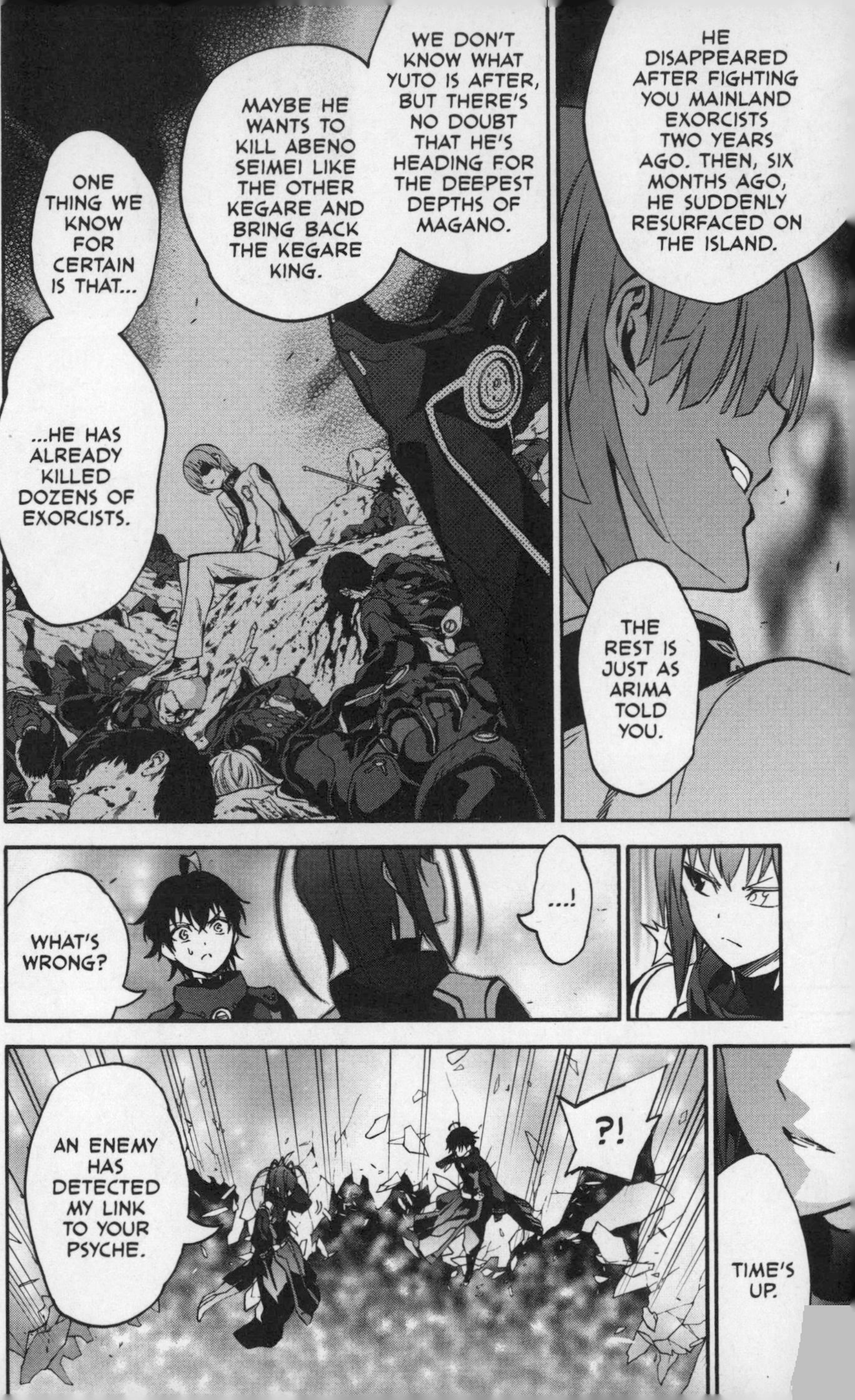
HE DISAPPEARED AFTER FIGHTING YOU MAINLAND EXORCISTS TWO YEARS AGO. THEN, SIX MONTHS AGO, HE SUDDENLY RESURFACED ON THE ISLAND.
THE REST IS JUST AS ARIMA TOLD YOU.
WE DON'T KNOW WHAT YUTO IS AFTER, BUT THERE'S NO DOUBT THAT HE'S HEADING FOR THE DEEPEST DEPTHS OF MAGANO.
MAYBE HE WANTS TO KILL ABENO SEIMEI LIKE THE OTHER KEGARE AND BRING BACK THE KEGARE KING.
ONE THING WE KNOW FOR CERTAIN IS THAT...
...HE HAS ALREADY KILLED DOZENS OF EXORCISTS.
...!
WHAT'S WRONG?
TIME'S UP.
?!
AN ENEMY HAS DETECTED MY LINK TO YOUR PSYCHE.

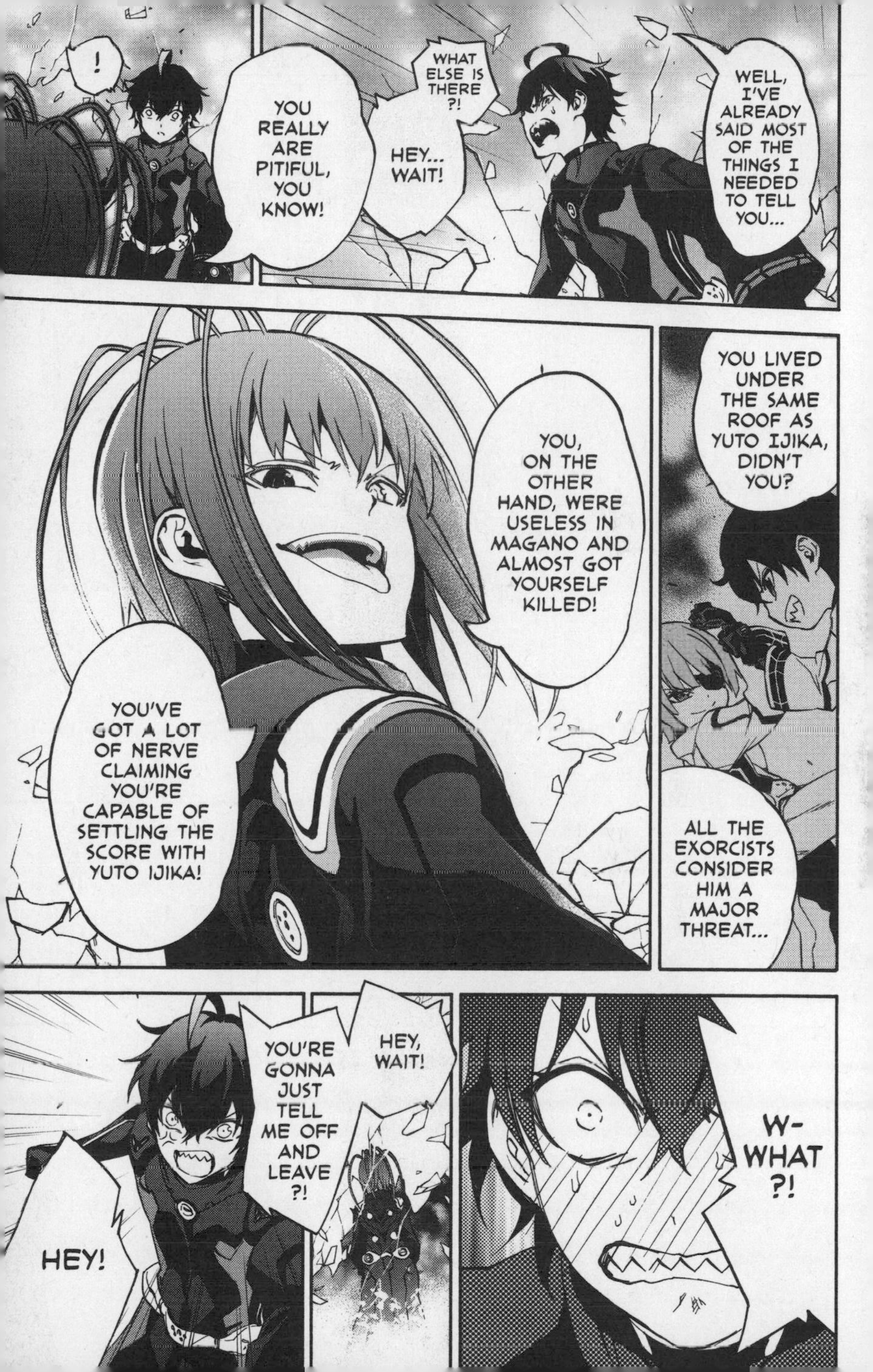
WELL, I'VE ALREADY SAID MOST OF THE THINGS I NEEDED TO TELL YOU...
WHAT ELSE IS THERE?!
HEY... WAIT!
YOU REALLY ARE PITIFUL, YOU KNOW!
!
YOU LIVED UNDER THE SAME ROOF AS YUTO IJIKA, DIDN'T YOU?
ALL THE EXORCISTS CONSIDER HIM A MAJOR THREAT...
YOU, ON THE OTHER HAND, WERE USELESS IN MAGANO AND ALMOST GOT YOURSELF KILLED!
YOU'VE GOT A LOT OF NERVE CLAIMING YOU'RE CAPABLE OF SETTLING THE SCORE WITH YUTO IJIKA!
W-WHAT?!
HEY, WAIT!
YOU'RE GONNA JUST TELL ME OFF AND LEAVE?!
HEY!

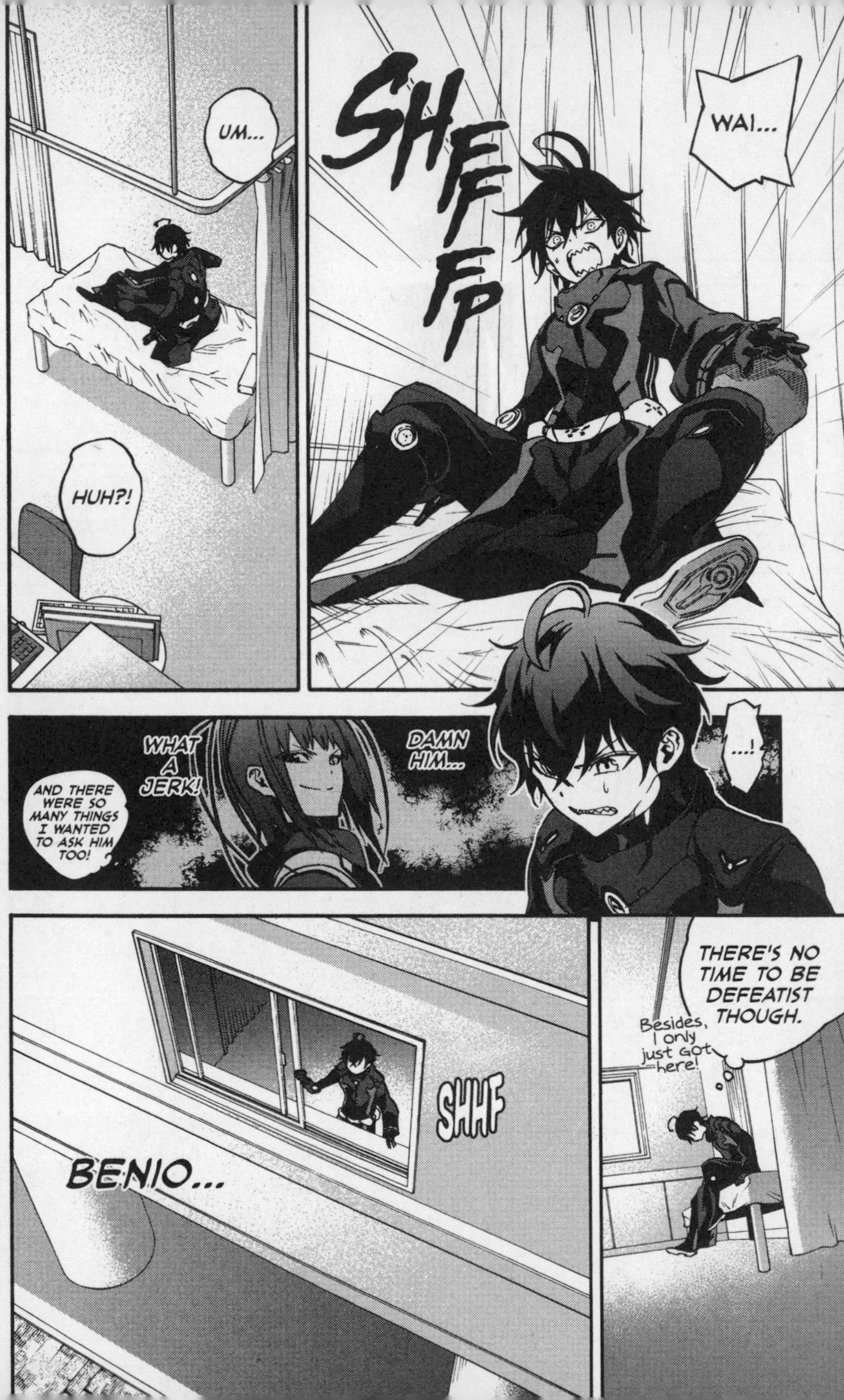
WAI...
SHFFFP
UM...
HUH?!
...!
DAMN HIM...
WHAT A JERK!
AND THERE WERE SO MANY THINGS I WANTED TO ASK HIM TOO!
THERE'S NO TIME TO BE DEFEATIST THOUGH.
Besides, I only just got here!
SHHF
BENIO...

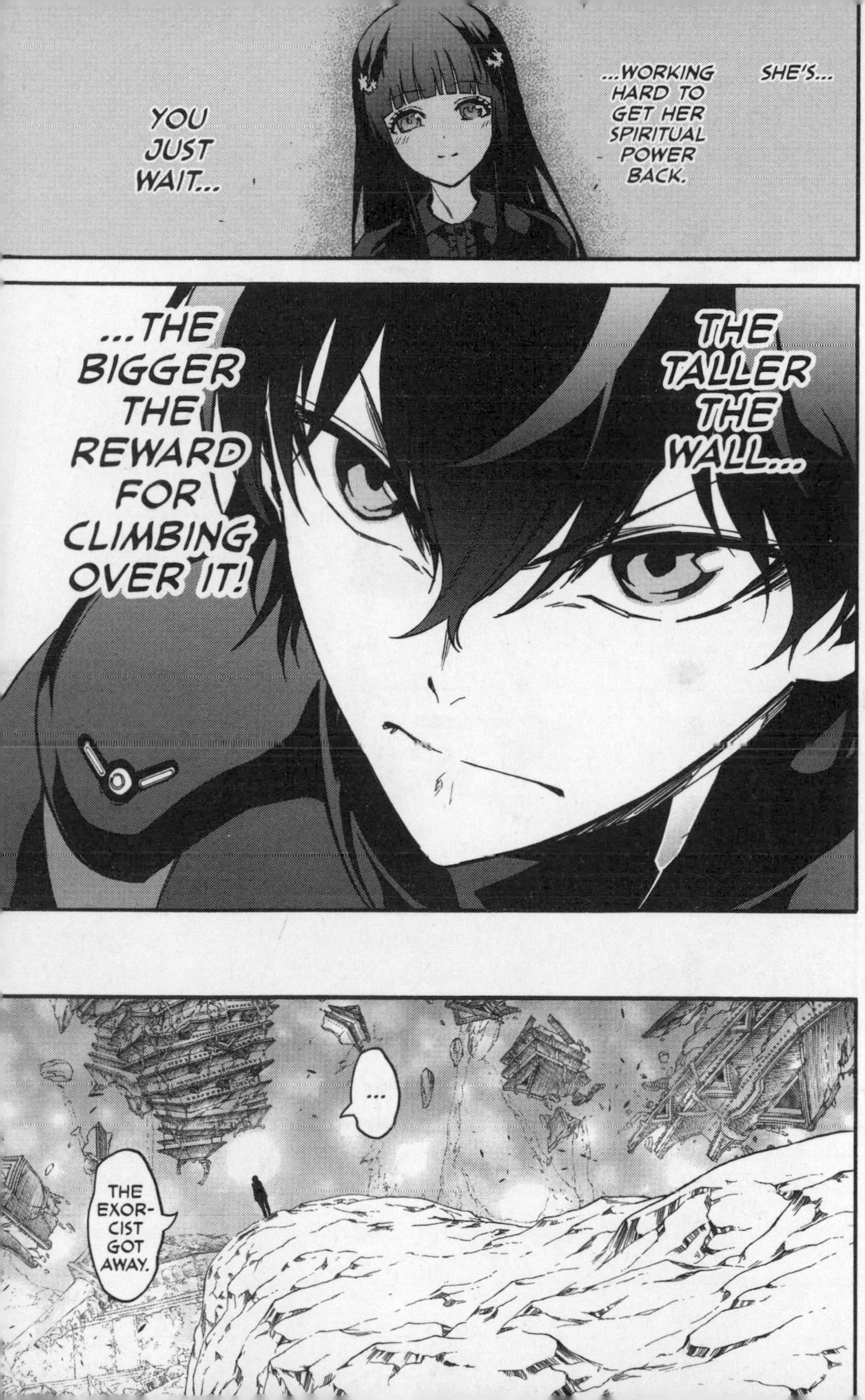
SHE'S...
...WORKING HARD TO GET HER SPIRITUAL POWER BACK.
YOU JUST WAIT...
THE TALLER THE WALL...
...THE BIGGER THE REWARD FOR CLIMBING OVER IT!
...
THE EXOR-CIST GOT AWAY.

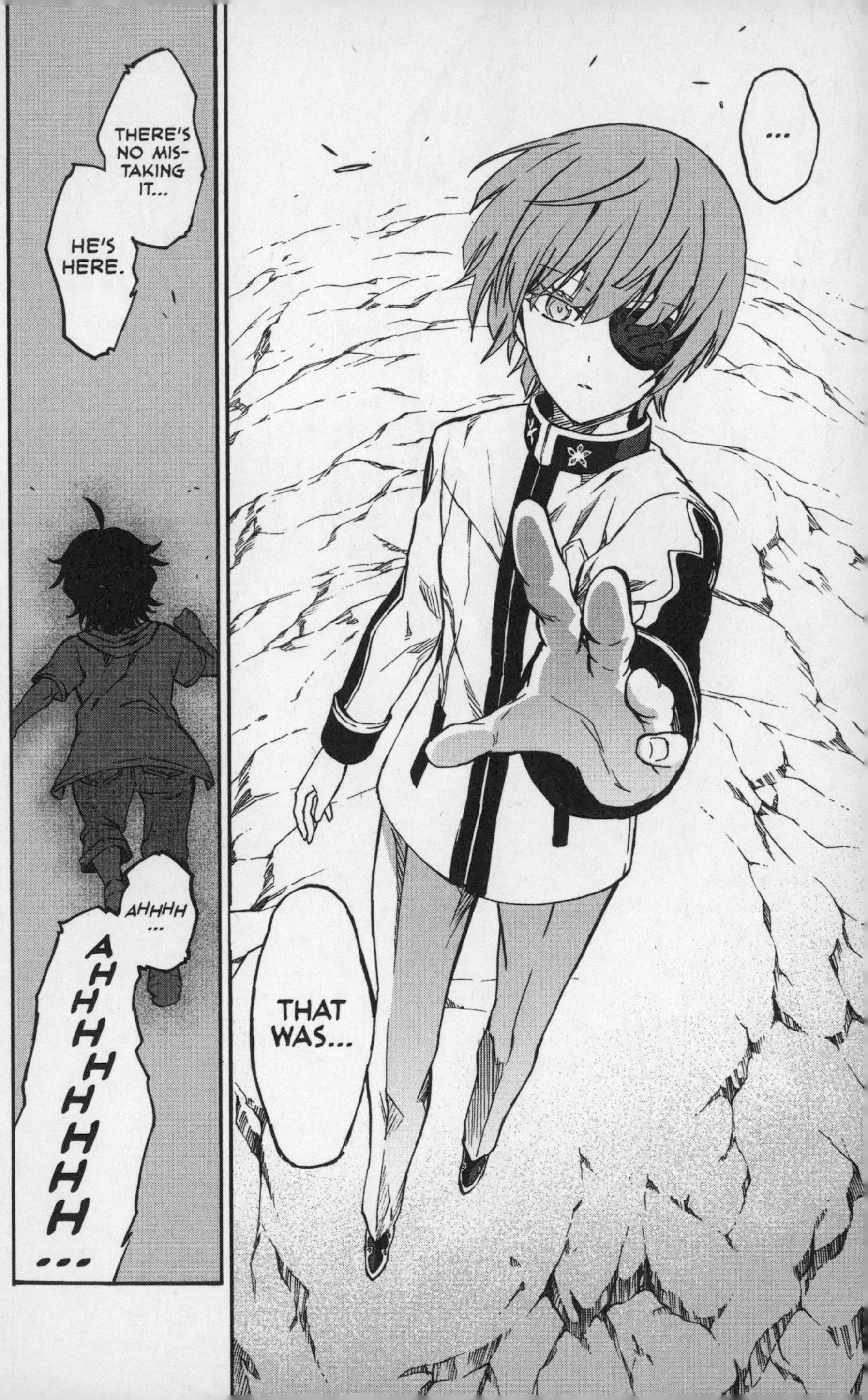
...
THAT WAS...
THERE'S NO MIS-TAKING IT...
HE'S HERE.
AHHHH...
AHHHHHHHHH...

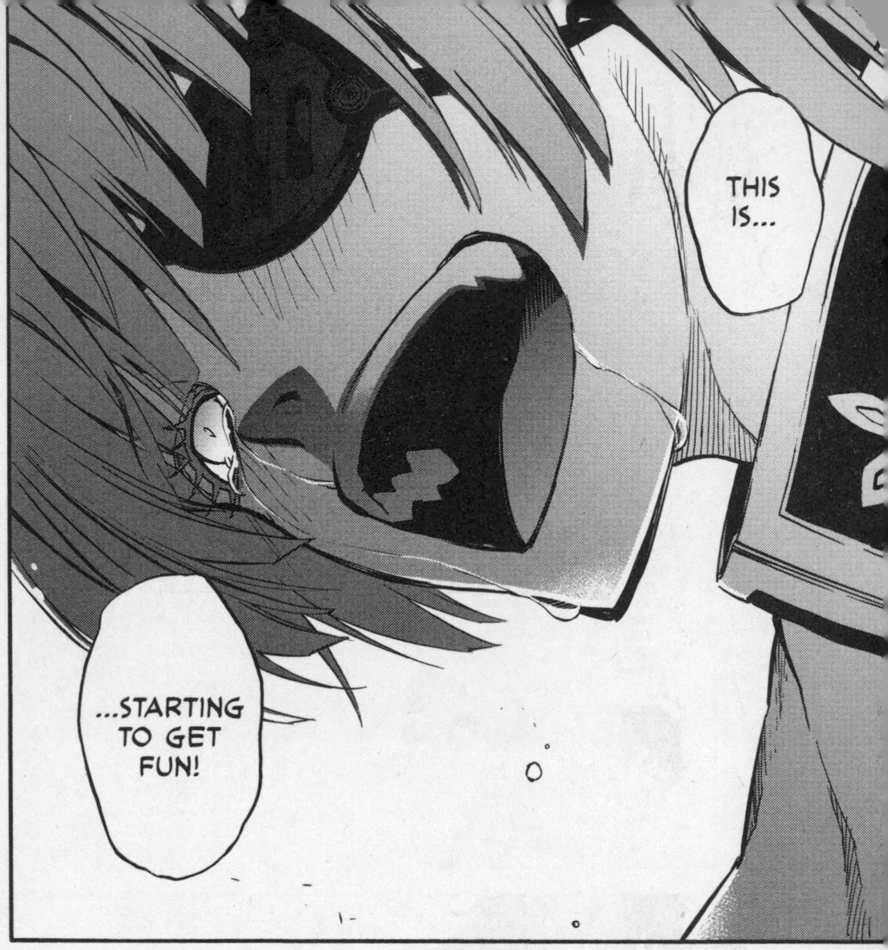
THIS IS...
...STARTING TO GET FUN!

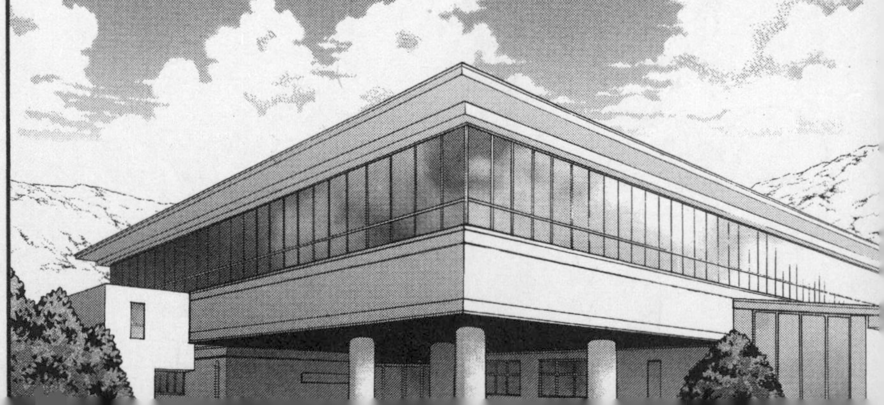

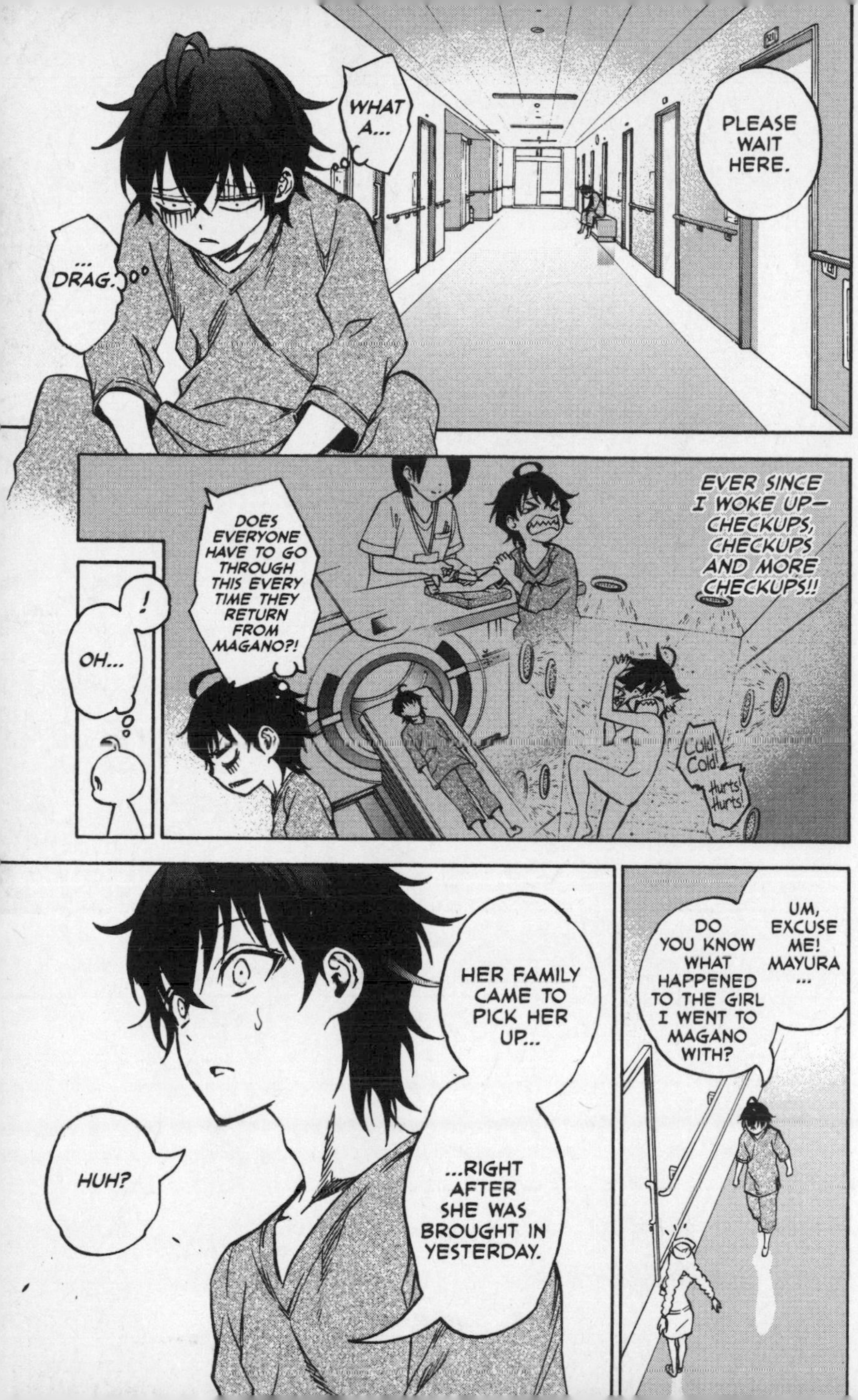
PLEASE WAIT HERE.
WHAT A...
...DRAG.
EVER SINCE I WOKE UP— CHECKUPS, CHECKUPS AND MORE CHECKUPS!!
Cold! Cold!
Hurts! Hurts!
DOES EVERYONE HAVE TO GO THROUGH THIS EVERY TIME THEY RETURN FROM MAGANO?!
!
OH...
UM, EXCUSE ME! MAYURA ...
DO YOU KNOW WHAT HAPPENED TO THE GIRL I WENT TO MAGANO WITH?
HER FAMILY CAME TO PICK HER UP...
...RIGHT AFTER SHE WAS BROUGHT IN YESTERDAY.
HUH?

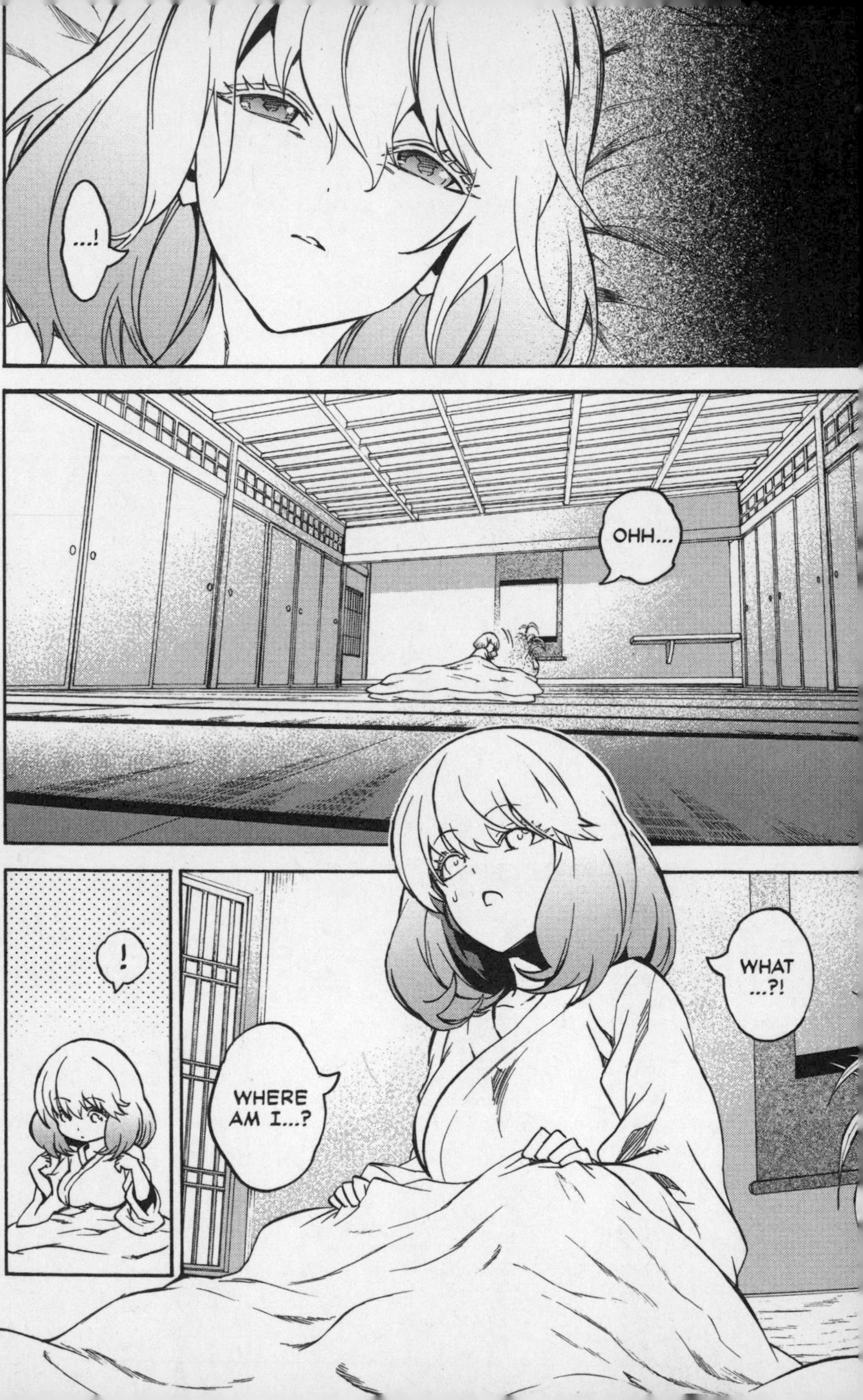
...!
OHH...
WHAT ...?!
WHERE AM I...?
!

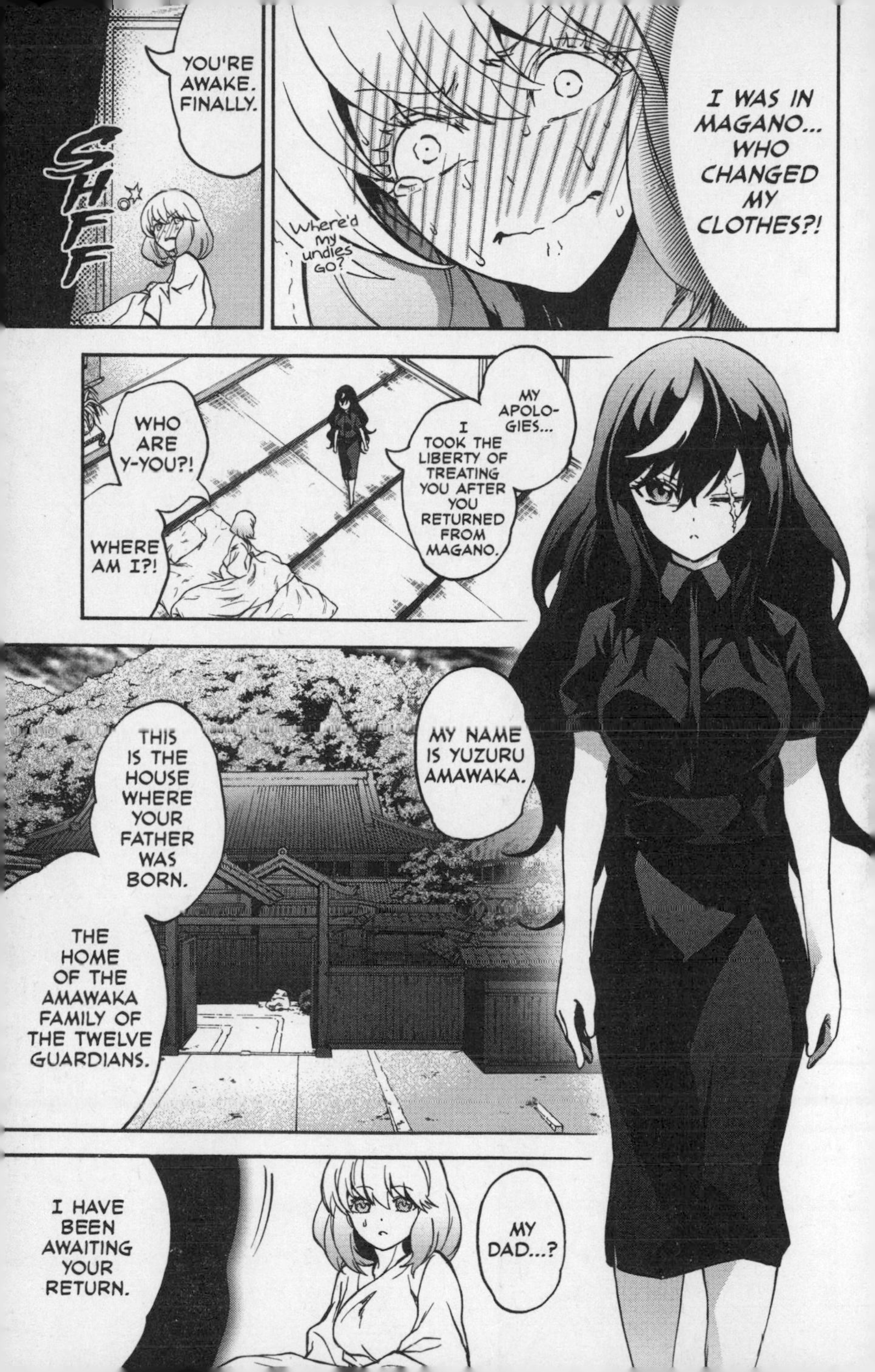
I WAS IN MAGANO... WHO CHANGED MY CLOTHES?!
Where'd my undies go?
YOU'RE AWAKE. FINALLY.
SHFF
WHO ARE Y-YOU?!
WHERE AM I?!
MY APOLOGIES... I TOOK THE LIBERTY OF TREATING YOU AFTER YOU RETURNED FROM MAGANO.
MY NAME IS YUZURU AMAWAKA.
THIS IS THE HOUSE WHERE YOUR FATHER WAS BORN.
THE HOME OF THE AMAWAKA FAMILY OF THE TWELVE GUARDIANS.
MY DAD...?
I HAVE BEEN AWAITING YOUR RETURN.

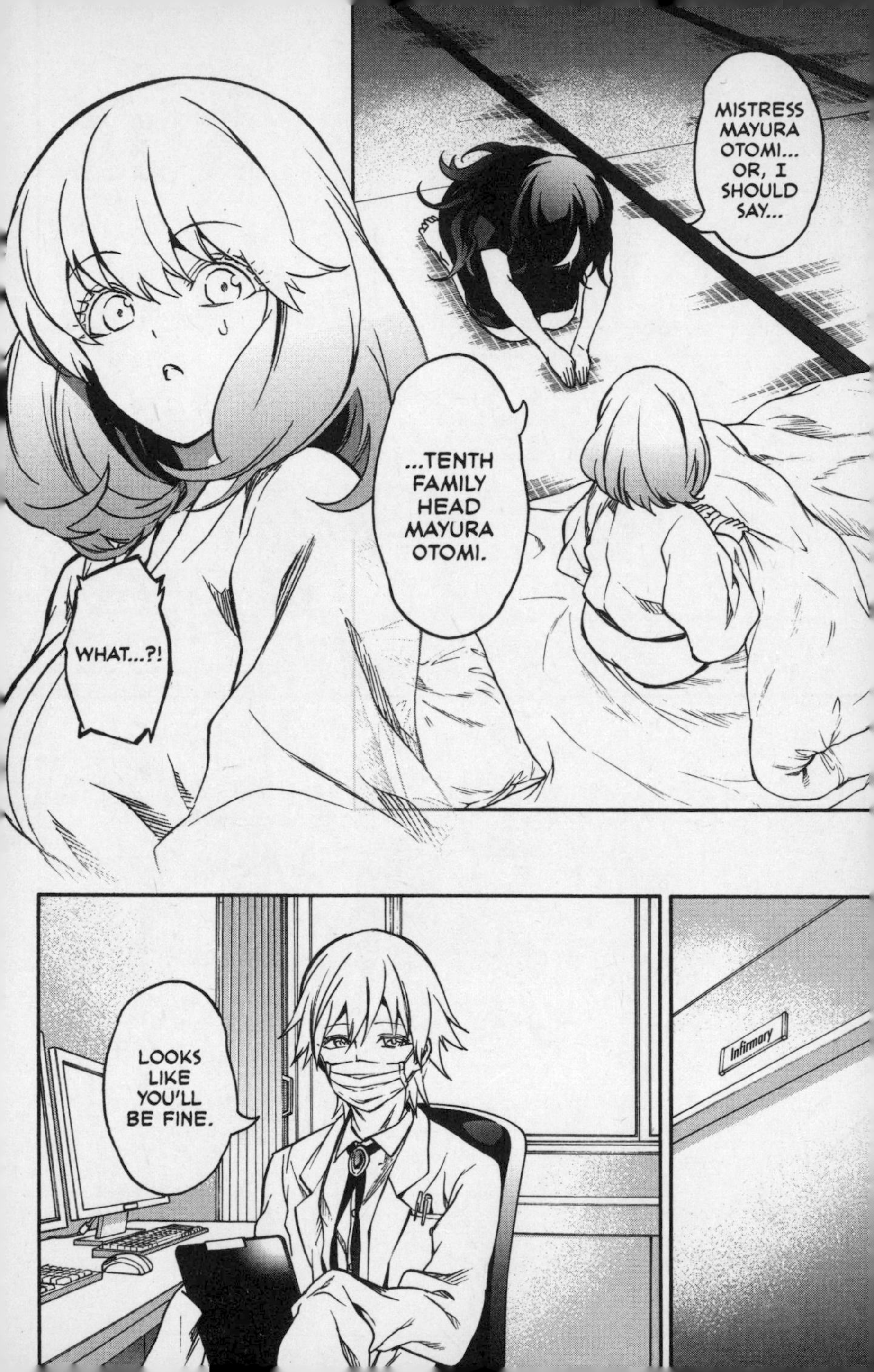
MISTRESS MAYURA OTOMI... OR, I SHOULD SAY...
...TENTH FAMILY HEAD MAYURA OTOMI.
WHAT...?!
Infirmary
LOOKS LIKE YOU'LL BE FINE.

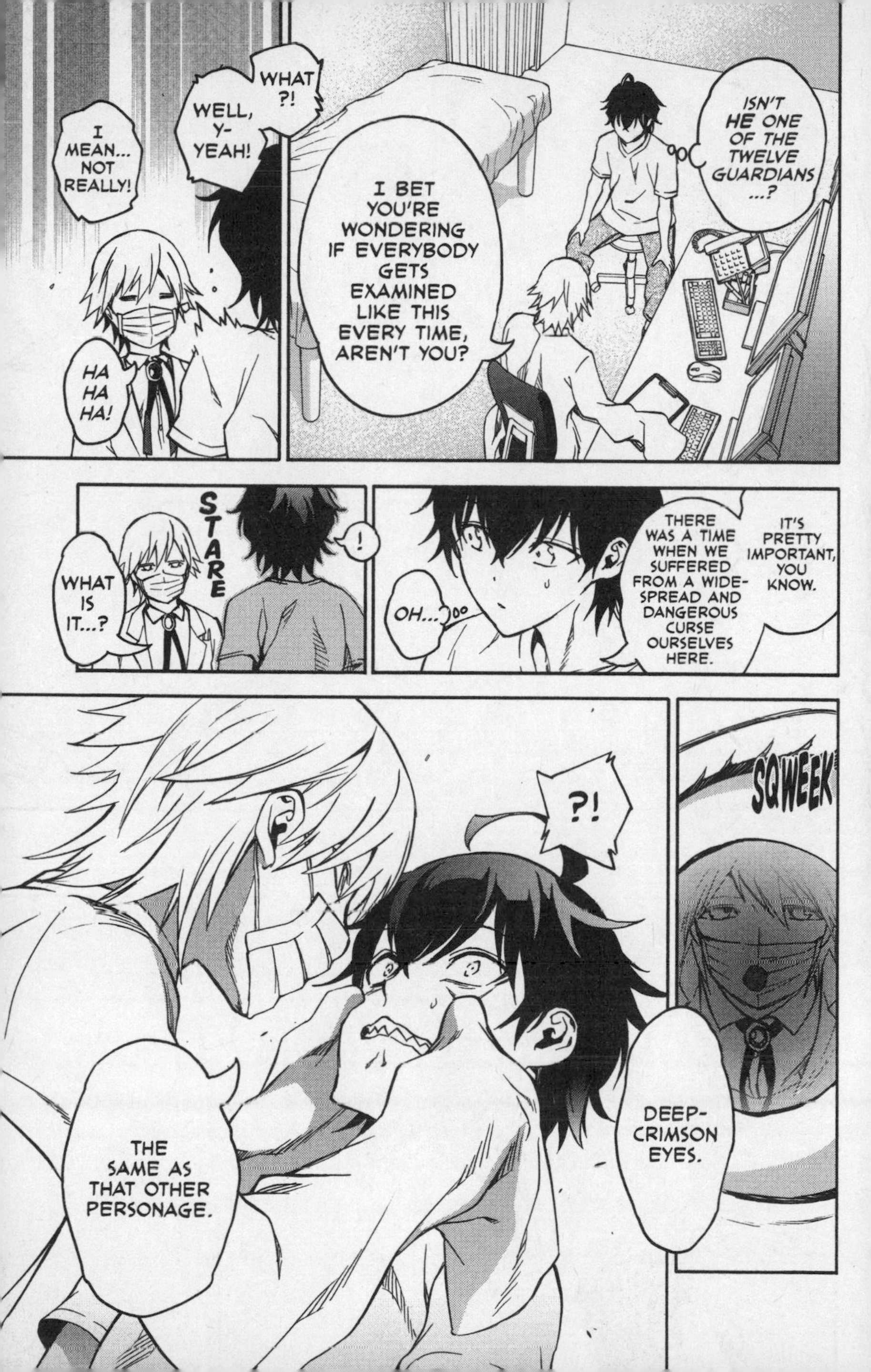
ISN'T HE ONE OF THE TWELVE GUARDIANS...?
I BET YOU'RE WONDERING IF EVERYBODY GETS EXAMINED LIKE THIS EVERY TIME, AREN'T YOU?
WHAT?!
WELL, Y-YEAH!
I MEAN... NOT REALLY!
HA HA HA!
IT'S PRETTY IMPORTANT, YOU KNOW.
THERE WAS A TIME WHEN WE SUFFERED FROM A WIDE-SPREAD AND DANGEROUS CURSE OURSELVES HERE.
OH...
!
STARE
WHAT IS IT...?
SQWEEK
DEEP-CRIMSON EYES.
?!
THE SAME AS THAT OTHER PERSONAGE.

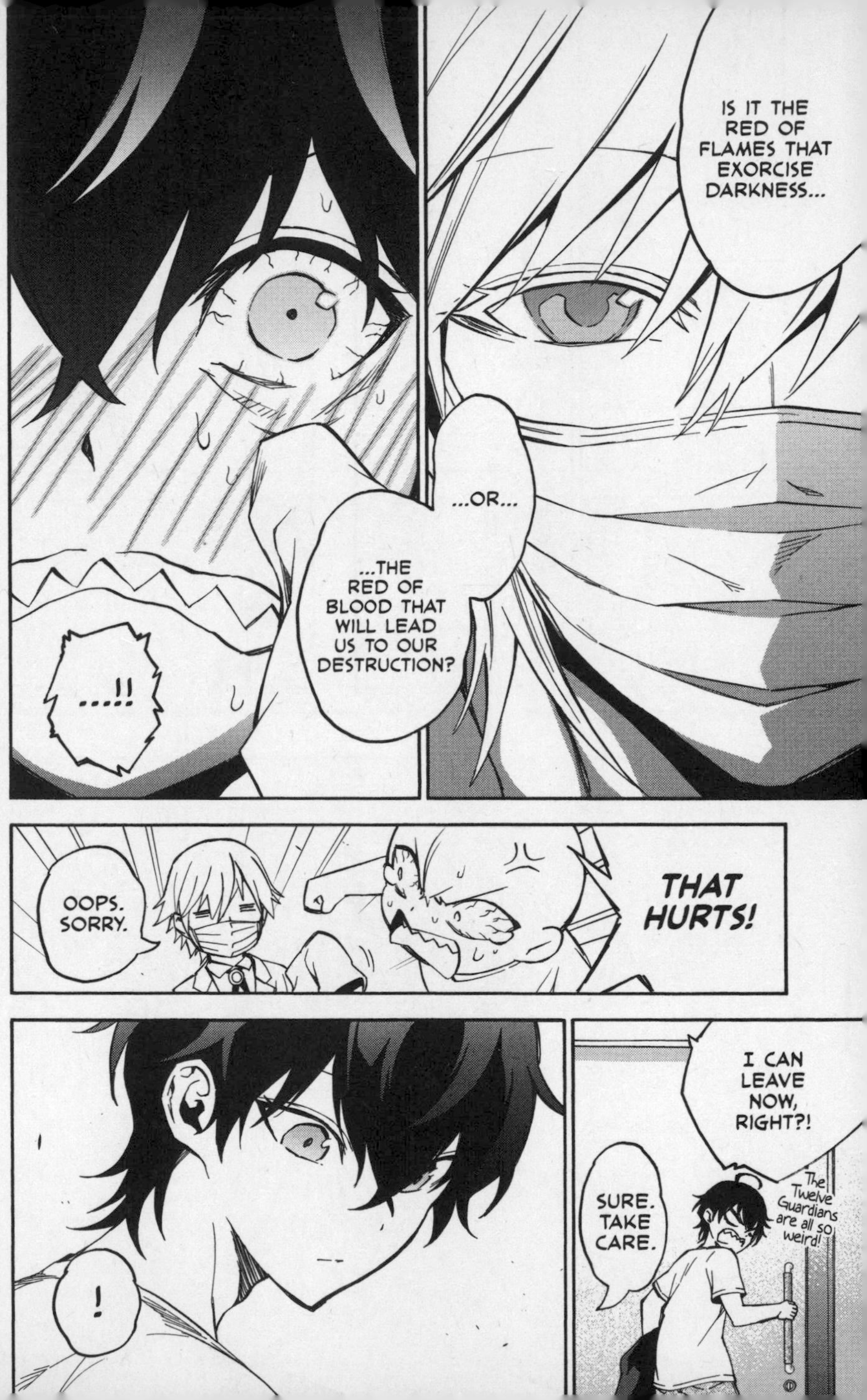
IS IT THE RED OF FLAMES THAT EXORCISE DARKNESS...
...OR...
...THE RED OF BLOOD THAT WILL LEAD US TO OUR DESTRUCTION?
...!!
THAT HURTS!
OOPS. SORRY.
I CAN LEAVE NOW, RIGHT?!
The Twelve Guardians are all so weird!
SURE. TAKE CARE.
!

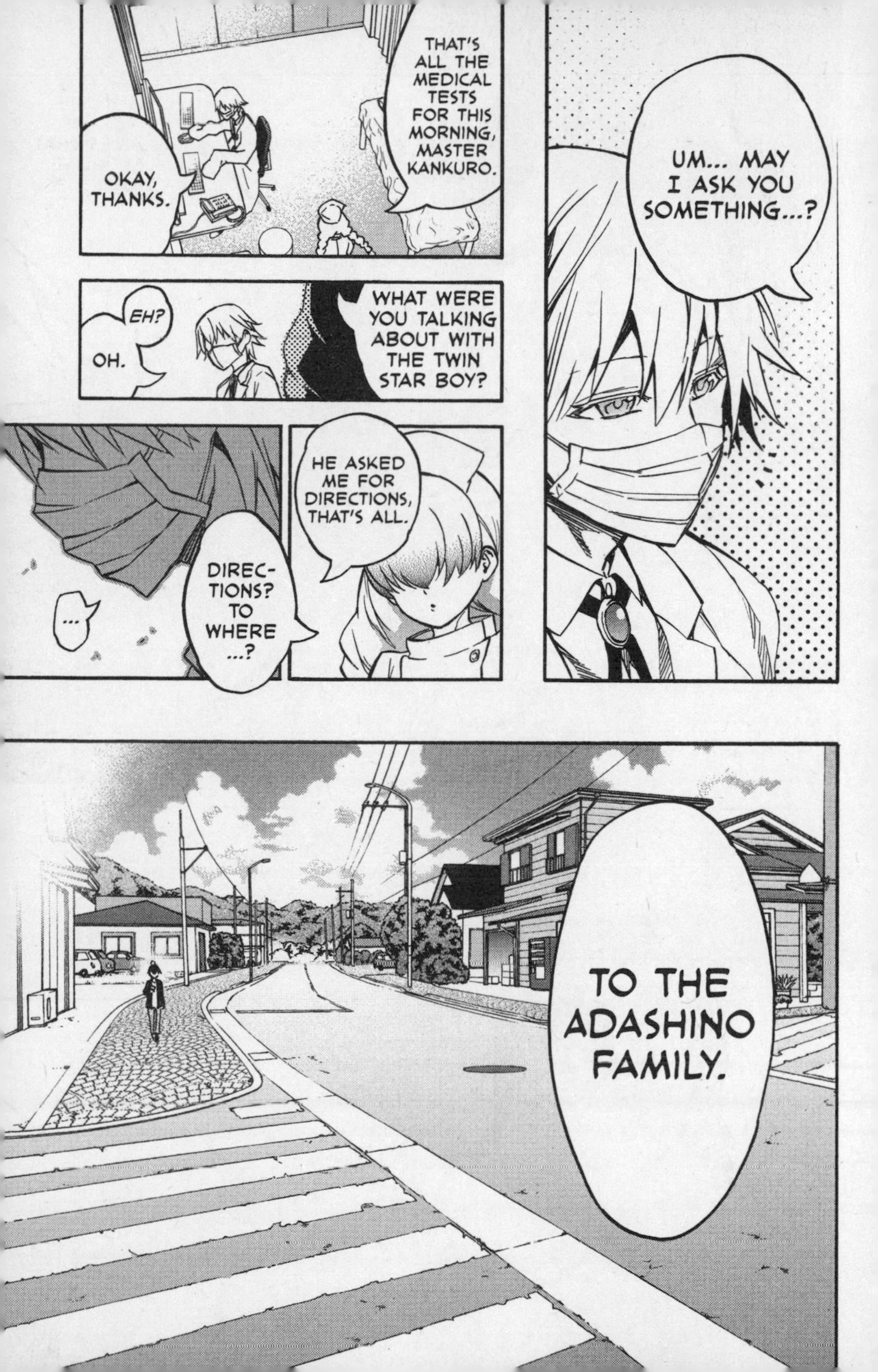
UM... MAY I ASK YOU SOMETHING...?
THAT'S ALL THE MEDICAL TESTS FOR THIS MORNING, MASTER KANKURO.
OKAY, THANKS.
WHAT WERE YOU TALKING ABOUT WITH THE TWIN STAR BOY?
EH?
OH.
HE ASKED ME FOR DIRECTIONS, THAT'S ALL.
DIREC-TIONS? TO WHERE ...?
...
TO THE ADASHINO FAMILY.

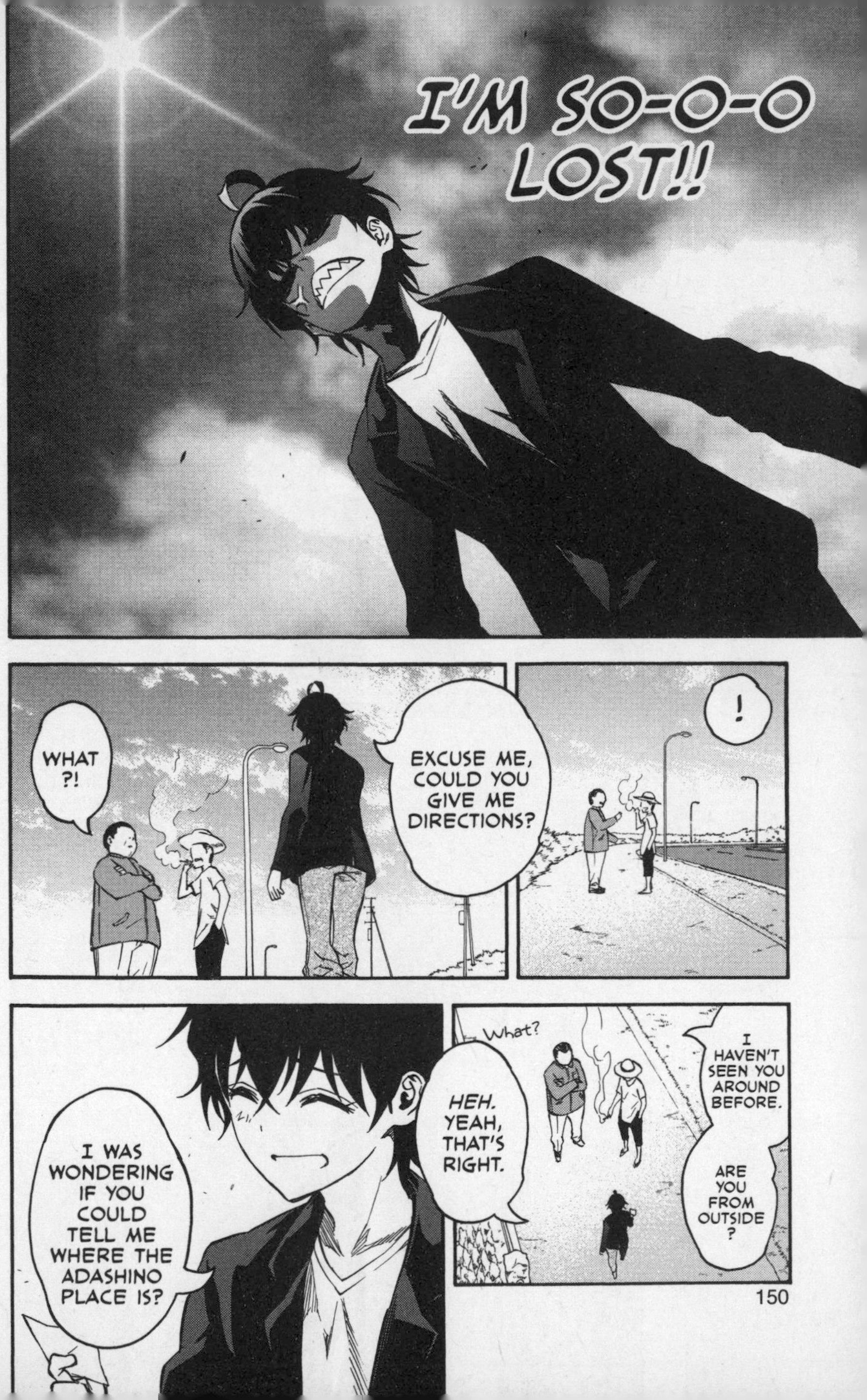
I'M SO-O-O LOST!!
!
EXCUSE ME, COULD YOU GIVE ME DIRECTIONS?
WHAT ?!
I HAVEN'T SEEN YOU AROUND BEFORE.
ARE YOU FROM OUTSIDE ?
What?
HEH. YEAH, THAT'S RIGHT.
I WAS WONDERING IF YOU COULD TELL ME WHERE THE ADASHINO PLACE IS?

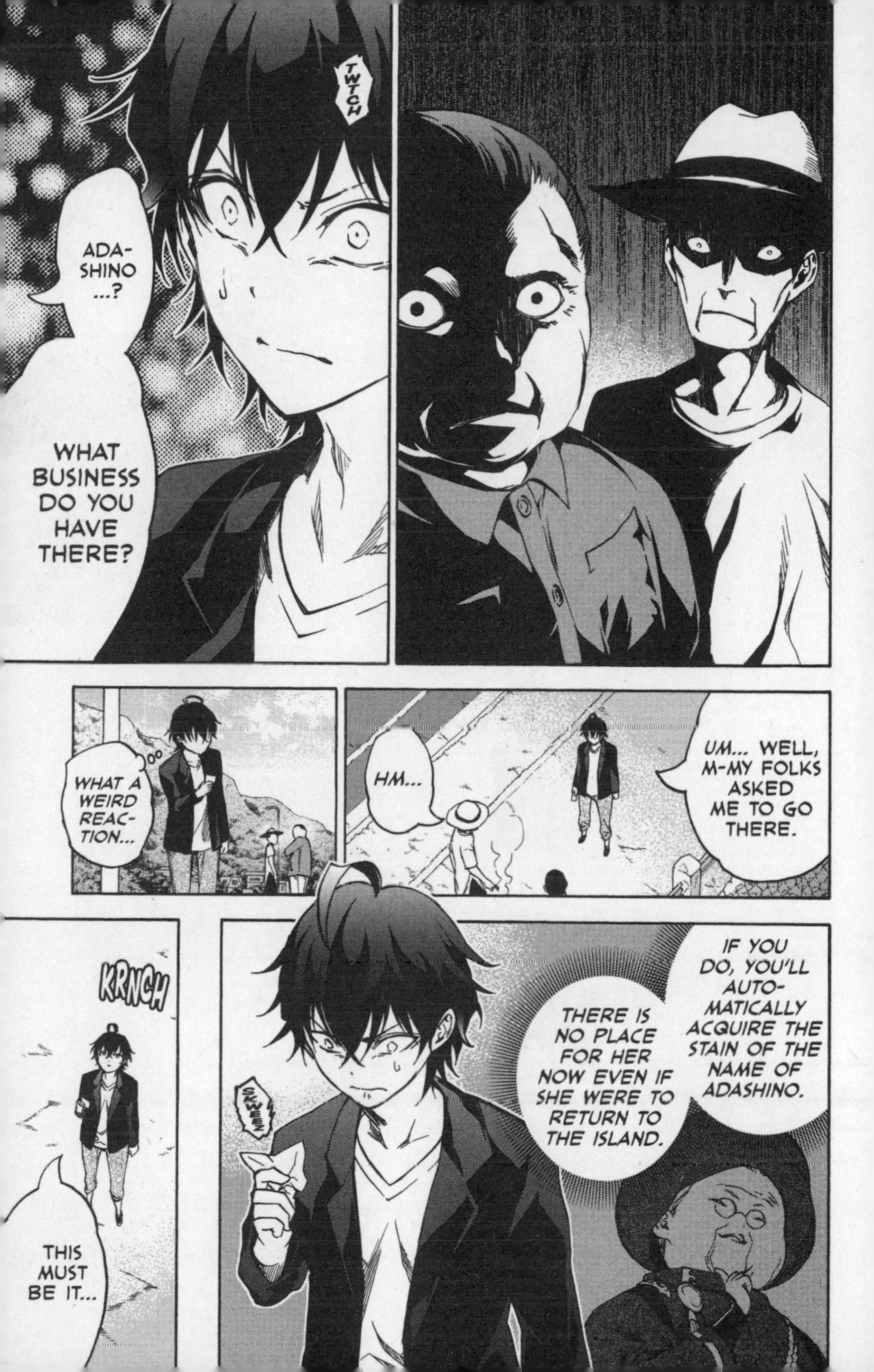
TWTCH
ADA-SHINO...?
WHAT BUSINESS DO YOU HAVE THERE?
UM... WELL, M-MY FOLKS ASKED ME TO GO THERE.
HM...
WHAT A WEIRD REACTION...
IF YOU DO, YOU'LL AUTOMATICALLY ACQUIRE THE STAIN OF THE NAME OF ADASHINO.
THERE IS NO PLACE FOR HER NOW EVEN IF SHE WERE TO RETURN TO THE ISLAND.
SKWEEZ
KRNCH
THIS MUST BE IT...

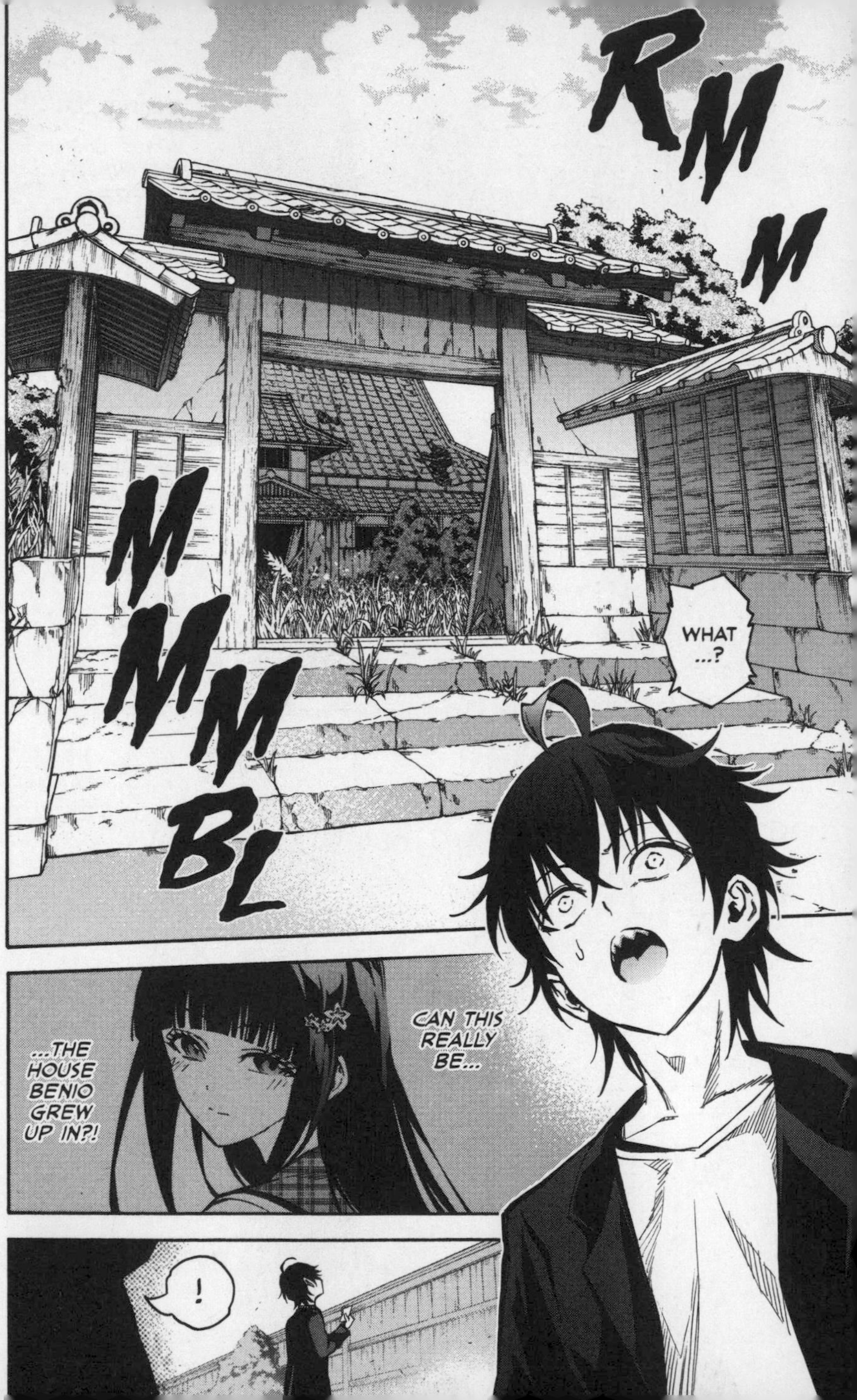
RMMM
MMMMBL
WHAT ...?
CAN THIS REALLY BE...
...THE HOUSE BENIO GREW UP IN?!
!

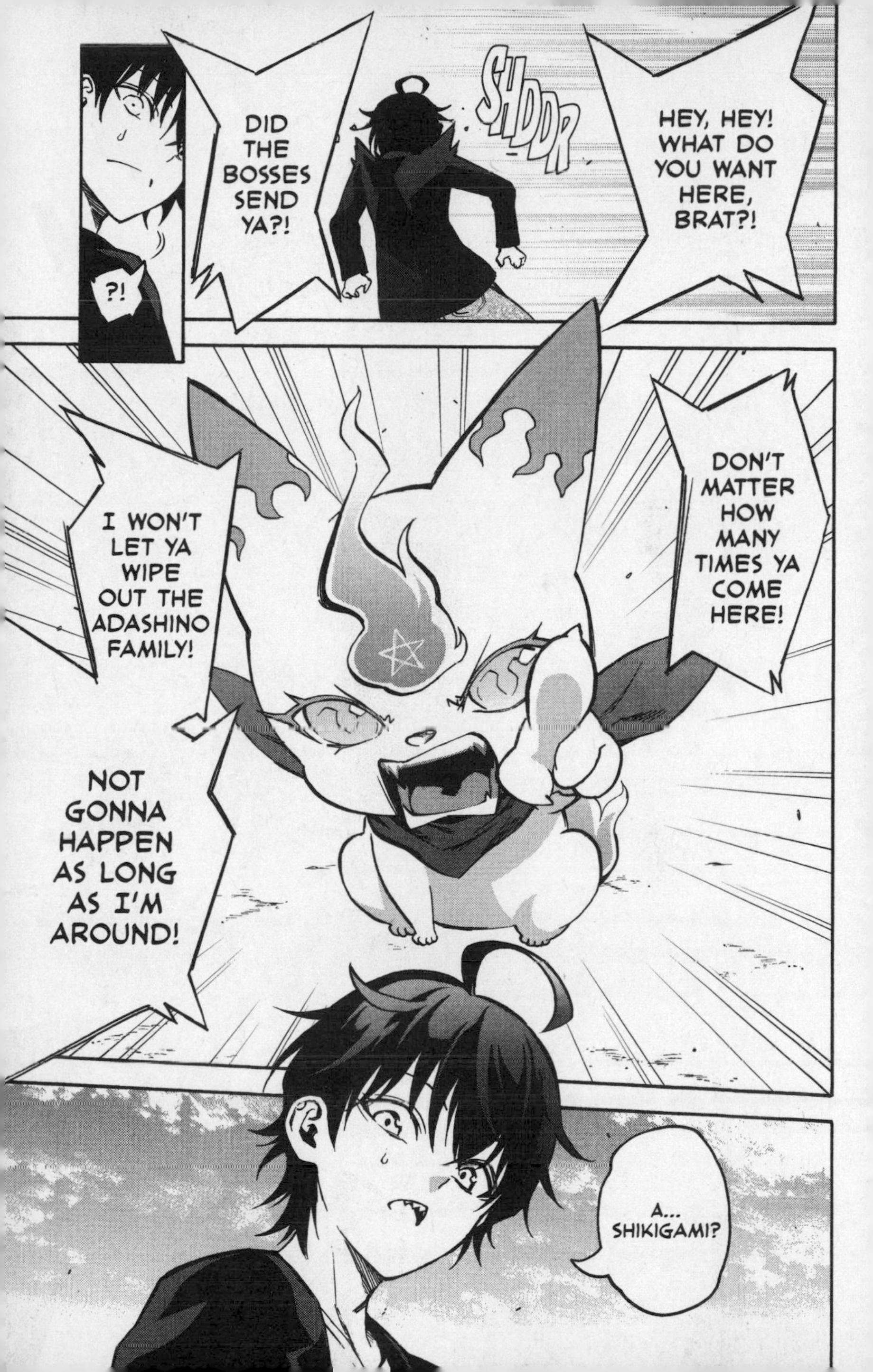
HEY, HEY! WHAT DO YOU WANT HERE, BRAT?!
SHDDR
DID THE BOSSES SEND YA?!
?!
DON'T MATTER HOW MANY TIMES YA COME HERE!
I WON'T LET YA WIPE OUT THE ADASHINO FAMILY!
NOT GONNA HAPPEN AS LONG AS I'M AROUND!
A... SHIKIGAMI?

Twin Star Exorcists

ONMYOJI

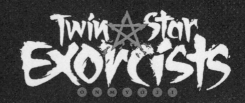

#37: The Little Giant of Adashino

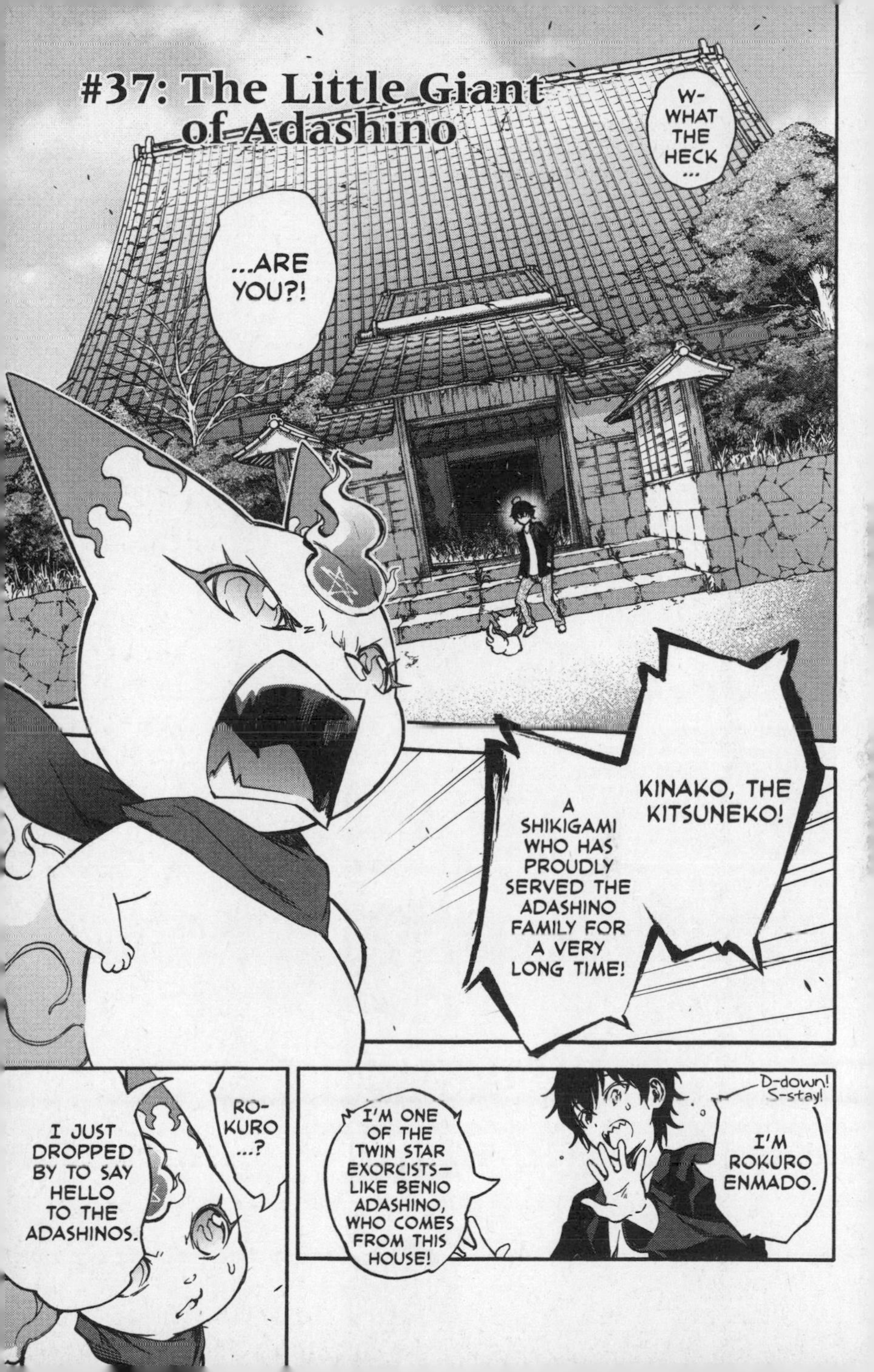
W-WHAT THE HECK...
...ARE YOU?!
KINAKO, THE KITSUNEKO!
A SHIKIGAMI WHO HAS PROUDLY SERVED THE ADASHINO FAMILY FOR A VERY LONG TIME!
D-down! S-stay!
I'M ROKURO ENMADO.
I'M ONE OF THE TWIN STAR EXORCISTS—LIKE BENIO ADASHINO, WHO COMES FROM THIS HOUSE!
RO-KURO...?
I JUST DROPPED BY TO SAY HELLO TO THE ADASHINOS.

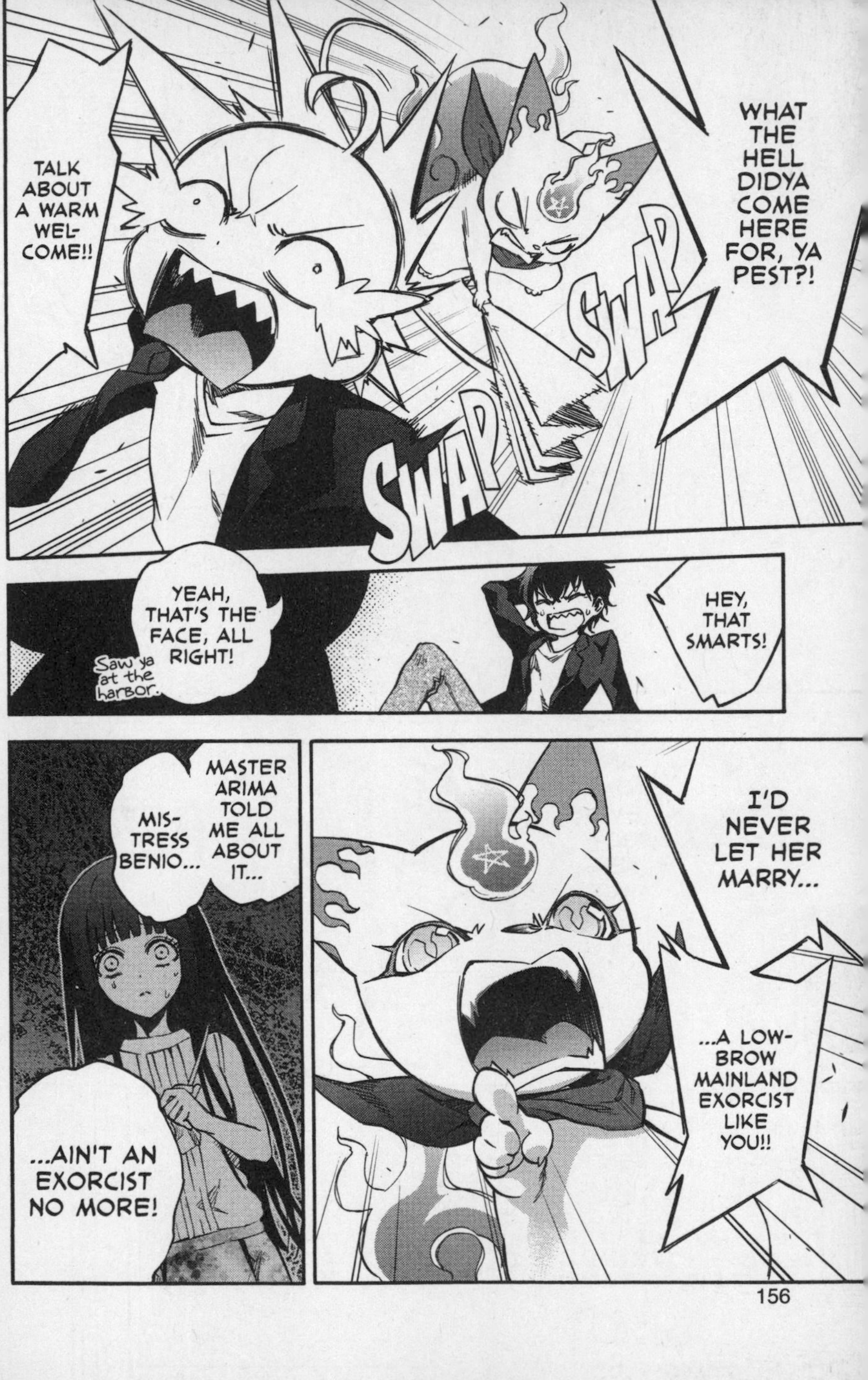
WHAT THE HELL DIDYA COME HERE FOR, YA PEST?!
SWAP
SWAP
SWAP
TALK ABOUT A WARM WEL-COME!!
HEY, THAT SMARTS!
YEAH, THAT'S THE FACE, ALL RIGHT!
Saw ya at the harbor.
I'D NEVER LET HER MARRY...
...A LOW-BROW MAINLAND EXORCIST LIKE YOU!!
MASTER ARIMA TOLD ME ALL ABOUT IT...
MIS-TRESS BENIO...
...AIN'T AN EXORCIST NO MORE!

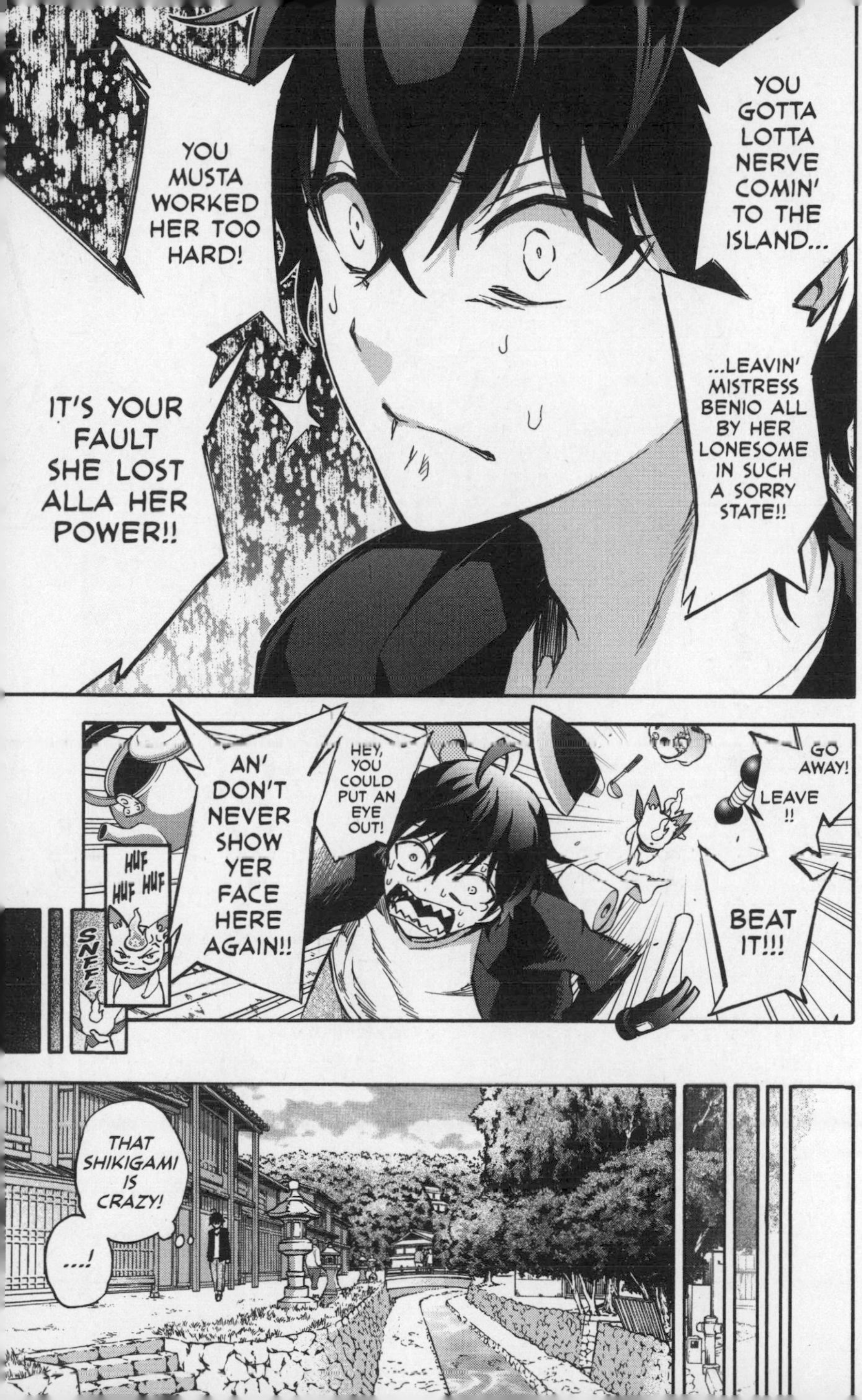
YOU GOTTA LOTTA NERVE COMIN' TO THE ISLAND...
...LEAVIN' MISTRESS BENIO ALL BY HER LONESOME IN SUCH A SORRY STATE!!
YOU MUSTA WORKED HER TOO HARD!
IT'S YOUR FAULT SHE LOST ALLA HER POWER!!
GO AWAY!
LEAVE!!
BEAT IT!!!
HEY, YOU COULD PUT AN EYE OUT!
AN' DON'T NEVER SHOW YER FACE HERE AGAIN!!
HUF HUF HUF
SNFFL
THAT SHIKIGAMI IS CRAZY!
...!

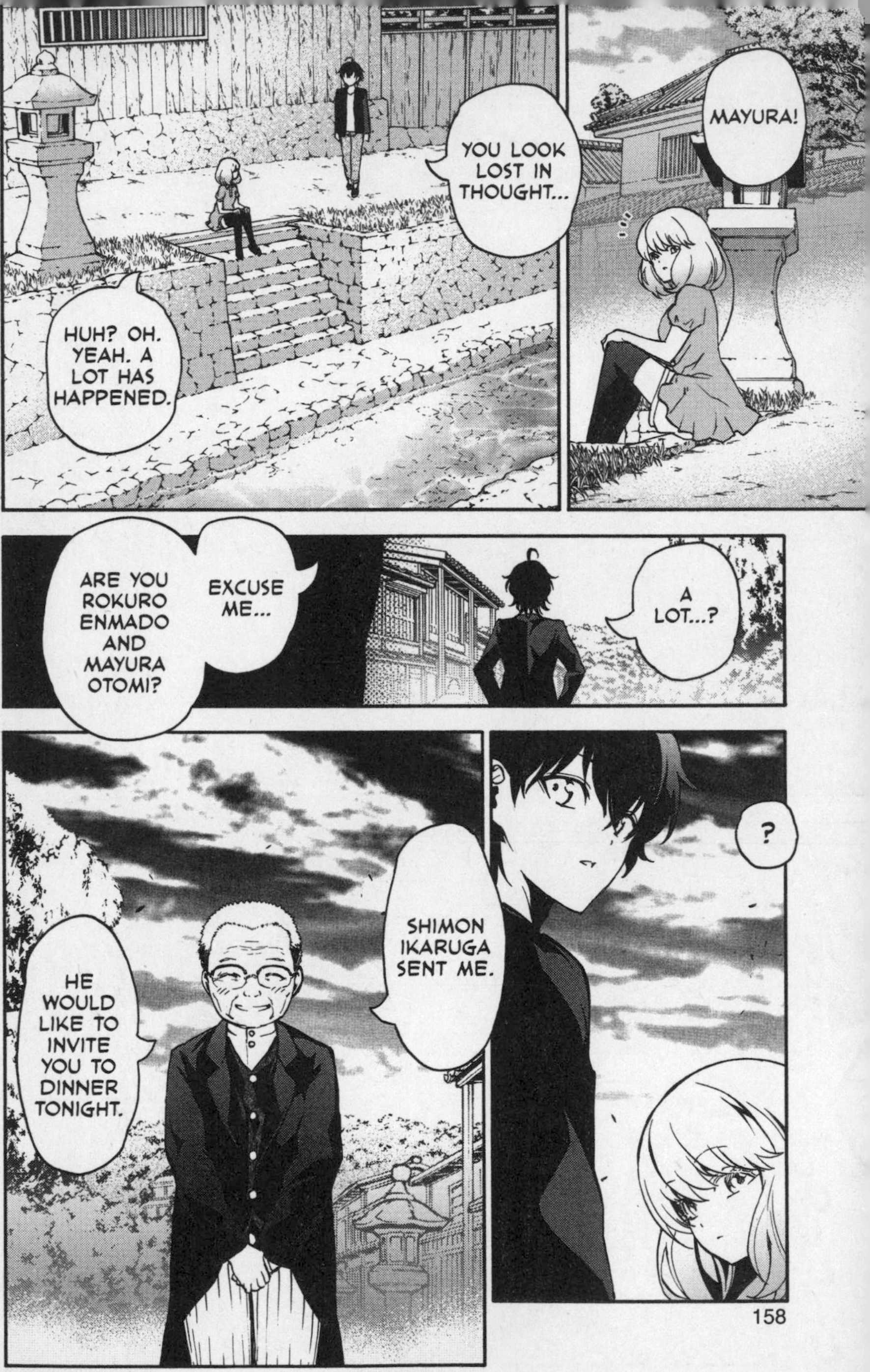
MAYURA!
YOU LOOK LOST IN THOUGHT...
HUH? OH. YEAH. A LOT HAS HAPPENED.
A LOT...?
EXCUSE ME...
ARE YOU ROKURO ENMADO AND MAYURA OTOMI?
?
SHIMON IKARUGA SENT ME.
HE WOULD LIKE TO INVITE YOU TO DINNER TONIGHT.

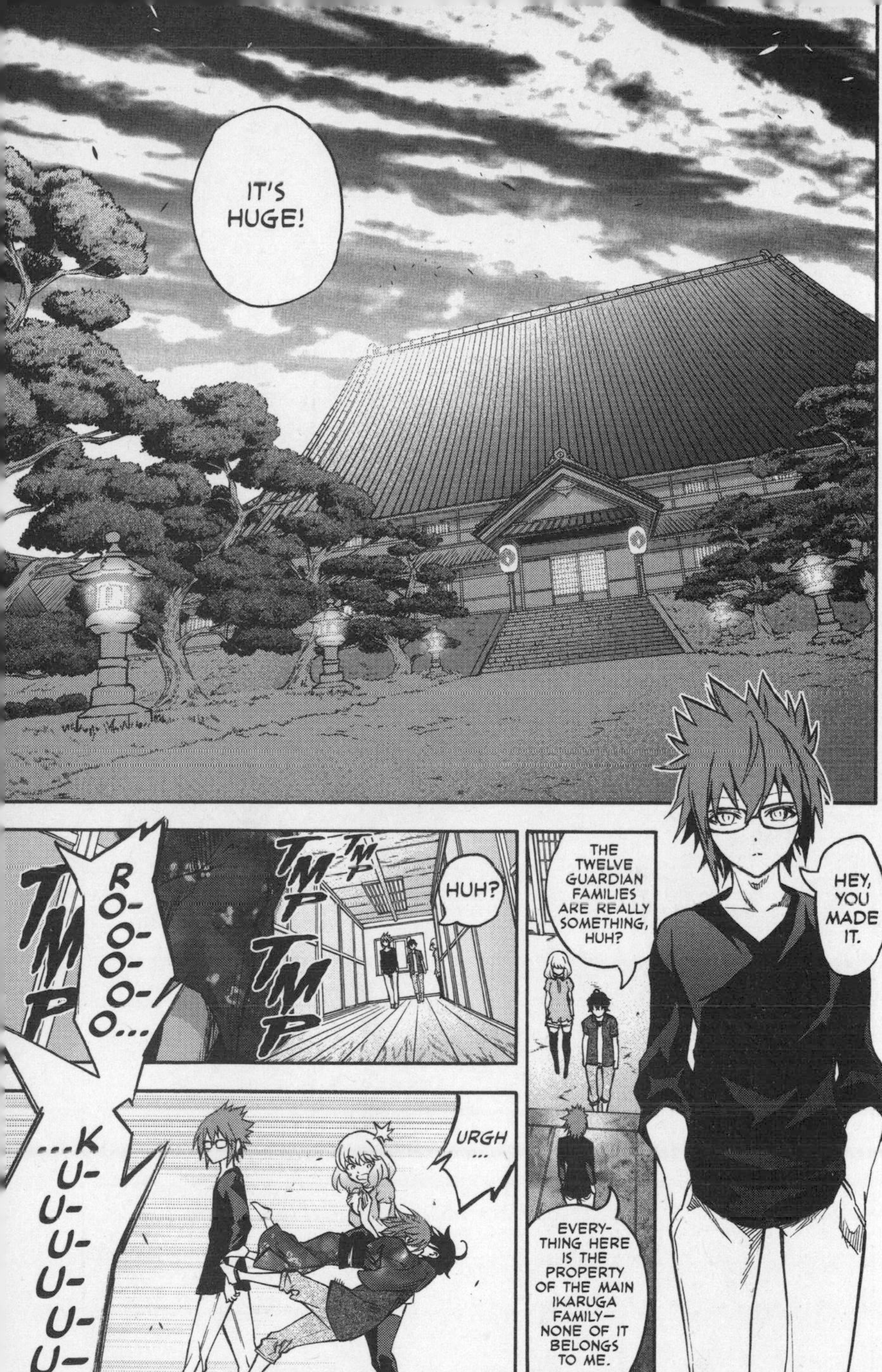
IT'S HUGE!
HEY, YOU MADE IT.
THE TWELVE GUARDIAN FAMILIES ARE REALLY SOMETHING, HUH?
EVERYTHING HERE IS THE PROPERTY OF THE MAIN IKARUGA FAMILY—NONE OF IT BELONGS TO ME.
TMP
HUH?
TMP TMP
RO-O-O-O-O-O...
TMP
URGH...
...KU-U-U-U-U-U-U–

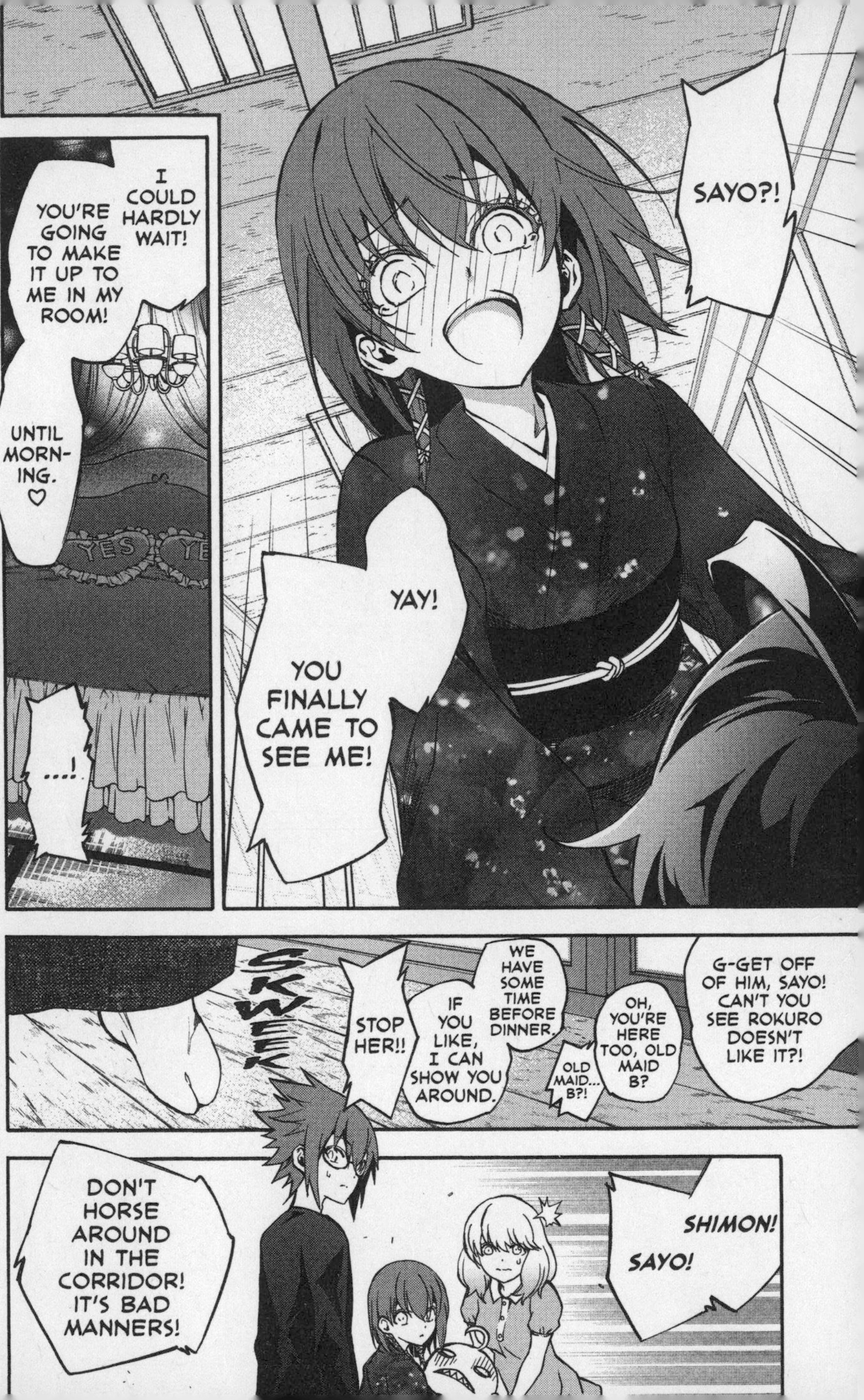
SAYO?!
YAY!
YOU FINALLY CAME TO SEE ME!
I COULD HARDLY WAIT!
YOU'RE GOING TO MAKE IT UP TO ME IN MY ROOM!
UNTIL MORNING. ♡
...!
G-GET OFF OF HIM, SAYO! CAN'T YOU SEE ROKURO DOESN'T LIKE IT?!
OH, YOU'RE HERE TOO, OLD MAID B?
OLD MAID... B?!
WE HAVE SOME TIME BEFORE DINNER.
IF YOU LIKE, I CAN SHOW YOU AROUND.
STOP HER!!
SKWEEK
SHIMON!
SAYO!
DON'T HORSE AROUND IN THE CORRIDOR! IT'S BAD MANNERS!

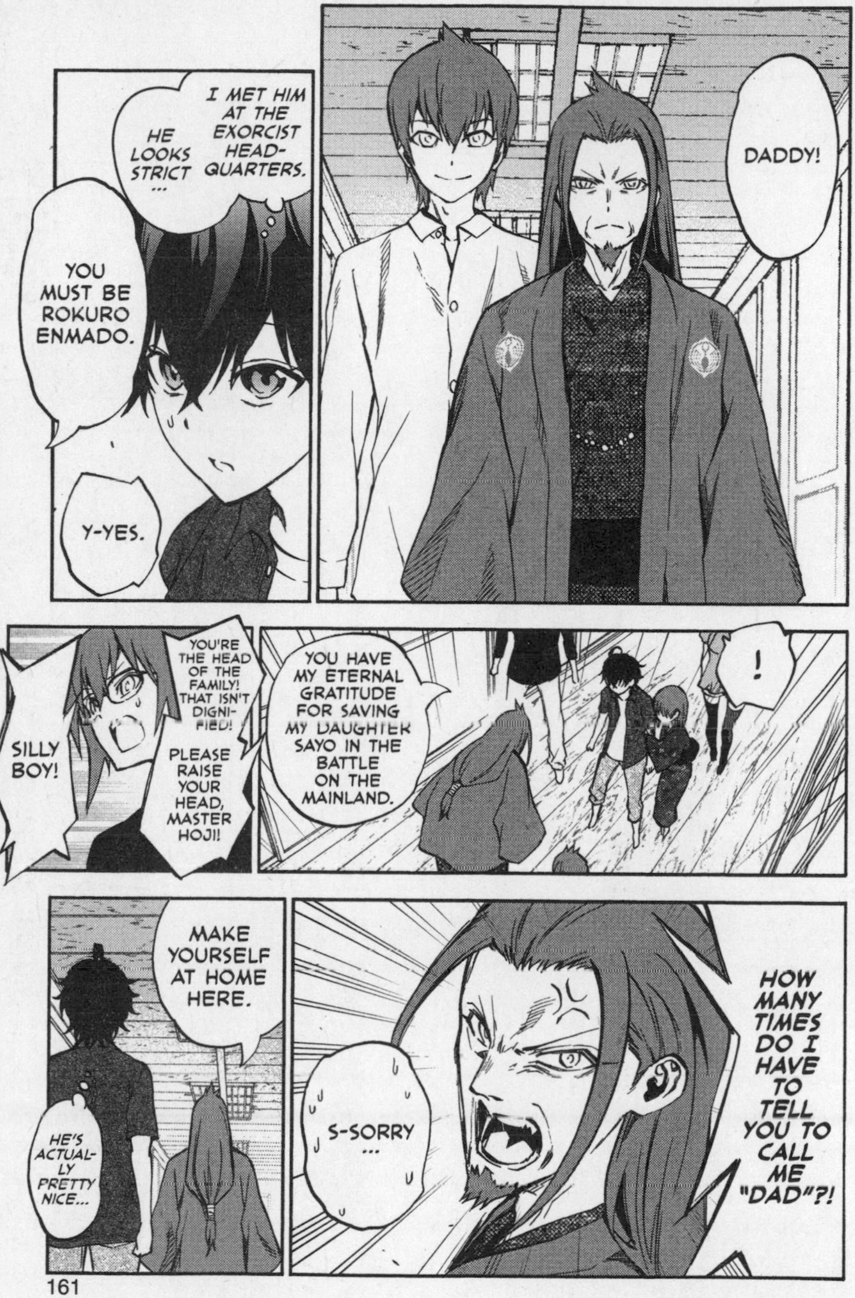
DADDY!
I MET HIM AT THE EXORCIST HEAD-QUARTERS.
HE LOOKS STRICT ...
YOU MUST BE ROKURO ENMADO.
Y-YES.
!
YOU HAVE MY ETERNAL GRATITUDE FOR SAVING MY DAUGHTER SAYO IN THE BATTLE ON THE MAINLAND.
YOU'RE THE HEAD OF THE FAMILY! THAT ISN'T DIGNI-FIED!
PLEASE RAISE YOUR HEAD, MASTER HOJI!
SILLY BOY!
HOW MANY TIMES DO I HAVE TO TELL YOU TO CALL ME "DAD"?!
S-SORRY ...
MAKE YOURSELF AT HOME HERE.
HE'S ACTUAL-LY PRETTY NICE...

I'M THE ELDEST SON, KEIJI IKARUGA.

THANK YOU FOR TAKING CARE OF SHIMON TOO.

IMPRESSIVE. IT'S NOT EASY GETTING OUR EMOTIONALLY REPRESSED FATHER TO SHOW APPRECIATION, YOU KNOW.

I'M PROUD TO HAVE A BROTHER LIKE SHIMON!

P-PLEASE STOP, YOUNG MASTER KEIJI...

SHIMON'S OLDER BROTHER?!

I'M THE OFFICIAL HEIR OF THE IKARUGA FAMILY...

...BUT SHIMON IS FAR MORE TALENTED THAN ME.

ANYWAY, LET'S SET ASIDE FORMALITY TODAY!

SORRY, SORRY...

HOW MANY TIMES DO I HAVE TO TELL YOU TO CALL ME "BIG BROTHER"?!!

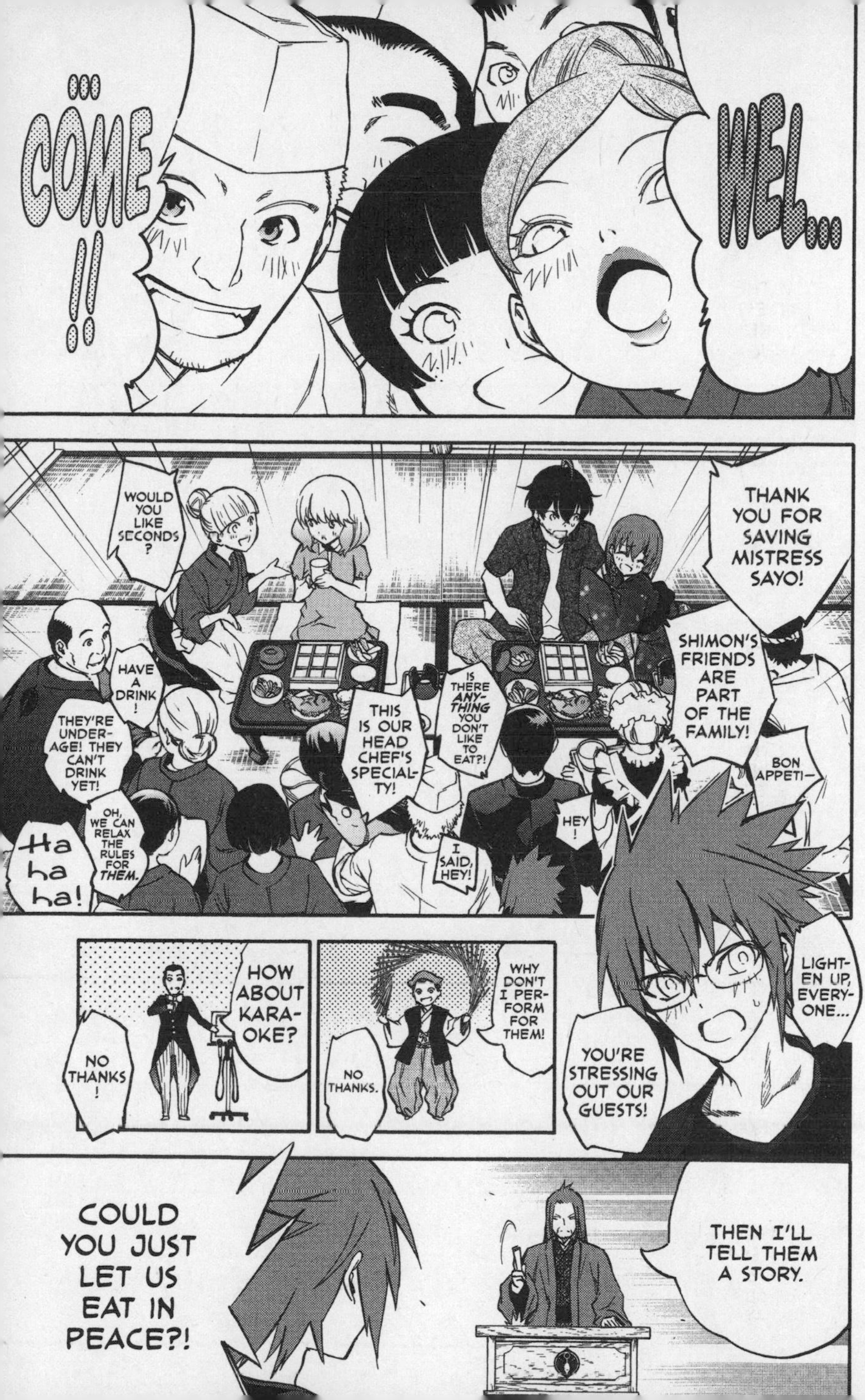
WEL...
...COME!!
THANK YOU FOR SAVING MISTRESS SAYO!
SHIMON'S FRIENDS ARE PART OF THE FAMILY!
BON APPETI—
IS THERE ANYTHING YOU DON'T LIKE TO EAT?!
HEY!
I SAID, HEY!
THIS IS OUR HEAD CHEF'S SPECIAL-TY!
WOULD YOU LIKE SECONDS?
HAVE A DRINK!
THEY'RE UNDER-AGE! THEY CAN'T DRINK YET!
OH, WE CAN RELAX THE RULES FOR THEM.
Ha ha ha!
LIGHT-EN UP, EVERY-ONE...
YOU'RE STRESSING OUT OUR GUESTS!
WHY DON'T I PER-FORM FOR THEM!
NO THANKS.
HOW ABOUT KARA-OKE?
NO THANKS!
THEN I'LL TELL THEM A STORY.
COULD YOU JUST LET US EAT IN PEACE?!

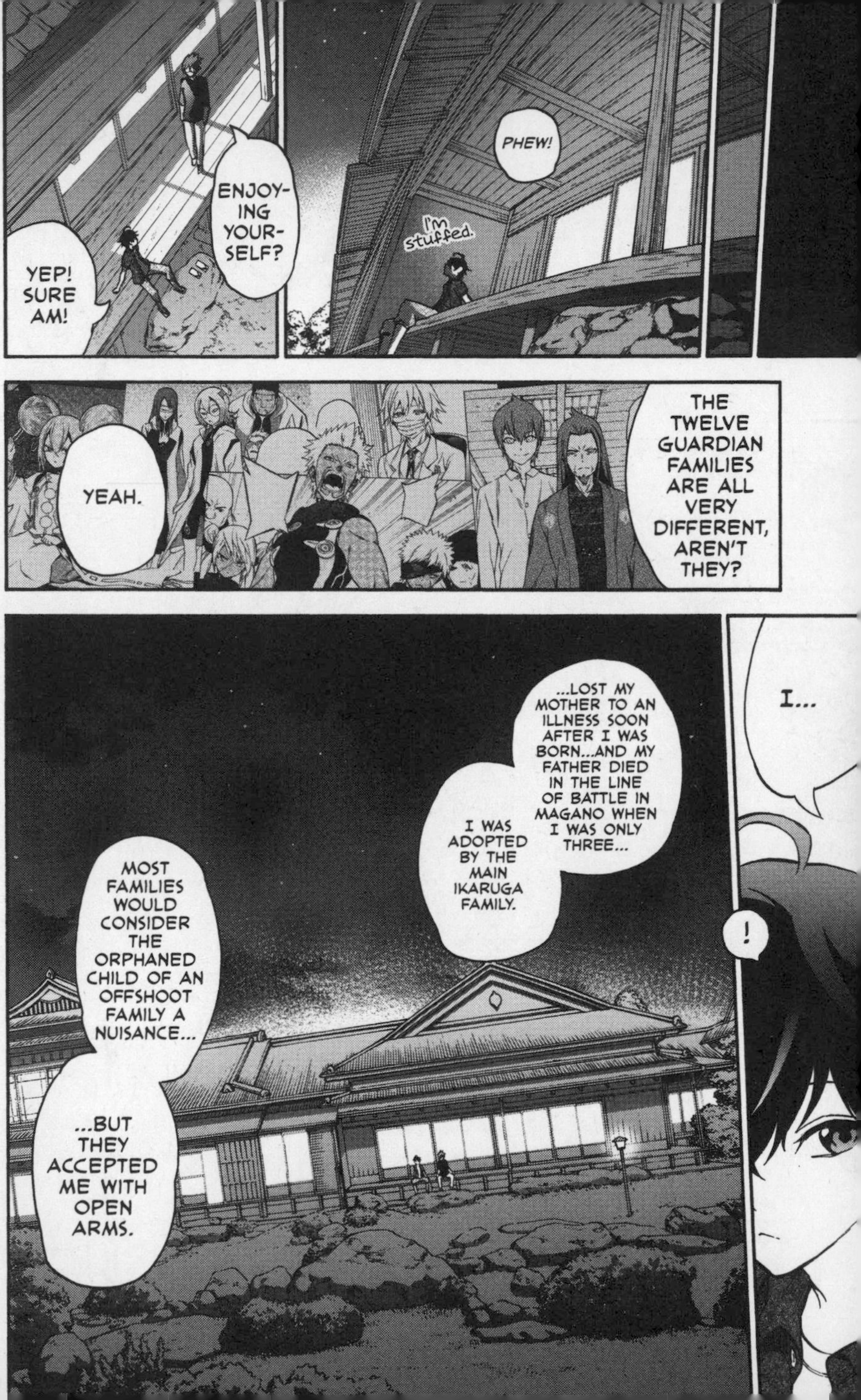
PHEW!
I'm stuffed.
ENJOYING YOURSELF?
YEP! SURE AM!
THE TWELVE GUARDIAN FAMILIES ARE ALL VERY DIFFERENT, AREN'T THEY?
YEAH.
I...
!
...LOST MY MOTHER TO AN ILLNESS SOON AFTER I WAS BORN...AND MY FATHER DIED IN THE LINE OF BATTLE IN MAGANO WHEN I WAS ONLY THREE...
I WAS ADOPTED BY THE MAIN IKARUGA FAMILY.
MOST FAMILIES WOULD CONSIDER THE ORPHANED CHILD OF AN OFFSHOOT FAMILY A NUISANCE...
...BUT THEY ACCEPTED ME WITH OPEN ARMS.

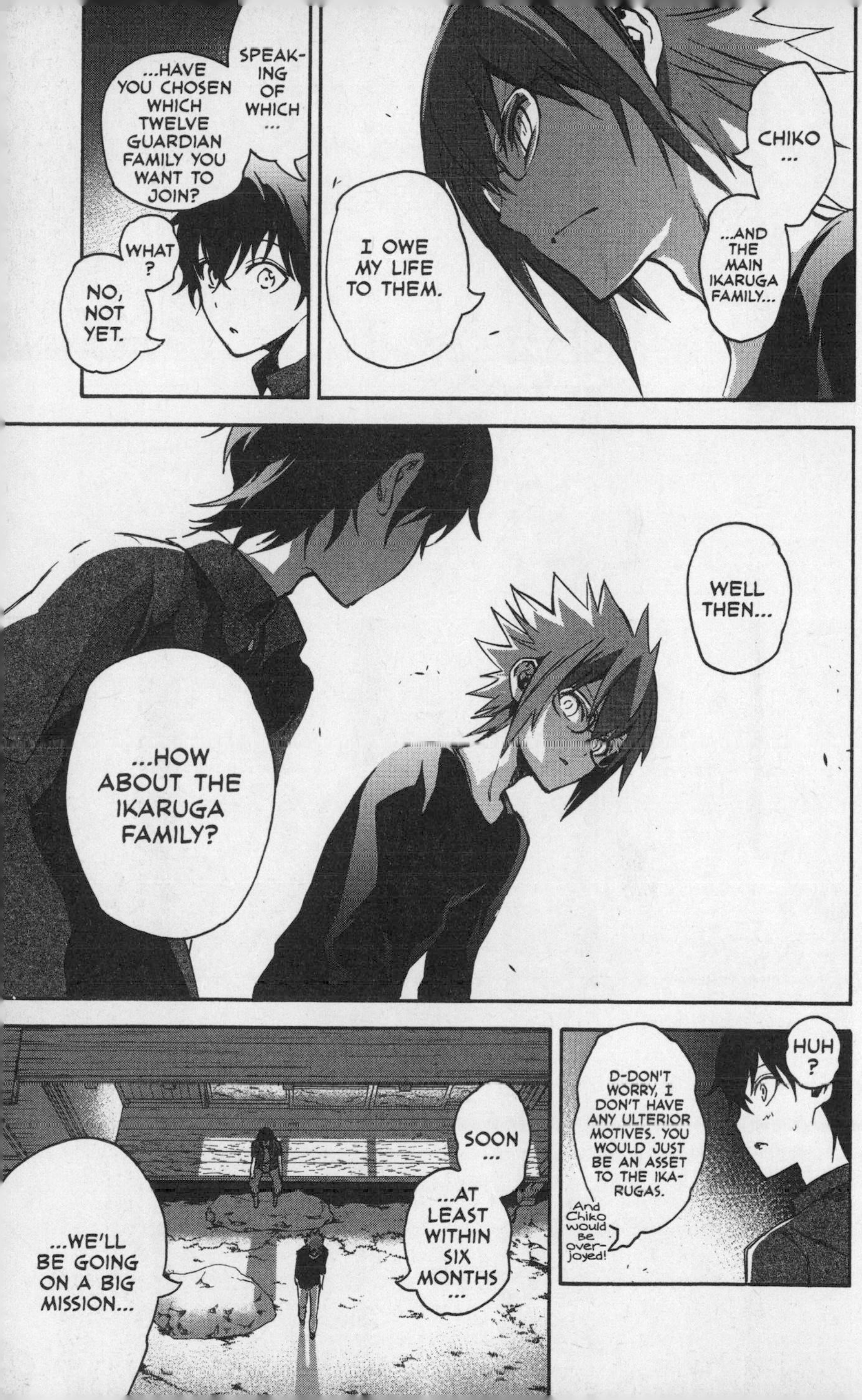
CHIKO...
...AND THE MAIN IKARUGA FAMILY...
I OWE MY LIFE TO THEM.
SPEAKING OF WHICH...
...HAVE YOU CHOSEN WHICH TWELVE GUARDIAN FAMILY YOU WANT TO JOIN?
WHAT?
NO, NOT YET.
WELL THEN...
...HOW ABOUT THE IKARUGA FAMILY?
HUH?
D-DON'T WORRY, I DON'T HAVE ANY ULTERIOR MOTIVES. YOU WOULD JUST BE AN ASSET TO THE IKARUGAS.
And Chiko would be overjoyed!
SOON...
...AT LEAST WITHIN SIX MONTHS...
...WE'LL BE GOING ON A BIG MISSION...

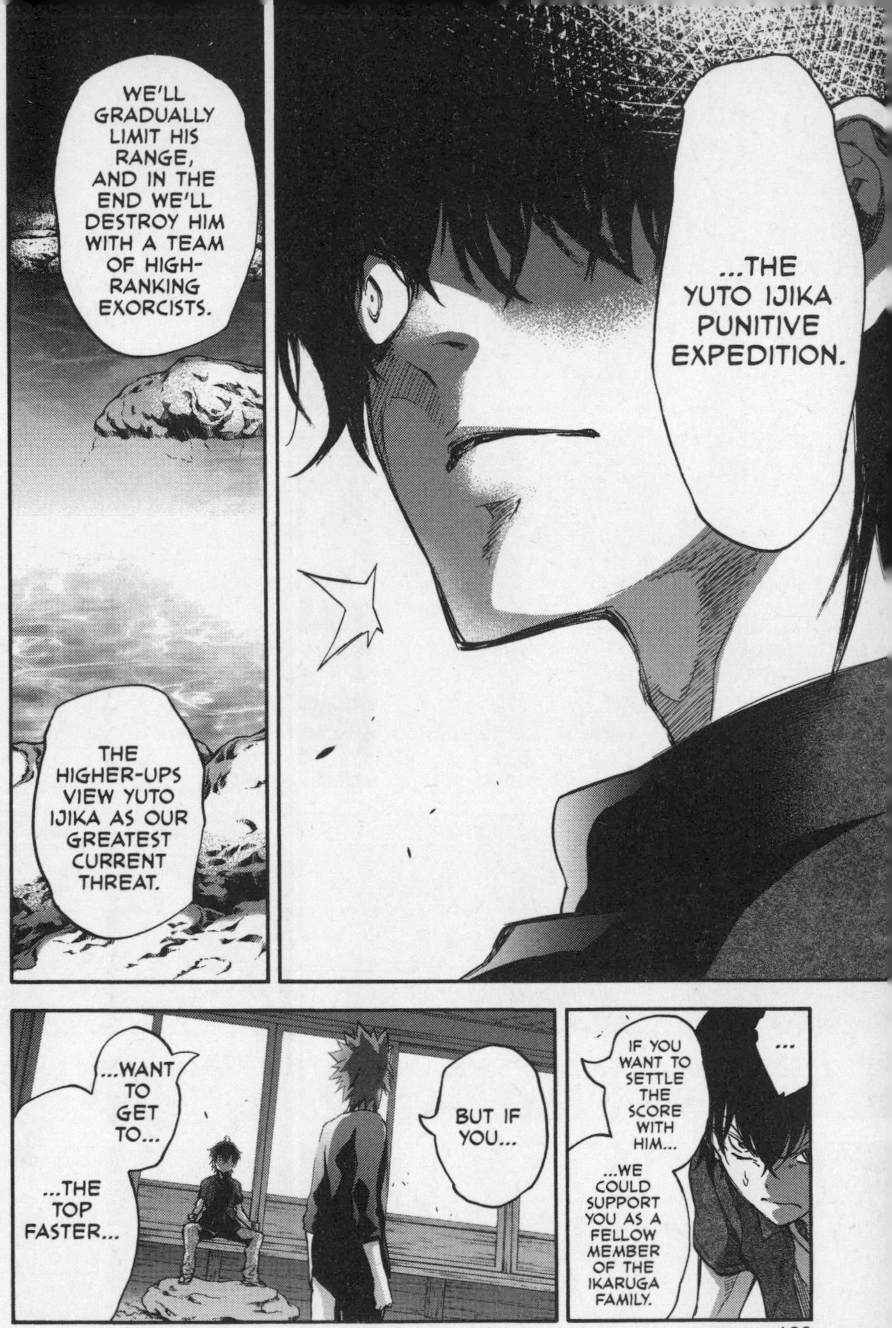
...THE YUTO IJIKA PUNITIVE EXPEDITION.
WE'LL GRADUALLY LIMIT HIS RANGE, AND IN THE END WE'LL DESTROY HIM WITH A TEAM OF HIGH-RANKING EXORCISTS.
THE HIGHER-UPS VIEW YUTO IJIKA AS OUR GREATEST CURRENT THREAT.
...
IF YOU WANT TO SETTLE THE SCORE WITH HIM...
...WE COULD SUPPORT YOU AS A FELLOW MEMBER OF THE IKARUGA FAMILY.
BUT IF YOU...
...WANT TO GET TO...
...THE TOP FASTER...

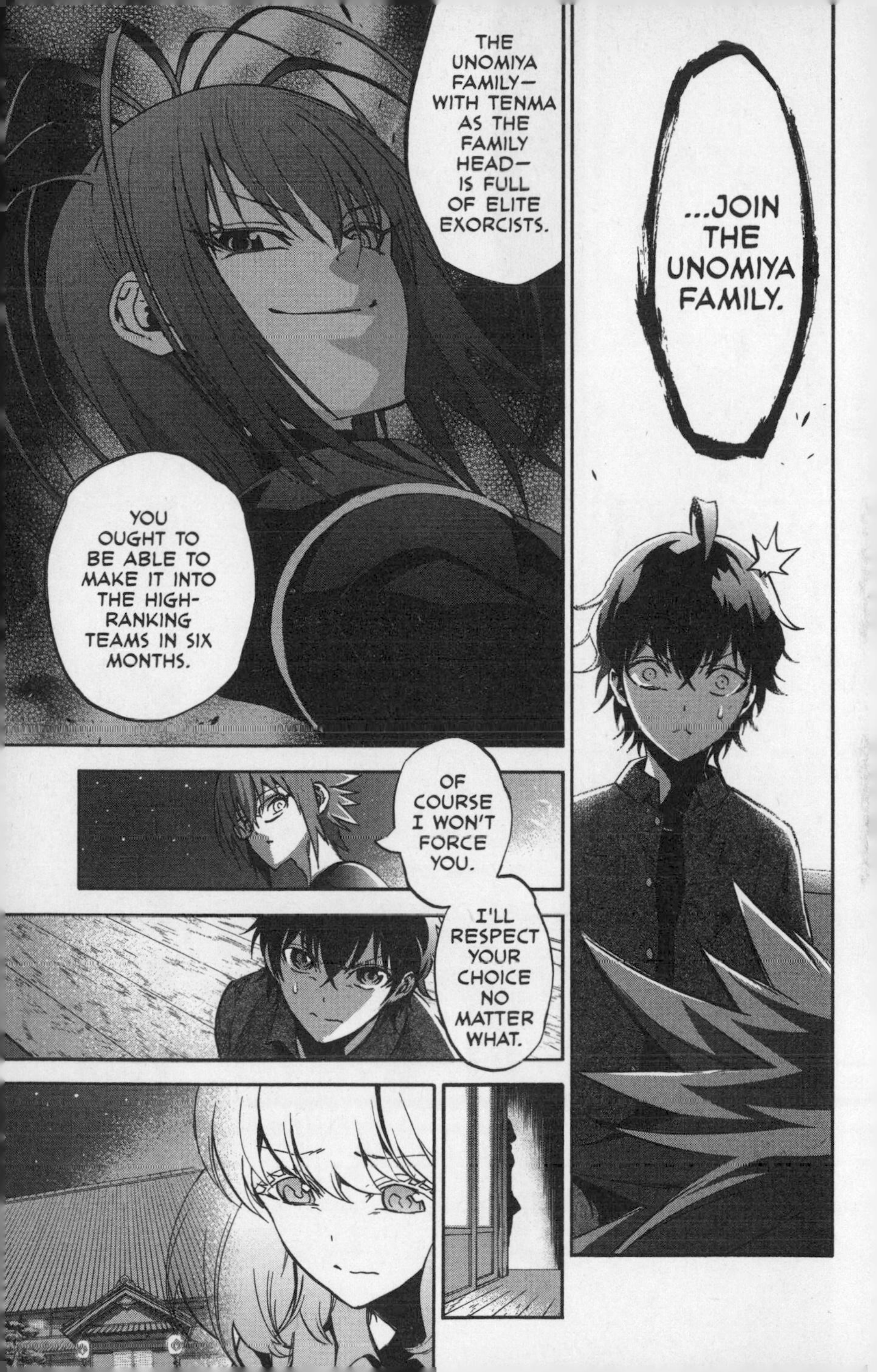
...JOIN THE UNOMIYA FAMILY.
THE UNOMIYA FAMILY—WITH TENMA AS THE FAMILY HEAD—IS FULL OF ELITE EXORCISTS.
YOU OUGHT TO BE ABLE TO MAKE IT INTO THE HIGH-RANKING TEAMS IN SIX MONTHS.
OF COURSE I WON'T FORCE YOU.
I'LL RESPECT YOUR CHOICE NO MATTER WHAT.

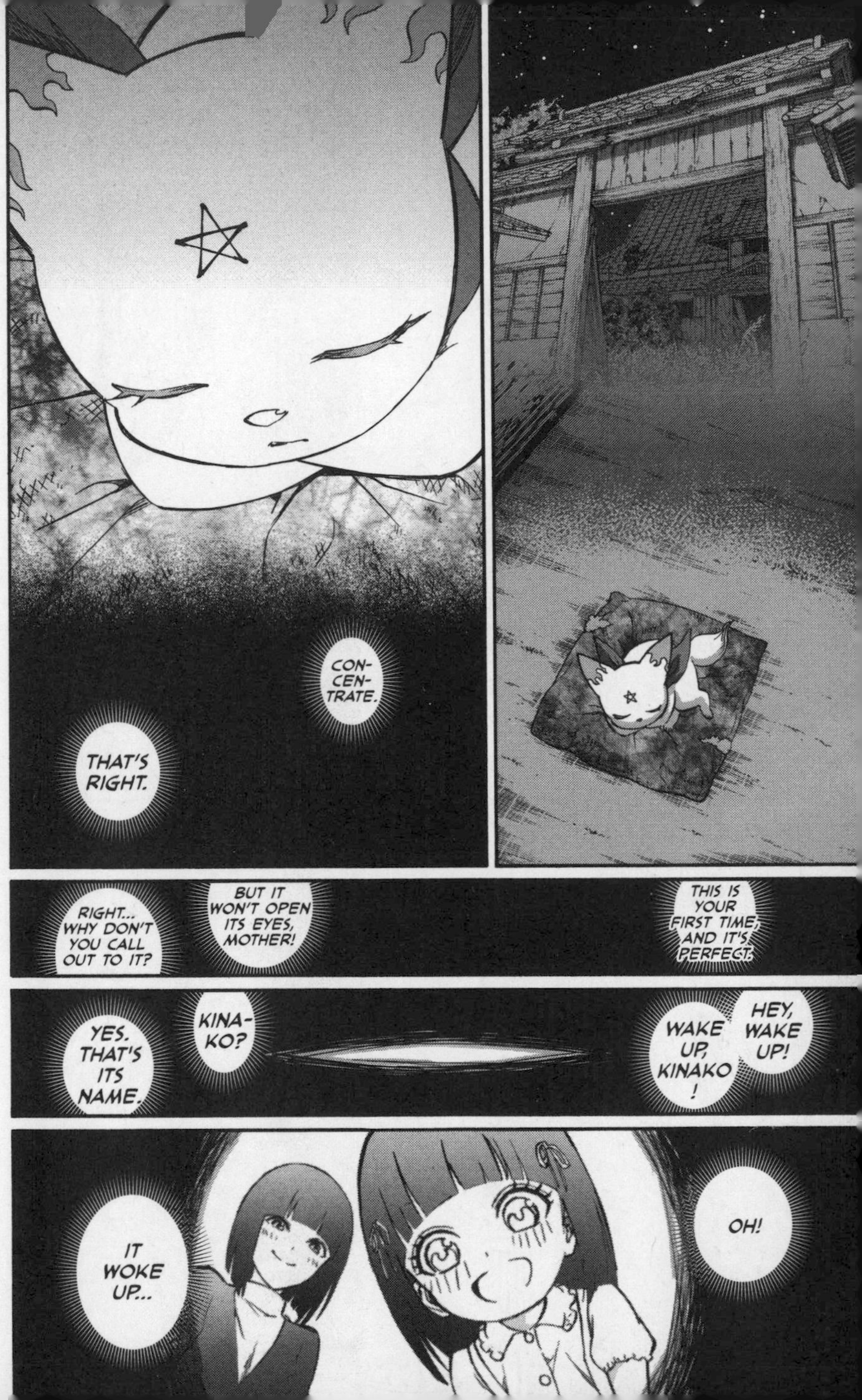
CON-CEN-TRATE.
THAT'S RIGHT.
THIS IS YOUR FIRST TIME, AND IT'S PERFECT.
BUT IT WON'T OPEN ITS EYES, MOTHER!
RIGHT... WHY DON'T YOU CALL OUT TO IT?
HEY, WAKE UP!
WAKE UP, KINAKO!
KINA-KO?
YES. THAT'S ITS NAME.
OH!
IT WOKE UP...

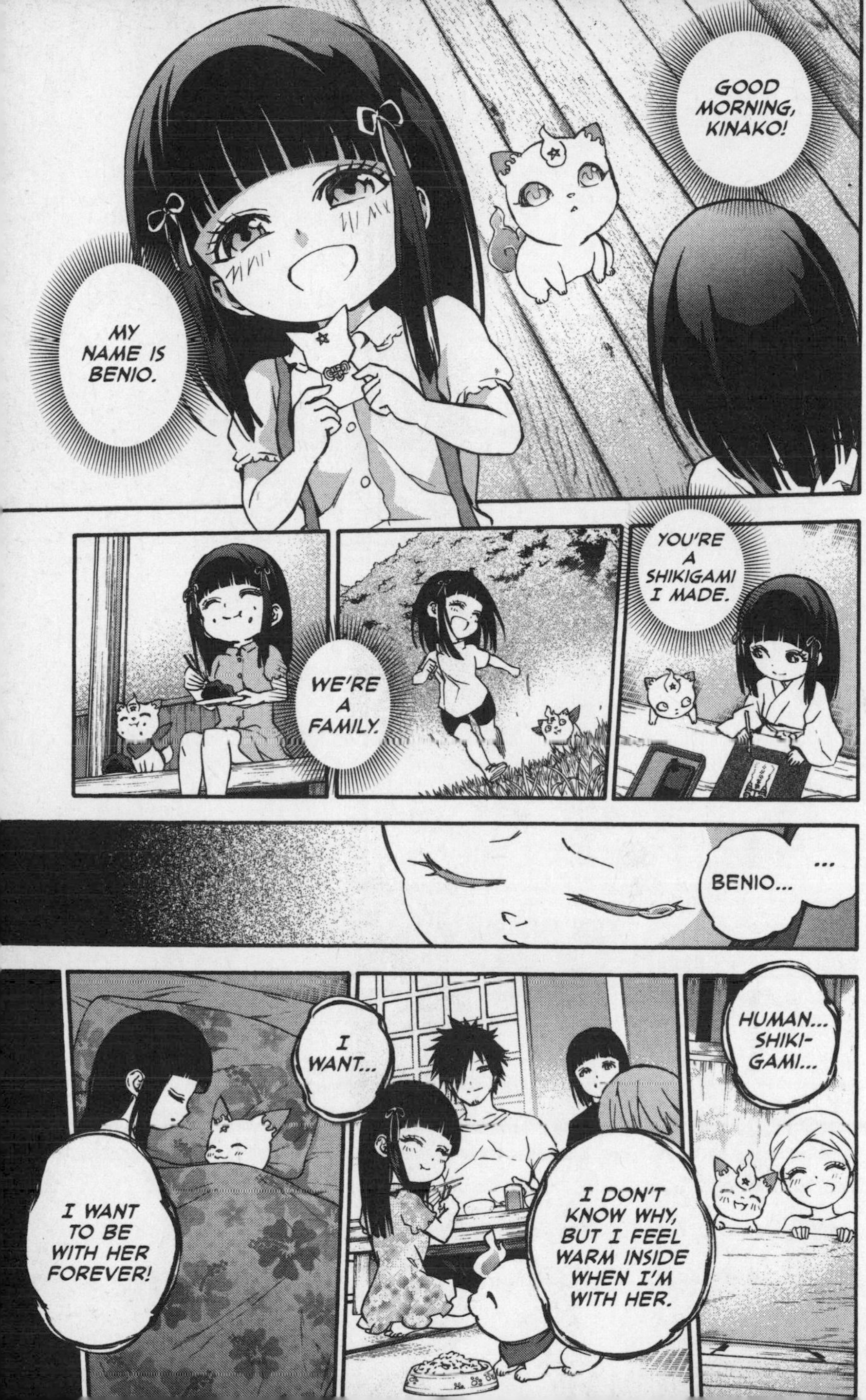
GOOD MORNING, KINAKO!
MY NAME IS BENIO.
YOU'RE A SHIKIGAMI I MADE.
WE'RE A FAMILY.
...
BENIO...
HUMAN... SHIKI-GAMI...
I DON'T KNOW WHY, BUT I FEEL WARM INSIDE WHEN I'M WITH HER.
I WANT...
I WANT TO BE WITH HER FOREVER!

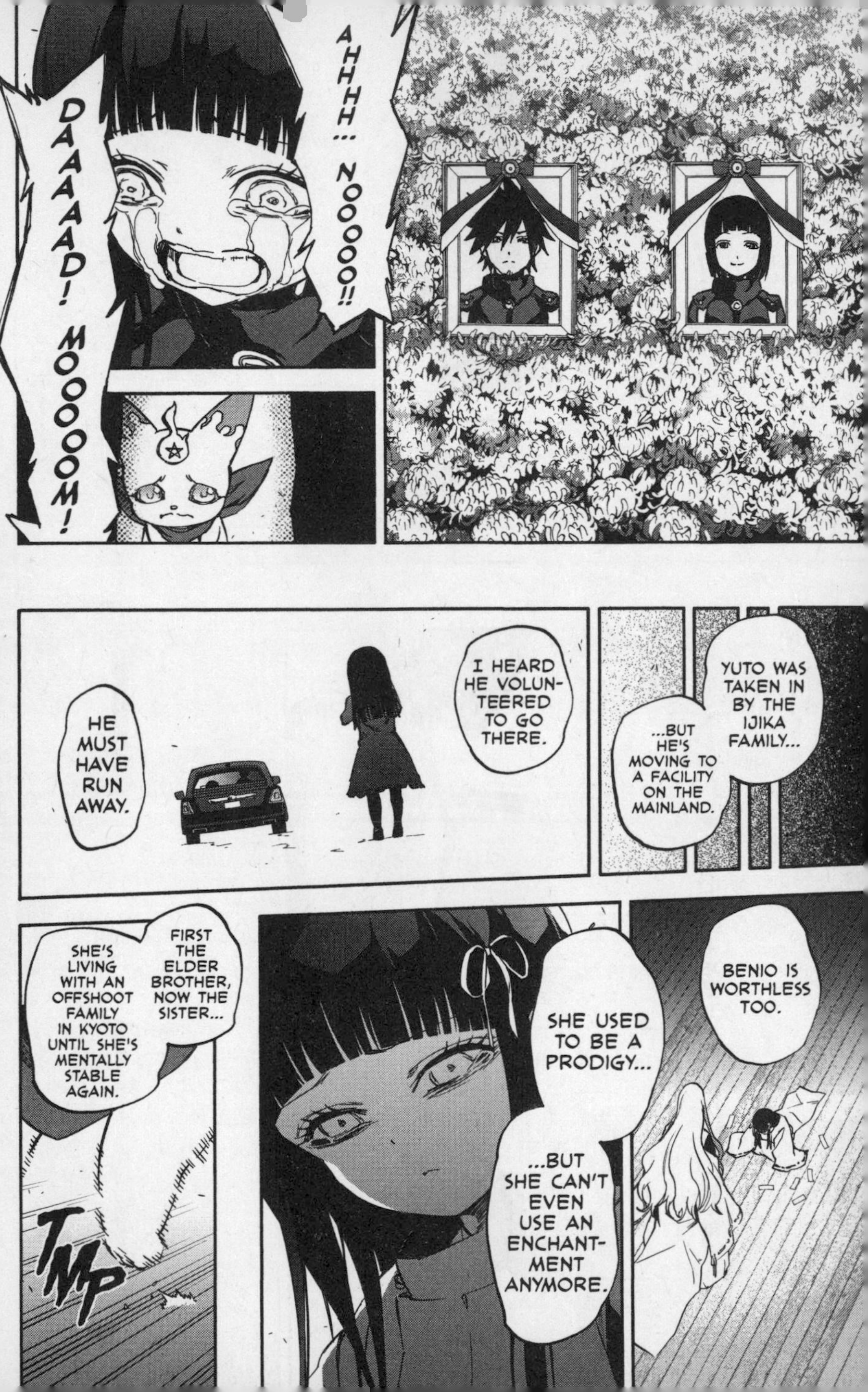
AHHHH... NOOOOOO!!
DAAAAAD! MOOOOOOM!
YUTO WAS TAKEN IN BY THE IJIKA FAMILY...
...BUT HE'S MOVING TO A FACILITY ON THE MAINLAND.
I HEARD HE VOLUNTEERED TO GO THERE.
HE MUST HAVE RUN AWAY.
BENIO IS WORTHLESS TOO.
SHE USED TO BE A PRODIGY...
...BUT SHE CAN'T EVEN USE AN ENCHANTMENT ANYMORE.
FIRST THE ELDER BROTHER, NOW THE SISTER...
SHE'S LIVING WITH AN OFFSHOOT FAMILY IN KYOTO UNTIL SHE'S MENTALLY STABLE AGAIN.
TMP

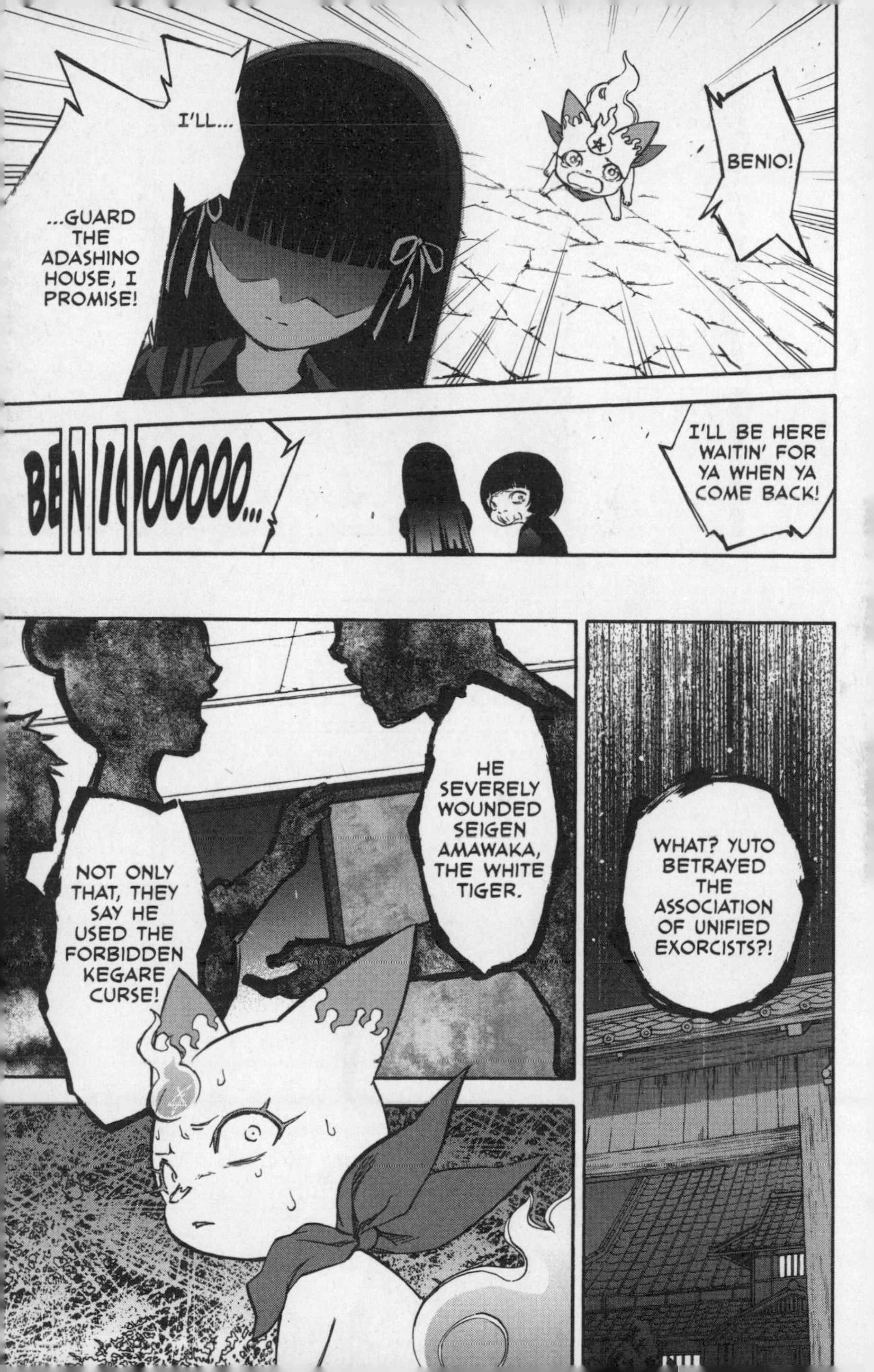
BENIO!
I'LL...
...GUARD THE ADASHINO HOUSE, I PROMISE!
I'LL BE HERE WAITIN' FOR YA WHEN YA COME BACK!
BENIOOOOO...
WHAT? YUTO BETRAYED THE ASSOCIATION OF UNIFIED EXORCISTS?!
HE SEVERELY WOUNDED SEIGEN AMAWAKA, THE WHITE TIGER.
NOT ONLY THAT, THEY SAY HE USED THE FORBIDDEN KEGARE CURSE!

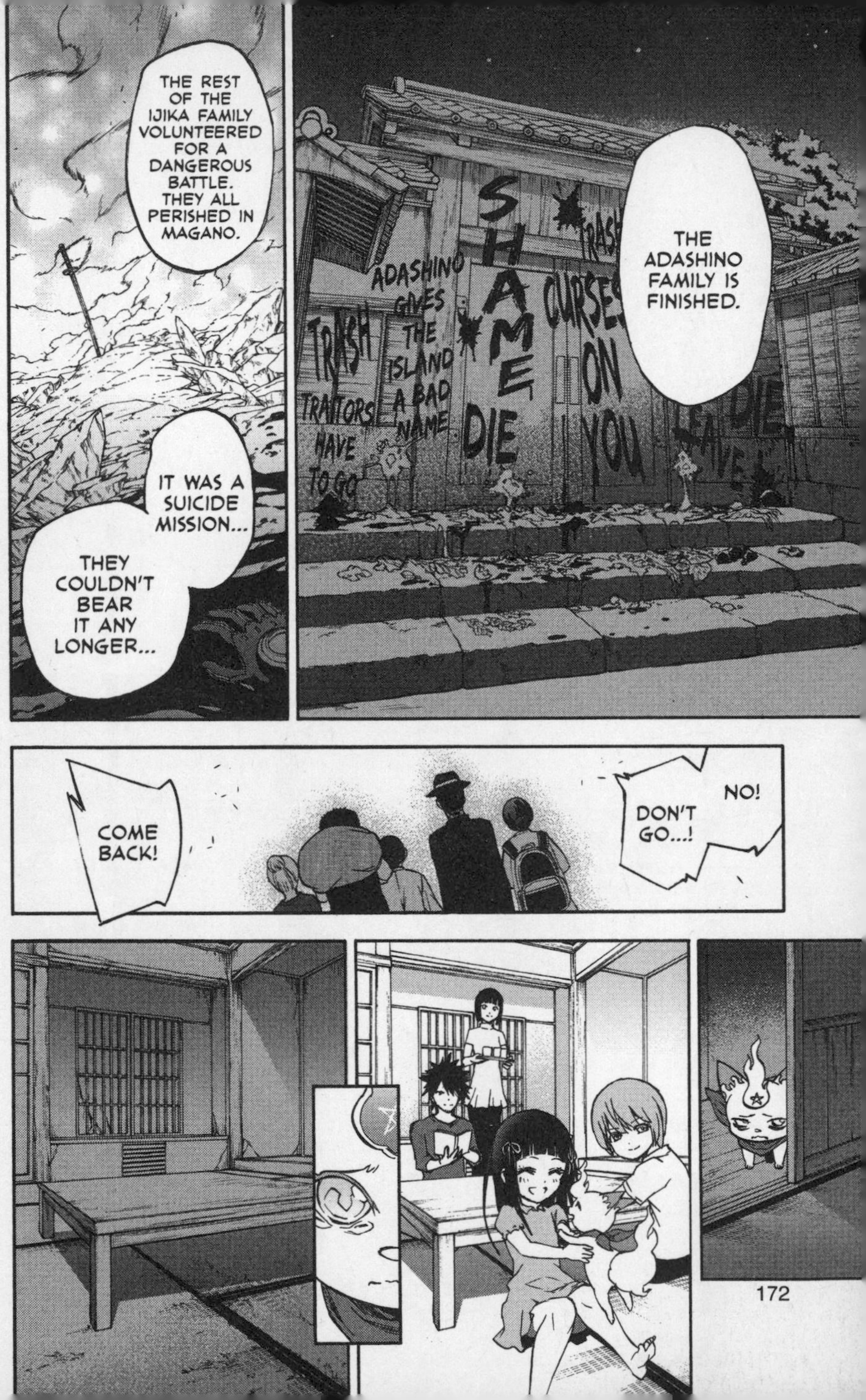
THE ADASHINO FAMILY IS FINISHED.
SHAME
DIE
TRASH
CURSES ON YOU
LEAVE
DIE
ADASHINO GIVES THE ISLAND A BAD NAME
TRASH
TRAITORS HAVE TO GO
THE REST OF THE IJIKA FAMILY VOLUNTEERED FOR A DANGEROUS BATTLE. THEY ALL PERISHED IN MAGANO.
IT WAS A SUICIDE MISSION...
THEY COULDN'T BEAR IT ANY LONGER...
NO!
DON'T GO...!
COME BACK!

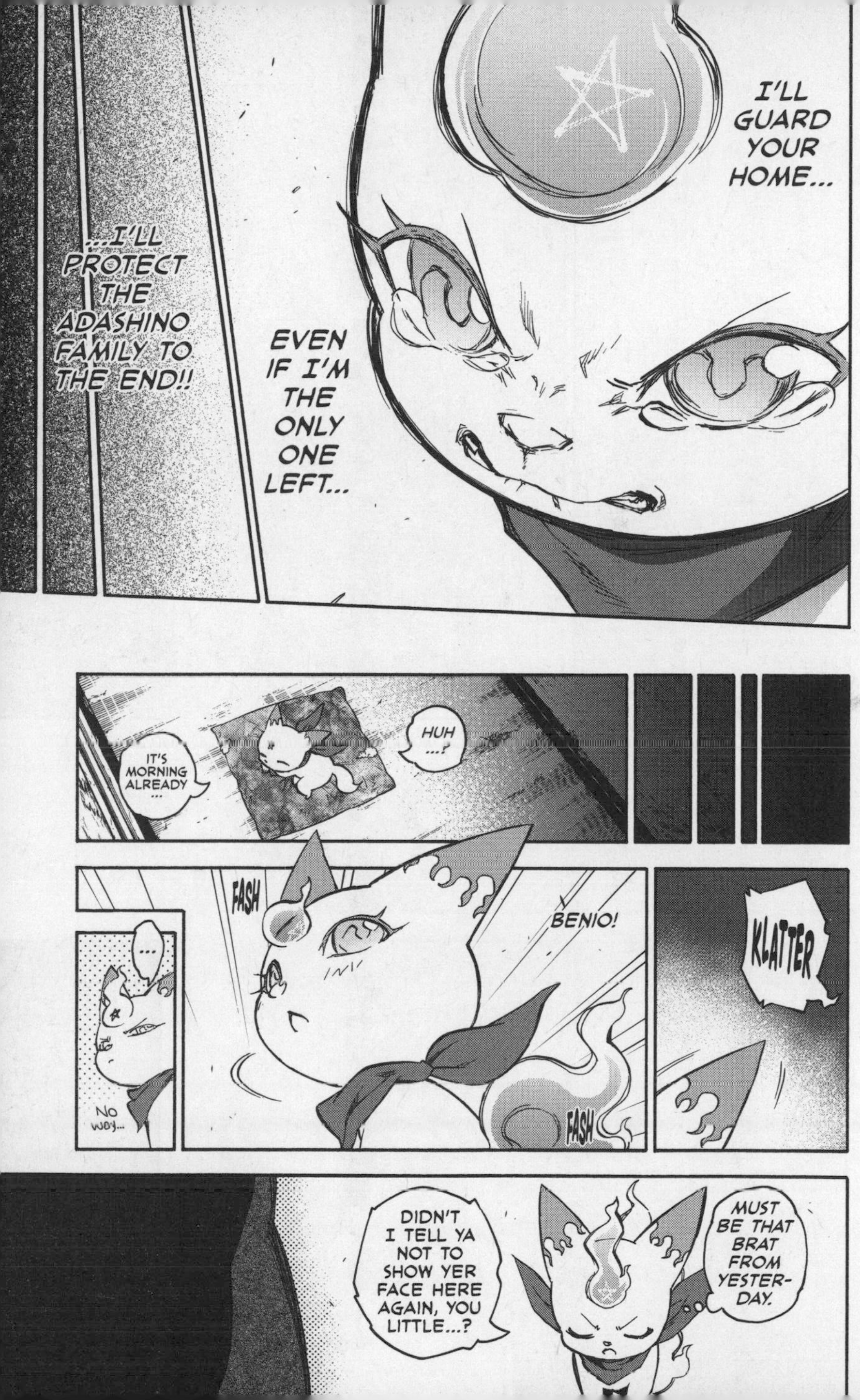
I'LL GUARD YOUR HOME...
EVEN IF I'M THE ONLY ONE LEFT...
...I'LL PROTECT THE ADASHINO FAMILY TO THE END!!
HUH ...?
IT'S MORNING ALREADY ...
KLATTER
BENIO!
FASH
FASH
...
No way...
MUST BE THAT BRAT FROM YESTER-DAY.
DIDN'T I TELL YA NOT TO SHOW YER FACE HERE AGAIN, YOU LITTLE...?

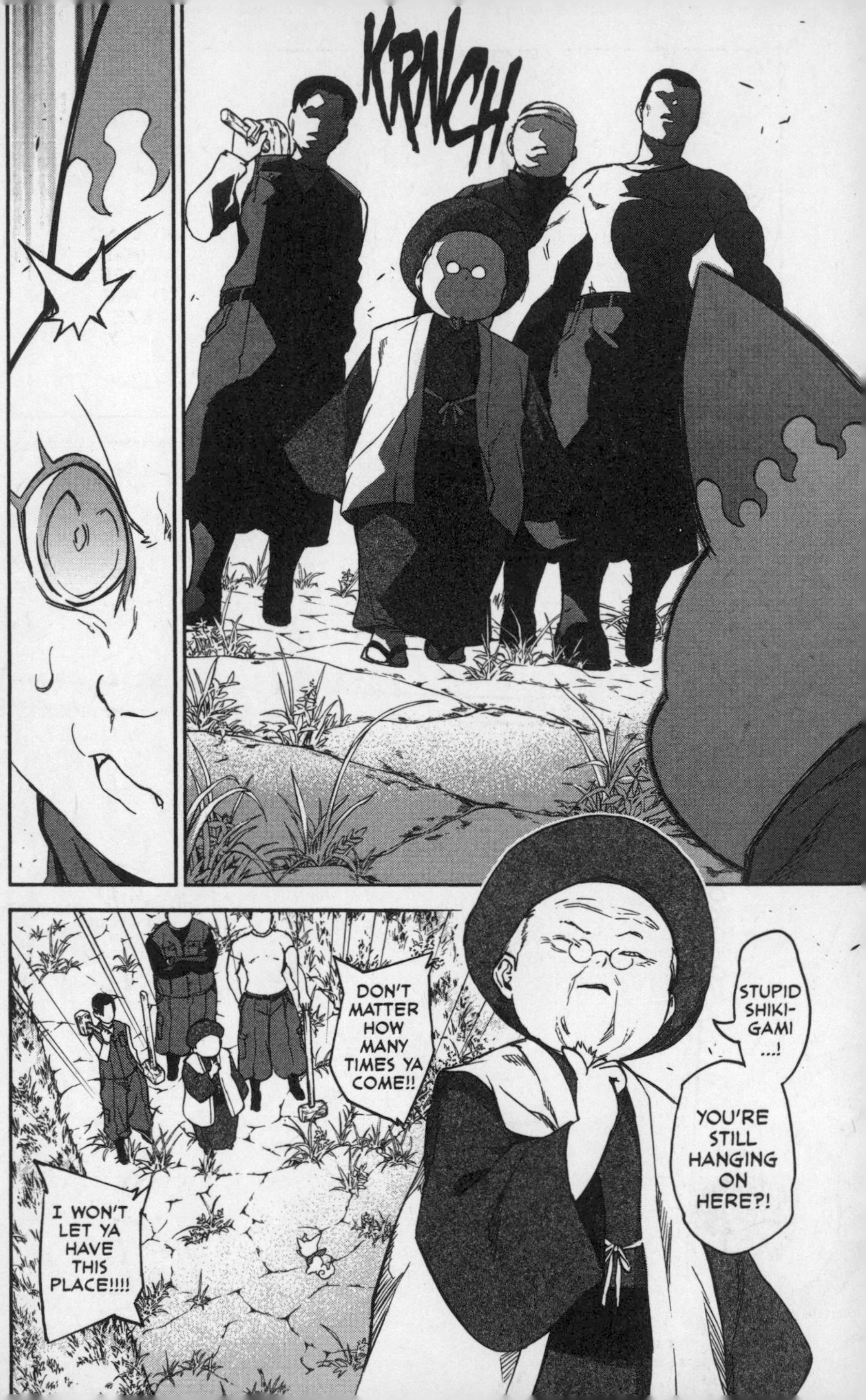
KRNCH
STUPID SHIKI-GAMI ...!
YOU'RE STILL HANGING ON HERE?!
DON'T MATTER HOW MANY TIMES YA COME!!
I WON'T LET YA HAVE THIS PLACE!!!!

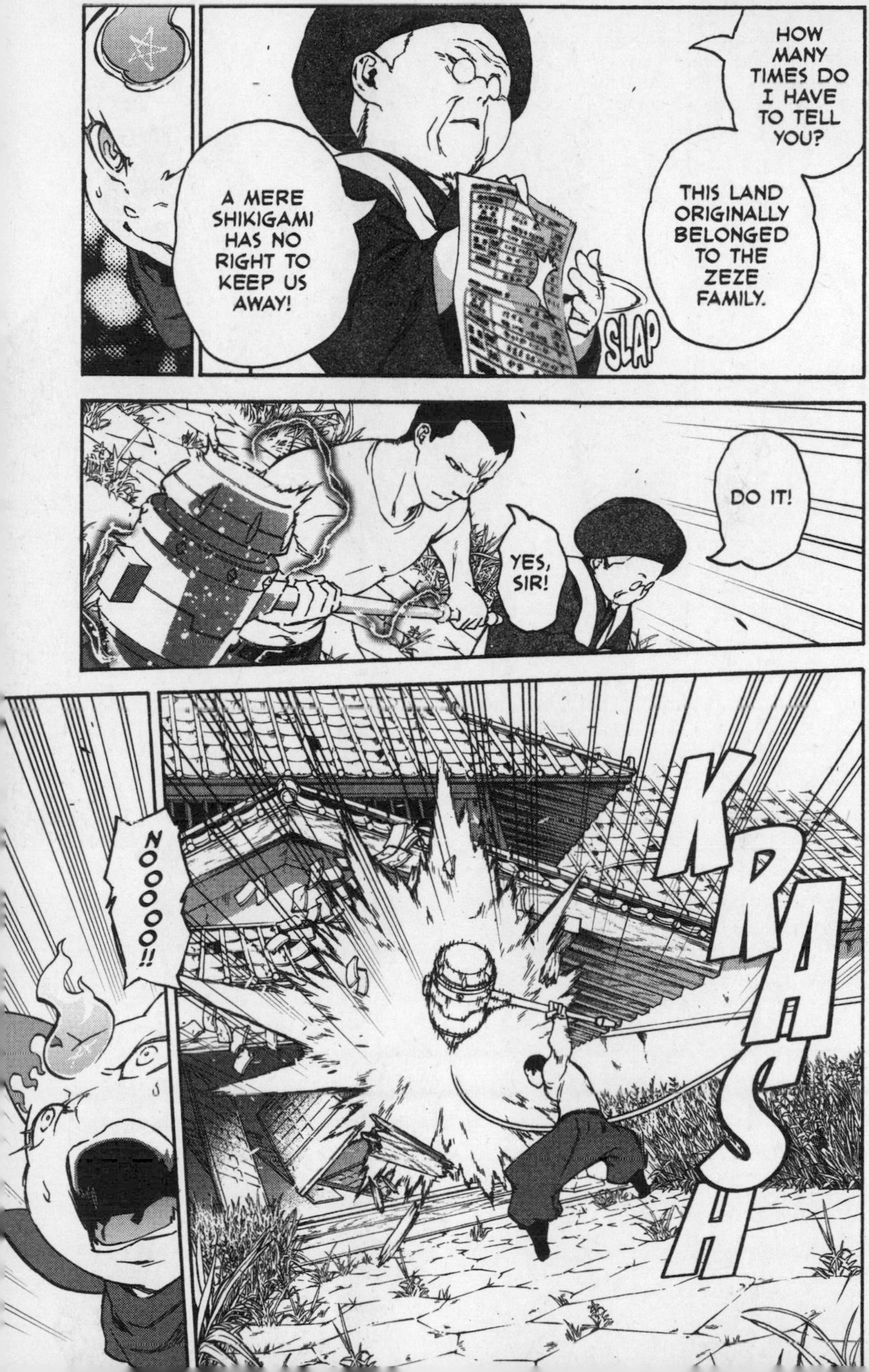
HOW MANY TIMES DO I HAVE TO TELL YOU?
THIS LAND ORIGINALLY BELONGED TO THE ZEZE FAMILY.
SLAP
A MERE SHIKIGAMI HAS NO RIGHT TO KEEP US AWAY!
DO IT!
YES, SIR!
KRASH
NOOOOO!!

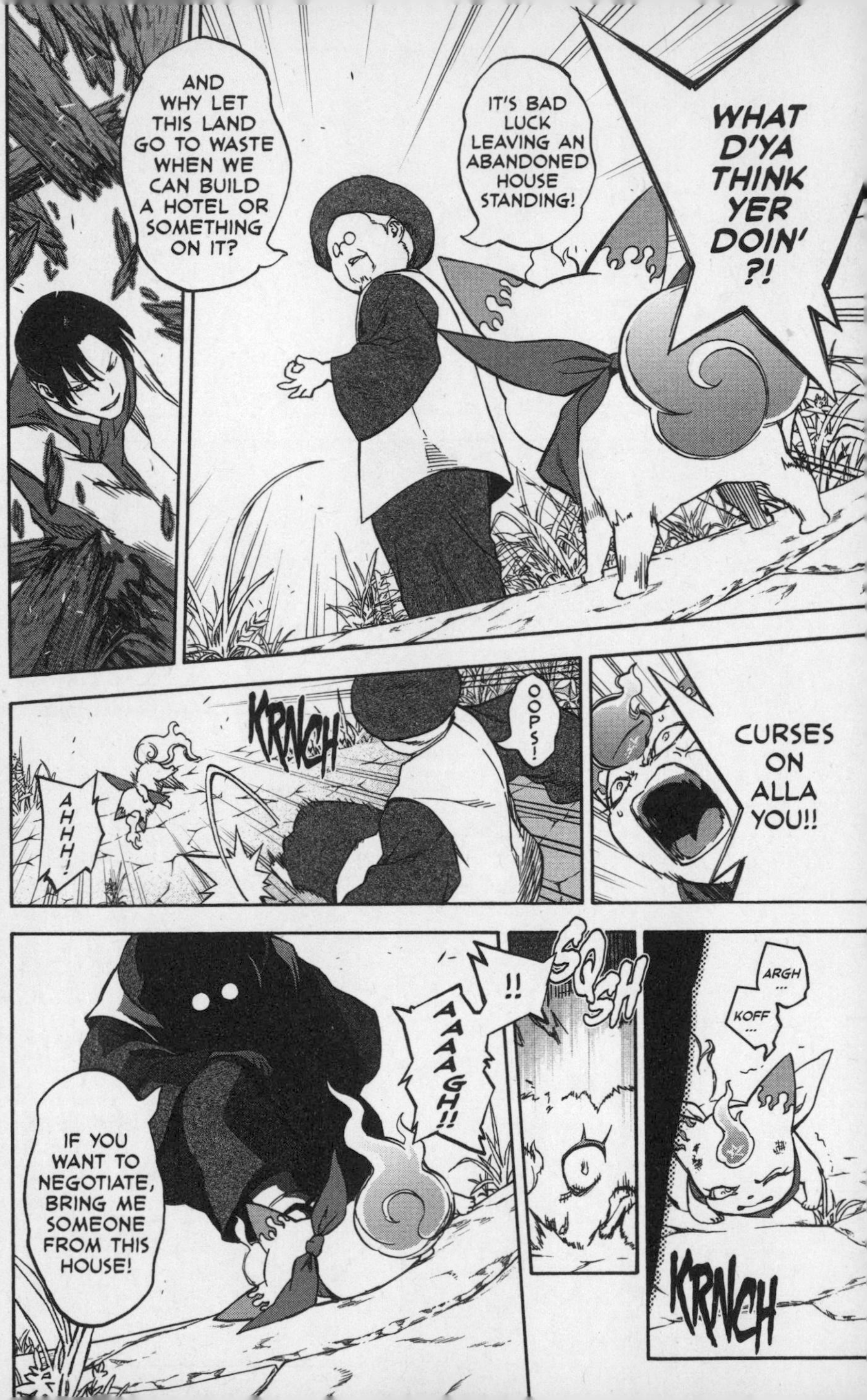
WHAT D'YA THINK YER DOIN' ?!
IT'S BAD LUCK LEAVING AN ABANDONED HOUSE STANDING!
AND WHY LET THIS LAND GO TO WASTE WHEN WE CAN BUILD A HOTEL OR SOMETHING ON IT?
CURSES ON ALLA YOU!!
OOPS!
KRNCH
AHHH!
ARGH... KOFF...
KRNCH
SQSH
!!
AAAAGH!!
IF YOU WANT TO NEGOTIATE, BRING ME SOMEONE FROM THIS HOUSE!

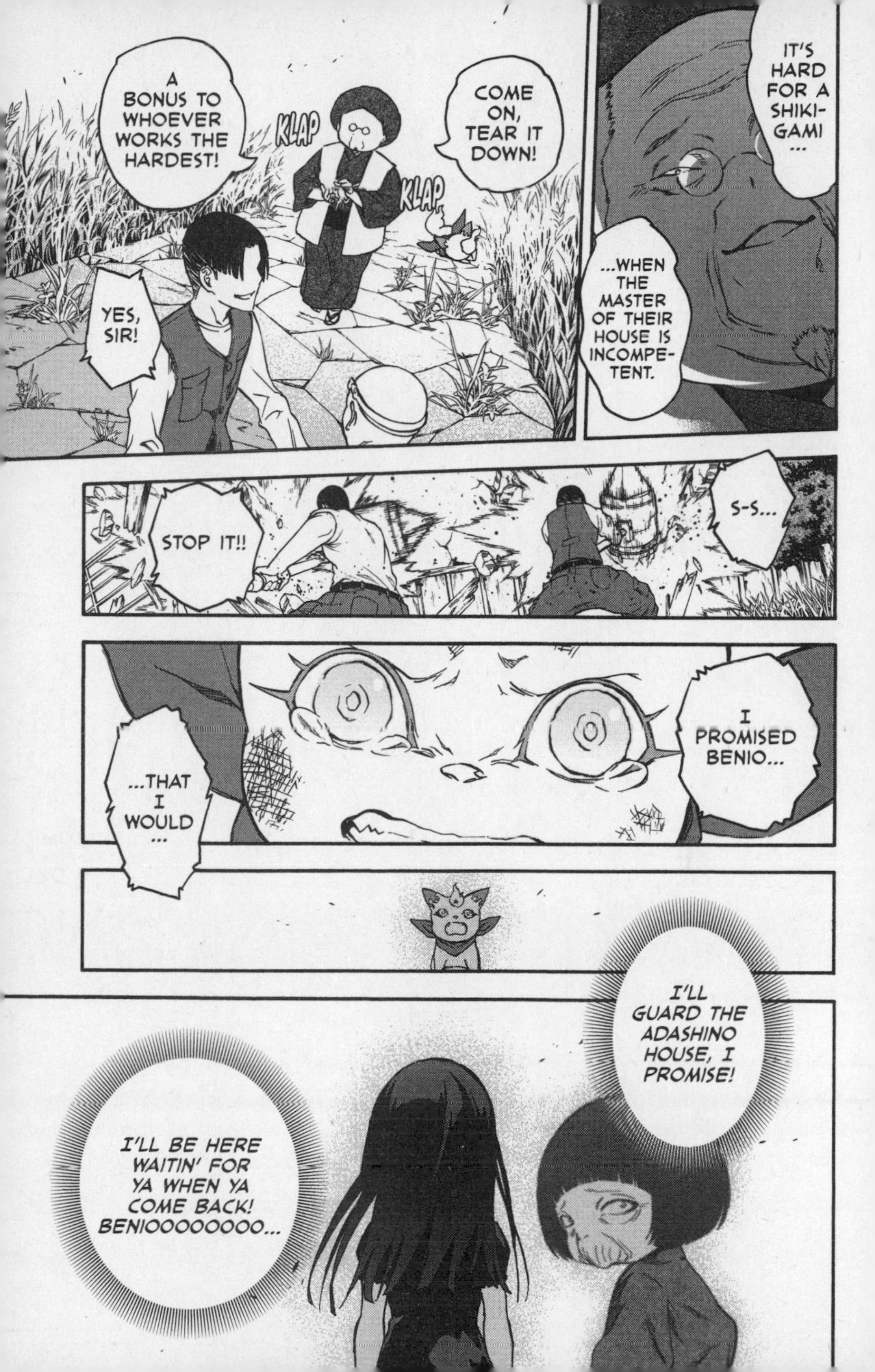
IT'S HARD FOR A SHIKIGAMI...
...WHEN THE MASTER OF THEIR HOUSE IS INCOMPETENT.
COME ON, TEAR IT DOWN!
KLAP
KLAP
A BONUS TO WHOEVER WORKS THE HARDEST!
YES, SIR!
S-S...
STOP IT!!
I PROMISED BENIO...
...THAT I WOULD...
I'LL GUARD THE ADASHINO HOUSE, I PROMISE!
I'LL BE HERE WAITIN' FOR YA WHEN YA COME BACK! BENIOOOOOOOO...

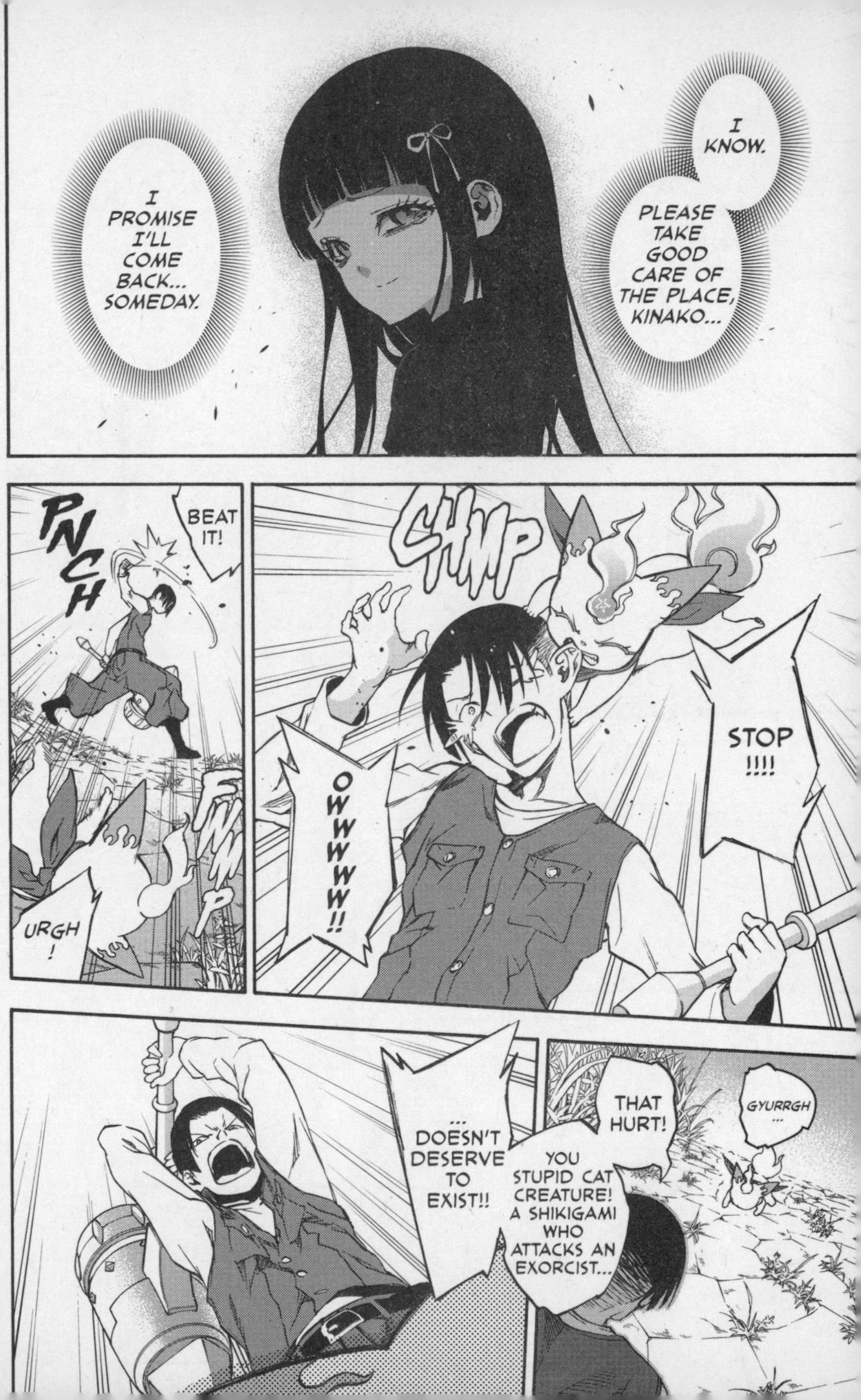
I KNOW.
PLEASE TAKE GOOD CARE OF THE PLACE, KINAKO...
I PROMISE I'LL COME BACK... SOMEDAY.
CHMP
STOP!!!!
OWWWWWW!!
BEAT IT!
PNCH
FWMP
URGH!
GYURRGH...
THAT HURT!
YOU STUPID CAT CREATURE! A SHIKIGAMI WHO ATTACKS AN EXORCIST...
...DOESN'T DESERVE TO EXIST!!

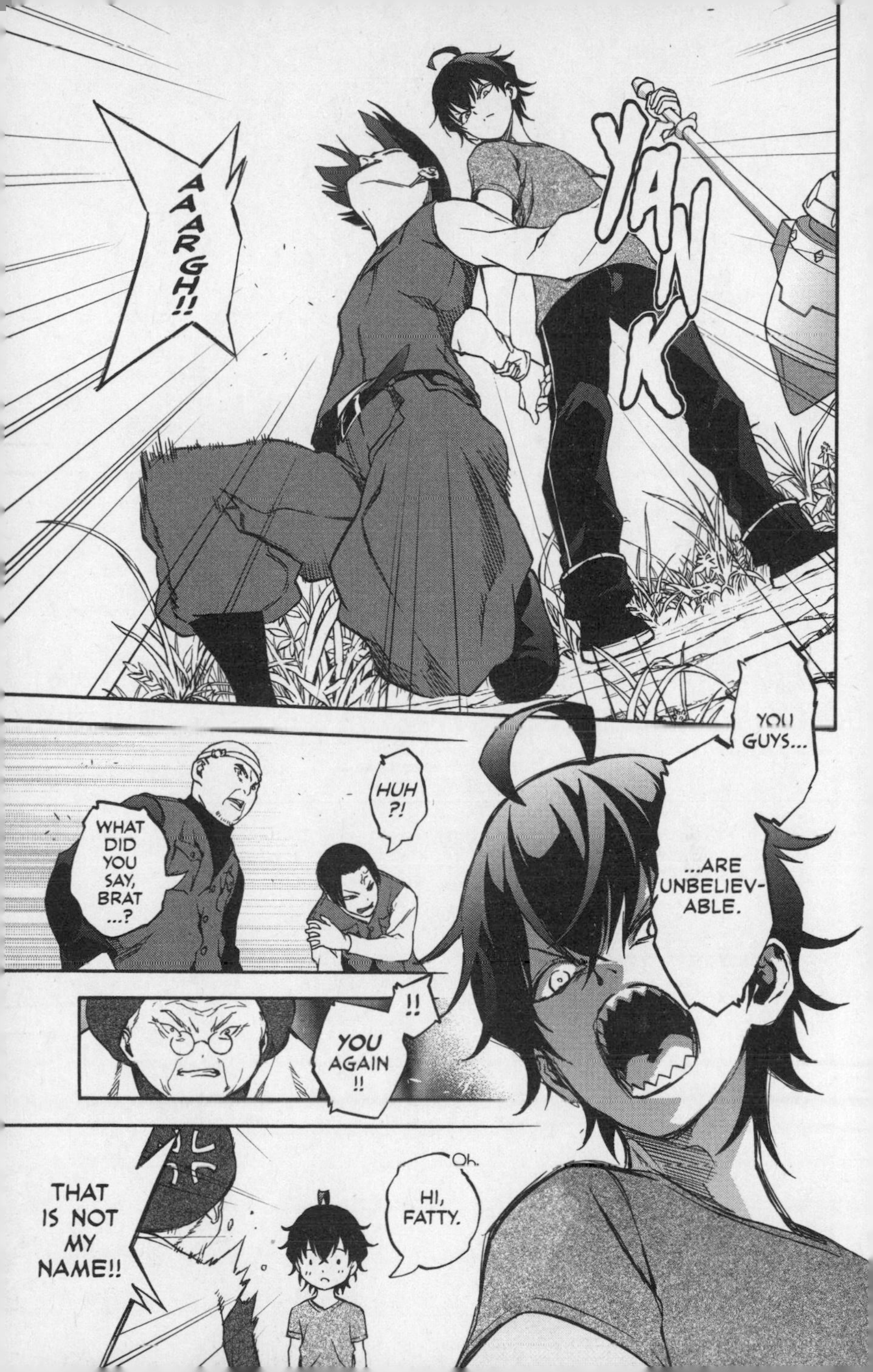
YANK
AARGH!!
YOU GUYS...
...ARE UNBELIEV-ABLE.
HUH ?!
WHAT DID YOU SAY, BRAT ...?
!!
YOU AGAIN !!
Oh.
HI, FATTY.
THAT IS NOT MY NAME!!

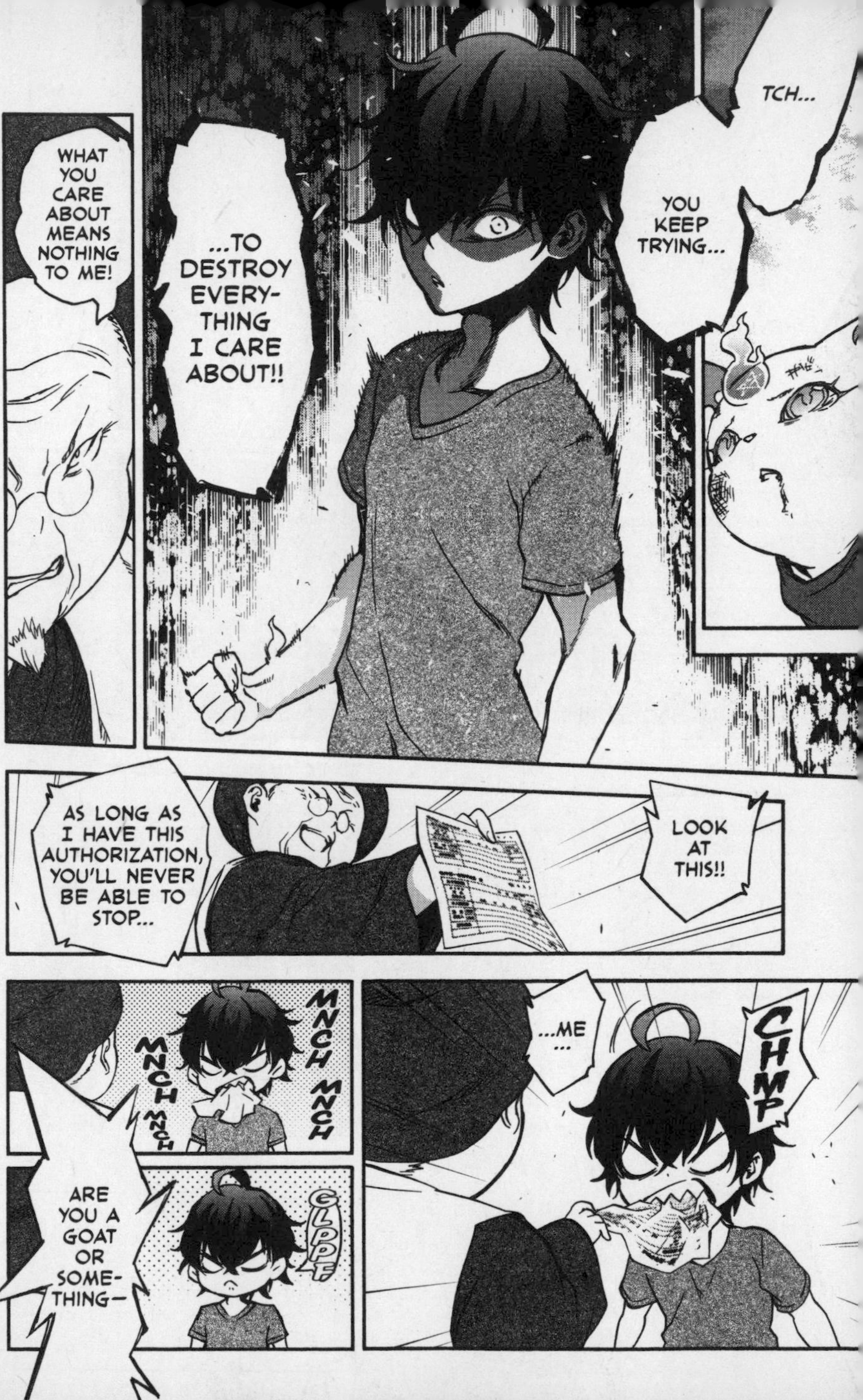
TCH...
YOU KEEP TRYING...
...TO DESTROY EVERYTHING I CARE ABOUT!!
WHAT YOU CARE ABOUT MEANS NOTHING TO ME!
LOOK AT THIS!!
AS LONG AS I HAVE THIS AUTHORIZATION, YOU'LL NEVER BE ABLE TO STOP...
CHMP
...ME ...
MNCH MNCH
MNCH MNCH
GLPPF
ARE YOU A GOAT OR SOMETHING—

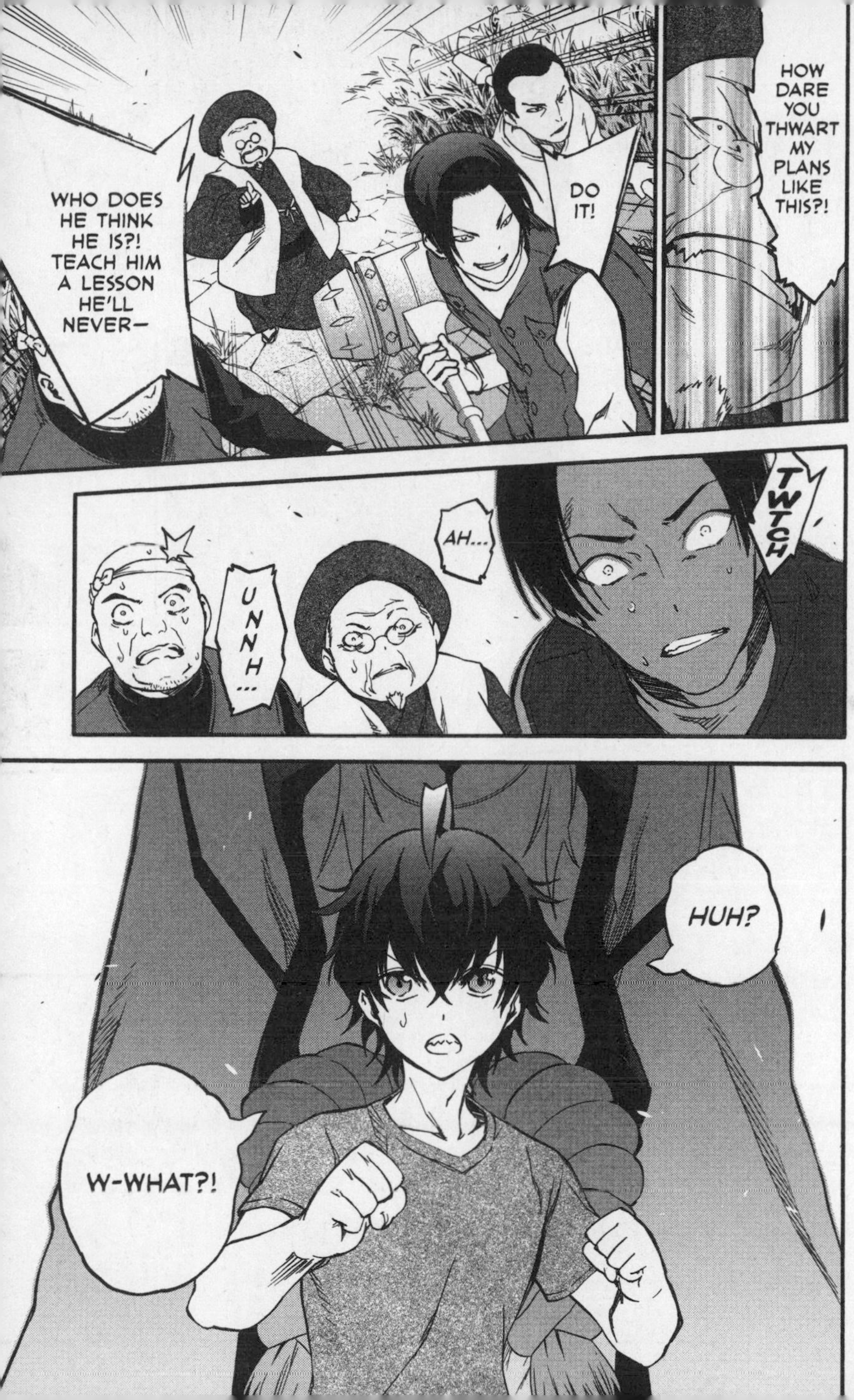
HOW DARE YOU THWART MY PLANS LIKE THIS?!
DO IT!
WHO DOES HE THINK HE IS?! TEACH HIM A LESSON HE'LL NEVER—
TWTCH
AH...
UNNH...
HUH?
W-WHAT?!

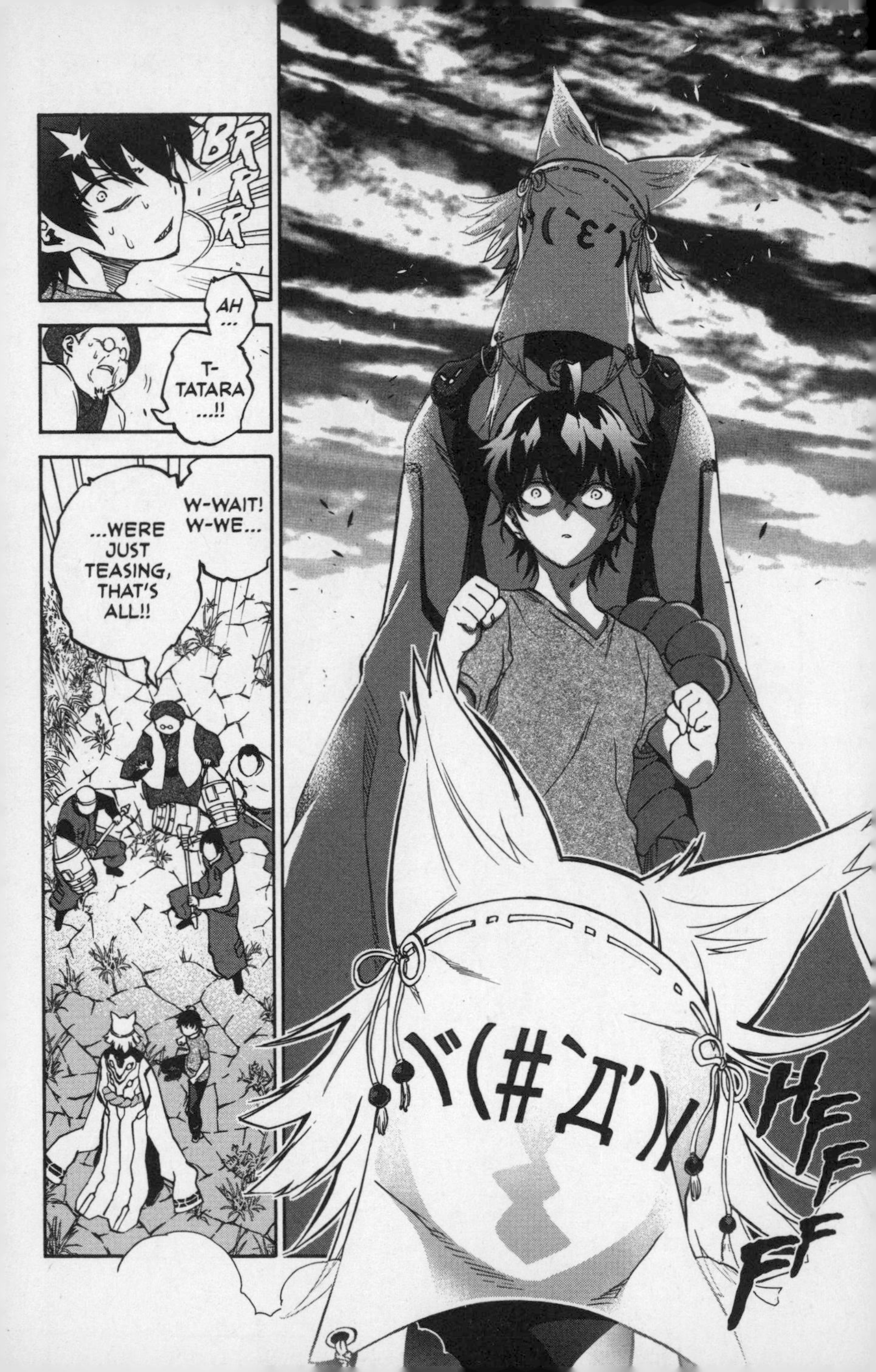
ヾ(#`Д´)ﾉ
HFFFF
BRRR
AH... T-TATARA...!!
W-WAIT! W-WE...
...WERE JUST TEASING, THAT'S ALL!!

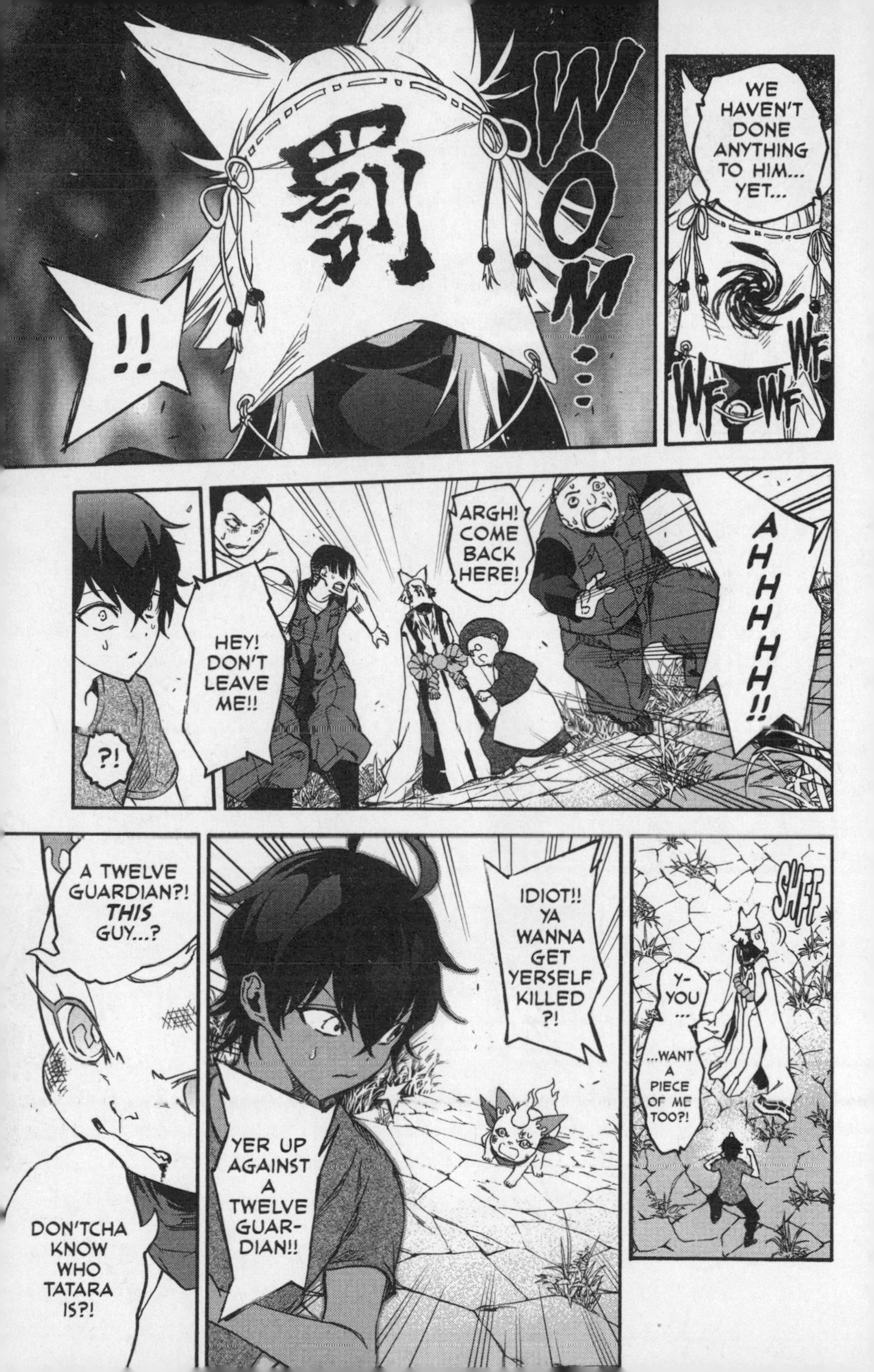
WE HAVEN'T DONE ANYTHING TO HIM... YET...
WF WF WF WF
WOM...
罰
!!
AHHHHHH!!
ARGH! COME BACK HERE!
HEY! DON'T LEAVE ME!!
?!
SHFF
Y- YOU ...
...WANT A PIECE OF ME TOO?!
IDIOT!! YA WANNA GET YERSELF KILLED ?!
YER UP AGAINST A TWELVE GUARDIAN!!
A TWELVE GUARDIAN?! *THIS* GUY...?
DON'TCHA KNOW WHO TATARA IS?!

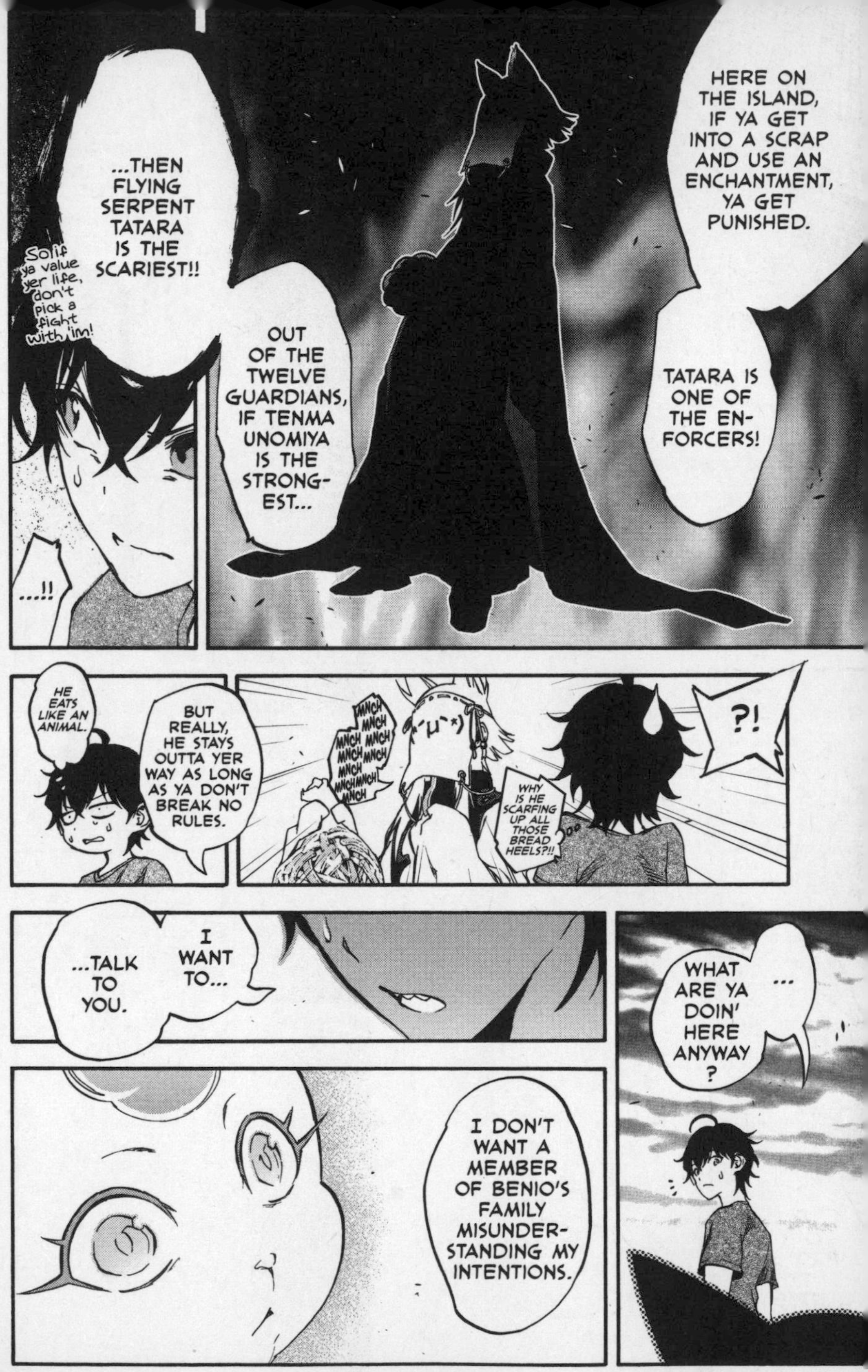
HERE ON THE ISLAND, IF YA GET INTO A SCRAP AND USE AN ENCHANTMENT, YA GET PUNISHED.
TATARA IS ONE OF THE EN-FORCERS!
OUT OF THE TWELVE GUARDIANS, IF TENMA UNOMIYA IS THE STRONG-EST...
...THEN FLYING SERPENT TATARA IS THE SCARIEST!!
So if ya value yer life, don't pick a fight with 'im!
...!!
?!
WHY IS HE SCARFING UP ALL THOSE BREAD HEELS?!!
MNCH MNCH MNCH MNCH MNCH MNCH MNCH MNCH MNCHMNCH MNCH
BUT REALLY, HE STAYS OUTTA YER WAY AS LONG AS YA DON'T BREAK NO RULES.
HE EATS LIKE AN ANIMAL.
WHAT ARE YA DOIN' HERE ANYWAY?
...
I WANT TO...
...TALK TO YOU.
I DON'T WANT A MEMBER OF BENIO'S FAMILY MISUNDERSTANDING MY INTENTIONS.

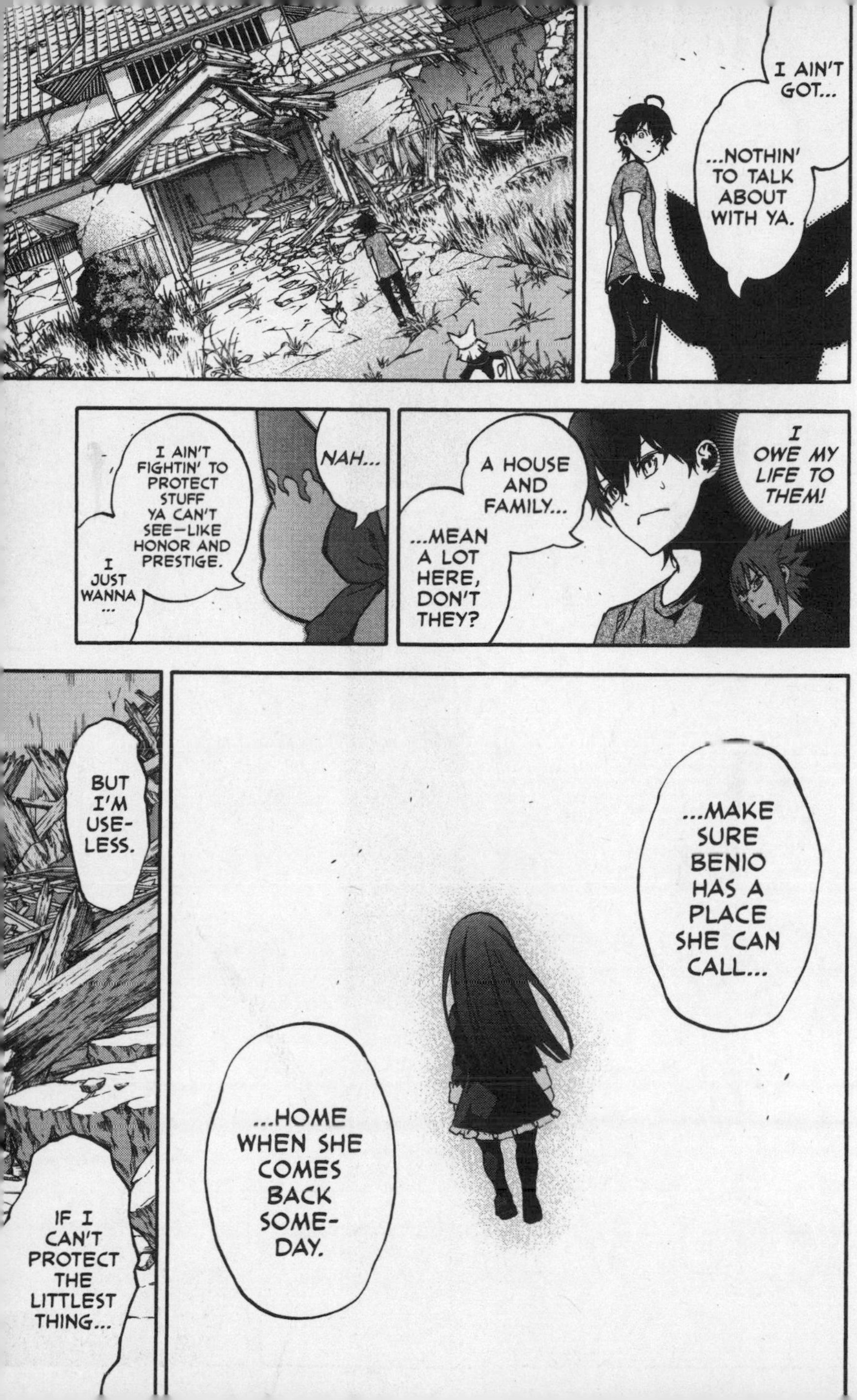
I AIN'T GOT...
...NOTHIN' TO TALK ABOUT WITH YA.
I OWE MY LIFE TO THEM!
A HOUSE AND FAMILY...
...MEAN A LOT HERE, DON'T THEY?
NAH...
I AIN'T FIGHTIN' TO PROTECT STUFF YA CAN'T SEE—LIKE HONOR AND PRESTIGE.
I JUST WANNA ...
...MAKE SURE BENIO HAS A PLACE SHE CAN CALL...
...HOME WHEN SHE COMES BACK SOME-DAY.
BUT I'M USE-LESS.
IF I CAN'T PROTECT THE LITTLEST THING...

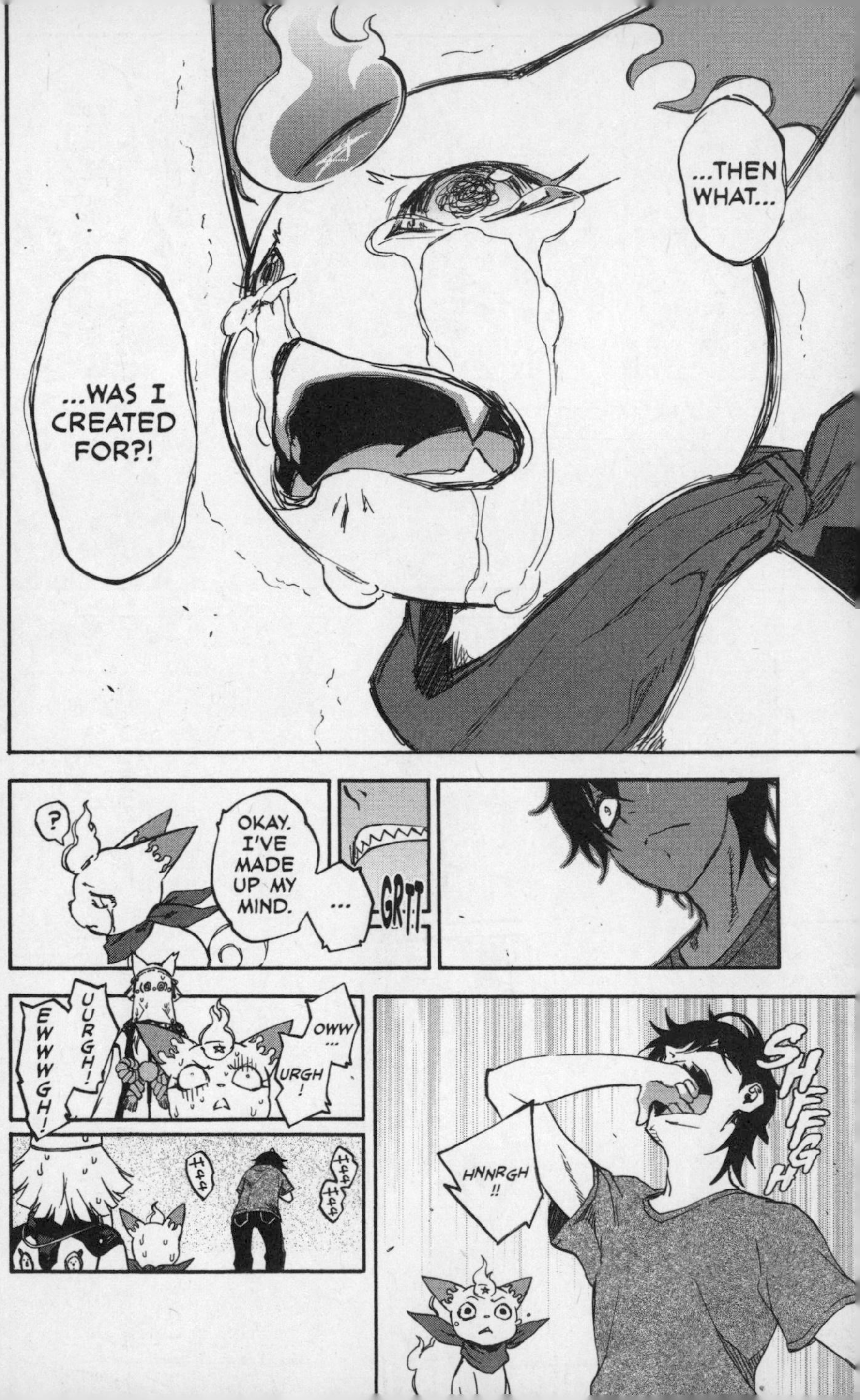
...THEN WHAT...
...WAS I CREATED FOR?!
GR-T-T
...
OKAY. I'VE MADE UP MY MIND.
?
SHFGH
HNNRGH !!
OWW ...
URGH !
UURGH!
EWWWGH!

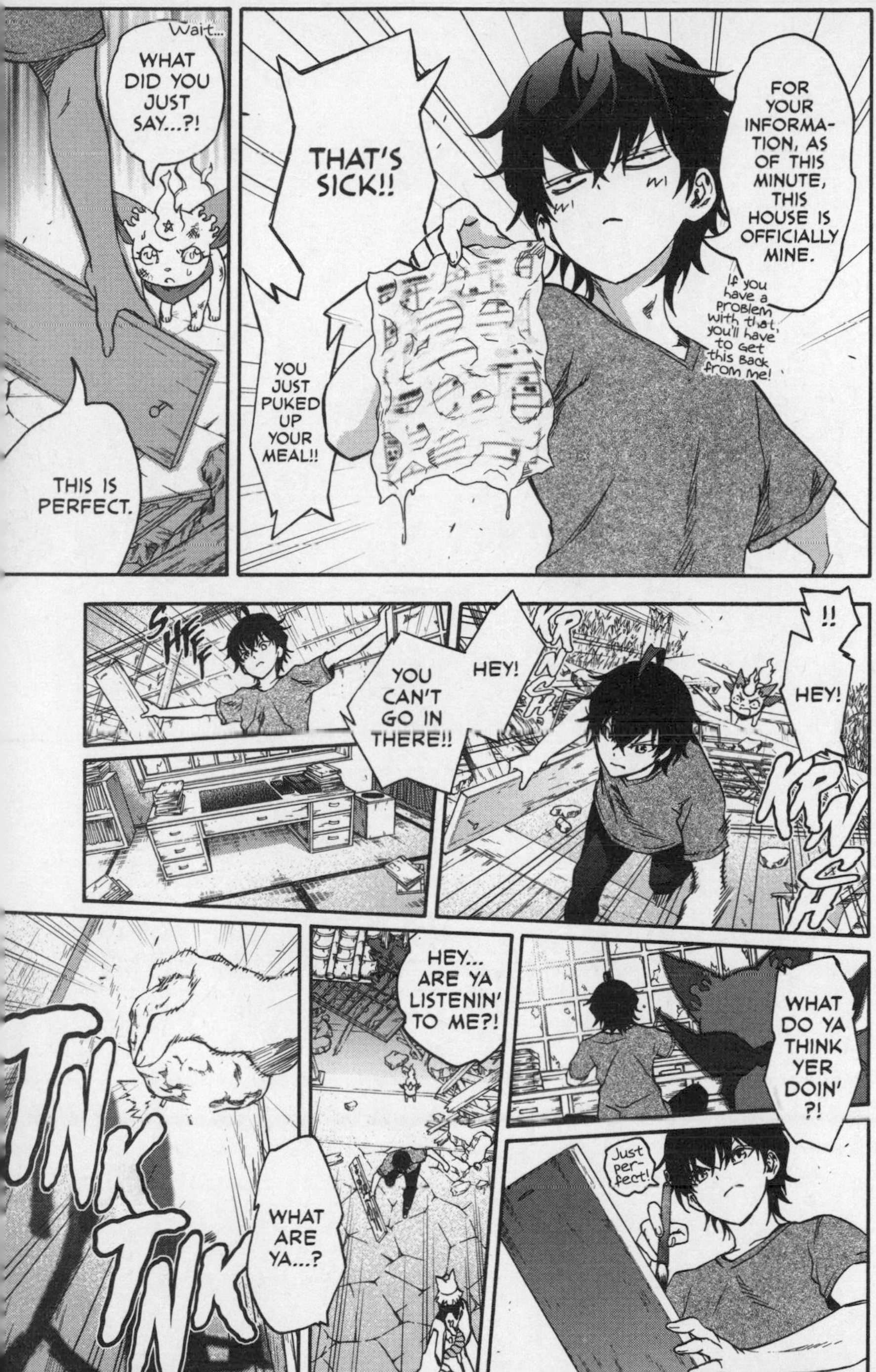
FOR YOUR INFORMATION, AS OF THIS MINUTE, THIS HOUSE IS OFFICIALLY MINE.
If you have a problem with that, you'll have to get this back from me!
THAT'S SICK!!
YOU JUST PUKED UP YOUR MEAL!!
Wait...
WHAT DID YOU JUST SAY...?!
THIS IS PERFECT.
!!
HEY!
KRNCH
HEY!
YOU CAN'T GO IN THERE!!
KRNCH
SHFF
WHAT DO YA THINK YER DOIN'?!
Just perfect!
HEY... ARE YA LISTENIN' TO ME?!
WHAT ARE YA...?
TNK
TNK

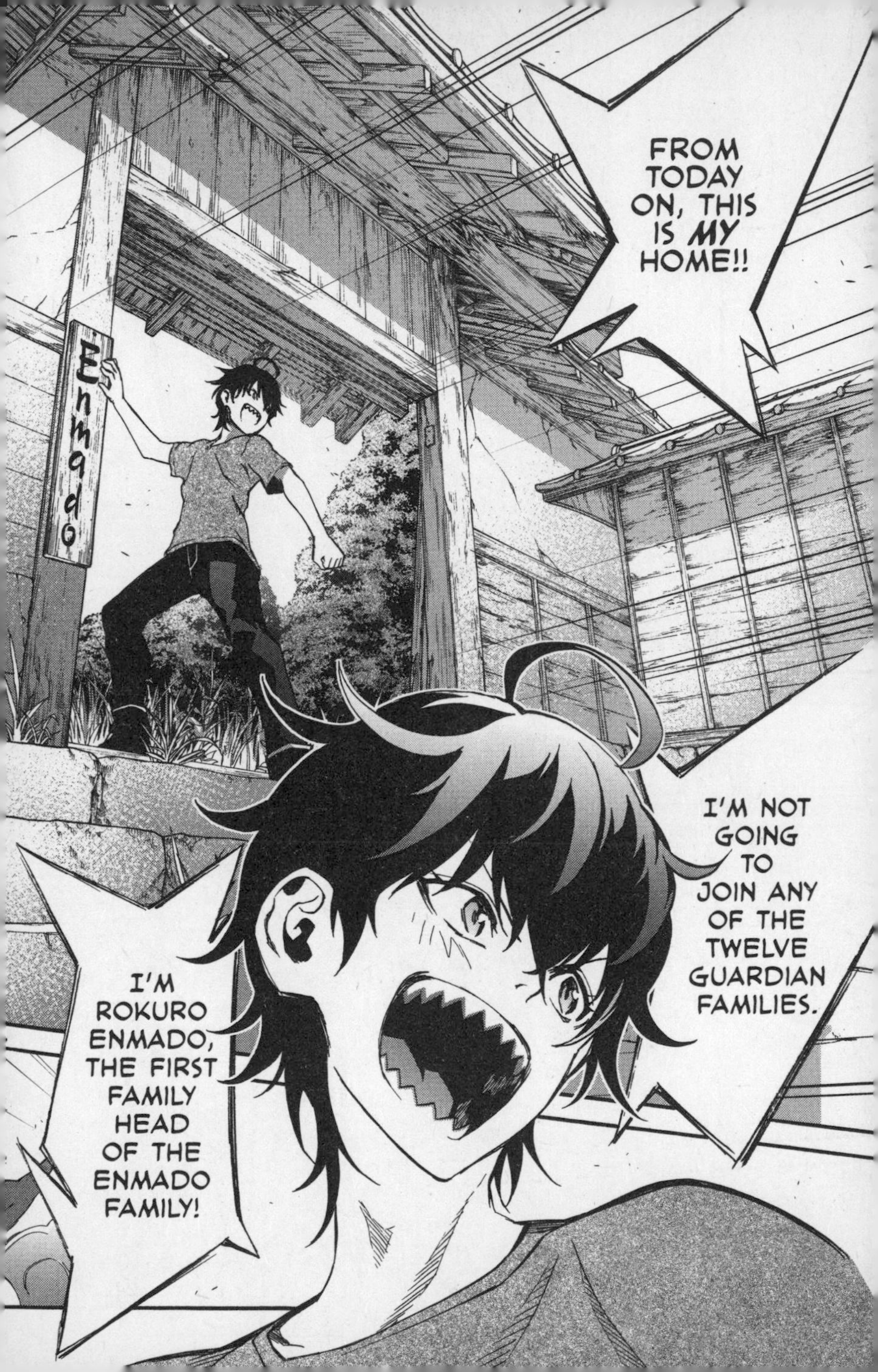
FROM TODAY ON, THIS IS *MY* HOME!!
Enmado
I'M NOT GOING TO JOIN ANY OF THE TWELVE GUARDIAN FAMILIES.
I'M ROKURO ENMADO, THE FIRST FAMILY HEAD OF THE ENMADO FAMILY!

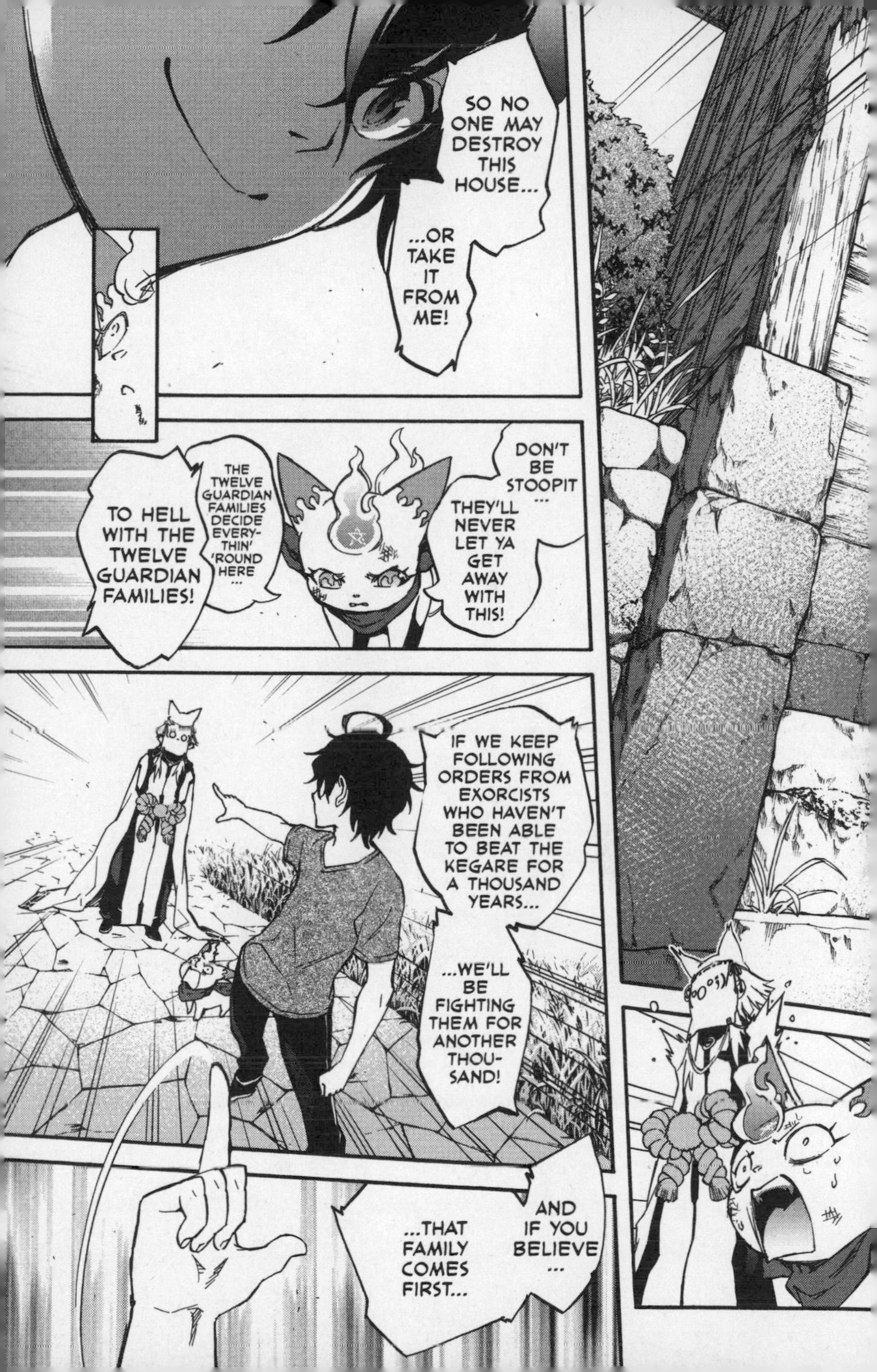
SO NO ONE MAY DESTROY THIS HOUSE...
...OR TAKE IT FROM ME!
DON'T BE STOOPIT ...
THEY'LL NEVER LET YA GET AWAY WITH THIS!
THE TWELVE GUARDIAN FAMILIES DECIDE EVERY-THIN' 'ROUND HERE ...
TO HELL WITH THE TWELVE GUARDIAN FAMILIES!
IF WE KEEP FOLLOWING ORDERS FROM EXORCISTS WHO HAVEN'T BEEN ABLE TO BEAT THE KEGARE FOR A THOUSAND YEARS...
...WE'LL BE FIGHTING THEM FOR ANOTHER THOU-SAND!
AND IF YOU BELIEVE ...
...THAT FAMILY COMES FIRST...

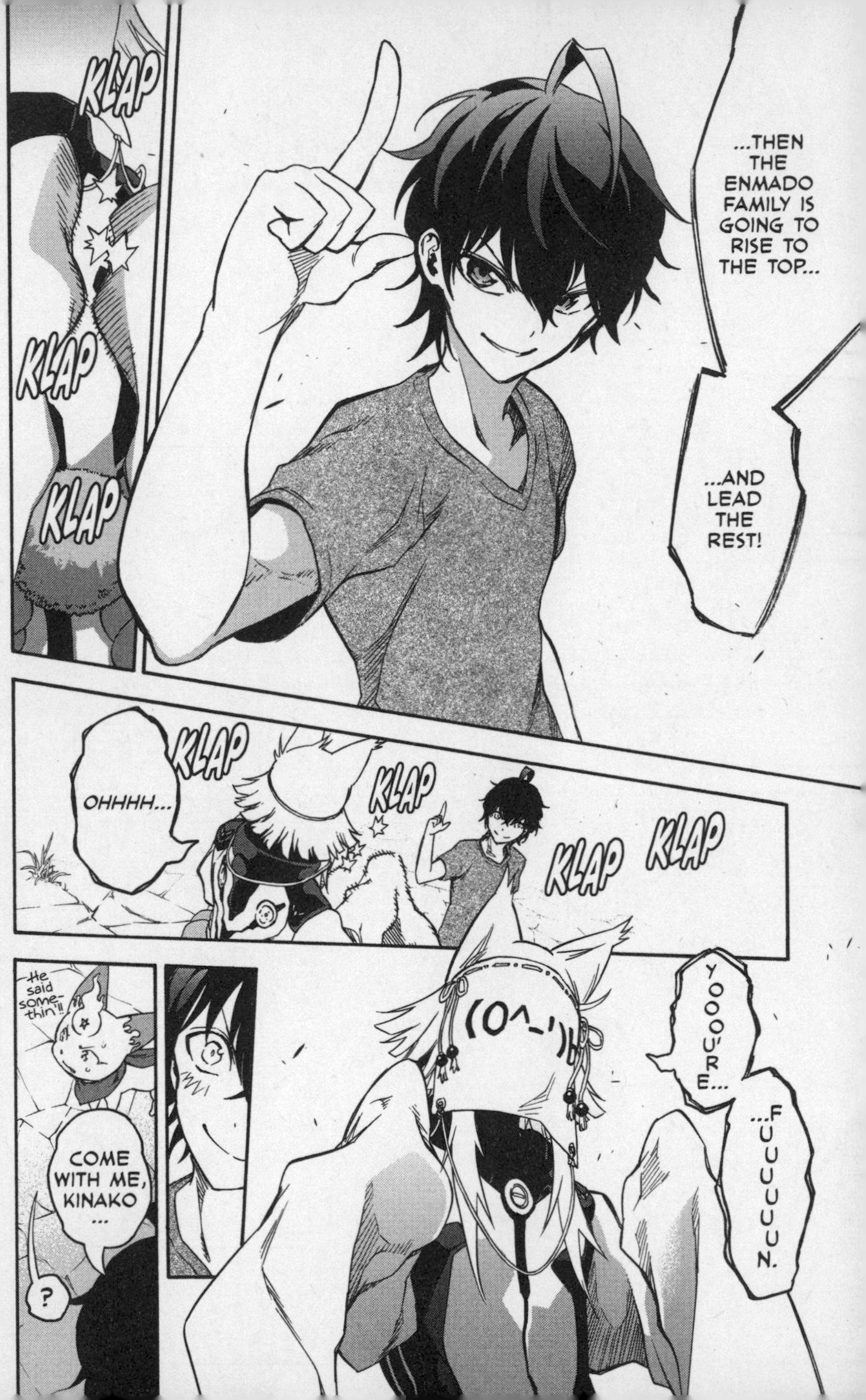
...THEN THE ENMADO FAMILY IS GOING TO RISE TO THE TOP...
...AND LEAD THE REST!
KLAP
KLAP
KLAP
KLAP
KLAP
KLAP
KLAP
OHHHH...
YOOOU'RE...
...FUUUUUUN.
He said somethin'!!
COME WITH ME, KINAKO...
?

LET'S FIX UP THE PLACE...

...TALK TO YOU.

I WANT TO...

...AND SURPRISE BENIO WHEN SHE COMES HOME!

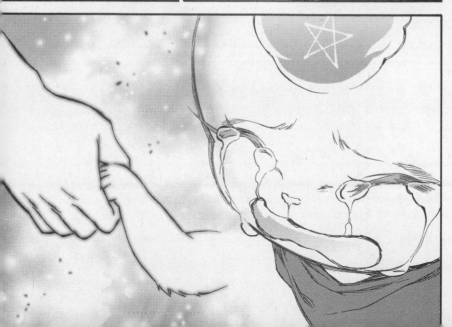

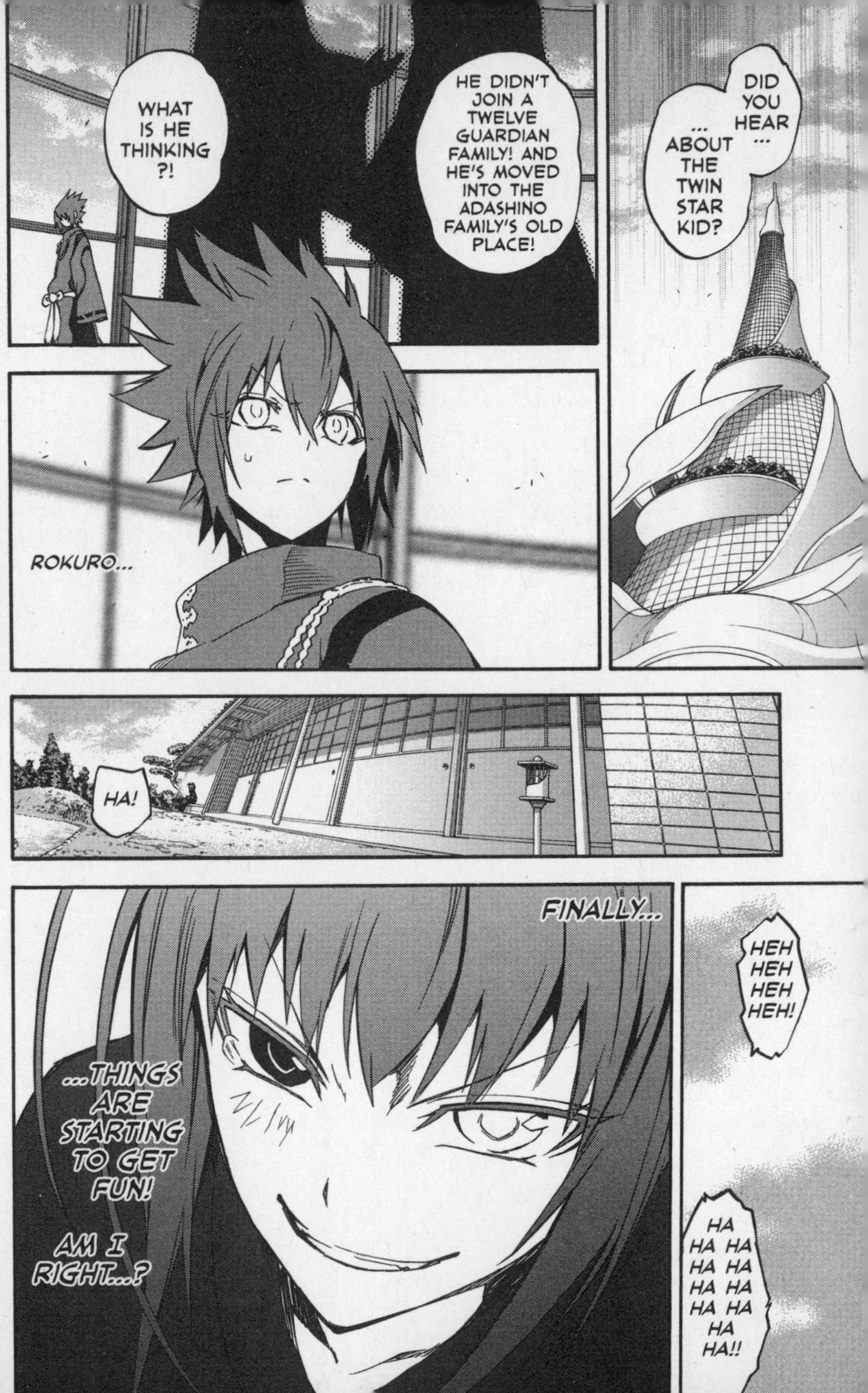
DID YOU HEAR ... ... ABOUT THE TWIN STAR KID?
HE DIDN'T JOIN A TWELVE GUARDIAN FAMILY! AND HE'S MOVED INTO THE ADASHINO FAMILY'S OLD PLACE!
WHAT IS HE THINKING ?!
ROKURO...
HA!
HEH HEH HEH HEH!
HA HA HA HA HA HA HA HA HA HA HA HA!!
FINALLY...
...THINGS ARE STARTING TO GET FUN!
AM I RIGHT...?

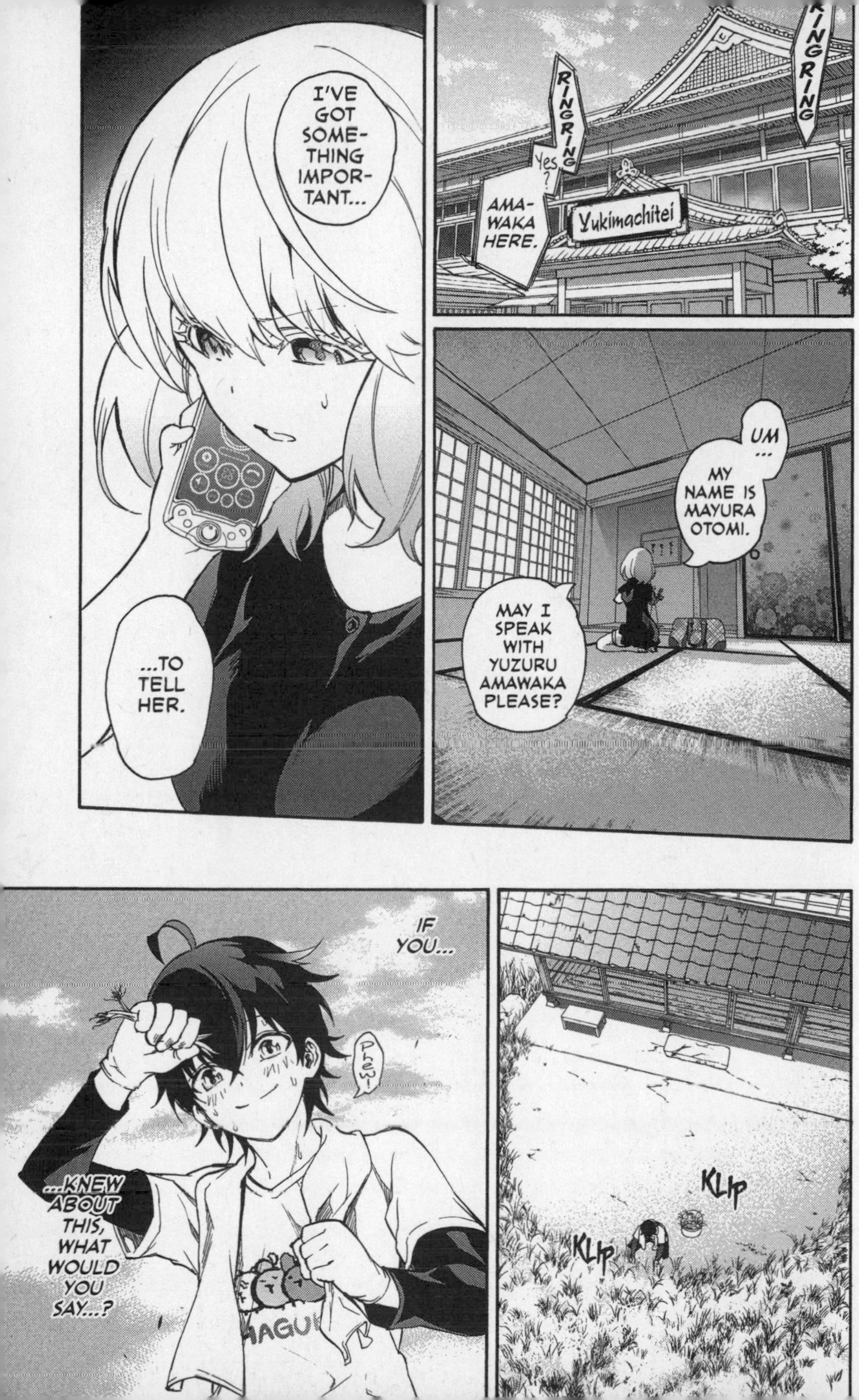
RINGRING
RINGRING
Yes?
AMAWAKA HERE.
Yukimachitei
UM...
MY NAME IS MAYURA OTOMI.
MAY I SPEAK WITH YUZURU AMAWAKA PLEASE?
I'VE GOT SOMETHING IMPORTANT...
...TO TELL HER.
KLIP
KLIP
IF YOU...
Phew!
...KNEW ABOUT THIS, WHAT WOULD YOU SAY...?

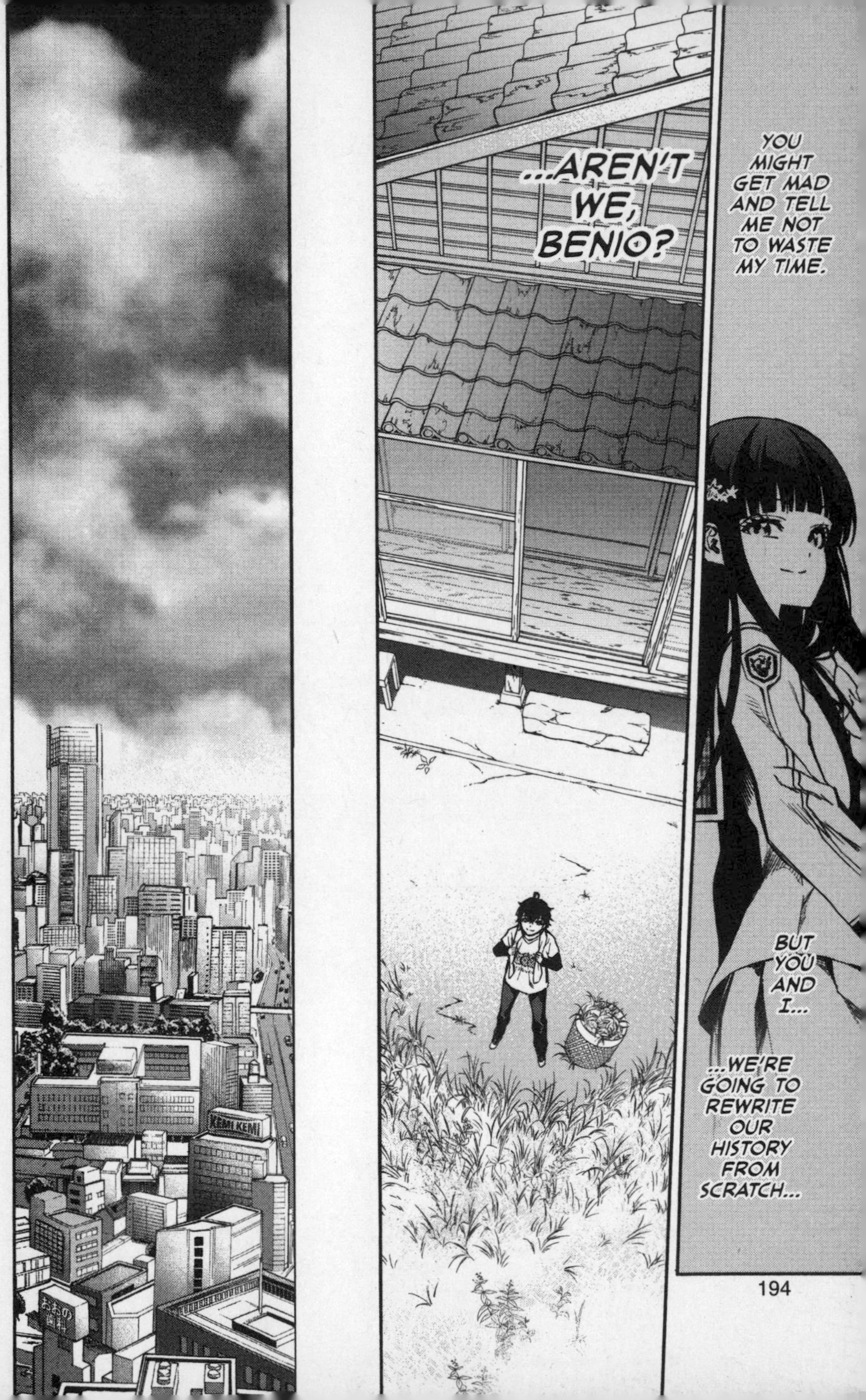
YOU MIGHT GET MAD AND TELL ME NOT TO WASTE MY TIME.
BUT YOU AND I...
...WE'RE GOING TO REWRITE OUR HISTORY FROM SCRATCH...
...AREN'T WE, BENIO?
KEMI KEMI

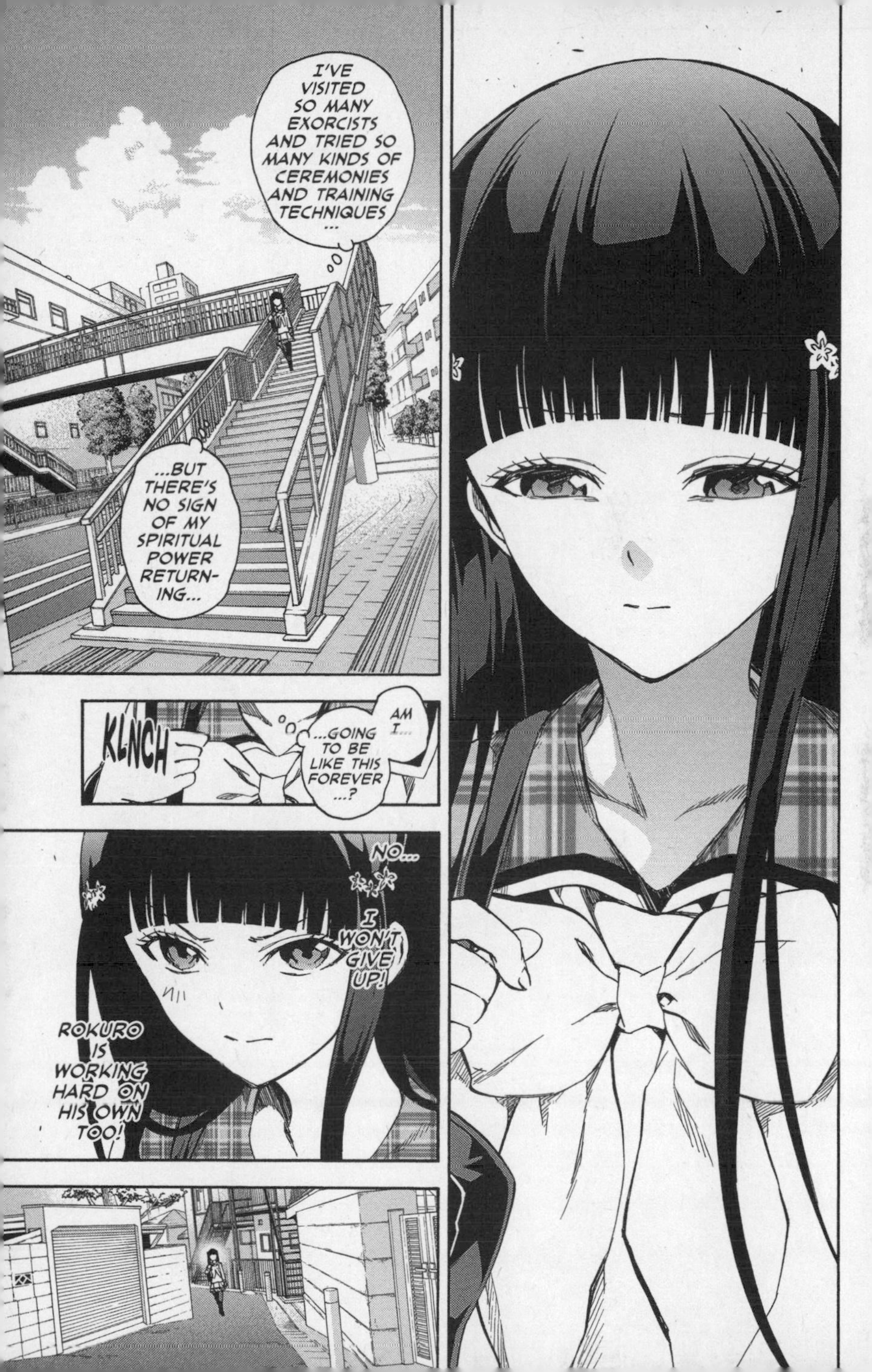
I'VE VISITED SO MANY EXORCISTS AND TRIED SO MANY KINDS OF CEREMONIES AND TRAINING TECHNIQUES ...
...BUT THERE'S NO SIGN OF MY SPIRITUAL POWER RETURN-ING...
AM I... ...GOING TO BE LIKE THIS FOREVER ...?
KLNCH
NO...
I WON'T GIVE UP!
ROKURO IS WORKING HARD ON HIS OWN TOO!

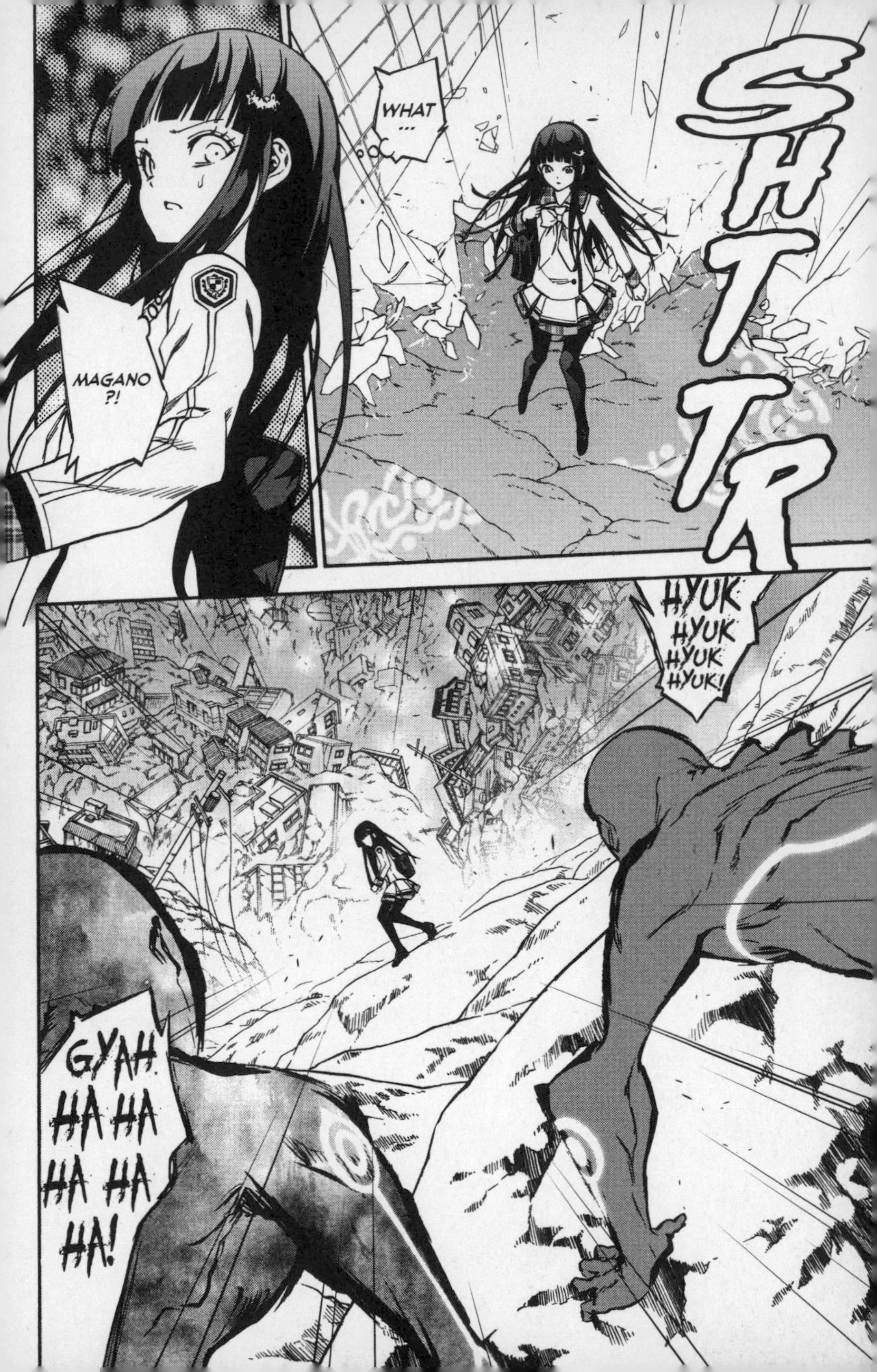
SHTR
WHAT ...
MAGANO ?!
HYUK HYUK HYUK HYUK!
GYAH HA HA HA HA HA HA!

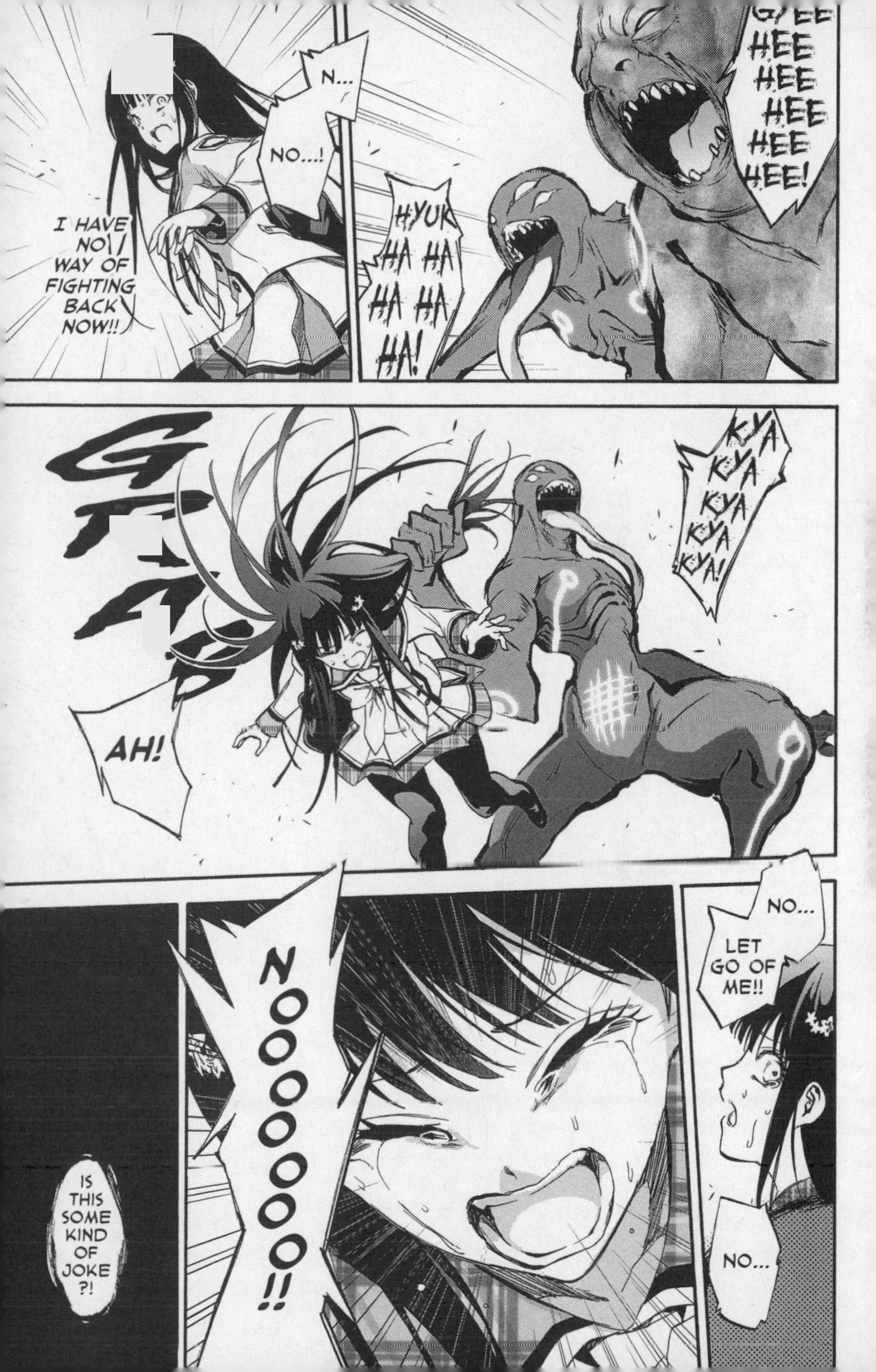
HEE HEE HEE HEE HEE!
HYUK HA HA HA HA HA!
N...
NO...!
I HAVE NO WAY OF FIGHTING BACK NOW!!
KYA KYA KYA KYA KYA!
AH!
NO...
LET GO OF ME!!
NO...
NOOOOOOOO!!
IS THIS SOME KIND OF JOKE?!

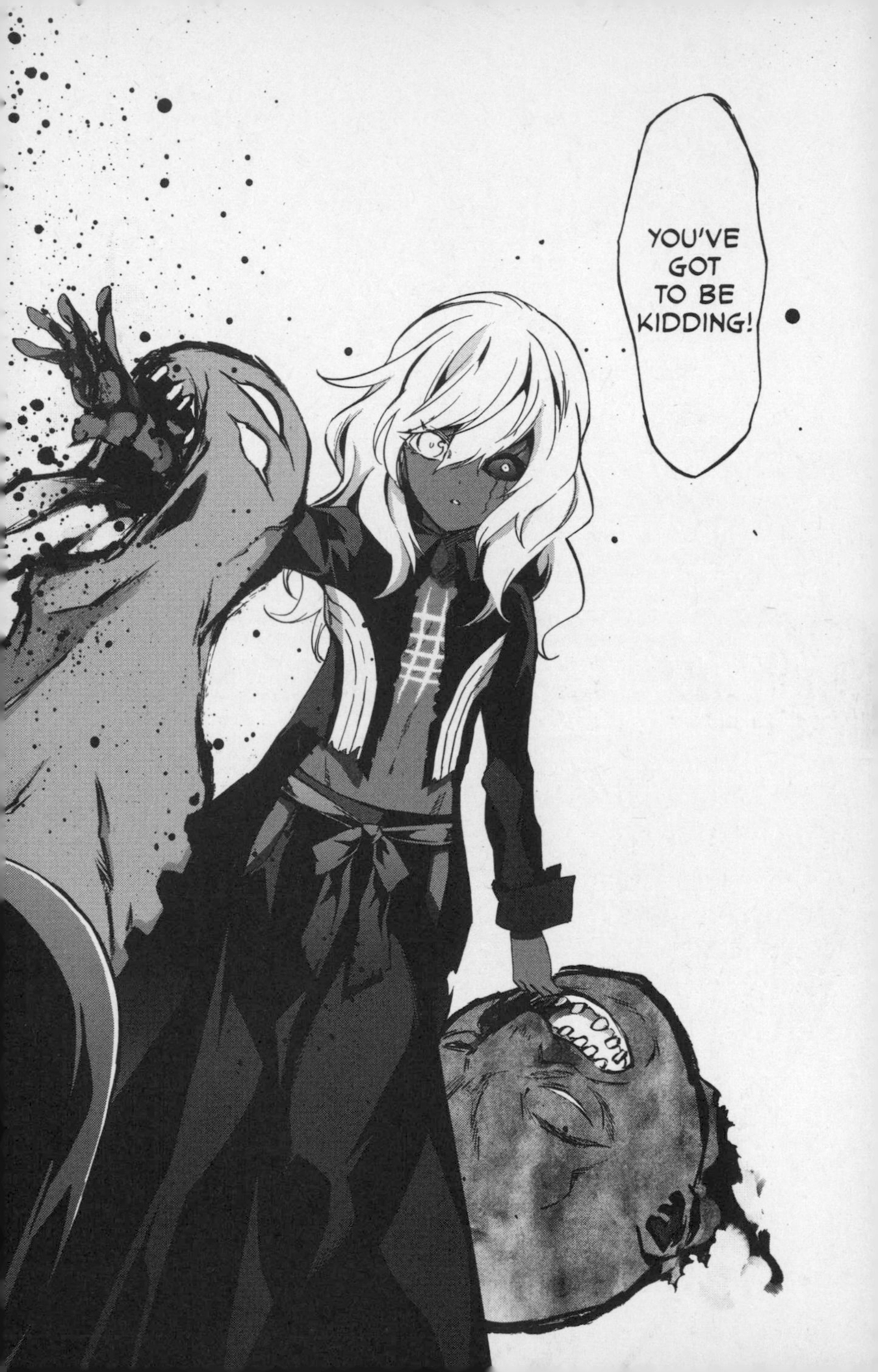
YOU'VE GOT TO BE KIDDING!

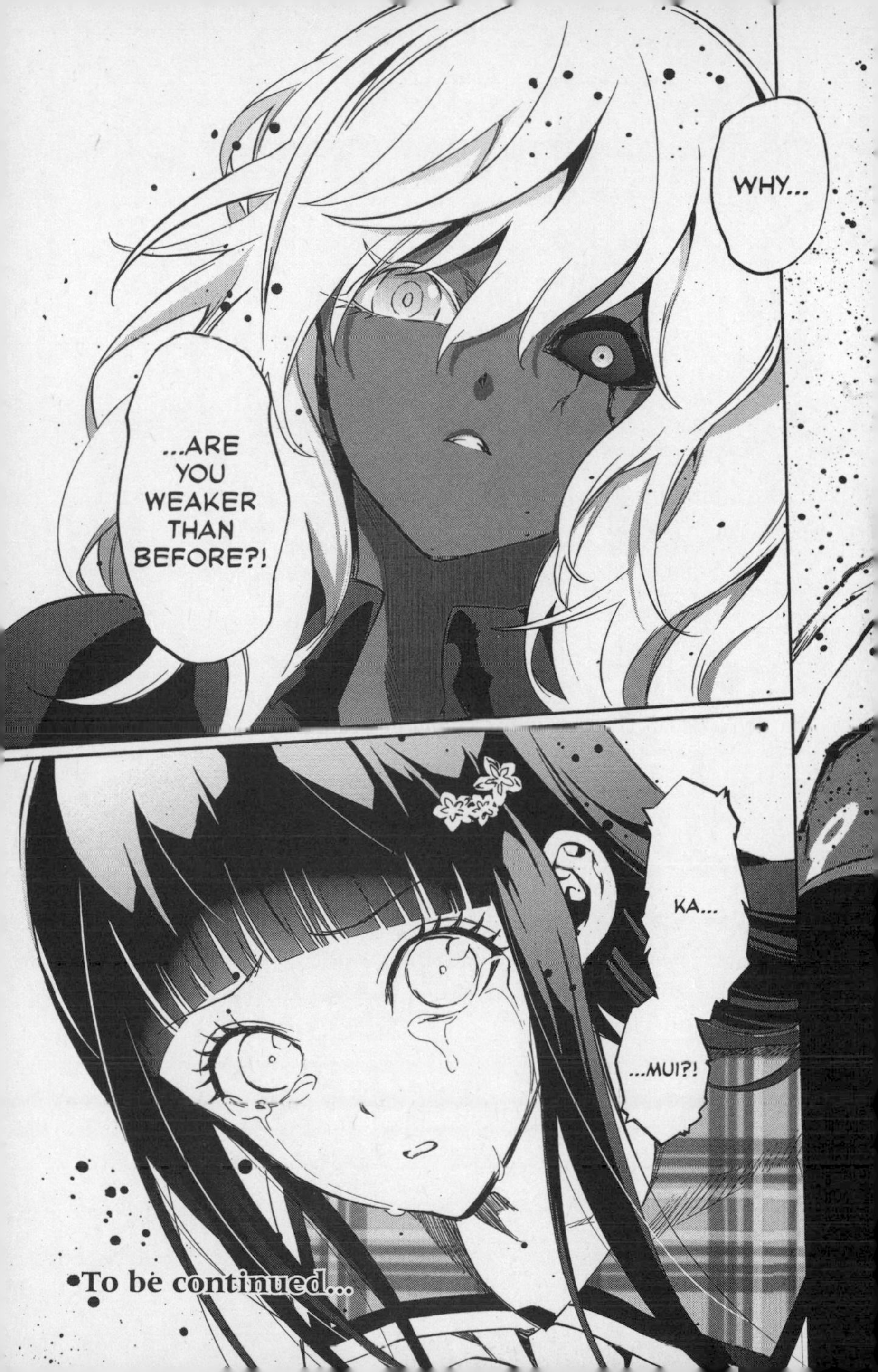
WHY...
...ARE YOU WEAKER THAN BEFORE?!
KA...
...MUI?!
To be continued...

QQnyoritsuryo! Question Corner

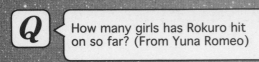

Q How many girls has Rokuro hit on so far? (From Yuna Romeo)

A Seventeen to 18...?

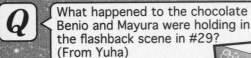

Q What happened to the chocolate Benio and Mayura were holding in the flashback scene in #29? (From Yuha)

Happy Valentine's D
Valenti

A They gave it away while repeating, "W-we're just giving this to you out of obligation!" 23 times.

Q In #33, "Separation of the Twin Stars," in the panel where Ryogo is hugging Rokuru before he leaves for the island, there's an image of the back of a woman in the background. Is that Miss Ayame City? (From Guren 15)

A That's right. Her name is Haruka Kaibara. She's a character who appears in the anime as well, and she just happens to be Ryogo's fiancée from his arranged marriage.

Q Will Tatara ever show his face? (From Assassin *Yuki*)

ヾ(#`Д´)ﾉ

A I've already decided what he looks like, so I'm sure he will. But you might get to see his face in the anime before the manga...!

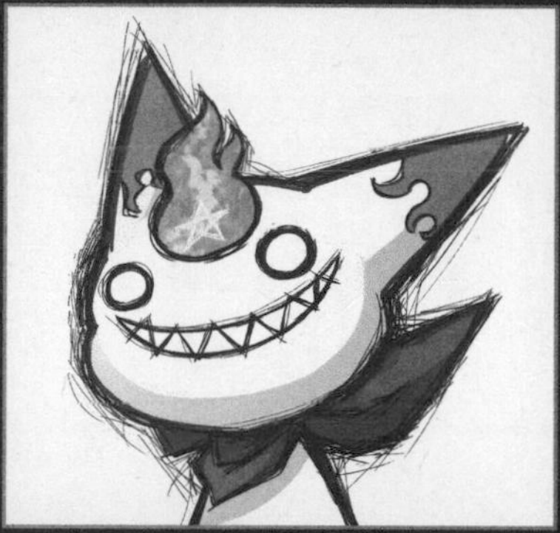

I'm on Twitter now!

Actually, I started a Twitter account around the time the previous volume was published... I upload tweets of rough sketches, plugs for my work, and little bits and pieces that I was unable to place in the extra pages of the graphic novels due to lack of space. I also draw requests! So rather than tweeting random things, I use it as a tool to have fun with my fans.

You'll probably find my account if you search for "Sukeno Twitter." Please drop by whenever you have time!

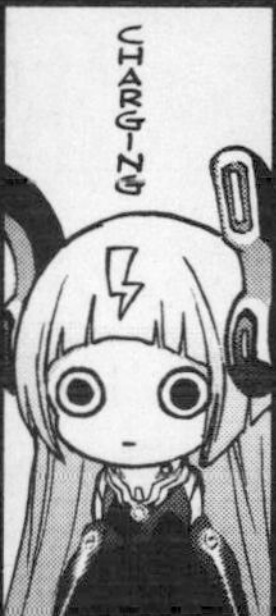
CHARGING

YOSHIAKI SUKENO was born July 23, 1981, in Wakayama, Japan. He graduated from Kyoto Seika University, where he studied manga. In 2006, he won the Tezuka Award for Best Newcomer Shonen Manga Artist. In 2008, he began his previous work, the supernatural comedy *Binbougami ga!*, which was adapted into the anime *Good Luck Girl!* in 2012.

SUPER-SHORT MANGA:

FROZEN WHITE TIGER

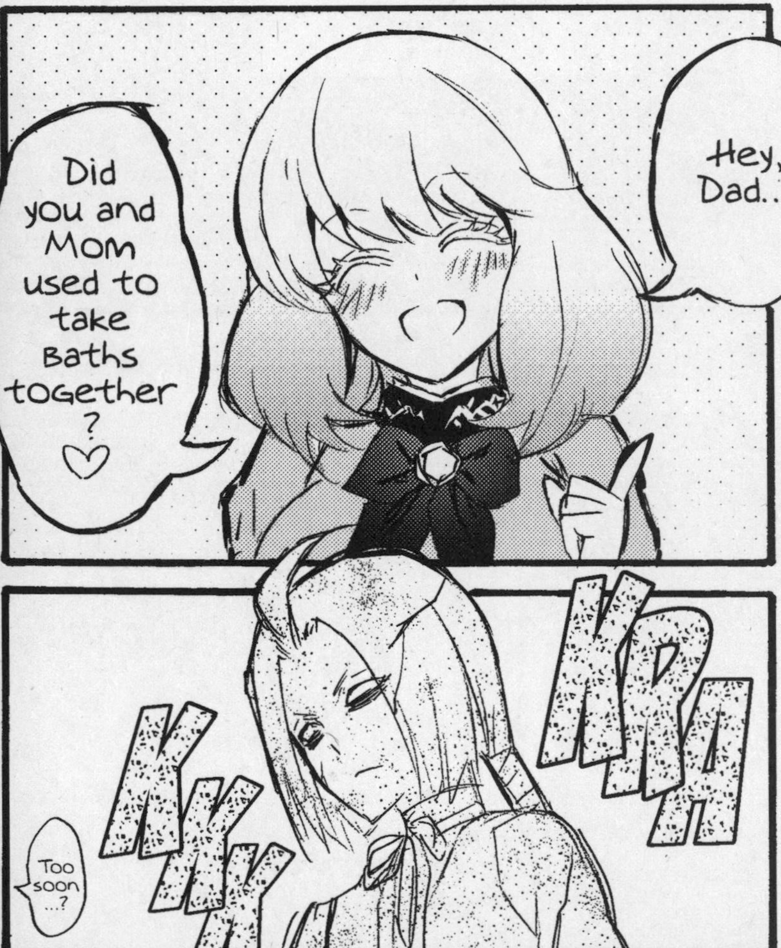
Hey, Dad...
Did you and Mom used to take baths together? ♡
KRA
KKKK
Too soon ...?

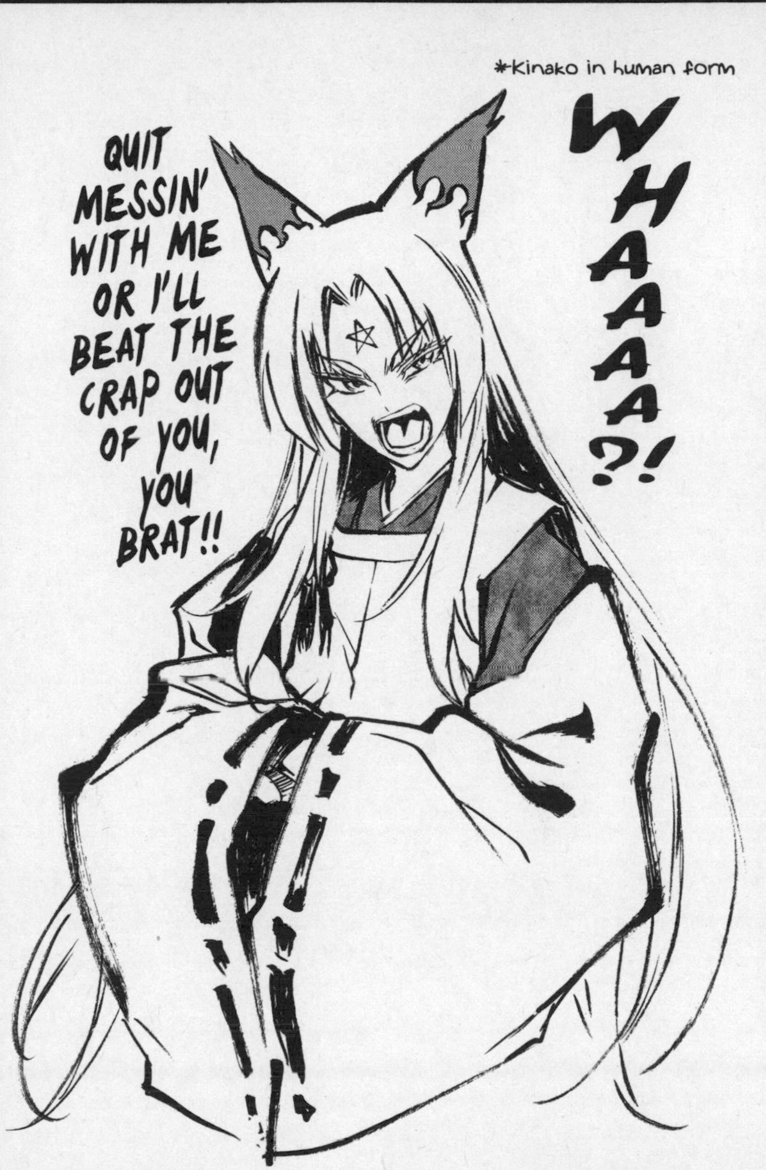
*Kinako in human form
WHAAAAA?!
QUIT MESSIN' WITH ME OR I'LL BEAT THE CRAP OUT OF YOU, YOU BRAT!!

—SHONEN JUMP Manga Edition—

STORY & ART **Yoshiaki Sukeno**

TRANSLATION **Tetsuichiro Miyaki**
ENGLISH ADAPTATION **Bryant Turnage**
TOUCH-UP ART & LETTERING **Stephen Dutro**
DESIGN **Shawn Carrico**
EDITOR **Annette Roman**

SOUSEI NO ONMYOJI © 2013 by Yoshiaki Sukeno
All rights reserved.
First published in Japan in 2013 by SHUEISHA Inc., Tokyo.
English translation rights arranged by SHUEISHA Inc.

Printed in the U.S.A.

Published by VIZ Media, LLC
P.O. Box 77010
San Francisco, CA 94107

10 9 8 7 6 5 4 3 2 1
First printing, October 2017

www.shonenjump.com

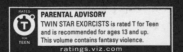

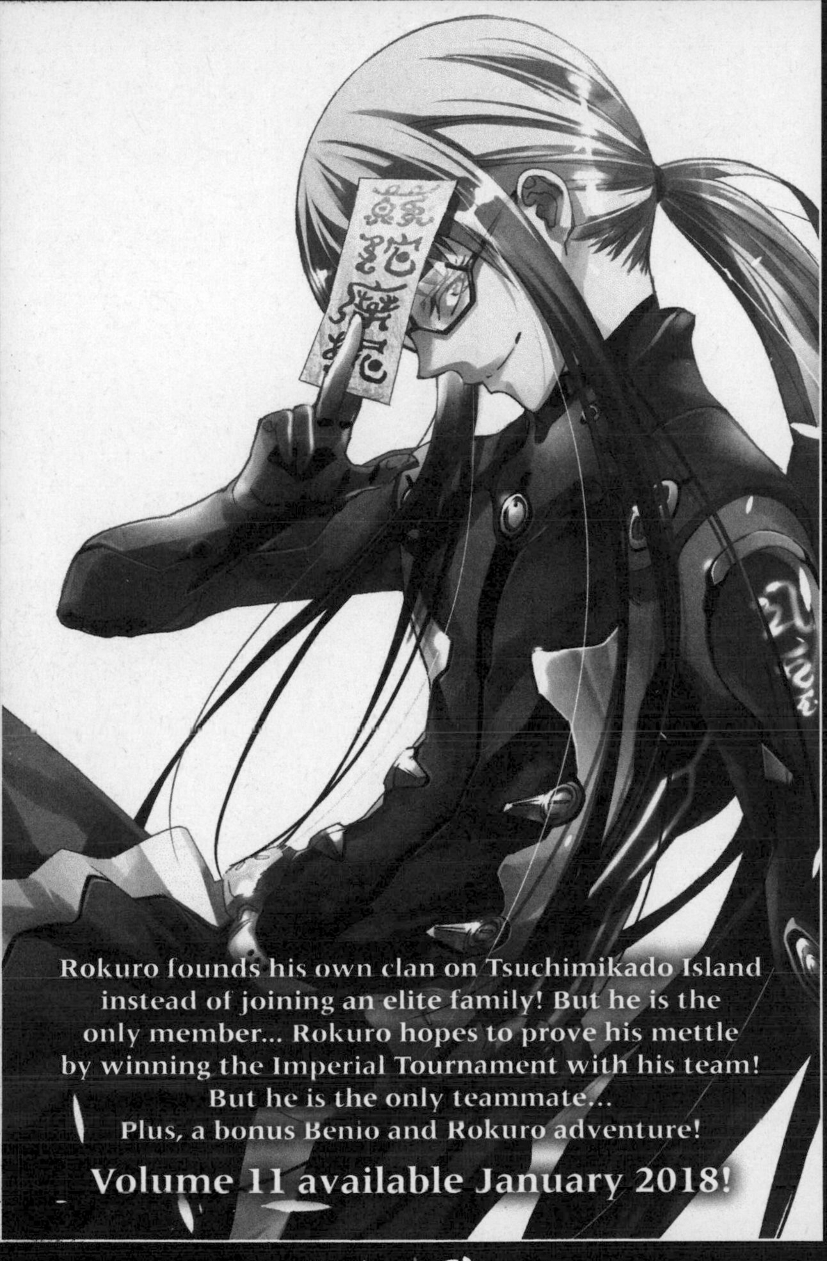
Rokuro founds his own clan on Tsuchimikado Island
instead of joining an elite family! But he is the
only member... Rokuro hopes to prove his mettle
by winning the Imperial Tournament with his team!
But he is the only teammate...
Plus, a bonus Benio and Rokuro adventure!
Volume 11 available January 2018!

Twin Star Exorcists

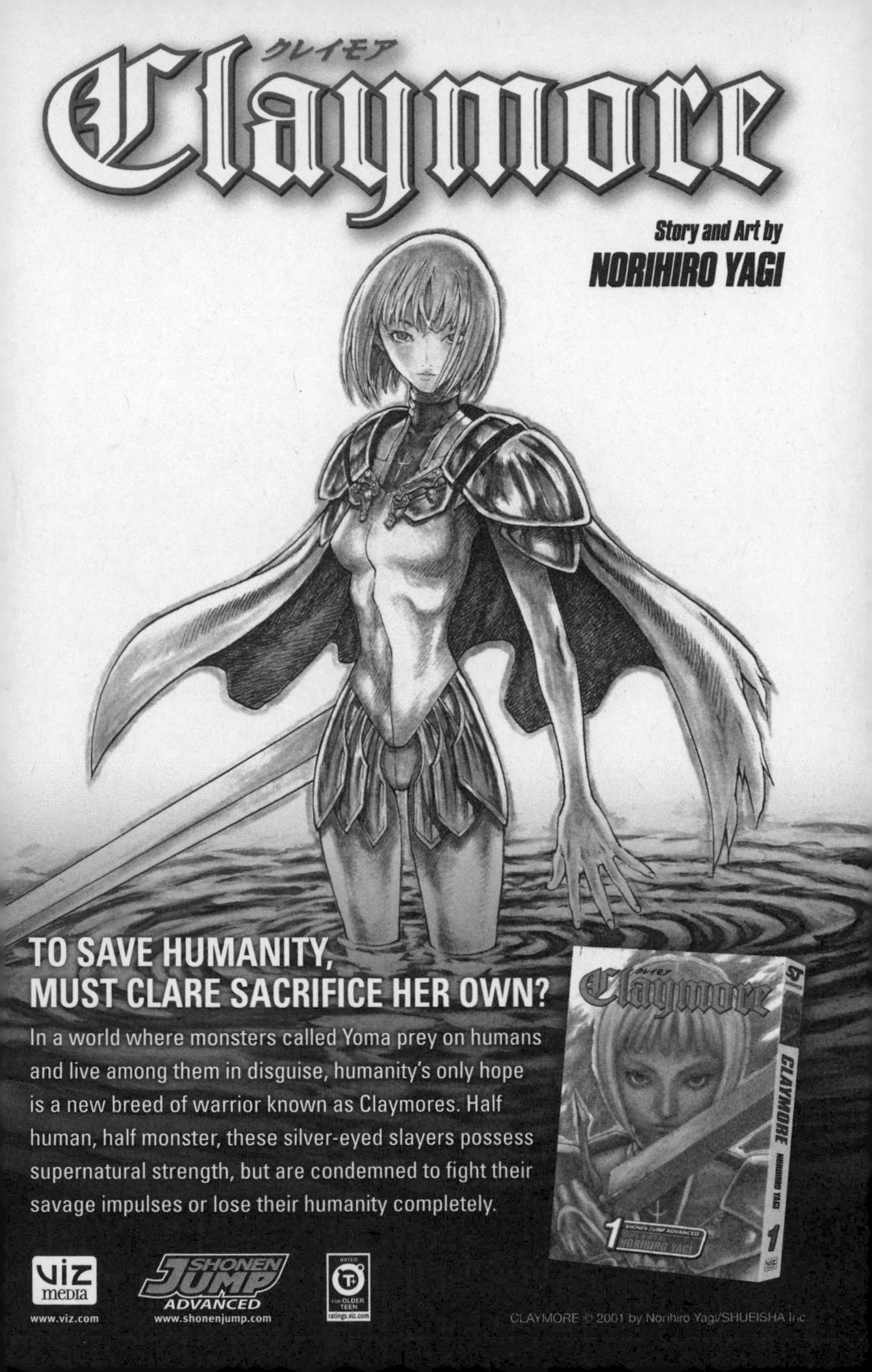
クレイモア
Claymore
Story and Art by
NORIHIRO YAGI
TO SAVE HUMANITY, MUST CLARE SACRIFICE HER OWN?
In a world where monsters called Yoma prey on humans and live among them in disguise, humanity's only hope is a new breed of warrior known as Claymores. Half human, half monster, these silver-eyed slayers possess supernatural strength, but are condemned to fight their savage impulses or lose their humanity completely.
viz media
www.viz.com
SHONEN JUMP ADVANCED
www.shonenjump.com
RATED T+ FOR OLDER TEEN
ratings.viz.com
CLAYMORE © 2001 by Norihiro Yagi/SHUEISHA Inc.

YOU'RE READING THE **WRONG WAY!**

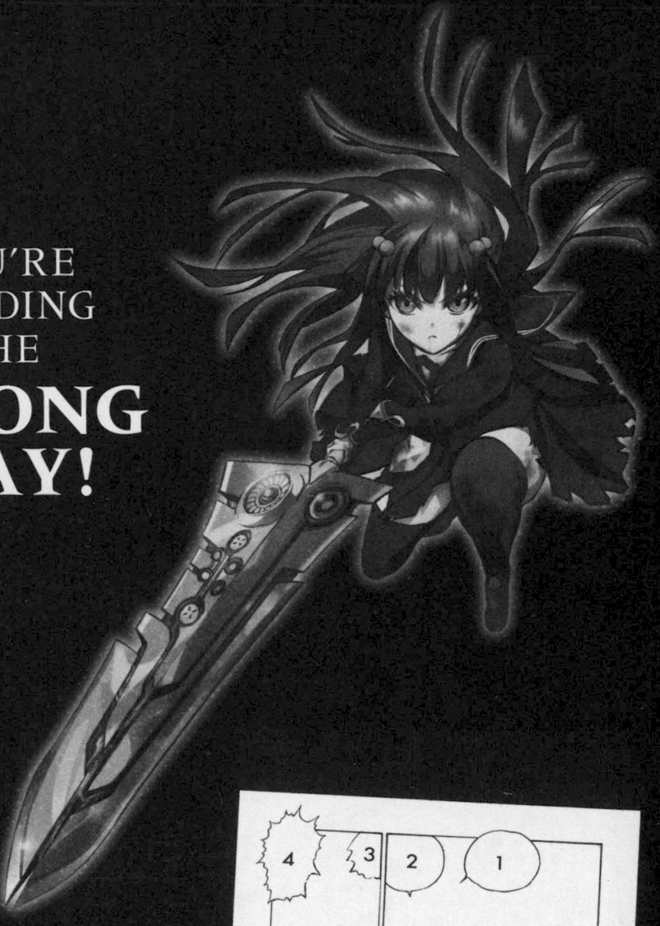

Twin Star Exorcists reads from right to left, starting in the upper-right corner. Japanese is read from right to left, meaning that action, sound effects and word-balloon order are completely reversed from English order.

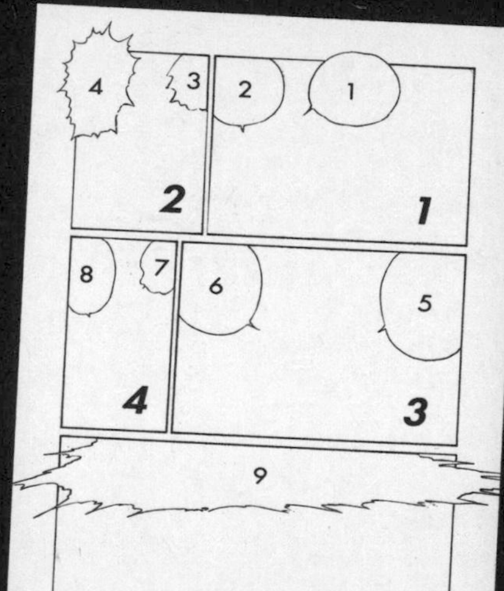
1
2
1
3
4
2
5
6
3
7
8
4
9
5
142